Corporate Concentration

Michigan Yearbook of International Legal Studies

VOLUME II

CORPORATE CONCENTRATION

National and International Regulation

Ann Arbor The University of Michigan Press

Library of Congress Cataloging in Publication Data
Main entry under title:

Corporate concentration.

(Michigan yearbook of international legal studies; v. 2)
Bibliography: p.
Includes index.
1. Antitrust law—Addresses, essays, lectures.
2. Corporation law—Addresses, essays, lectures.
3. Antitrust law—United States—Addresses,
essays, lectures. 4. Corporation law—United
States—Addresses, essays, lectures. 5. Indus-
trial concentration—Addresses, essays, lectures.
I. Krauland, Edward J. II. Smith, Stephanie M.
III. Green, Joseph T. IV. Series.
K3856.Z9C67   343'.072   80-25646
ISBN 0-472-09250-2

To John H. Jackson,
Professor, University of Michigan Law School

Preface

This is the second volume of a new international and comparative law periodical of the University of Michigan Law School—the *Michigan Yearbook of International Legal Studies*. The *Yearbook* is an annual student publication intended each year as a comprehensive sourcebook on an international and comparative law topic of particular current interest. Volume II contains the written contributions of foreign and American scholars who gathered at the law school in the autumn of 1979 to discuss the issues associated with the existence and regulation of corporate concentration.

Volume I of the *Yearbook* examined "Antidumping Law"—an extensive body of law regulating a particular and concrete aspect of international trade and commerce. With volume II, the *Yearbook* accepted a new and different challenge, for the antitrust problems of corporate concentration, particularly in the transnational context, are of relatively recent vintage and are hence less well formulated.

The term *concentration* describes various forms of industrial structure and organization: *horizontal* concentration refers to the control of a given industry or market by a small number of producers, *vertical* concentration refers to the results of mergers between companies that operate in different phases or stages of the production and distribution process, *aggregate* concentration refers to the overall aggregation of national economic power or assets in the hands of major producers. As large multinational business enterprises expand through takeovers and mergers, national and international attention has begun to focus on corporate concentration in national and transnational markets.

Those advocating strict regulation of corporate concentration are concerned that concentration of productive capacity reduces competition, blocks the entry of new companies into the market, hinders innovation, and insulates corporate decision making and conduct from governmental and public scrutiny. Politically there is a fear that large corporations exert quasi-governmental authority in making decisions that affect social welfare and the process of economic development. The issue of corporate concentration becomes more attenuated in the transnational business environment due to the incorporeal character of multinational corporations and the disparate economic and political values of foreign governments.

Although the topic of corporate concentration plunges us into the established and well-documented field of antitrust law, there is a noticeable dearth of law and legal writing addressed to the specific social, political, and economic considerations of industrial structure and organization. In the United

States (where free enterprise is so much a part of the social fabric), as well as in other industrialized countries, concentration of economic assets, market shares, and managerial power has not attracted the type and breadth of scrutiny that corporate behavior in the marketplace has garnered.

Upon perusing the collected articles and notes, the reader may gather that the topic is one of indefinite proportions and contours, contains troublesome and unresolved issues of social and economic policy, and evinces a distressing absence of political consensus regarding the "concentration problem." Accordingly, volume II seeks to serve the traditional purposes of legal scholarship: to state the issues, identify particular problems, discuss these issues and problems, and posit possible solutions. However, since the *Yearbook* concerns itself with a nascent and developing area of law and social policy, its flavor is descriptive and provocative, with a view to stimulating additional discussion and analysis.

To this end, volume II begins with a discussion of current U.S. antitrust enforcement policy in the area of national and transnational corporate concentration. A recent legislative proposal that offers an innovative structural approach to aggregate concentration is followed by a brief but engaging economic essay. The first section closes with an examination of the regulation of controlled-economy enterprises operating in the Unites States's free market economy. The second section contains a series of articles dealing with selected foreign efforts to regulate corporate concentration in the domestic and transnational settings. These articles demonstrate the wide variety of regulatory perspectives toward concentration that exist at the national level. The European Economic Community (EEC) article also illustrates the difficulty of applying a supranational regulatory framework to national economic systems that ascribe to different economic and competitive policies. The ensuing corporate perspective expands upon the foreign analysis by highlighting some of the peculiarities of doing business in nonmarket economies, and asks whether the concern over corporate concentration is nothing but a chimera in the context of East-West trade and investment. The scholarly discourse ends with a description and assessment of current international efforts to regulate multinational corporate behavior and structure; in particular the activities of the Organisation for Economic Cooperation and Development (OECD) and the United Nations, and the difficulties in obtaining multilateral consensus on antitrust policy are cogently examined. The final feature of the *Yearbook* is a collection of appendixes that summarize selected foreign antitrust laws, outline recent U.S. legislative proposals relevant to corporate concentration, and list a selected annotated bibliography.

Volume II, like its predecessor, is the progeny of a symposium held at the University of Michigan Law School under the joint auspices of the International Law Society and the *Yearbook* organization. The faculty committee and editorial board of the *Yearbook* would again like to express their gratitude to those who participated at the symposium and made such extremely interesting and valuable contributions.

The symposium itself was an endeavor of tremendous proportions. Many students, faculty, and law school administrators made the symposium possible through their labor, advice, moral support, and financial assistance. We appreciate the kind help given us throughout the year by Helen Betts, Ann LaVacque, and Henrietta Slote.

We would like to thank the following people for their assistance in preparing the manuscript: Michelle Johnson, Vicki Scoggins, Edith Horvath, Pat Root, and Mary Gladstone.

Special thanks are in order for University of Michigan President Allan Smith and Law School Dean Terrance Sandalow; the members of our faculty advisory committee—Professor Emeritus William W. Bishop, Jr., and professors Alfred F. Conard, Eric Stein, Whitmore Gray, John H. Jackson, and Gerald M. Rosberg; and special advisors professors Thomas E. Kauper and William James Adams. The editorial board of volume II would like to express its deepest appreciation to Professor Kauper for his help in organizing the symposium and his advice on the articles and notes. It was our pleasure to be able to work with Professor Kauper, as well as all the other faculty members who shared their time and thoughts with us. We believe the collective effort has resulted in a valuable contribution to the legal literature.

Contents

APPENDIXES

Abbreviations

ARC	Act Against Restraints of Competition (Federal Republic of Germany)
CEE	Controlled Economy Enterprise
CMEA	Council for Mutual Economic Assistance
CTC	United Nations Commission on Transnational Corporations
ECSC	European Coal and Steel Community
EEC	European Economic Community
FCO	Federal Cartel Office (Federal Republic of Germany)
FIRA	Foreign Investment Review Act (Canada)
FTO	Foreign Trade Organization (Soviet Union)
GATT	General Agreement on Tariffs and Trade
IME	International Investment and Multinational Enterprise
MNC	Multinational Corporation
OECD	Organisation for Economic Cooperation and Development
OFT	Office of Fair Trading
RBP	Restrictive Business Practice
RTPC	Restrictive Trade Practices Commission
TNC	Transnational Corporation
UNCTAD	United Nations Conference on Trade and Development

This volume should be cited as:
2 Mich. Y.B. Int'l Legal Stud._____(1981)

Introduction: Transnational Corporate Concentration—The Issues

THOMAS E. KAUPER

Competition policy in the United States, particularly reflected in antitrust policy, in recent years has focused on corporate structure. To some, this emphasis simply reflects a belief in a close correlation between corporate structure and behavior. A single firm monopoly inevitably will restrict output and raise prices above levels that would prevail under competition conditions, distorting allocative efficiency. The behavioral pattern is a direct consequence of structure.[1] Many believe that high corporate concentration, even short of single firm monopoly, is at least conducive to, if not a cause of, monopolistic behavior.[2] Some also view high corporate concentration, and the aggregation of economic as well as political and social power identified with it, as a threat to democratic institutions and individual liberty.[3] Not surprisingly, there are dissenters who view high corporate concentration in particular markets as facilitating successful collusive behavior, but of no necessary competitive consequence.[4] The latter view focuses simply on behavior. The relationship between corporate concentration and behavior is thus not clearly understood, and is the subject of vigorous debate in the United States. Of course, this debate is directly relevant to the need for, and contours of, government policy directed toward control of concentration. Antitrust policy directed toward concentration, and particularly mergers that directly increase concentration, is at the heart of the controversy.

The articles in this volume carry the debate a step further. As corporate enterprises extend their activities across international boundaries, so too, problems of corporate concentration take on an international quality. New issues come to the fore. Is transnational corporate concentration an identifiable problem that presents policy issues beyond those posed by concentration measured in particular national markets? If there is a separate problem, can it be sufficiently defined to formulate an intelligent public policy response? And are there now, or in the future likely to be, national or international control mechanisms capable of implementing any such policy intiatives?

Thomas E. Kauper is a professor of law at the University of Michigan and the former Assistant Attorney General, Antitrust Division, Justice Department.

This volume presents the views of scholars, government and international organization officials, and private practitioners, on these questions. The reader will not find a consensus, either on the nature of the problem or on any proposed solution. But hopefully the exchange will contribute to the public discussion which is already well under way, and provide valuable insights to those who must bear the responsibility for policy formulation.

Many of the issues to be discussed in this volume are unresolved. This is not because they are unimportant, for it is abundantly clear that they are of extraordinary significance. But they are issues on the frontier of both legal development and international relations. They are also issues which tend to provoke emotional responses and assertions of very strong national interests. The very word *multinational,* a word that we now manage to avoid to some extent, tends to evoke images of corporate giants operating on such a large international scale that they are for all practical purposes beyond the control of any national authority. The *multinational problem,* as some describe this absence of unified control, relates, to the extent that we can define any problem at all, to a number of public policy concerns ranging from formulation of tax policy to concerns about full employment. The focus in this volume will be primarily upon competition policy and the need to preserve free and open markets.

Within the context of corporate enterprises operating across one or more national boundaries, the initial issues will relate to the degree of danger to competition such enterprises create. Do they pose a peculiar threat to competition in national markets? Indeed, is it even realistic to think in terms of national markets? If such a threat can be identified, what remedies might presently be available? If these remedies are inadequate, for jurisdictional or other reasons, what sort of mechanisms might be capable of assuring an adequate measure of international control? These questions are all obviously interrelated. If multinational enterprises pose a particular danger to free markets, it is either because they have a power not common to domestic businesses, or because national policies, implemented in a variety of ways, are not capable of checking the exercise of that power because it transcends national boundaries. An assessment of the effectiveness of national control mechanisms in dealing with multinational enterprises thus is central to the determination that such enterprises pose a peculiar competitive problem calling for additional national or international control mechanisms. This conference focused on the competitive threat, if any, caused by the enterprises operating on a large international scale and on the need for additional means to assure their control.

Several articles in this volume focus on national efforts to deal with corporate concentration in terms of competition policy. An examination of such efforts is useful both in determining whether there is any broad-scale consensus on the competitive effects of concentration, and in evaluating the need for further national or international remedies. In the United States, for example, antitrust control of mergers under Section 7 of the Clayton Act has been sufficiently severe that significant mergers between competing firms, the category of mergers which most directly increase concentration, seldom occur.[5] Merger policy clearly reflects a direct concern with concentration in purely structural terms. But other nations view concentration within their domestic markets differently, and may go so far as to promote mergers which, while significantly increasing concentration, are thought to promote efficiency. The French policy, for example, seems far more in accord with the latter approach than with that followed in the United States. The long-standing effort within the European Economic Community to develop a merger control guideline acceptable to member nations, an effort still largely unsuccessful, reflects the difficulty of accommodating such divergent views.[6]

It will readily become apparent that there is little consensus over the nature of the problem or the need for, or nature of, a solution. Empirical data on concentration and its effects, both in national markets and internationally, is lacking. Different nations start, therefore, with different data bases, making comparisons difficult. More importantly, the international community lacks consensus not only over what competition is, but also over its desirability. Aggressive competition to one nation is ruinous to another. Competition policy may, to some, include what to others are trade policy concerns. The concern of underdeveloped nations with the need for "antitrust" rules to govern parent-subsidiary relationships is but one example. Concerns over national sovereignty may dictate noncompetitive results, particularly where state-owned enterprises are involved. There is thus no consensus over the standards by which the problems, if any, can be identified and measured. The same lack of consensus causes different national authorities to focus on different problems. Conflict necessarily results. This absence of consensus today makes any international solution difficult, if not impossible.

Related to the identification of competitive concerns about transnational concentration is an assessment of the adequacy of existing national remedies. National antitrust authorities in some countries, particularly in the United States, have not been wanting, at least for effort, in protecting their own interests and markets from conduct undertaken outside their own boundaries. But how far can such authorities reach? The application of extraterritorial principles has resulted in increasingly vocal protest, both from affected business enterprises and from sovereigns who view their own interests quite differently. This simply reflects, in part, the lack of consensus alluded to earlier. It also reflects concern over national sovereignty and a nation's need to control conduct within its own geographic boundaries. Assuming a nation's ability to apply extraterritorial principles to specific conduct, how relevant are those principles to matters of structure if structure is in fact the ultimate determinant of behavior? The difficulty of dealing with structure in one or more countries in order to eliminate concomitant behavioral effects in another is obvious. The result may well be that the country in which effects are felt has little real choice but to deal only with the behavioral symptoms.

Mergers might afford the best example. Mergers can affect structure, and thus competition, on an international scale. But how far may any national authority go in dealing with mergers beyond its own boundary? Sovereigns in whose territory one or more of the merging partners is located may view the merger as procompetitive within their own national markets. Or the merger may be viewed as serving some other public need, such as full employment or technological growth, which in the view of that nation makes the transaction desirable, even if anticompetitive. Not all nations, after all, value competition as highly as the United States. An attempt on an extraterritorial basis to prohibit the merger thus provokes sovereign conflict, conflict which might mean either that no action is taken, or that the nation whose policy is offended can at best regulate the behavior of the merged firm within its own territory. This conflict in national interests may manifest itself in a variety of ways. Nations objecting to the extraterritorial application of the antitrust laws of others may take steps to block investigative efforts by antitrust authorities of other nations within their territory or of their nationals, perhaps even to the point of legislatively directing noncooperation.[7] Judicial relief orders that require action or attempt to regulate behavior in another nation can be obstructed or even formally blocked by the latter. The relief problem is particularly acute in dealing with mergers, where implementation of a decree requiring divestiture abroad would be at issue. Several articles in this volume consider such practical questions.

To a substantial degree, conflicts of this sort reflect a lack of consensus over the desirability of competition, and over the competitive consequences of particular behavior. This gives the outsider the perception that multinational enterprises are beyond the control of authorities who would like, but are unable, to exert some degree of control. In reality, however, the fundamental issue is a lack of agreement on the need for such control in the first instance. Yet it is also true that where there is international agreement on the need to deal with a particular act, or pattern of behavior, the ability of the affected enterprise to use the multiplicity of interested national authorities to its own advantage can operate to obstruct such efforts. From a national perspective, an inability to reach such enterprises can also pose significant domestic issues. Firms operating within a local market peopled in part by multinational enterprises, and thus directly competitive with them, may perceive what is in reality an inability to deal with these competitors as a form of conscious favoritism. Political pressure may then be exerted to lessen the severity of the antitrust rules applicable within the domestic market to permit local firms to compete more effectively with multinational enterprises that are thought, rightly or wrongly, not to be subject to the same rules.

For these reasons, among others, consideration is now being given to a variety of international solutions, solutions predicated on the ineffectiveness of piecemeal and often inconsistent national efforts. Guidelines, standards, and even international enforcement mechanisms have been proposed. So far, such efforts have been directed solely toward anticompetitive behavior. Can the national interests of states with fundamentally different economic policies and concerns, some of whom deal through state-owned enterprises, some of whom do not, and some of whom are far less developed than others, reach a sufficiently precise consensus on both the nature of the problem and substantive remedial standards sufficiently precise to afford any promise of workability? If no consensus can be reached with respect to behavior, how less likely is it that concentration can ever be dealt with on an international basis in structural terms? Standards which do reflect a consensus may be so generalized as to be of little value. The discussion in this volume of the efforts of the OECD[8] and the United Nations Conference on Trade and Development (UNCTAD)[9] to prepare international guidelines and standards will focus on this kind of question, as well as on the utility of a voluntary guideline approach which contains no real obligation and no enforcement mechanism. To some, voluntary guidelines for corporate behavior are a cynical illusion, designed to alleviate pressure from underdeveloped nations without in fact offering any real prospect of change. But conversely, if consensus on a relatively specific set of guidelines can be achieved, the accomplishment of the consensus alone may make the exercise meaningful.

Ultimately, however, the question of some new type of international antitrust cooperation or even enforcement authority, must be addressed. These questions themselves make the complexity of the answers obvious. Clearly we do not know the answers. We are not sure we even know the problem. Thus, the only realistic response may well be one of "time will tell." Certainly, however, the issues to be discussed in this volume are both contemporary and evocative of controversy. The uranium cartel investigation,[10] the Organization of Petroleum Exporting Countries (OPEC) case, [11] the indictment of Atlantic shipping companies,[12] the proposed removal of the International Air Transport Association's (IATA) U.S. antitrust immunity,[13] all actions under United States antitrust laws, have provoked strong international protests. American firms doing business abroad continue to press for antitrust immunity under our own antitrust laws for conduct abroad. They also occasionally assert that competition policy of other sovereigns has been applied against them in a discriminatory manner. At the same time, the Congress of the United States continues to press for more far-reaching application of our own statutes, and the Justice Department always seems to find itself caught in the middle. Careful analysis and reflection outside the political arena is necessary before new courses can be set. This volume is intended to aid such deliberations.

NOTES

1. *See* R. POSNER, ANTITRUST LAW 8–18 (1976); F.M. SCHERER, INDUSTRIAL MARKET STRUCTURE AND ECONOMIC PERFORMANCE (1980).

2. Areeda and Turner, *Conglomerate Mergers: Extended Interdependence and Effects on Interindustry Competition as Grounds for Condemnation,* 127 U. PA. L. REV. 1082 (1979).

3. Brown Shoe v. United States, 370 U.S. 294, 344 (1962).
   It is competition, not competitors, which [the Clayton] Act protects. But we cannot fail to recognize Congress' desire to promote competition through the protection of viable, small, locally owned businesses. Congress appreciated that occasional higher cost and prices might result from the maintenance of fragmented industries and markets. It resolved these competing considerations in favor of decentralization.
   Blake & Jones, *In Defense of Antitrust*, 65 COLUM L. REV. 377, 382–84 (1965); Elzinga, *The Goals of Antitrust: Other than Competition and Efficiency, What Else Counts?*, 125 U. PA. L. REV. 1191 (1977).

4. R. POSNER, *supra* note 1, at 78–95.

5. 15 U.S.C. § 18 (1976).

6. Temple Lang, *Regulating Transnational Corporate Concentration— The European Economic Community, post.*

7. *See, e.g.,* Business Records Protection Act, 1947, ONT. REV. STAT. c. 54 (1970); Great Britain's Protection of Trading Interest Bill, 1979, ANTITRUST & TRADE REG. REP. (BNA) F–1.

8. Stockmann, *Reflections on Recent OECD Activities: Regulation of Multinational Corporate Conduct and Structure, post.*

9. Kurek, *Supranational Regulation of Transnational Corporations: The UNCTAD and CTC Efforts, post.*

10. *See, e.g.,* United States v. Gulf Oil Corp. [1970–1979 Transfer Binder] TRADE REG. REP. (CCH) ¶ 45,078.

11. International Association of Machinist and Aerospace Workers v. Organization of Petroleum Exporting Countries [1979] TRADE REG. REP. (CCH) ¶62,868.

12. United States v. Atlantic Container Line, Ltd. [1970–1979 Transfer Binder] TRADE REG. REP. (CCH) ¶ 45,079.

13. 44 Fed. Reg. 29,509 (1979).

United States Perspectives

Doctrines and Problems Relating to U.S. Control of Transnational Corporate Concentration

DOUGLAS E. ROSENTHAL, STUART E. BENSON, & LISA CHILES

The Committee of Experts on Restrictive Business Practices for the Organisation for Economic Cooperation and Development (OECD) has recently published a report on corporate concentration among OECD member states.[1] The OECD report, which was four years in preparation, has drawn on data supplied by nine member states. Among its conclusions are the following:

1. Substantially more increases than decreases in concentration occurred in Canada, Germany, Japan, and the United Kingdom, and in the industries analyzed by the EEC;
2. In the United States, over the period 1958 to 1972, concentration tended to remain stable in already highly concentrated industries but increased in the low to medium concentrated industries in a sample of 183 comparable manufacturing industries . . . ;
3. The relationship between industry concentration and growth confirmed the theoretical prediction that at high rates of growth, concentration decreased, but that at low to medium growth rates, concentration tended to increase;
4. In general, the evidence of most studies is that high [arguably monopoly] profits are associated with concentrated industries;

The views expressed are entirely those of the authors and do not represent an official position of any agency of the U.S. government.

Mr. Rosenthal is a partner, Sutherland, Asbill and Brennan, Washington, D.C.; former chief, Foreign Commerce Section, Antitrust Division, U.S. Department of Justice.

Mr. Benson is deputy assistant secretary of commerce for trade agreements; former deputy assistant legal adviser, Economic and Business Affairs, U.S. Department of State.

Ms. Chiles is senior attorney, Office of the General Counsel, Agency for International Development, U.S. Department of State; former attorney-adviser, Office of Policy Planning, Antitrust Division, U.S. Department of Justice.

5. Imports did not restrain the ability of larger firms to raise their margins relative to the smaller firms unless there was a very high degree of import penetration;[2] and

6. One United States study found that a two firm concentration ratio of 35 percent or more correlated significantly with high price/cost margins. Structure itself "as measured by different concentration ratios explain more than about one-fifth of the variance in industry price/cost margins."[3]

Given this evidence it is not surprising that "high or rapidly growing levels of concentration are increasingly becoming a matter of concern in many countries,"[4] including the United States. However, a subject of intense controversy within the United States has been with what should U.S. antitrust authorities be concerned, how concerned should they be, and how reliable are the data on which concerns are based. The greatest controversy surrounds the question of whether aggregate industrial concentration in modern societies is increasing rapidly and dangerously. According to David G. Gill of Exxon Corporation, a member of the Business and Industry Advisory Committee to the OECD which monitors official OECD activities, no inference should be drawn from the OECD report that aggregate concentration is becoming a problem.[5]

While it is generally conceded that the problem of aggregate concentration is controversial among antitrust experts,[6] as well as the general public, it is perhaps less well appreciated whether (and to what extent) there is a problem in the United States of intraindustry concentration (concentration among the manufacturers of the same goods) and if it is itself controversial. The conclusions of the OECD report are at variance with those of other analysts.[7]

It is the principal thesis of this article that important recent case decisions in U.S. antitrust law reflect just this conflict over the extent to which intraindustry (horizontal) concentration is economically harmful. We are at a point where the future direction of the law is difficult to discern. Until there is greater U.S. policy agreement, and consistency within U.S. law itself, it is unlikely that any common transnational response will emerge to even horizontal corporate concentration. Ironically, it may not be possible to clarify U.S. antitrust law as long as the underlying policy conflict remains so sharp. For the present, there is an impasse in the United States regarding the question of corporate concentration.

The initial section of this article focuses on some existing legal impasses in the United States with respect to concentration (1) by mergers between manufacturers of the same product, especially where the failing company's defense and considerations of potential competition are involved, (2) by technology licensing between noncompeting firms manufacturing comparable products, and (3) by traditional and shared monopolies.

Four topics, deserving attention in a more comprehensive analysis, will not be discussed. The first of these is conglomerate mergers. Conglomerate mergers have generally been permitted under U.S. antitrust law. Since they promote aggregate concentration, they are subject to criticism by those who see aggregate concentration as a danger. As already indicated, there is enough controversy over the problem of horizontal concentration to leave this even more divisive topic to others.[8]

The second topic is vertical mergers. While conceptually distinct and the subject of a large literature in its own right,[9] a vertical merger may frequently be analyzed in the same manner as a horizontal merger between a potential competitor and an existing firm in an industry. In vertical merger cases, customer or supplier enterprises are often the most likely actual or perceived potential entrants into a particular product market.

The third excluded topic is transnational corporate concentration by private international cartel.[10]

The fourth topic is the role of governments in promoting corporate concentration through the implementation of anticompetitive laws and policies. It is sufficient to point out that governments often undo with one hand what they undertake with the other. As antitrust authorities from several nations are considering how concentration might be lessened to promote competition, others in these same governments are devising programs to increase concentration and stabilize markets, sometimes in the service of the same ultimate objective of greater productivity and allocative efficiency.

Next, the article touches more briefly on a few of the special problems of applying United States law to foreign firms operating within the United States and to U.S. transnational enterprises operating in foreign countries. United States antitrust enforcement policy seeks evenhanded application of U.S. law to foreign as well as domestic enterprises.[11] However, this is not always possible because of special problems raised by (1) the so-called extraterritorial assertion of U.S. jurisdiction where doing so conflicts with important laws and policies of other nations, (2) the difficulties in obtaining relevant information from foreign jurisdictions, (3) the difficulties of obtaining effective relief from excessive concentration outside one's sovereign territory, and (4) the erosion of the "potential competition" doctrine in recent decisions by the United States Supreme Court.[12] These problems combine to give foreign enterprises certain advantages over domestic enterprises in avoiding U.S. antitrust regulation.

The Conclusion shows that given the current impasse in U.S. antitrust enforcement against horizontal concentration, especially where it involves conduct beyond our shores, there are no imminent prospects for defining transnational enforcement standards or establishing transnational enforcement institutions. Nonetheless, some modest transnational collaboration is possible and desirable to clarify policy choices and build a foundation for future progress.

THE CONCENTRATION PART OF THE PROBLEM OF
TRANSNATIONAL CONCENTRATION

The identification of a concentration problem is founded on the assumption that if one or a few firms acquire the power to control prices as to distinct products in a geographically-defined market, competition will be suppressed, product quality will decline (as will the range of consumer choice and producer productivity, including the development of new technology), and prices will reflect some degree of monopoly profits. On the other hand, other considerations may tend to vitiate the characterization of industrial concentration as a problem. For example, large-scale markets and production experience may increase rather than decrease efficiency; industrial competition in a high-growth phase may consolidate the industry into a few strong competitors with the weakest firms having to drop out; in the international setting, domestic concentration may be necessary and therefore desirable in order to maintain an internationally competitive position. There is as yet no strong consensus on either the characterization of concentration as a problem, or on what approaches to the problem so defined are most effective.

Nonetheless, U.S. antitrust law takes a certain cognizance of industrial concentration as a problematic phenomenon. The prototypical illustration of this phenomenon in the antitruster's demonology is that of the U.S. steel industry over the course of this century. Antitrust authorities sometimes view the relative concentration and lack of competition in the steel industry as a primary cause of its present state of technological retardation and resultant difficulty in competing with imported steel.[13]

Statutory Overview

Three principal antitrust statutes are directly relevant to the effort to deal with this problem of concentration, but Section 7 of the Clayton Act is probably the most powerful tool in the antitrust regulatory regime.[14] Section 1 of the Sherman Act [15] and Section 5 of the Federal Trade Commission Act[16] require evidence of conspiracies in restraint of trade or unfair trade practices respectively, in order to obtain remedial prohibitions. Similarly, Section 2 of the Sherman Act[17] requires a showing of affirmative action to obtain or restrain market power by exclusionary or predatory conduct.[18]

Section 7 of the Clayton Act, however, only requires evidence that a corporation engaged in commerce in the United States is seeking to acquire another and, by so doing, may substantially lessen competition or tend to create a monopoly. Moreover, when applied prior to the consummation of an acquisition, Section 7 permits quick, clean, and effective relief to avert anticompetitive effects by prohibiting the merger. One of the many vexing problems subsumed by the general issue of concentration is that of formulating an appropriate remedial order for anticompetitive mergers that have already been consummated between firms of signficant size in a concentrated market.[19]

Mergers Between Producers of the Same Product

Although Section 7 seems to be, in theory, the most effective of the present antitrust statutes, its enforcement by the Justice Department appears to be declining. According to an unpublished study by the Antitrust Division there were twenty-three Section 7 prosecutions filed by the Department of Justice in 1969, sixteen in 1973, and only eleven in 1979.[20] The meaning of this decline is unclear. At least as to horizontal mergers between actual competitors, the decline may be a reflection of the only locus of consensus on horizontal concentration doctrine—the general validity of the 1968 Merger Guidelines of the Department of Justice (Merger Guidelines).[21] The Merger Guidelines, twelve years ago, announced that they are to be read "only as a statement of current Department policy, subject to change at any time without prior notice"[22] and, of course, are not binding on courts.

Nonetheless, not only the Antitrust Division and Federal Trade Commission (FTC), but also the courts and private antitrust practitioners have been heavily influenced by the relative clarity and precision of the guidelines. Illustrative of this precision is the instruction given in the guidelines for analyzing a possible merger by one of the four largest firms making a product as to which they share 75 percent of a geographic market. According to the guidelines, if the acquiring firm possesses a 4 percent market share, the Department of Justice will ordinarily challenge the acquisition of a competitor with another 4 percent market share.[23] If the acquiring firm's share is 15 percent, then an acquisition of a firm with only a 1 percent market share is likely to be challenged.[24]

Since September 5, 1978, when the premerger regulations went into effect, companies with substantial sales into, or assets within, the United States must give prior notice to federal antitrust enforcement agencies when planning to merge.[25] Of the approximately sixty proposed transnational mergers referred to the Foreign Commerce Section of the Antitrust Division, during the first eighteen months of this new notification requirement, only one involved firms with proportionate market shares close to the standards set forth in the guidelines. In fact, only three raised any substantial antitrust question at all and none of these appeared, based on traditional enforcement considerations, to warrant prosecution.[26]

It appears that this consensus in merger law was formed largely because of the conclusion by the private antitrust bar and its clients that the standards are reasonable and reduce uncertainty in business planning.

Professor William James Adams has identified two distinct modes of analysis for reviewing mergers. He calls one "competition as a quasi-goal of society." The other is "competition for the sake of efficiency." According to the former, competition is always desirable. According to the latter, competition is only desirable when it yields net benefits.[27] This distinction strikes to the heart of the current debate over horizontal concentration. If antitrust lawyers, their clients, and judges conclude that some horizontal mergers involving a big firm in a concentrated market are economically beneficial ("competition for the sake of efficiency") the present consensus on the validity of the guidelines may dissolve. In fact, there already is evidence that the consensus is eroding in two special horizontal merger situations.

Acquisition of the "Failing Company"

The first involves the acquisition of an allegedly failing company. Where the firm to be acquired is likely to withdraw from the market by ceasing operations, it is no more anticompetitive, in many instances, to let another firm buy it out than to let it go under. The Merger Guidelines state that the department will accept the defense only where the firm to be acquired has (1) "depleted resources," (2) only "remote prospects for rehabilitation," and (3) made "good faith efforts . . . to elicit a reasonable offer of acquisition more consistent with the purposes of Section 7."[28]

How badly off must the acquired firm be? How hard must it try to find a more eligible suitor? In *General Dynamics*,[29] the Supreme Court may have suggested that it will entertain arguments about the lack of competitive harm from a merger which violates the Merger Guidelines, especially where the acquired firm is competitively weak, with depleted resources, even if not failing. In that case the acquired company owned substantial coal reserves that were committed under long-term requirements contracts. Because the reserves of the acquired firm were spoken for, the Court concluded that the acquisition was not anticompetitive.

In a recent decision, *United States v. International Harvester Co.*,[30] the Seventh Circuit read *General Dynamics* to permit a merger of two companies with more than 20 percent sales in the concentrated market for high-powered farm tractors. Apparently, the court felt that while the acquired company, Steiger, was not failing, it was competitively weak for lack of adequate access to funds for investment. Since *Harvester*, the purchaser of 40 percent stock interest in Steiger, had a deep pocket, the court reasoned that the acquisition would serve Steiger's needs.[31]

Department of Justice officials have criticized this decision and its suggestion that the failing company defense is now reduced to a "weakened competitor" defense.[32] They correctly point out that the Supreme Court in *General Dynamics* did not conclude that the contractual commitment of its coal reserves made the acquired firm a weak competitor. It only concluded that the committed reserves were not a factor in the market and that the relevant product market was properly narrowed to reserve coal mining capacity for future sales.[33] There is now a direct conflict between two circuit courts and the issue remains for future resolution.

Acquisition by a Potential Competitor

The second horizontal situation in which there appears to be erosion of the Merger Guidelines involves acquisitions by potential future (but not present) competitors. According to the guidelines, the threat of entry, either through internal (de novo) expansion or toehold acquisition of a small firm already present, "may often be the most significant competitive limitation on the exercise of market power by leading firms, as well as the most likely source of additional actual competition."[34] In two important decisions, one domestic—the *Marine Bancorporation* case,[35] the other international—the *British Oxygen* case,[36] some doubt has been cast on the vitality of that proposition.

In *Marine Bancorporation*, the Supreme Court established two tests for a successful challenge to an acquisition of one firm by another based on the acquirer being an actual potential entrant by de novo or toehold entry. First, there must be proof that the entrant could feasibly enter the market by other routes. Second, and more demanding, there must be proof that entry by another route would have a "substantial likelihood of ultimately producing deconcentration of that market or other significant procompetitive effects."[37] Implicitly, by setting this condition, the Supreme Court adopted what Adams has called the "competition for the sake of efficiency" mode of concentration analysis. However, the Department of Justice in the Merger Guidelines usually employs the "competition as a quasi goal of society" standard.[38] Competition is thought to be facilitated when unjustified concentration is frustrated. It is not necessary, appropriate, or even perhaps possible to demonstrate that the acquirer will clearly establish a significant independent presence in the market if its acquisition plans are blocked. The Supreme Court's test puts the law enforcer in the perverse position of having to know better than the acquirer itself what its true prospects are for entry by means other than acquisition. It would make more sense to put the burden of proof on the acquirer to justify why independent entry is not feasible. Either way, this decision makes a departure from the clear structural guidelines of excessive horizontal concentration—a major purpose and benefit of the guidelines.

At present, the law of potential competition—especially as to transnational mergers—is at an impasse. In *British Oxygen*, the world's second largest producer of industrial gases—with no prior sales in the United States—acquired the third largest producer, Airco (a U.S. company), that occupied 16 percent of a product market in which the top three firms held 60 percent of the market.[39] In upholding the acquisition, the Second Circuit found that the Federal Trade Commission did not show that British Oxygen was a potential entrant in the reasonably near future. The court held that a showing of "eventual" entry was not sufficient.[40] While not discussed in the opinion, it is worth noting that both the British government and the European Commission filed papers with the court supportive of the merger, arguing that foreign potential entrants are handicapped by cultural and social barriers that make independent entry even more difficult for them than for domestic potential entrants.[41] This decision would lead one to expect easy access to American markets by major foreign firms acquiring large American firms.

However, a recent decision by the Federal Trade Commission indicates that the issue has not been finally settled. *In the Matter of Brunswick Corporation,*[42] involved a joint venture to manufacture less expensive outboard motors. One of the partners was Brunswick. Its Mercury Division had approximately 20 percent of the market[43] which made it the second largest of four domestic manufacturers jointly occupying 95 percent of the market.[44] The other partner was the Japanese firm Yamaha. Yamaha manufactured and sold outboard motors everywhere in the world but the United States—the largest market.[45] Yamaha was already established as a successful seller of motorcycles and snowmobiles throughout the United States, but had failed twice before to penetrate the outboard motor market de novo.[46] The FTC found (on relatively compressed analysis) that by 1973 Yamaha had the technology to compete effectively in the United States.[47]

Late in 1972, the two firms had formed a joint venture, Sanshin, to make outboard motors in Japan. These were to be marketed in Japan under a Yamaha label and in the United States under a Mariner label. The joint venture was for a period of ten years with automatic three-year renewals (unless revoked with three years' notice).[48] The FTC decision found that the three burdens of proof imposed by the decisions in *Marine Bancorporation* and *British Oxygen* had been met. First, Yamaha's technical capability and market experience demonstrated the feasibility of its entry.[49] De novo entry was found to be possible through (1) its national network of motorcycle and snowmobile dealers, (2) private label mass merchandisers, or (3) camping and sports supply stores.[50]

Second, the likelihood of significant procompetitive effects was found in Yamaha's overall financial strength, development of an advanced motor, successful expansion history worldwide, and intention to compete effectively at the time the joint venture was entered.[51]

Finally, the FTC took the fact of the joint venture itself as proof that Yamaha was an imminent potential entrant.[52]

There is a second potential competition theory besides that of actual potential entry. It is the theory of the perceived potential entrant "waiting in the wings" as a threat of competition, keeping present competitors from giving in to the temptation of oligopoly or collusive pricing.[53] This theory for control of concentration is even more tenuous, as it depends upon perceptions that are subjective and therefore likely to be ambiguous if enough people are canvased. Nevertheless, the FTC explicitly held that Yamaha alone among noncompeting enterprises was able "to inspire the fear of competition in the hearts of U.S. manufacturers" before it entered the joint venture.[54]

The case is now on remand to the Administrative Law Judge for a relief determination, since the Commission had reversed the initial decision on liability. The difficulty reconciling *Brunswick* with *British Oxygen* suggests that the potential competition doctrine will stand or fall on the weight given to particular facts of particular adjudications. By applying the three conservative tests of liability and finding it as to a nonpermanent joint venture (even where Yamaha had twice previously failed to effect de novo entry) the FTC has boldly attempted to reestablish the vitality of the position taken in the Merger Guidelines—that is, competition as a quasigoal of society.

Whether or not the potential competition doctrine is applied in U.S. law, can have a profound impact upon the U.S. domestic economy as well as the transnational economy. If foreign enterprises that are only potential competitors are virtually free to make horizontal domestic acquisitions, the trend toward foreign takeovers in U.S. markets is stimulated at a time when U.S. companies appear to be substantially undervalued. It also suggests the possibility that international concentration by merger may reach problem proportions before concentration reaches the trigger point in any national market. Consider a hypothetical case of a Canadian acquirer not competing in the U.S. market which acquires a U.S. target not selling in Canada. The Canadian firm is the fifth largest in Canada, and the U.S. firm is fifth largest in America. There would be no increase in the five-firm concentration ratio in either Canada or the United States, but there may be a significant increase in concentration in the aggregate North American market.

Concentration by Technology License

The preceding discussion of the *Brunswick* case demonstrates that many of the effects of a merger, including anticompetitive concentration, can be achieved by joint venture.[55] The same is true of technology licensing by one firm to another, or reciprocally, where the effects of the arrangement may be not only the reduction of competition *inter se* but the reduction of significant consumer choice in the product market generally.

In this area of the law there is something of an impasse as to what types of technology-sharing arrangements between large firms in concentrated markets should be and are illegal. Three current and contradictory theories of excessively anticompetitive concentration are discernible.

The first, and most dubious, is reflected in the most recent decision to consider the issue. In *United States v. Westinghouse Elec. Corp.*,[56] Judge Weigel held that a fifty-year-old reciprocal know-how agreement between two billion-dollar worldwide enterprises (Westinghouse and Mitsubishi), as to virtually their full line of hundreds of electrical products, was not illegal even though the two enterprises generally did not compete in each other's home market and the agreement had so provided. His decision was based on two considerations: (1) it is necessary to prove anticompetitive intent to render such an agreement illegal, *regardless of the anticompetitive effect*,[57] and (2) no such intent is shown here because the most plausible explanation for the failure of Mitsubishi to sell in the United States in competition with Westinghouse is fear of infringing on Westinghouse patents.[58]

The first consideration, as the Department of Justice has argued on appeal to the Ninth Circuit,[59] flatly contradicts the Supreme Court decision in *National Society of Professional Engineers v. United States*, which held that the legality of agreements must be tested against their effect on competition.[60] Judge Weigel's second finding is undercut by the fact that the case was decided immediately after the government presented its case, before the defendants had intoduced specific evidence showing that there were Westinghouse patents actually blocking Mitsubishi sales. There is no precedent for imposing on the plaintiff the burden of proving the negative—in this case, that patents must have blocked licensee entry into the U.S. market.[61]

An alternative theory of liability is argued by the United States on appeal.

> A major manufacturer in a highly concentrated market may not repeatedly renew broad, multiproduct, multipatent license agreements that have the effect of disabling major potential competitors from providing badly needed additional competition in the United States.[62]

In its brief, the United States offers evidence demonstrating that Mitsubishi, but for the long-term, multiproduct license, was an actual potential entrant into the U.S. market. It argues that:

> The court need not determine how long competitors may renew patent license agreements before the antitrust laws are violated. There is no single answer to that question. Rather, under a rule of reason analysis, the answer in each case will depend on the economic factors relevant to the parties and markets involved. The issue in this case is, however, whether the restraints imposed for over fifty years can now be justified as reasonable in light of the relevant present day economic realities.[63]

The caution of this statement suggests that reciprocal licensing agreements between large firms in concentrated markets that may have a restrictive effect may still be legal if their duration is somewhat less than fifty years or covering a somewhat smaller range of products than several hundred. Recent experience of the senior author in Department of Justice decision making in the technology licensing area demonstrates that this has been the recent enforcement philosophy of the department. The department has not filed a single suit following up on its theory in the *Westinghouse* case. Such a view encourages long-term restrictive technology-sharing agreements between the largest transnational enterprises, even in oligopolistic industries. While such licensing does promote some efficient dissemination of technology, one wonders whether the disincentives to independent research in concentrated industries, stemming from dependence on a licenser effectively eliminated from the competitive market for perhaps two or three decades, do not outweigh the benefits of collaboration.

The Department of Justice appeared to take a more aggressive position in its *Antitrust Guide for International Operations*, now more than three years old.[64] The essential problem in this area of antitrust enforcement is determining whether a licensee could become a competitor of the licenser without the benefit of the license. Recognizing this problem as others have,[65] the guide suggests that it may be relevant to ask whether the restraint on competition exceeds "the time it would take [for the licensee] to develop equivalent know-how itself (the reverse engineering period)."[66] Unfortunately, this "reverse engineering" test begs the question. There is no objective or precise measure of the reverse engineering capability of a licensee. Perhaps the most effective approach for exercising greater control over excessive concentration by technology licensing would be to shift the burden of proof to the licensing parties where the territorial restraint exceeds a period of, say, fifteen years, and the parties are large, well-financed, technologically sophisticated, and operating in noncompetitive industries with significant barriers to entry.[67]

Confusion as to which of these three antitrust enforcement approaches to restrictive technology licensing (or yet another) will be used in the future reflects the conflict between Adams's two modes of competition analysis.[68] Those who believe that seeking competition for itself increases the economic efficiency of a society will probably favor a policy to limit restrictive technology licensing between large potentially competitive enterprises. On the other hand, those who believe that many technological problems are too difficult and too costly for efficient competitive solutions, will tend to favor a less aggressive policy. Again, there is something of an impasse.

Traditional and Shared Monopolies

The word *control* in describing existing concentration in the United States is a misnomer. Dealing with concentration per se as a restraint of trade or a monopoly is difficult under the Sherman Act and the Federal Trade Commission Act. When monopolies do violate statutes, however, traditional U.S. antitrust theory is not content with mere restraint of the monopoly power. The earliest antitrust cases made it clear that the primary purpose of Sherman Act Section 2 is to break up, dissolve, or dissipate monopoly power. In the 1911 *Standard Oil* case, the Supreme Court recognized that remedial relief must not only prevent the conduct that created and maintained a monopoly, but eliminate the monopoly and restore or recreate competition in the affected market.[69] The National Commission for the Review of the Antitrust Laws and Procedures (Commission), recently supported this view.[70]

In its January 1979 report the Commission urged the use of structural relief in Section 7 and Section 2 cases.[71] The Commission's report relied on two major factors to support this view. First, the commissioners agreed that structural relief is more effective in restoring competition to an affected market. If the only relief is an injunction prohibiting certain conduct, the concentrated market will remain; subsequent abuses will be likely, since the basic market conditions persist, and no court could possess the foresight to enjoin all possible forms of abuse that a monopolist may contrive. Second, use of structural relief avoids the need for continuing judicial or administrative supervision of a monopolist to determine whether it is abusing its position or engaging in various practices designed to enhance its position in the market.[72]

One question that was not addressed by the Commission is whether the need to maintain international competitiveness should be a defense to an order of dissolution. For example, under Japan's comparable antitrust statute, the Japanese Fair Trade Commission may not order divestiture when it may make it "difficult for the firm to maintain international competitiveness."[73] This issue has not yet been raised in a U.S. antitrust case.[74]

The Commission emphasized that persistent monopoly power, except in extraordinary circumstances, can be maintained only by culpable conduct.[75] This accords with the view expressed in *Alcoa*[76] and *United Shoe*,[77] among others, that monopoly power itself creates a presumption of culpable conduct which can only be rebutted by evidence of superior skill and foresight. As a result, a number of the commissioners believed that the requirement that conduct to enhance or maintain power should be eliminated by legislation, so that evidence of persistent monopoly power would lead to dissolution unless significant economies of scale were shown.[78] Others believed it was important to retain the conduct element.[79] Nevertheless, the commissioners agreed that persistent monopoly can only be maintained by culpable conduct.[80]

Some recent cases indicate that the trend is just the other way; that is, U.S. courts may be more willing to tolerate monopolies and are raising the burden of proof accordingly for those attacking such power. The courts appear most tolerant of monopoly power when design changes or product innovations are involved. California Computer Products (CalComp) recently sued IBM for appropriating its market share in peripheral equipment that CalComp manufactures to fit into IBM's central processing units.[81] IBM manufactures both the central units and the peripheral equipment itself. CalComp was in the business through the process of reverse engineering, whereby it would buy a product from IBM, break it down and copy it, and then undersell IBM since IBM's research and design costs were avoided. IBM made design changes that effectively prevented CalComp from competing on the peripheral units for new machines. Some of the design changes, such as integration of the add-on functions into the main unit, meant not only a lag time, but that CalComp could not compete at all.

The Ninth Circuit Court of Appeals rejected CalComp's argument that these technological manipulations violated the antitrust law.[82] CalComp argued that the changes did not improve performance, but the court found both cost savings to the consumer and improved performance in the new units.[83]

The recent Second Circuit Court of Appeals decision overturning most of the district court's award in *Berkey Photo v. Eastman Kodak*,[84] presents a similar case. In 1972, Kodak introduced the 110 photographic system, including a camera and new film format to go with it. Those companies, including Berkey, that manufactured cameras using film provided by Kodak, could not immediately compete with Kodak's new camera, and Berkey claimed that Kodak had unlawfully monopolized the market. The 110 system had been an immediate success, and Kodak's market share for amateur cameras did not fall below 50 percent for four years.

Berkey presented evidence that the new film product was actually inferior (at least initially) to existing products. The court avoided making any determination of the value of the new product, deciding that this was a matter of individual taste. The important question for the court was whether some coercion was involved.[85] Was the desire to use the new format motivated by desire to impede competition? The court found no evidence that Kodak attempted to persuade customers to purchase the 110 camera because it was the only camera that could take the new film.[86] The court concluded there was no coercive behavior and no violation of the antitrust laws.

In neither of these cases did the court seek to assess the value of the new product. Both courts indicated that the antitrust laws are aimed at unreasonable business behavior such as predatory pricing or coercive practices. In *CalComp*, the court concluded that price cuts by IBM were not predatory since they were profitable to IBM and were responsive to competition from the peripherals manufacturers such as CalComp.[87]

The Commission report also urged the courts to take a tougher stand in "attempt to monopolize" cases, under Section 2 of the Sherman Act. The Commission was primarily concerned about the approach taken in *United States v. Empire Gas*,[88] where the conduct was particularly anticompetitive, but was not actionable since the defendant's market share was not large enough to present a "dangerous probability of success" of monopolization of the market.[89]

The Commission concluded that a legislative change to clarify the "dangerous probability" requirement may be necessary,[90] because the Supreme Court has declined to reconcile various circuit court decisions that have construed the "dangerous probability" requirement differently.[91] The Commission's proposed legislation would require courts, in determining the existence of a dangerous "risk" of monopoly, to weigh several factors including the defendant's intent, its present or probable market power, and the anticompetitive potential of the conduct involved.[92] Moreover, under the proposal, the evidence by defendants that prices were not below average variable or marginal cost would not be an absolute defense, but just another factor to be considered.[93]

Successful prosecution of an "attempt to monopolize" case is most difficult because of the burden of proving a "dangerous probability of success." Inasmuch as courts evince greater tolerance of monopoly power, they may also increase the existing burden of proof for attempt cases. These concerns are evident in the FTC action against *Dupont*,[94] in which it is alleged that Dupont was employing illegal strategies to expand its production of titanium dioxide to meet or capture all growth in the market. These strategies included pricing low enough to prevent other companies from expanding production and refusing to license its technology, which permitted DuPont to preserve its technological advantage over competitors.[95] The administrative law judge agreed that DuPont would probably acquire a monopoly share, but refused to hold any of DuPont's actions to be unfair or unreasonable. The opinion concluded that even if DuPont knew it would gain a monopoly share, such knowledge was not enough to turn legitimate business conduct into an illegal practice or to presume an intent to lessen competition or create a monopoly.[96]

Another current problem in U.S. antitrust law concerns shared monopolies. Justice Department officials[97] acknowledge that antitrust theorists differ on the nature and extent of the problem, and whether it is structural[98] or behavioral;[99] some theorists warn that enforcement agencies should distinguish between contrived and natural oligopolistic pricing;[100] still others argue that there is no problem at all.[101] The concern of the Antitrust Division is that a few dominant firms in a market, aware of their oligopolistic interdependence, may also be able to coordinate their decision making so as to achieve a monopolylike level of performance without an overt agreement.

The Antitrust Division has had underway for more than two years a systematic examination of concentrated industries in the United States.[102] Several concerns have motivated the division to undertake this study. First, concentration improves the firms' ability to coordinate behavior leading to anticompetitive results. In order to circumvent the rigors of competition, these firms must be able to reach some consensus as to the right noncompetitive price structure. In addition, they must be able to detect rivals who might otherwise succeed in gaining increased profits by undercutting the consensus price.[103]

Concentration alone may not be enough to enable the firms to coordinate their activities. These firms may have to adopt *facilitating mechanisms,* which the Antitrust Division has defined as any practice (often developed over time and perhaps even serving a legitimate business purpose) which facilitates interdependent or cooperative behavior.[104] Facilitating mechanisms will vary within each industry. An illustration of the type of activity that may be classified as a facilitating mechanism can be found in the Westinghouse–GE consent decree entered with the United States in 1976.[105] Westinghouse and GE made available to each other current price and other competitive information through price books containing simplified procedures for pricing turbogenerators, along with a multiplier that could be used to determine the price each would use in any given sales situation. Both also introduced price protection policies designed to ensure treatment to all customers, but also published outstanding orders and price quotations. As a result, both companies had a means to coordinate prices and avoid accidental or intentional price undercutting.

Shared monopolies appear to be a matter of considerable concern outside the United States as well. The Treaty of Rome establishing the European

Economic Community contains a provision addressed to abuses of a dominant position by one or more enterprises.[106] A bill is pending before the Canadian Parliament that would authorize civil review of *joint monopolization,* defined as any situation where a small number of firms account for more than 50 percent of a relevant market and pursue closely parallel policies.[107] Japan recently enacted a law that presumes an industry to be monopolized when the market share of one company exceeds 50 percent or the combined share of two companies exceeds 75 percent.[108] In 1978, the Japanese Fair Trade Commission announced that twenty-six lines of manufacturing industries were considered in a state of monopoly or shared monopoly.[109] At present, there is very little practical experience with these laws, but interest in shared monopoly among various antitrust agencies appears to be increasing.[110]

United States antitrust agencies are acquiring more extensive information about concentration through the recently enacted premerger notification requirement of the Clayton Act.[111] These notification requirements extend to certain foreign transactions, including those involving major foreign sellers doing business in the United States or those with significant assets located here.[112] The Hart-Scott-Rodino Act (the Act) does not cover all acquisitions or mergers that should be reviewed by antitrust authorities. Rather the Act purposely limited the reporting requirements to the activities most likely to raise antitrust concerns. Thus, obtaining information about trends in concentration as such, both here and abroad, will only be assisted partially by this mandatory requirement.[113]

THE TRANSNATIONAL PART OF THE PROBLEM

If little agreement exists on the definition of the concentration problem, there is even less on what assertions of extraterritorial jurisdiction are considered appropriate to limit transnational concentration. That, in essence, is the transnational part of the problem. The Justice Department's active enforcement of the antitrust laws in U.S. foreign commerce has met some resistance, especially from foreign governments. The most recent *causes célèbres* involved the so-called international uranium cartel and the North Atlantic shipping case.[114] A corollary of the jurisdictional problem is that the difficulties of enforcing U.S. antitrust law over foreign enterprises, especially when they do not operate in the United States, sometimes gives such enterprises a type of antitrust immunity that domestic enterprises do not enjoy.[115] Largely in response to the uranium and shipping cases, the British government has recently adopted legislation that increases the powers of the British Secretary of State to prevent compliance with foreign (read United States) demands for evidence or other orders that offend British jurisdiction or sovereignty, limits enforcement in Great Britain of foreign antitrust and multiple damage judgments, and (perhaps of most interest) enables British persons and companies to recover damages paid under foreign judgments in excess of actual damages to the foreign plaintiff.[116]

The problem, of course, is not new. Laws blocking foreign access to evidence have been on the books in Great Britain and elsewhere for some time,[117] and the Australian government recently prohibited the enforcement of foreign antitrust judgments that offend its jurisdiction and sovereignty.[118]

Two suggestions seem in order. First, as State Department Legal Adviser John Stevenson noted in 1970,

> In the overwhelming majority of cases, where problems [of jurisdiction] have arisen they have not been the result of invalid exercises of jurisdiction but rather of two valid, conflicting exercises of jurisdiction.[119]

Antitrust cases have generally not been brought either by enforcement agencies or private parties unless there was a substantial U.S. connection.

Second, the objection of foreign countries is often not to the extraterritorial application of U.S. law per se, but rather to its unilateral application. Where international agreement exists, even the United Kingdom applies its law extraterritorially.[120] The contracting parties of the General Agreement on Tariffs and Trade (GATT) permit the application of each others' antidumping and countervailing duty laws to conduct abroad and generally permit the gathering of evidence by other countries in their territories in order to enforce these laws.[121]

Unfortunately, the differences among nations (even our major trading partners) regarding antitrust enforcement have made similar agreements in the antitrust field impossible. The recently concluded 1979 OECD Council Recommendation on Cooperation in Restrictive Business Practices Affecting International Trade calls for member states to cooperate with foreign investigations where national laws and national interests permit.[122] Even this constructive step forward necessitates a sometimes painful case-by-case approach that is not always successful in resolving conflict.

The shipping and uranium cases illustrate these points. In the former, heavy fines were assessed against a number of U.S. and foreign firms and individuals for fixing rates and otherwise restraining competition among them in the North Atlantic shipping trade. Since the case involved shipments to and from U.S. ports there was little question that the U.S. government had jurisdiction in a legal sense; U.S. antitrust authorities have the power, and we believe the right, to set and enforce rules for the conduct of those who wish to do business in the United States. However, the United States was not the only country with both a direct interest in the activity and legitimate jurisdiction to regulate it. Foreign governments argued, as they have persistently done in the past, that the United States should not unilaterally regulate this inherently international industry.

In the case of the so-called uranium cartel, certain foreign governments in 1972 sponsored the establishment of an international arrangement for the setting of floor prices for uranium exported by their domestic producers. This was in response to an embargo imposed by the United States against all importation of uranium for U.S. domestic consumption, which eliminated well over half the world's uranium market for foreign producers. There was some evidence that the cartel had an indirect effect on uranium prices in the U.S. domestic market, and that members of the cartel attempted to prevent U.S. middleman uranium dealers from selling uranium abroad. The Department of Justice conducted an extensive grand jury investigation into the activities of the cartel and brought a criminal prosecution against the Gulf Oil Corporation.[123] It did not, however, sue the foreign members of the cartel.

In both of these cases, foreign governments resisted all attempts by the grand juries to obtain evidence in their countries. Nonetheless, substantial evidence was obtained from documents located within the United States and in the case of the uranium cartel, from inspection of documents obtained from Australia by the environmental organization Friends of the Earth.

The Justice Department's decision in the uranium case not to take criminal action against the foreign defendants, over which it believed it had jurisdiction, was taken primarily because of considerations of comity[124] that weighed against the application of U.S. antitrust law to foreign participants in the cartel.[125] Among the factors leading to this conclusion were: (1) the impact of the uranium cartel on United States commerce was not found to be substantial, (2) the cartel was formed pursuant to clear and important policies of the involved foreign states, and (3) these policies sought the reasonable objective of preserving foreign uranium industries from the otherwise devastating blow of the protectionist U.S. uranium import embargo. However, a different standard was applied to Gulf because its first obligation as a U.S. corporation was to comply with the law of the United States and it could be expected to be aware of and to act in conformity with that law.

Transnational mergers and joint ventures can raise similar problems. On the whole, U.S. law enforcement in this area has been quite circumspect. This is due in part to considerations of comity and to the fact that Section 7 of the Clayton Act applies only to mergers between firms that are actually engaged in U.S. commerce.[126] However, several additional factors are involved when one or both parties to a merger are foreign companies. First, differences in language and custom, and uncertainties connected with foreign trade and investment, constitute additional barriers to entry into the U.S. market; foreign companies are thus less likely to be considered potential competitors. This may have been a factor in the *British Oxygen* decision[127] as well as in a recent FTC decision not to oppose the acquisition by J. I. Case Company, (a subsidiary of Tenneco) of the French firm Poclain. Case proposed to acquire a 40 percent interest in Poclain assuring control of its U.S. assets (including a U.S. subsidiary). The Poclain group of companies is Europe's largest manufacturer of heavy construction equipment. However, the firm was in some financial difficulty.[128] Both Case and Poclain produced hydraulic excavators and cranes, though Poclain had not produced or sold these products in the United States. The French government had approved the acquisition, presumably to increase the economic vitality of an important French manufacturing entity.

Considerations of comity, the importance of the merger to the French economy, as well as the improbability that a foreign company in financial difficulty would enter the U.S. market, may have led to the FTC's decision to permit the merger.

In another instance, the Justice Department objected to a proposed international joint venture, despite the significant adverse impact its decision had on the interests of two foreign governments. Pratt & Whitney of Canada and Rolls Royce of Britain proposed a joint venture whose purpose was to produce an executive jet engine largely for sale in the United States.[129] Pratt & Whitney of Canada was a wholly owned subsidiary of United Technologies, a U.S. firm. The Justice Department found that United Technologies and Rolls Royce were the two largest manufacturers of jet engines in the non-Communist world, and the world market was very concentrated. The Justice Department reasoned that these two companies could each produce the engines and that the joint venture would preclude potential competition between them. It rejected the argument that the venture was so costly that independent development was unlikely. It also rejected the argument that there already were several viable competitors in the market who would remain unaffected by the joint venture. While this was true, the combination of the Rolls Royce and Pratt & Whitney names was likely to overwhelm the less well-known competitors.

This decision led to abandonment of the venture, thereby frustrating a significant investment in Canada that would have been welcomed by the Canadian government. One could argue that the United States should have ignored this joint venture, since Pratt & Whitney Canada was not a U.S. company. But it was wholly owned and controlled by United Technologies; there was every reason to treat them as one entity. This economic unit notion, though objected to by many foreign governments, is not exclusively American.[130] Furthermore, the original joint venture proposal brought to the department involved a Pratt & Whitney plant in the United States. It appears that the Canadian plant was suggested as a new location for manufacturing after the U.S. situs joint venture was rejected. It should be pointed out that while the Justice Department opposed this joint venture it approved a more speculative and costly collaboration between Rolls Royce and United Technologies to produce a different size jet turbofan engine.

Second, U.S. antitrust enforcement against foreign enterprises is also somewhat limited by the difficulties in obtaining evidence abroad. The British bill[131] is a reminder that foreign governments can and do block U.S. enforcement efforts. In many merger and joint venture cases, the involvement of one U.S. firm will be a sufficient avenue to challenge the transaction; this is especially true since the Premerger Notification Law[132] gives U.S.

agencies the chance to investigate and obtain information concerning proposed mergers and joint ventures. Further, the Justice Department now has the power to issue Civil Investigative Demands to persons abroad.[133]

When a U.S. agency or court serves compulsory process on a foreign party, and that party, acting in good faith, is prohibited by local law from complying with it, one nation's interests must give way. U.S. courts have so far held that the relative interests must be weighed and that, where the foreign national interest is strong, and the consequences for the private party under the foreign law for compliance are severe, they will often not require compliance.[134] This problem further differentiates the application of U.S. antitrust laws between U.S. and foreign firms operating in transnational commerce.

Finally, there is sometimes a problem in formulating an appropriate remedy in international merger cases. If a U.S. firm proposes to merge with a foreign firm or enter into a joint venture with it, this can be easily enjoined. However, if two foreign firms with no U.S. affiliates combine, there may be no practical way to attack the transaction, even if one or both parties have substantial sales in the United States. Suppose, on the other hand, that both these foreign firms have U.S. subsidiaries that have a relatively small share of the U.S. market that is, however, subject to scrutiny under the Justice Department's Merger Guidelines. Should the United States and other countries in similar positions require divestiture of the U.S. subsidiaries? Again, a weighing of the relative interests in the transaction may hold the only principled solution.

Because of all these factors—comity, jurisdiction, additional barriers to entry, evidence, and remedies—U.S. antitrust laws concerning economic concentration affect domestic firms more than foreign firms. Whether this places U.S. companies at a disadvantage vis-a-vis their foreign competitors here or abroad is beyond the scope of this brief discussion. It should be remembered, however, that U.S. companies are generally free to conduct joint operations in foreign markets and to merge with foreign firms if in the process they do not restrain or tend to suppress competition in the United States.

The clearer problem is that these factors substantially increase the uncertainties of antitrust analysis, a problem aggravated by the fact that decision making is not centralized. Antitrust enforcement involves not only the Department of Justice and the FTC, but also the courts and sometimes other agencies. Moreover, private suits may be filed regardless of whether the government takes any action. In both the uranium and shipping cases, massive treble damage actions are underway[135] and, in the shipping case, the Federal Maritime Commission is investigating whether the alleged arrangements violated the Shipping Act of 1916.[136]

It has been argued that antitrust enforcement in foreign commerce should be treated as an element of U.S. foreign economic policy and should be handled by diplomacy rather than by legal process.[137] This would work a substantial modification, both procedural and substantive, of the antitrust laws as they apply to foreign commerce. It is, quite frankly, unlikely to occur. However, it may be that, at a minimum, the federal government should take a more active role in private litigation. In certain cases, it may be appropriate for the government to provide its views to the courts on questions of jurisdiction and comity through *amicus curiae* briefs. This could promote a more consistent U.S. approach in an area of great concern to our allies and to the United Staes. To date, the federal government has hesitated even to appear to take sides in private suits; however, some cases may have such international economic and political significance that they should become the legitimate concern of the executive branch.

CONCLUSION

While we have tried to demonstrate that the lack of consensus within the United States, and among other nations, on what is and is not the concentration problem is a fundamental impediment to the establishment of transnational standards or institutions for addressing it, there is still a basis for present collaboration leading to possible future consensus. At the least, increasing horizontal and aggregate concentration leads to new economic relationships and dependencies that may in some respects be both less efficient and more harmful to important social and political values. Accordingly, these phenomena should be better measured and understood.

The OECD report[138] may be a watershed document. If it is possible to agree that obtaining a better understanding of the nature and impact of industrial concentration is a shared problem for developed countries, then a necessary basis for further international collaboration will be established.

Five developing stages of international collaboration are possible. The first stage is expanding the collection and reporting of concentration data within the various nation states. The OECD report recognizes this objective as essential to further action. It suggests that:

(a) Concentration statistics should be expanded by, for example, calculating several different measures, and by introducing new size variables, studying enterprise and local concentration, defining industries more finely, taking into account foreign trade, and by studying concentration outside the industrial sector; . . .

(c) studies should be undertaken into the relationships between the structure of an industry and its behavior and performance; and

(d) where Member countries have not produced concentration studies, they should either undertake such studies themselves or encourage private research into the causes and effects of concentration . . . . [139]

The second stage is sharing, comparing, and analyzing data across national boundaries. If the Japanese experience is relevant to U.S. law enforcement and vice versa, more uniform data and data gathering is necessary, as are institutions to collect and disseminate this information, such as the OECD, GATT, UNCTAD and the U.N. Centre on Transnational Corporations, as well as private research bodies. There is a clear and disconcerting absence of relevant comparative data and important analytical studies of industrial organization.[140] Furthermore, only recently have U.S. antitrust enforcers (and even more recently, a handful of private U.S. antitrust lawyers) agreed that something can be learned from foreign antitrust experience. Foreign data should be utilized in more U.S. analysis and foreign legal developments should be referred to more frequently in developing U.S. enforcement policy and common law jurisprudence.

The third stage is compiling information on and reflecting upon industrial concentration in international markets. Progress in the first two developmental stages will facilitate this process. Such action may assist U.S. antitrust authorities in determining appropriate enforcement policy as to concentration in the U.S. submarkets of larger world markets, such as the automobile industry. The OECD Steel Committee, acting independently of the work of the Restrictive Business Practices Committee, is accumulating and analyzing such aggregate data to assist member states in coping with the international economic difficulties of that industry.[141] The International Energy Agency is performing a similar task as to the world oil industry.[142] Further progress at this stage requires greater willingness to share data across national boundaries and to accommodate the conflicting goals of promoting knowledge and progress on the one hand, while providing some protection to national security and private proprietary interests on the other.

The fourth stage is greater cooperation between nation states in facilitating the investigations and prosecutions of national enforcement agencies against transnational enterprises acting outside that nation's territory with a significant adverse impact within its territory. It is becoming increasingly clear that extraterritorial law enforcement is an inevitable and increasing fact of life in an interdependent world. Absent any extraterritorial enforcement, transnational enterprises possess the theoretical ability to at least partially evade the enforcement of laws of a nation affected by their conduct.

The main problem with extraterritorial antitrust enforcement is not so much that it is extraterritorial, but that it involves direct conflicts between sovereign jurisdictions over fundamental policies. If greater consensus does develop that there is a phenomenon of excessive concentration, it may be desirable for one nation to defer to the law enforcement efforts of another in particular instances for the purposes of gathering information across boundaries or asserting jurisdiction over one's nationals. This type of cooperation is increasing not only with respect to organized crime and drug smuggling, but also with respect to unfair trade practices as defined in the GATT codes.[143] While cooperation on international cartel activity would be expected to come sooner, this stage becomes plausible when the other three have been well established.

Finally, progress to that extent would make it possible to consider a joint enforcement effort by teams of enforcers from two or more national antitrust agencies, or even by employees of an international antitrust agency dealing with excessive concentration by transnational enterprises in several national markets. For those who consider this a utopian vision, consider what the Competition Directorate of the EEC has accomplished in just fifteen years. It has fleshed out a multilateral treaty into an organic body of developing case law—with strong common standards and multinational enforcement experience.[144] Twenty-five years ago, few scholars would have expected such progress for a joint antitrust agency working to promote competition among such a diversity of European states, *inter alia,* by increasing collaboration with national antitrust agencies.

The work of a distinguished political scientist, Inis Claude, suggests that this proposed agenda follows a fifty-year-old theory in international relations called *functionalism.*[145] Most fully developed by David Mitrany,[146] its cornerstone is the proposition that "a major prerequisite for the ultimate solution of political conflicts" is the development of ad hoc institutions of economic and social cooperation.[147] The Mitrany thesis should be acceptable to antitrust authorities who are skeptical about comprehensive planning for social and economic organizations. It is not yet possible to define clearly and commonly the *concentration problem,* let alone fashion a viable remedy for it; however, government officials can at least commit themselves to learn and share.

This volume may be an important early step on the road to cooperatively solving the problem, for it provides a basis in Mitrany's words for ". . . binding together those interests which are common, where they are common and to the extent to which they are common."[148]

NOTES

1. OECD, Report of the Committee of Experts on Restrictive Business Practices, Concentration and Competition Policy (1979).
2. *Id.* at 130–38.
3. *Id.* at 138, citing Kwoka, Jr., Staff Report to the Federal Trade Commission: Market Shares, Concentration and Competition in Manufacturing Idustries (1978).
4. *Id.* at 138.
5. OECD Document DAF/RBP/3798 transmitted to Experts of the Restrictive Business Practices Committee on October 16, 1979. A copy is reprinted *infra,* Annex 1.
6. *See* Ky P. Ewing, Jr., Deputy Assistant Attorney General, Antitrust Division, "Remarks on Where the Justice Department Is Heading and Why: Some Thoughts on Proposals for Conglomerate Merger Legislation," Conference, New York City (June 22, 1979).
7. *See, e.g.,* Kaiser Aluminum & Chemical Corporation, At Issue: The Controversy Over Concentrated Industries (October, 1978).

8. Much of the current debate about the problem of conglomerate mergers centers on two pieces of legislation introduced by Senator Kennedy. *See* Boies, *International Implications of Limitations on Aggregate Concentration, post.* One is S. 600, the *Small and Independent Business Protection Act of 1979*, introduced March 8, 1979, 96th Cong., 1st Sess. The other is S. 1246, the *Energy Antimonopoly Act of 1979*, introduced May 24, 1979, 96th Cong., 1st Sess.

9. *See, e.g.*, L. SULLIVAN, ANTITRUST 657–67 (1977).

10. J. Rahl, "International Cartels and Their Regulation," Columbia University Center for Law and Economic Studies, Conference on International Regulation of Restrictive Business Practices. (November 9, 1979) (Unpublished).

11. *Testimony on Foreign Investment in the United States: Hearings on S. 1284 Before the Subcomm. on International Trade, Investment and Monetary Policy of the Senate Comm. On Banking, Currency and Housing.* 94th Cong., 1st Sess. 3–17 (1975) (statement of Thomas E. Kauper).

12. *See* text accompanying notes 114–40, *infra.*

13. *See, e.g.*, EXECUTIVE OFFICE OF THE PRESIDENT, COUNCIL ON WAGE AND PRICE STABILITY, A STUDY OF STEEL PRICES, Ch. 2 (1975); FTC, BUREAU OF ECONOMICS, STAFF REPORT ON THE UNITED STATES STEEL INDUSTRY AND ITS INTERNATIONAL RIVALS, Ch. 2, II and Ch. 4, I (1977); United States v. Columbia Steel Co., 334 U.S. 495, 534 (1948) (Douglas, J. dissenting); United States v. Bethlehem Steel Corp., 168 F. Supp. 576 (S.D.N.Y. 1958).

14. 15 U.S.C. §18 (1976).

15. 15 U.S.C. § 1 (1976).

16. 15 U.S.C. § 45 (1976).

17. 15 U.S.C. § 2 (1976).

18. United States v. Grinnell Corp., 384 U.S. 563 (1966).

19. Elzinga, *The Antimerger Law: Pyrrhic Victories*, 12 J. L. & ECON. 43 (1969).

20. *See* ANTITRUST DIVISION WORKLOAD REPORT, submitted to the staff of the Senate Subcomm. on Antitrust Monopoly and Business Rights of the Comm. on the Judiciary 96th Cong., 1st Sess. (December 7, 1979) (unavailable at date of printing).

21. MERGER GUIDELINES OF THE DEP'T OF JUSTICE, 1 TRADE REG. REP. (CCH) ¶4510 (1968).

22. *Id.* at 6881.

23. *Id.* at 6884.

24. *Id.*

25. FTC, HART-SCOTT-RODINO ANTITRUST IMPROVEMENTS ACT OF 1976—PREMERGER NOTIFICATION; REPORTING AND WAITING PERIOD REQUIREMENTS; 43 Fed. Reg. 33450 (1978).

26. This information is based on unpublished records retained by the Antitrust Division. During this eighteen-month period approximately 1,340 premerger notifications were received by the Antitrust Division as a whole.

27. Adams, *The "Economic" Analysis of Transnational Mergers, post.*

28. MERGER GUIDELINES, *supra* note 21, at 6884.

29. United States v. General Dynamics Corp., 341 F. Supp. 534 (N.D. Ill. 1972), *aff'd*, 415 U.S. 486 (1974).

30. 564 F.2d 769 (7th Cir. 1977).

31. *Id.* at 777.

32. *Testimony Concerning the Failing Company Defense before the Subcomm. on Antitrust, Monopoly, and Business Rights of the Senate Comm. on the Judiciary*, 96th Cong., 1st Sess. (1979) (statement

of John H. Shenefield) (available from the Legal Procedure Unit of the Antitrust Division).

33. 415 U.S. at 506.

34. MERGER GUIDELINES, *supra* note 21, at 6887–88.

35. United States v. Marine Bancorporation, 418 U.S. 602 (1974).

36. BOC Int'l Ltd. v. FTC, 557 F.2d 24 (2d Cir. 1977).

37. 418 U.S. at 633 (1974).

38. Adams, *supra* note 27.

39. 557 F.2d at 25.

40. *Id.* at 29.

41. *See* J. Griffin, *Antitrust Constraints on Acquisitions by Aliens in the United States*, 13 INT'L LAW. 427 (1980).

42. 3 TRADE REG. REP. (CCH) ¶ 21,623 at 21,773.

43. *Id.* at 21,779.

44. *Id.* at 21,782.

45. *Id.* at 21,779.

46. *Id.* at 21,778.

47. *Id.* at 21,782.

48. *Id.* at 21,779.

49. *Id.* at 21,783.

50. *Id.* at 21,784.

51. *Id.* at 21,784–85.

52. *Id.* at 21,783.

53. United States v. Falstaff Brewing Corp., 410 U.S. 526, 532–33 (1973).

54. In the Matter of Brunswick, 3 TRADE REG. REP. (CCH) ¶ 21,623 at 21,785.

55. *See* text accompanying notes 129–30, *infra,* for a discussion of the proposed joint venture between Rolls Royce and Pratt & Whitney in the manufacture of two types of jet engines.

56. 471 F. Supp. 532 (N.D. Cal. 1978).

57. *Id.* at 537–38.

58. *Id.* at 539.

59. Brief for the Appellant, United States v. Westinghouse Elec. Corp., No. 79–4109 (9th Cir., filed July 13, 1979).

60. 435 U.S. 679, 691 (1978).

61. Brief for the Appellant, *supra* note 59, at 26–31.

62. *Id.* at 32–33.

63. *Id.* at 33 n.78.

64. ANTITRUST DIVISION, U.S. DEP'T OF JUSTICE, GUIDE FOR INT'L OPERATIONS (1977).

65. *See especially,* M. BLECHMAN, FOREIGN LICENSING MONOGRAPH, 27 *et seq.* (1977) (unpublished draft submitted to the Monograph Committee of the Antitrust Section of the American Bar Association).

66. GUIDE FOR INT'L OPERATIONS, *supra* note 64, at 31.

67. *See, e.g.,* Turner, *Territorial Restrictions in the International Transfer of Technology,* TOKYO CONFERENCE ON INT'L ECON. AND COMPETITION POL'Y 151, 156 (1973).

68. *See* Adams, *supra* note 27.

69. Standard Oil Co. v. United States, 221 U.S. 1, 78 (1911).

70. The Commission was organized in 1978 and directed by the president to study and make recommendations on ways to improve the conduct of large antitrust cases, including ways to improve relief in such cases.

71. NATIONAL COMMISSION FOR THE REVIEW OF ANTITRUST LAWS AND PROCEDURES, REPORT TO THE PRESIDENT AND THE ATTORNEY GENERAL 114, 119 (January 22, 1979) (COMMISSION REPORT). This preference for structural relief may be fundamental in U.S. antitrust law and theory, but it is not reflected in competition laws of other countries. Most of these statutes attempt to control the behavior of dominant firms; for the most part, they do not include provisions for directly attacking the power that has been abused.

    See, e.g., the Treaty Establishing the European Community, No.

4300, U.N.T.S. Article 86, which proscribes abuses by one or more dominant undertakings within the Common Market or in a substantial part of it; Federal Republic of Germany's Act Against Restraints of Competition, Sections 22(1) and 22(2), *discussed in* Edwards, *American and German Policy Toward Conduct by Powerful Enterprises: A Comparison,* 23 ANTITRUST BULL. 83 (1978), which prohibits abusive conduct by dominant enterprises. Similar statutes can be found in the United Kingdom, the Netherlands, and Canada.

The antimonopoly law of Japan is a notable exception, in that it does provide for dissolution of monopolists, but only as a last resort if no other remedy would be sufficient, and not as the first remedy to be thought of in cases involving market power. ANTIMONOPOLY LAW OF JAPAN OF 1977 § 8–4 (Counselor's Office of Fair Trade Commission, ed.) (1977).

72. *See, e.g.,* the decision entered in United States v. United Shoe Mach. Corp., 391 U.S. 244 (1968) in which the Supreme Court granted the government's motion to add a divestiture provision to a decree entered ten years earlier. *Discussed in* COMMISSION REPORT, *supra* note 71, at 117–19.

73. ANTIMONOPOLY LAW OF JAPAN (1977), *supra* note 71, at § 8–4(1).

74. Boies, *supra* note 8.

75. COMMISSION REPORT, *supra* note 71, at 156.

76. United States v. Aluminum Company of America, 148 F.2d 416 (2d Cir. 1945).

77. United States v. United Shoe Mach. Corp., 110 F. Supp. 295 (D. Mass 1953), *aff'd per curiam* 347 U.S. 521 (1964).

78. COMMISSION REPORT, *supra* note 71, at 158–59.

79. These commissioners believe that a "no conduct" standard might discourage firms with a near-monopoly position from undertaking legitimate competitive actions, and that the emphasis on proving efficiencies as a defense to structural relief would only protract litigation. COMMISSION REPORT, *supra* note 71, at 161–62.

80. COMMISSION REPORT, *supra* note 71, at 156.

81. California Computer Products v. International Business Machine Corp., 1979–1 TRADE CASES (CCH) ¶ 62,713 (9th Cir. 1979).

82. *Id.* at 77,982.

83. *Id.*

84. 603 F.2d 263 (2d Cir. 1979).

85. *Id.* at 287.

86. *Id.*

87. California Computer Products, Inc., 1979–1 TRADE CASES at 77,983.

88. 537 F.2d 296 (8th Cir. 1976), *cert. denied.,* 429 U.S. 1122 (1977).

89. Empire Gas threatened to put a competitor out of business if he refused to raise his prices, followed through with price cuts; refused to mail a distributor invoices so he could pay his bills, then on this pretense, refused to sell him the propane he needed. It also went door-to-door soliciting a competitor's customers by saying the competitor had gone out of business, even though the competitor had not. Although the court agreed that this conduct was anticompetitive, it concluded that there was no reasonable probability that Empire Gas would ever get much more than its existing 50 percent market share, primarily because of easy entry in the liquid petroleum gas retail business.

90. Commission Report, *supra* note 75, at 150–51.
91. *See, e.g.,* Sulmeyer v. Coca Cola Co., 515 F.2d 835 (5th Cir. 1975), *cert. denied,* 424 U.S. 934 (1976); George R. Whitten, Jr., Inc. v. Paddock Pool Builders, Inc., 508 F.2d 547 (1st Cir. 1974), *cert. denied,* 421 U.S. 1004 (1975); Dearney & Trecker Corp. v. Giddings & Lewis, Inc., 452 F.2d 579, 579 (7th Cir. 1971), *cert. denied* 405 U.S. 1066 (1972); Lessig v. Tidewater Oil Co., 327 F.2d 459 (9th Cir. 1964), *cert. denied,* 377 U.S. 993 (1964).
92. Commission Report, *supra* note 71, at 165–66. The word *risk* of monopolization rather than *probability* was used in order to avoid the implication that the term refers to a greater than 50 percent chance that monopoly will occur. *Id.* at 151.
93. *Id.* at 149–50.
94. *In re* E.I. duPont de Nemours & Company, No. 9108, FTC (filed Sept. 4, 1979), 3 Trade Reg. Rep . (CCH) ¶ 21,613.
95. DuPont's records indicated it planned to extend its market share from 42 percent in 1977 to 53 percent in 1985.
96. DuPont, 3 Trade Reg. Rep. (CCH) ¶ 21,613 at 21,750.
97. See Ky P. Ewing, Jr., Deputy Assistant Attorney General, Antitrust Division, "Remarks on Shared Monopoly and Concentration," Conference, New York City (December 1, 1978) (available from the Legal Procedure Unit of the Antitrust Division).
98. *Id. See, e.g.,* Weiss, "The Structure-Conduct-Performance Paradigm and Antitrust," presentation at the Conference on Antitrust Law and Economics, University of Pennsylvania, November 17, 1978; Qualls, *Stability and Persistence of Eco-*

nomic Profit Margins in Highly Concentrated Industries, 40 S. Econ. J. 604 (1974); Scherer, Industrial Market Structure and Economic Performance 184 n.3 (1st ed. 1971).
99. Hart, *A Forecast of Antitrust Policy Regarding Economic Concentration,* 10 Antitrust Bull. 51 (1965); Hart, *Restructuring the Oligopoly Sector: The Case for a New "Industrial Reorganization Act,"* 5 Antitrust L & Econ. Rev. 35 (1975) (Pt. 1); 6 Antitrust L. & Econ. Rev. 47 (1972) (Pt 2).
100. Winn & Leabo, *Rates of Return, Concentration and Growth—Question of Disequilibrium,* 17 J. L. & Econ. 97 (1974); Mancke, *Causes of Interfirm Profitability Differences: A New Interpretation of the Evidence,* 88 Q. J. Econ. 191 (1974); Weston, *Pricing Behavior of Large Firms,* 10 W. Econ. J. 1 (1972).
101. Handler, *Some Unresolved Problems of Antitrust,* 62 Colum. L. Rev. 930 (1962).
102. One purpose is to provide some information on concentration in the United States. Secondly, of course, the Division is interested in prosecutable cases. The intital survey began with a universe of 717 manufacturing industries in the United States selected on the basis of a four-digit Standard Industrial Classification, which possessed one or more five-digit product categories, and with a four-firm concentration ration of 40 percent or more in 1972. Roughly one-half were excluded, either because they were not known to be shared monopolies, or because their SIC code did not constitute a product *market* in any reasonable antitrust sense. A year ago, the division announced that from these, approximately sev-

enty product lines had been pegged for immediate inquiry; the remainder will be examined over time. Ewing, *supra* note 97, at 6–8.

103. *Id.* at 9.

104. *Id.* at 11.

105. United States v. General Electric Co., [1977–2] TRADE CASES (CCH) ¶¶ 61,659–60.

106. *Supra* note 71; *See* Schroder, *Le Concept de Position Dominante dans l'Application des Articles 66 paragraphe 7 du Traite CECA et 86 Traite CEE,* in LA REGLEMENTATION DU COMPORTEMENT DES MONOPOLES ET ENTERPRISES DOMINANTES EN DROIT COMMUNANTAIRE, (J.A. Van Damme ed. 1977) 186; Temple Lang, *Regulating Multinational Corporate Concentration: The European Economic Community, post.*

107. Competition Act C–13, 30th Parliament, 3d Sess., § 29 (1977). *See* Gressman, *Canadian Merger Policy and Its International Implications, post.*

108. Laws Concerning the Prohibition of Private Monopolization and the Preservation of Fair Trade, *as amended,* ANTIMONOPOLY LAW OF JAPAN, Ch. 1 § 2 (7) (1977).

109. Japan Times, Nov. 30, 1977.

110. A related issue is whether the use of a shared monopoly theory may bring about changes in "attempt to monopolize" law: Could certain conduct of a single firm be held an attempt to create a shared monopoly situation?

111. 15 U.S.C. § 18 (1976).

112. The application of the Act to foreign persons raises a number of issues. For example, will the full penalty of $10,000 a day be imposed against a foreign person for each day of noncompliance? 15 U.S.C. § 18a(g) (1). Will there be secrecy problems: Where domestic companies alone are involved, there are confidentiality requirements. 15 U.S.C. § 18a(h). But where a foreign company is involved, will the intital inquiry be an "antitrust action" that requires notification to foreign governments under existing OECD notification and consultation commitments? Will there be an opportunity for consultation about the economic implications of pending mergers or acquisitions? This is not built into the statutory timetable for review.

113. United States purchasers of foreign assets or voting securities are exempt from reporting unless $10 million or more sales in or into the United States can be attributed to the acquired person in the most recent fiscal year. If a foreign issuer is acquired, the acquisition must be reported if, together with all the entities it controls, the foreign issuer holds assets located in the United States having an aggregate book value of $10 million or more, or made sales in or into the United States of $10 million or more in its most recent fiscal year. Certain investment assets and securities of another person are excluded from this computation.

Similarly, acquisitions by a foreign person must be reported if it acquires assets in the United States of $10 million or more (excluding investment assets). Certain acquisitions by a foreign person outside the United States must be reported as well if it acquires voting securities of a foreign issuer which will give the acquiring foreign person either control of an issuer that holds assets in the United States of $10 million or more, or control of a U.S. issuer with annual net sales or total assets of $10 million or more. In addition, the acquisition must be reported if the aggregate annual sales of the foreign acquirer and the foreign acquired person in or into the United States total $110 million or more, or if their aggregate total assets located in the United States total $110 million or more. *Supra* note 25.

114. United States v. Atlantic Container Line, Crim. No. 79–271, 79–272 (indictment filed June 1, 1979, D.D.C.).

115. As noted at p.17, weakening the vitality of the potential competitor doctrine can have the same effect.

116. [1979] ANTITRUST & TRADE REG. REP. (BNA) F–1.

117. *See, e.g.,* Business Records Protection Act of 1947, ONT. REV. STAT. c. 54 (1970); Netherlands Economic Competition Act of June 28, 1957 *as amended by* Act of July 16, 1958, Art. 39.

118. Foreign Proceedings (Prohibition of Certain Evidence) Act of 1976, Austl. Acts. No. 121 (1976).

119. *Extraterritoriality in Canada— United States Relations,* 63 DEP'T STATE BULL. 425 (1970).

120. An example of this is the British export embargo to Rhodesia, *see* Southern Rhodesia Act, 1965, c. 76; Director of Public Prosecutions v. Doot, [1973] 1 All E.R. 940 (H.L.).

121. *See generally* General Agreement on Tariffs and Trade, October 30, 1947, 61 Stat. (5) (6), T.I.A.S. No. 1700, 55 U.N.T.S. 194 (effective Jan. 1, 1948) *as amended* T.I.A.S. No. 1890; *Agreements Reached in the Tokyo Round of the Multilateral Trade Negotiation: Documents to the United States House of Representatives, 96th Cong., 1st Sess.* 257–307, 309–37 *(1979) (message from the president).*

122. OECD Council Recommendation Document No. C(79)154 (1979).

For a full text of this recommendation, *see* Stockmann, "Reflections on Recent OECD Activities: Regulation of Multinational Corporate Conduct and Structure," *post. See also,* Agreement Between the Government of the United States of America and the Government of the Federal Republic of Germany Relating to Mutual Cooperation Regarding Restrictive Business Practices, signed June 23, 1976, entered into force September 11, 1976, [1976] 27 U.S.T. 1956, T.I.A.S. No. 8291.

123. United States v. Gulf Oil Corp., No. 78–123 (W.D.Pa.) (Crim. information filed May 9, 1978).

124. The principle of comity is one of deference to the interests of foreign sovereign authorities where the application of one's own national law could work a disproportionate harm to those foreign interests. The principle is analogous to the "weighing of interests" test for resolving conflicts of law between the states of our federal system. *See, e.g.,* Timberlane Lumber Co. v. Bank of America, 549 F.2d 597 (9th Cir. 1976); Mannington Mills, Inc. v. Congoleum Corp., 595 F.2d 1287 (3d Cir. 1979); A. VON MEHREN & D. TRAUTMAN, THE LAW OF MULTINATIONAL PROBLEMS 80 (1963). It is most clearly enunciated as to international conflicts between nation states in *Restatement (2d) of the Foreign Relations Law of the United States.* RESTATEMENT (2d) OF FOREIGN RELATIONS LAW OF THE UNITED STATES §§ 18, 39, 40 (1965). The Restatement provides that, among other factors to be taken into account are:

(b) *the extent and the nature of the hardship that inconsistent enforcement actions would impose . . . ,* (c) *the extent to which the re-*

quired conduct is to take place in the territory of the other state,

(d) the nationality of the person, and

(e) the extent to which the enforcement of either state can reasonably be expected to achieve compliance of the rule prescribed by that state. Id. at §40.

125. *Testimony Regarding Department of Justice Uranium Investigation Before the Subcomm. on Antitrust, Monopoly and Business Rights of the Senate Comm. on the Judiciary,* 96th Cong., 2d Sess. (1980) (Statement of John H. Shenefield) (unavailable at date of printing).

126. 15 U.S.C. §18 (1976).

127. 557 F.2d 24; *See* text accompanying notes 39–41.

128. It is not known whether the difficulty rose to the level of a possible "failing company defense". *See* text accompanying notes 28–33, *supra.*

129. Letter from then Assistant Attorney General Thomas E. Kauper to attorneys Phil E. Gilbert, Jr. and Thomas A. Dieterich, December 15, 1975, regarding two proposed joint ventures between Rolls Royce (1971) and United Technologies Corp.

130. *See, e.g.,* Imperial Chemical Industries, Ltd. v. E.C. Commission, [1971–1973 Transfer Binder] Comm. Mkt. Rep. (CCH) ¶ 8161.

131. *Supra* note 116.

132. 15 U.S.C. § 18a (1976).

133. Antitrust Procedures Improvement Act, Pub. L. 96–90 Stat. 1383, §102 amending §3 of the Antitrust Civil Process Act (15 USC 1312)

134. *See* Societe Internationale v. Rogers, 357 U.S. 197 (1958); *In re* Westinghouse Electric Corp. Uranium Contracts Litigation, Ancillary

Proceedings, 563 F.2d 992 (10th Cir. 1977).

135. *See, e.g.,* Uranium Trust Litigation, MDL 342 (Westinghouse Electric Corp. v. Rio Algom Ltd., No. 76-C-3830) (N.D.Ill.); *In re* Ocean Shipping Antitrust Litigation, MDL 395 (S.D.N.Y. M–21–26–CES, [all cases]).

136. 46 U.S.C. § 814 (1976); Order of Investigation August 14, 1979, Federal Maritime Commission Doc. No. 79–83.

137. *See, e.g.,* Mann, *Anglo-American Conflict of International Jurisdiction,* 13 Int. & Comp. L.Q. 1460 (1964).

138. *Supra* note 1.

139. *Id.* at 144.

140. As the OECD report recommends, *id.* at 144, "concentration data should be made more uniform for the purposes of international comparison, since experience in other countries can be helpful in the development of [national] competition policy."

141. 14 Weekly Comp. of Pres. Doc. 1915 (Nov. 1, 1978).

142. International Energy Agency, Oil Market Information System (1979).

143. Multilateral Trade Agreements, *supra* note 121.

144. *See,* Temple Lang, *supra* note 106.

145. I. Claude, Swords into Plowshares: The Problem and Progress of International Organization 344–68 (3d ed. 1964).

146. D. Mitrany, The Progress of International Government (1933).

147. *Supra* note 148, at 345.

148. D. Mitrany, A Working Peace System 40 (1946).

ANNEX 1: REMARKS ON THE OECD CONCENTRATION REPORT

Remarks on the OECD report "Concentration and Competition Policy", by Mr. D. G. Gill, member of the group of Experts on Restrictive Business Practices of the Business and Industry Advisory Committee to the OECD, made to the members of the Bureau of the OECD Committee of Experts on Restrictive Business Practices at a meeting held on June 27, 1979. *See* Summary Record of the 36th meeting of the Committee, OECD Doc. No. RBP/M(79)1 at item XI.

OECD Report on Concentration and Competition Policy

I recently received the draft of chapter 4 dated 19 April. I have not had an opportunity to read the other sections of the OECD's study on concentration and competition policy and will confine most of my comments to those portions of the report dealing with the U.S.

I should note initially that, while the chapter contains a number of comments with which I disagree, overall I found much in the report with which I would agree. Paras. 4 and 5 discuss the many technical problems involved in measuring concentration, and I certainly agree with and endorse the description of the many great difficulties involved in this exercise. The problem, at least in the U.S., is that the data derives from different bases, is non-comparable over time, and includes non-comparable numerators and denominators. Usually, the data is contaminated: for example, foreign operations may or may not be included in numerators or denominators, and much non-manufacturing data is always included for manufacturing companies. The definitions of industries are extremely artificial. Many of my criticisms of the report stem from precisely these inadequacies. I note the following:

(1) Para. 11 observes that in the U.S. from 1958 to 1972 "concentration tended to remain stable in already highly concentrated industries but increased in the low to medium concentrated industries in a sample of 183 comparable manufacturing industries for which data were available". Many economists and university professors in the U.S. question whether any such trend is really observable. Betty Bock, Yale Brozen, Harold Demsets and Fred Weston are representative of the many economists in the U.S. who challenge the interpretations of concentration figures issued by the U.S. Department of Justice and the Federal Trade Commission.

(2) Para. 15 states that overall concentration in the U.S. in manufacturing increased significantly in the post-war period from 1947 to 1952. The report goes on to say that "most of this increase appears to have occurred in the early part of the period". In fact, when one looks at the data, the latter sentence is a clear understatement. The data (and I here refer to The Conference Board's 1978 study, p. 3, of The Relativity of Concentration Observations) show that the hundred largest U.S. firms grew not at all in their share of total value added by manufacturing during the period from 1963 to 1972.

The OECD report goes on to say that the percentage of total manufacturing assets held by the Fortune 500 largest industrial corporations rose from 73 to 83% from 1972 to 1977. In fact, the official statistics of the U.S., contained in the 1978 Statistical Abstract, at p. 576, show that the share of the 200 largest firms (no data is furnished for the 500 largest corporations) declined from 60% in 1972 to 58.4% in 1977. As my economist friends say, it is very difficult to observe much of a trend here.

(3) Para. 29 of the OECD report says that in the U.S. a considerable amount of research confirms Bain's finding of a positive correlation between concentration and profitability. I am sure that you are all aware that a considerable amount of research does *not* confirm Bain's "finding"; indeed, more recent and complete economic studies flatly reject it. I will here cite only Messrs. Brozen, Singer, Stigler and McGee. These and other academics have severely criticized the smallness and the lack of comparability of Professor Bain's sample. Indeed, when one examines the definition of "price-cost margin", one finds that it includes all sorts of things: taxes, overhead, depreciation, distribution expense, research and development, everything other than costs of materials and payrolls. Again, concentration statistics tend to be extremely artificial in both their components and interpretations.

(4) Para. 31 says that it is "apparent" that high concentration is increasing in the recent past. Most of the economists whom I have quoted would reject any such simplistic conclusion for the U.S. I call your attention to an interesting article on Aggregate Concentration, published last month by Betty Bock, Jack Farkas, Deborah Weinberger of The Conference Board. The Conference Board makes the obvious points about the inadequacies of the statistics, the non-comparability of numerators and denominators and the artificiality of the industry classifications. They also point out that the identity of the 50 or 100 or 200 largest manufacturing corporations changes from year to year. For example, between 1947 and 1977, 21 of the 50 largest in assets in 1947 had been replaced by other corporations by 1977. Eighty-five of the 200 largest in sales had been replaced by 1977. The pattern is similar for sales and assets for whatever group you chose to examine. Is it reasonable then to talk about the common characteristics of the 50, 100 or 200 largest corporations over a period of time when the identity of the group is changing? The Conference Board concludes by suggesting that "far from witnessing signals of agglomeration of corporate power in fewer and fewer hands—we are seeing data showing an apparent explosion above the standard cut-offs. And we are witnessing this proliferation without significant support from conglomeration or large-scale acquisition. Are we, then, viewing numbers that show increasing power in a few hands—or signals of a dispersion of size at the top?

(5) Para. 43 states that studies in the U.S. "have concluded" that mergers account for a varying but significant proportion of increases in concentration. In fact, for the 200 largest corporations the annualized ratio of acquisitions as a percentage of change in assets varied from .60 of 1% in

1947–54 to 1.04% in the 1972–1977 period. The figures for all manufacturing corporations were somewhat lower but roughly equivalent in all periods. Para. 43 goes on to observe that conglomerate mergers have been increasingly in evidence as a percentage of merger activity in the U.S., a far from surprising phenomenon when one considers the enthusiastic and effective enforcement of the U.S. antimerger statute against horizontal and vertical acquisitions. Finally, the report goes on to suggest that the profits of the leading firms in concentrated industries tend to be higher than required to attract capital. The generality of this last observation almost defies analysis and, insofar as it is based upon price-cost margin figures, is virtually without meaning. As Betty Bock has observed, "until we have profit and concentration data that match, mechanical mating of the two types of information can produce only hybrid conclusions."

    (6) In conclusion, let me make three points:

        (a) The report observes that "in the absence of conclusive evidence on concentration and its effect", we should all take note of the politically important point concerning the danger of centralization of power in the hands of a few enterprises. Fair enough—but perhaps equally relevant is the danger of the centralization of economic power in the hands of government and government ministries who regulate economic enterprises on the basis of hopelessly inexact economic data or interpretations thereof. Misleading or poorly interpreted data can provide a convenient excuse to those regulators who wish to substitute their personal social or political judgments in place of the economic judgment of the market.

        (b) One is also struck, in reading the report, at the lack of reference to international economic competition. Para. 3 mentions the relevance of such competition but then focuses on the various domestic markets which obviously have higher concentration ratios. In the U.S. context, for example, discussion of domestic automobile industry concentration ratios without reference to increasing international competition makes no economic sense at all.

        (c) In remarks last year at an antitrust seminar, Ms. Betty Bock cited an illustration to demonstrate her contention that economic theories based solely on structure and so-called objective economic statistics can be extremely dangerous. Some years ago the U.S. antitrust authorities, noting that the two top U.S. tire companies accounted for a high percentage of all tires manufactured in the U.S. and had previously lowered their prices for premium tires to the disadvantage of small competitors, brought a suit against the two companies, essentially claiming that they were behaving in a monopolistic fashion. After careful examination, the Antitrust Division, conceding that it had failed to consider a number of very important factors in bringing suit, asked for the dismissal of the suit. These factors included such facts as the shift of tire buyers away from premium to regular brands and the presence in the tire market of the huge automobile companies which were the principal customers for tires. The presence of this countervailing customer power effectively regulated the tire manufacturers. The point I am making is that statistics and concentration figures alone are no substitute for adequate economic analyses.

International Implications of Limitations on "Aggregate Concentration"

DAVID BOIES

Traditionally, antitrust laws have been concerned with competition and concentration within a single market. In the past few years, however, increasing attention has been given to economywide or *aggregate* concentration–especially when such concentration is accomplished by merger rather than by internal growth. In 1979 and 1980, Congress considered Senate Bill S. 600 which would limit mergers based on size criteria that are unrelated, at least directly, to proof of a lessening of competition within any given market.[1] The international implications of applying this principle are complex and difficult, and have yet to be fully addressed. It is the purpose of this article to articulate the contours of this area of emerging importance.

AGGREGATE CONCENTRATION

The term *concentration,* as it traditionally has been used in the antitrust area, has usually referred to concentration within a particular product or geographic market—concentration in the steel industry, the computer industry, the automobile industry, or the drug industry. Traditionally, that has been the sole focus of the antitrust laws with respect to concentration. Yet there is another sense in which economists and legislators (and to some extent, antitrust lawyers) talk about concentration—concentration in an economywide sense or *aggregate* concentration as it is referred to by some economists.[2] Aggregate concentration is not a measure of the extent to which a particular company or group of companies controls a specific market share of a given industry; rather it refers to the concentration of the entire economy in the hands of a limited number of corporations.[3] When used in that sense, concentration of industry within the United States has increased significantly by most measures.

Mr. Boies is a member of the New York Bar and former chief counsel and staff director, Senate Judiciary Committee.

RECENT INCREASES IN AGGREGATE CONCENTRATION

In 1955 the top 500 manufacturing corporations in the United States controlled aproximately 65 percent of all the manufacturing and mining assets in the United States.[4] Only ten years later, in 1965, the top 500 manufacturing and mining corporations controlled somewhat over 70 percent of those assets,[5] and by 1977 the percentage of all manufacturing and mining assets controlled by the top 500 corporations had increased to over 80 percent[6]—an increase in concentration of nearly 34 percent in twenty-two years. This is a phenomenon with which the antitrust laws have not been traditionally concerned; it is, however, a phenomenon that many in Congress and elsewhere believe to be a serious economic, social, and political problem entirely apart from the incidence of concentration within particular markets.

If in this country 100 companies each had only 1 percent of each market but together controlled the entire manufacturing sector of the economy, most people would be viscerally troubled, even though, from a traditional antitrust standpoint, the markets might be said to be rather deconcentrated since 100 companies were actively competing in each of the markets.[7] Though this exact scenario is improbable, the U.S. Chamber of Commerce estimates that by the year 2000 a few hundered international corporations will control 54 percent of the worldwide manufacturing, mining, and service income and assets.[8] Thus there is a demonstrable trend toward very substantial aggregate concentration in the United States and, if the Chamber of Commerce's forecasts are correct, on a worldwide basis as well.[9]

EFFECTS OF INCREASED CONCENTRATION

As the economy becomes more concentrated, the number of independent businesses declines. This loss of diversity can limit the choices available to consumers and stunt the process of growth through innovation. Moreover, the loss of diversity has economic effects. As conglomerates acquire companies that were formerly independent, a new layer of business bureaucracy is imposed on the acquired companies, which results in a marked increase in intracorporate bureaucratic review, and the number of independent decision-making centers is reduced. Moreover, applying to economic affairs the principle of federalism that innovation and experimentation are promoted by the dispersion rather than the concentration of decision-making power, these characteristic objectives of the free enterprise system would be impeded. Further, a loss of corporate independence may adversely affect company-community and employer-employee relations as absentee management becomes increasingly distant and isolated from employee and community interests.[10]

Particularly in considering the scale on which mergers are taking place today, economic concentration and the loss of diversity can have significant social and political implications as well as economic effects. One of the perceptible trends over the last five years, and in some respects a healthy trend, has been the increasing political activity of business political action committees, or PACs. Corporate executives may play a proper role in political and election activities by establishing and contributing to a PAC which then acts as effectively as the corporation's political arm.[11] There were about 700 corporate lobbies registered in 1978.[12] If the resources and actitivities of those 700 groups were suddenly concentrated in seventy, or in seven, the concomitant loss of diversity of political opinion and the concentration of political power is something that would be very troubling in any society, but particularly in the United States, which prides itself on diversity and political, social, and economic democracy.[13]

Apart from the effect on organized political activity, large corporations have profound effects on our society—the tastes we acquire, the activities that are encouraged or discouraged, the attitudes that are advertised or attacked, the products and services that are offered or discontinued, the charities and public activities that are supported or starved for funds. Only the most naive among us would suggest that in these areas large corporations are guided and controlled wholly by the "invisible hand" of the marketplace. How much discretion large corporations have in exercising their power is debatable—but there is no doubt that they have significant influence.[14] It is an article of democratic faith that such discretionary power is best when it is dispersed and most troubling when it is concentrated in a few hands, however benign.

THE EFFECT OF MERGERS ON AGGREGATE CONCENTRATION

Mergers of large enterprises have contributed significantly to the level of industrial concentration. In 1975 there were fourteen mergers with a value in excess of 100 million dollars. In 1977 there were forty-one such mergers; in 1978 there were eighty such mergers; and in 1979 at least ninety such mergers were consummated.[15]

There are various ways to measure changes in the level of industrial concentration. Whether concentration is greater today than it was five years ago or ten years ago depends to some extent on what figures are used.[16] It is nonetheless clear that U.S. enterprise is more highly concentrated than it would have been in the absence of the recent merger activity.

There may, of course, be economic and social benefits from the process that lead to increased industrial size. This is particularly so where the increases in size result from the internal growth of successful firms.[17] Growth may encourage firms to reduce their prices, improve their product, and generally serve consumers more effectively. Tampering with such an incentive is particularly dubious in a time when a priority concern of the country is its apparent long-run inability to sustain increased productivity.

There are also important benefits that can be obtained from growth through merger—such as economies of scale, strengthening of competitors, and transfer of technology.[18] However, there are many mergers—including many of the largest mergers—where such justifications are weak, if they are pertinent at all. Many large mergers are more a product of tax planning,[19] accounting and stock market considerations,[20] and corporate empire building[21] than they are a product of economic rationales that serve consumer interests. This is particularly true of so-called conglomerate acquisitions that, by definition, involve companies in unrelated markets, and therefore are less likely to result in economies of scale or other efficiencies common to related market mergers.

PROBLEMS UNDER THE EXISTING LAW

Congress first started to address the issue of conglomerate acquisitions in the late 1960s and early 1970s. At the confirmation hearings for Assistant Attorney General McLaren, the Senate Judiciary Committee received a commitment that large conglomerate mergers would be attacked by the Justice Department under Section 7 of the Clayton Act.[22] And a few months later, such a suit was commenced to bar the proposed merger of Ling-Temco-Vought and the Jones & Laughlin Steel Corporation.[23]

The Justice Department's activity in this area, however, has met with little success. For example, from 1974 through 1978, twelve conglomerate mergers were challenged in court; the government lost all twelve cases.[24] The failure of the Justice Department to prevent such mergers under existing antitrust laws underscored the inadequacy of Section 7 of the Clayton Act; it focuses solely on concentration within a "line of commerce."[25] If the trend toward aggregate concentration is to be halted, new legislation must be enacted to constrain conglomerate merger activity.[26] Accordingly, throughout the last decade, Congress intensively studied this problem, holding hearings on conglomerate mergers, the related topic of multinational corporations,[27] and on specific concentrated industries, most notably the oil industry.[28]

THE PROPOSED LEGISLATION: S. 600

One piece of legislation to come out of this congressional inquiry is the Small Business Protection Act of 1979 (the Act), Senate Bill S. 600, which was introduced in 1979 by Senator Edward Kennedy. The bill imposes limitations on mergers based on the size of the participating corporations, irrespective of the consequences of those mergers within a particular market. The basic purpose of the bill is to impose threshold size limitations on changes in concentration through mergers regardless of whether the increase in concentration is economywide or within a particular market.

The bill recognizes, however, that some mergers might enhance economic efficiency. Accordingly, except for the very largest mergers, in which case it is presumed that further concentration of economic power cannot be justified on any grounds, the bill provides the acquiring companies with potential affirmative defenses.

The bill has three separate prohibitory sections. Section 2(a) completely prohibits the merger or consolidation of any two companies when each has assets or sales exceeding $2 billion. No affirmative defenses are available when the merger or consolidation reaches these proportions. It is important to note, however, that this is not an absolute limitation on corporate size. It only limits industrial giants from making huge leaps in size by combining with another industrial giant. Expansion through internal growth is not hindered since the bill only addresses merger activity.

Section 2(b) prohibits mergers or consolidations between companies when each has assets or annual sales in excess of $350 million. Section 2(c) is a combination of traditional antitrust principles and the new aggregate concentration concept. It prohibits mergers when one company has assets or sales exceeding $250 million and the other company has 20 percent or more of the sales in any significant market during the calendar year immediately preceding the acquisition.

For mergers covered by Sections 2(b) and 2(c), the bill now provides three independent affirmative defenses. The acquisition may occur if: (1) its preponderant effect is to enhance competition substantially, or (2) substantial efficiencies will result,[29] or (3) the parties divest themselves, within one year, of assets equal to or greater than those acquired.

To discourage the sort of aggressive acquisition programs which ran rampant in the last decade, the bill provides that these affirmative defenses are not available if either party to the transaction has, within the past year, been a party to another transaction that was within Section 2(b) or 2(c).

The purpose of the legislation is to prohibit those mergers that have an undesirable impact on increasing industrial concentration, yet permit those mergers that either increase efficiencies or enhance competition. The provision allowing for the spin-off of comparable assets permits a company to acquire a particular corporation under circumstances that would otherwise be barred, as long as it does not increse concentration in the aggregate sense.

INTERNATIONAL IMPLICATIONS OF S. 600

Studying the international impact of the application of this legislation, one encounters the same difficulties that occur in other antitrust contexts.[30] Analytically, the international aspects of U.S. concentration regulation fall into two broad areas. First, to what extent should the application of those concentration principles be relaxed in favor of foreign corporations or foreign entities as a result of jurisdictional and comity issues or related concerns?[31] Second, to what extent should the principles that we might otherwise want to apply in the United States be modified by recognizing the realities of the worldwide market conditions in which our corporations must compete? In its present form, S. 600 addresses the first of these questions and concludes that there should be no lesser standard for foreign corporations.

A few examples will serve to illustrate the sort of problems that might arise. Suppose a large conglomerate acquisition is proposed in the United States: Mobil Oil Company seeks to acquire Marcor, a company with more than $350 million but less than $2 billion in assets or sales. Section 2(b) of S. 600 would limit, but not necessarily prohibit, this type of merger. If the corporations could demonstrate some economies of scale or substantial enhancement of competition resulting from the merger, the merger would be allowed; but given the circumstances of this hypothetical merger, it is probable neither can be demonstrated. Accordingly, we can assume that this merger would be precluded by the application of the anticonglomerate merger bill. Should or would the bill similarly prohibit a foreign giant, such as British Petroleum, from acquiring Marcor? The answer to that question lies in another question: To what extent does it make sense to impose this type of restriction on U.S. companies if it would be permissible for a foreign company with no U.S. assets to enter the United States and effect the otherwise prohibited purchase of Marcor? In other words, is it desirable to prevent U.S. companies that compete in the United States from acquiring other U.S. companies if the result is simply to have those U.S. companies available for sale to foreign corporations?[32]

The authors of S. 600 concluded that if a U.S. company had assets or sales in excess of the $350 million jurisdictional threshold amount, then the acquisition of that company ought to be subject to the constraints of the statute whether the acquiring company was inside or outside the United States. Therefore, if a foreign corporation, even one that has no assets in the United States, sought to acquire Marcor, that acquisition would be covered by the legislation whenever the foreign corporation had the requisite jurisdictional amount of assets anywhere in the world.

Two major concerns argue for this approach. First, it means that U.S. companies and foreign companies are to be treated similarly when they seek to acquire a U.S. concern except when jurisdictional or comity considerations are paramount. Second, the statute seeks to prevent the aggregation of assets by regulating the acquisition of U.S. corporations, irrespective of the identity of the acquirer. In this way, the purpose of the legislation is broader than the means. Since the principle underlying the legislation is to prevent the kind of loss of diversity and loss of independence that occurs with the conversion of an independent corporation into a subsidiary or a division of another corporation, both the purposes and the jurisdictional basis of the statute are met regardless of whether the acquiring corporation is a U.S. corporation or a foreign corporation.

A second, more difficult problem, is whether antitrust officials should regulate the acquisition of a foreign corporation by a U.S. corporation; that is, where a U.S. company acquires a foreign company with no assets in the

United States and both companies have the requisite jurisdictional asset value. As presently drafted, the legislation would apply to the acquisition abroad by a U.S. company even though the acquired foreign company does not have the requisite jurisdictional amount of assets in the United States, but does have sufficient assets in its worldwide operation.

This result is troubling to those persons concerned with the legislation. Yet it would be difficult to exempt such acquisitions as a practical matter and still be able to enforce the ban against the acquisition of U.S. companies by foreign companies. First, this sort of discrimination in favor of U.S. companies might cause serious diplomatic problems. Foreign governments have become increasingly sensitive about U.S. interference with the acquisition policies of their domestic firms.[33] Their attitude is understandable. For years other nations have watched U.S. firms profit by investment abroad. By acquiring existing firms in foreign markets, U.S. firms have increased their worldwide presence. In light of this, foreign governments would be offended by a statute that created restrictions on acquisitions of American firms by foreign companies, but had no restrictions on foreign acquisitions by U.S. firms.[34] Second, excluding acquisitions of foreign companies from the bill's coverage would tend to drive U.S. capital abroad, a result which certainly should be avoided.

A third and critical reason to include such transactions in the bill is the practical problem of making sure all domestic acquisitions are covered. If foreign acquisitions are exempted, it might permit companies to structure their acquisitions to avoid the clear intent of the bill. Corporate lawyers would simply arrange the transaction so that the acquired corporation was always a foreign entity; the intent of the bill would thus be nullified. It would be possible for the courts to attempt to make a factual determination of who is the acquirer and who is the acquired company, but that would be a difficult task and would still present the problems raised by the issue of discrimination.

Whether this legislation should apply to merger activity between two companies when neither company has the requisite jurisdictional amount of assets within the United States is one of the most difficult questions facing the Congress. The question remains open. It will be the focus of considerable discussion and debate during the markup sessions that will occur throughout 1980, and presumably during the next Congress, at which time this legislation will probably reach the floor of the Senate and the House.[35]

A different, but equally difficult question is the extent to which foreign competitive effects can or should be taken into account in providing the affirmative defenses of enhancement of competition, economies of scale, or other efficiencies. On the one hand, it is desirable to have symmetry when applying the same principles in both foreign and domestic contexts. On the other hand, the bill is primarily a domestic statute with particular concerns about U.S. concentration and the benefits of competition and efficiencies within the United States. This too is an issue that remains unresolved.

LIMITATIONS ON LEGISLATIVE SOLUTIONS

These are areas in which it is much easier to raise questions than it is to formulate solutions. The same is true in the area referred to earlier—the extent to which U.S. antitrust authorities should take into account the effects of enforcing U.S. antitrust laws against U.S. corporations in the international market. One might conclude that the ideal of our antitrust laws is a competitive model that should be applied not only in the United States but outside the United States as well. Congress, however, lacks the power to impose that competitive model on the rest of the world,[36] and many nations have embraced monopoly rather than competition as a model for industrial growth.[37] Given the fact that this competitive model cannot be imposed on the rest of the world and that competition in the worldwide market continues to increase, to what extent should United States antitrust laws continue to be applied to the maximum extent possible in an attempt to bring this country closer to that competitive model? To put it differently, to what extent must United States antitrust and enforcement policies be modified in recognition of the kind of international conditions that face our domestic corporations?[38] A couple of illustrations will be helpful. The first relates to the concern of traditional antitrust laws with intramarket concentration; the second relates to aggregate concentration that would be regulated by Senate Bill S. 600. Consider first a U.S. company that seeks to acquire a foreign manufacturer in a related business—to take a specific fact situation, if Gillette in the United States wishes to acquire Braun, a German producer of electric shavers.[39] In making the decision whether this acquisition violates U.S. antitrust law,[40] should the inquiry be tempered by the probability that if the Gillette acquisition is prohibited, another foreign shaver producer will make the acquisition; or must the focus of scrutiny be limited to the particular transaction in question and its domestic economic effect?[41] If attention is directed only to the particular transaction, it may be concluded that the merger would inhibit actual competition, at least in some broad market, or might prohibit potential competition since the two companies may enter into each other's more narrow markets. And if the world was controlled uniformly by the U.S. antitrust laws, it might very well be concluded that the hypothetical merger should be stopped (although in the facts of the proposed case this author has some doubt). Such a conclusion was in fact made by U.S. enforcement authorities[42] (but tempered by the consent decree) in a case involving Gillette.

On the other hand, if the German shaving company is not acquired by Gillette, it may still be acquired by some large foreign shaver manufacturer with an equal effect on competition not only outside the United States but inside the United States as well. That acquisition is likely to be beyond the traditional reach of U.S. antitrust laws either for jurisdictional or comity reasons. In that case, it is not clear that U.S. antitrust laws should be applied to a foreign acquisition by a U.S. company (and therefore, within our jurisdiction), if the alternative is simply to have the acquisition occur between another foreign company with equal or perhaps even greater impact on competition when compared with the impact of an acquisition by the U.S. company.[43]

The second example is even more difficult. Consider U.S. companies that operate in a concentrated U.S. industry (such as the drug, steel, or automobile industry) but also compete against foreign companies in international markets. Does it make sense from the U.S. antitrust standpoint to enforce deconcentration laws against U.S. corporations without looking at the extent to which those rules affect companies as they compete outside of the United States, confront larger international markets and foreign corporations, and deal with foreign governments that appear to favor concentration within particular industries? Government policies that favor high levels of concentration are much more firmly established in Europe and Japan than they are in the United States. When formulating U.S. antitrust policy, such as S. 600, a serious issue is whether, and to what extent, the international or non-U.S. circumstances surrounding major U.S. industries (including the major industries that are most concentrated in the United States) can or should be ignored. That is, how does U.S. antitrust policy take into account the realization that U.S. corporations must compete in an international environment and compete against companies that have different incentives, different motivations, and different domestic controls in their home countries.

CONCLUSION

None of these problems can be easily or precisely resolved. Unfortunately, most of them seem to rest on factual circumstances that are peculiar to individual cases and result in ad hoc determinations, although that raises problems not only for foreign countries and corporations, but for U.S. companies as well. It is an area where a certain amount of vagueness is desirable, so as to allow the courts to operate flexibly within a broad framework of national policy, on a case by case basis, and flesh out the details of U.S. policy by implementing it in the most principled and reasonable fashion.[44] However, a certain amount of predictability, that would attend a more precise codification by statute, is also needed. Congress will be attempting to balance these two competing and to a large extent conflicting desires, both with respect to the conglomerate merger legislation, which is a new effort in the area of the control of concentration, and with respect to conventional antitrust laws as they affect international events or as international events and issues affect the application of those laws in the United States.

NOTES

1. S. 600, 95th Cong., 1st Sess., 125 Cong. Rec. 2417 (1979). The bill is reprinted as annex 1, *infra.* S. 600 does, however, provide that it shall be

an affirmative defense under the Act to show that the merger will result in a substantial enhancement of competition. The affirmative defenses are delineated more fully *infra*.

2. One commentator has explained the terms as follows:
   "*[A]ggregate concentration . . . refers to the centralization of productive resources in the economy as a whole rather than in a particular market . . .*"
   Fishbein, *Conglomerate Mergers and Economic Concentration*, 62 YALE REV. 507, 508 (1973).
   See also, STAFF OF THE ANTITRUST SUBCOMM. OF THE HOUSE COMM. ON THE JUDICIARY, 92d CONG., 1st SESS., REPORT ON INVESTIGATION OF CONGLOMERATE CORPORATIONS 20 (Comm. Print 1971).

3. Whether aggregate concentration in itself inevitably leads to market concentration is an open question. *See* Bryan, *Conglomerate Mergers: Proposed Guidelines*, 11 HARV. J. LEGIS. 31, 33–35 (1973).

4. 125 CONG. REC. 2418 (1979) (statement of Senator Kennedy on S. 600).

5. *Id.*

6. *Id.*

7. *See* INVESTIGATION OF CONGLOMERATE CORPORATIONS, *supra* note 2, at 49:
   Growth of these vast corporate structures, even though, at the same time, they are accompanied by an increase in number of the much smaller and less powerful corporate organizations that operate under the umbrella of the major companies in markets served by the major companies, presages imposition of a cartel-like structure to American business. Some observers foresee a situation where the American economy will be dominated by a few hundred business suzerainties, under whose influence a multitude of small, weak,
   quasi-independent corporations will be permitted a subsidiary and supplemental role.

8. Kennedy, *supra* note 4.

9. Undoubtedly, as international trade increases the concept of market under the present law will be modified and expanded to reflect the broader context in which the existing statutes must be applied. Commentators have already suggested several alternative approaches to the question of the proper market in foreign commerce cases. *See, e.g.,* W. FUGATE, FOREIGN COMMERCE AND THE ANTITRUST LAWS 254 (1958); K. BREWSTER, ANTITRUST AND AMERICAN BUSINESS ABROAD 85 (1958).
   If enacted into law, the concept of aggregate concentration should also be interpreted and reinterpreted in accordance with worldwide changes in industrial concentration.

10. Mueller, *The Merger's Impact on the Community*, AM. FEDERATIONIST, June 1971, at 14. *See* United States v. Falstaff Brewing Corp., 410 U.S. 526, 541–43 (1973) (J. Douglas, concurring):
    "*Preservation of a competitive system was seen as essential to avoid the concentration of economic power that was thought to be a threat to the Nation's political and social system.*" Control of American business is being transferred from local communities to distant cities where men . . . with only balance sheets and profit and loss statements before them decide the fate of communities with which they have little or no relationship. . . . The antitrust laws favored a wide diffusion of corporate control. . . ." *[T]he desirability of retaining 'local control' over industry and the protection of small businesses*" was our comment in Brown Shoe Co. v. United States. . . .

11. *See* Federal Election Campaign Act of 1971, 2 U.S.C. §§ 431–55 (1976).
12. Kennedy, *supra* note 4, at S. 2419.
13. "It is fundamental to the American creed that political democracy cannot coexist with economic oligarchy." Mueller, *supra* note 10, at 18.
14. *See, e.g.*, Ehrbar, *"Bigness" Becomes the Target of the Trustbuster,* FORTUNE, March 26, 1979, at 34, 38.
15. *See* Kennedy, *supra* note 4.
16. *See Hearings on the Small and Independent Business Protection Act, S. 600, Before the Senate Comm. on the Judiciary,* 96th Cong., 1st Sess. 7 (1979) (statement of John H. Shenefield) (forthcoming).
17. Conglomerate acquisitions are often made in industries that are already highly concentrated. *See* FTC, ECONOMIC REPORT ON CORPORATE MERGER §§ 123–26 (1969). When a conglomerate acquires a company that has a large market share in a concentrated industry, the opportunities for interdependent behavior are multiplied; such acquisitions do not revitalize competition within the industry, they only entrench the status quo. *Accord,* Areeda & Turner, *Conglomerate Mergers: Extended Interdependence and Effects on Interindustry Competition as Grounds for Condemnation,* 127 U. PA. L. REV. 1082 (1979). Internal expansion, on the other hand, often does result in a return to the competitive model:
    One of the best prospects for deconcentrating concentrated industries— in fact, perhaps the only one of any significance—is new entry. And, by and large, those companies who are most capable of new entry into most other industries are the very large companies. Therefore, I think, if over a period of ten or fifteen years, these companies had to go the internal expansion route or the route of relatively minor acquisitions to get a foothold in an industry and then build up, that over the economy as a whole, fifteen years from now, you would have less concentration in a good many markets than you would otherwise have.
    An Interview with the Honorable Donald F. Turner, 37 ANTITRUST L.J. 290, 299–300 (1968).
18. Bryan, *supra* note 3, at 36.
19. *See generally* Sinrich, *Tax Incentives and the Conglomerate Merger: An Introduction,* 44 ST. JOHN'S L. REV. 1009 (spec. ed. 1970).
20. *See generally* Briloff, *Financial Motives for Conglomerate Growth,* 44 ST. JOHN'S L. REV. 872 (spec. ed. 1970); H. LYNCH, FINANCIAL PERFORMANCE OF CONGLOMERATES 280 (1971).
21. *Cf.* W. BAUMOL, BUSINESS BEHAVIOR, VALUE AND GROWTH (rev. ed. 1967). (A study of oligopolistic decision making and objectives, and of the forces behind economic growth in modern capitalist economies).
22. *Hearings on the Nomination of Richard W. McLaren Before the Senate Comm. on the Judiciary* 91st Cong. 1st Sess. 36 (1969) (statement of Richard W. McLaren).
23. United States v. Ling-Temco-Vought, 315 F. Supp. 1301 (W.D. Pa. 1970) (consent decree).
24. REPORT OF THE ATTORNEY GENERAL PURSUANT TO SECTION 10(e) OF THE SMALL BUSINESS ACT, *as amended,* CONGLOMERATE MERGERS, SMALL BUSINESS, AND THE SCOPE OF EXISTING ANTIMERGER STATUTES 16 (1979). *See also* Bauer, *Challenging Conglomerate Mergers Under Section 7 of the Clayton Act: Today's Law and Tomorrow's Legislation* 58 B. U. L. REV. 199–201 (1978).
25. 15 U.S.C. § 18 (1976).
26. *See* Interview with Donald F. Turner, *supra* note 17, at 298.

27. *International Aspects of Antitrust Hearings on S. Res. 191 Before Subcomm. on Antitrust and Monopoly of the Senate Comm. of the Judiciary* 89th Cong. 2d Sess. (1966).

28. *Competition and Public Policy in the Petroleum Refining Industry, Hearing before the Subcomm. on Antitrust and Monopoly of the Senate Comm. on the Judiciary.* 95th Cong. 2d Sess. (1978)

29. Because the facts in each case will vary and cannot be anticipated, the task of developing standards for applying these defenses on a case-by-case basis has been left to the courts.

30. *See generally* Donovan, *The Legality of Acquisitions and Mergers Involving American and Foreign Corporations Under the United States Antitrust Laws,* 39 S. Calif. L. Rev 526 (pt 1), 40 S. Calif. L. Rev. 38 (pt 2) (1966–67).

31. The general principles of international comity were summarized by James R. Atwood, Acting Legal Adviser, Department of State:

    Even where there is a basis in international law for exercising jurisdiction, principles of comity often suggest that forebearance is appropriate. Under those principles, states should consider and weigh the legitimate interests of other states when taking action that could affect those interests, and should leave the regulation of conduct to the state with the primary interest. Thus, our foreign partners expect that in general they have the right to regulate the climate for investment within their territories and to establish energy and competition policies for their own economies and firms. By refraining from intruding upon these spheres more than is necessary, we can avoid many unnecessary foreign relations frictions. . . .

    Where the rules two states prescribe may require inconsistent conduct upon the part of a person, each state is required by international law to consider, in good faith, moderation in the exercise of its enforcement jurisdiction. Each state should take into account relevant factors such as the vital national interests of the states involved, the extent and nature of the hardship created by inconsistent enforcement actions, the extent to which the conduct takes place in another state's territory, the nationality of the persons involved, the relative significance of the effects in each territory, the extent to which adverse effects on the enforcing state are explicitly intended or reasonably foreseeable, and the extent to which enforcement action can reasonably be expected to achieve compliance. This jurisdictional rule of reason, or balancing test, is a commonsense rule and, of course, states may differ in their judgments of how it should be applied in a given instance. The international legal obligation is . . . to consider these interests in good faith and, where appropriate in light of all circumstances, to temper the exercise of enforcement jurisdiction. Hearings on the Energy Antimonopoly Act of 1979, H.R. 4295 Before the Senate Comm. on the Judiciary, 96th Cong., 1st Sess. 5–7 (1979) (Department of State Print). *Cf.* Hansen, *The Enforcement of the United States Antitrust Laws by the Department of Justice to Protect Freedom of United States Foreign Trade,* 11 ABA Antitrust Section 75 (1957).

32. *See, e.g.,* United States v. Standard Oil Co., 1970 Trade Cases, ¶ 72,988 (N.D. Ohio 1969) (consent decree).

33. The Antitrust Division concluded early on that acquisitions of American firms should be treated no differently when the acquiring firm is a

foreign national. *See* Wall St. J., Nov. 18, 1969, at 3, col. 1 (quoting Richard McLaren, then Asst. Att'y Gen'l, Antitrust Div.).

34. E. KINTNER & M. JOELSON, AN INTERNATIONAL ANTITRUST PRIMER 119 (1974).

35. Analogous problems are raised by the proposed Energy Antimonopoly Act of 1979, S. 1246, 96th Cong., 1st Sess., 125 CONG. REC. S. 6703 (1979). *See, e.g.,* Amendment to S. 1246 Proposed by the Department of Justice, Letter to Senator Edward M. Kennedy from John H. Shenefield, Assistant Attorney General, Antitrust Division (September 18, 1979). *Reprinted in* Annex 2, *infra*.

36. *Limitations on the power, size and structure of the supranational firm may ultimately be imposed through worldwide uniform standards developed by the United Nations or a similar multinational body, but until agreement is reached on the nature or desirability of such control, the burden of regulation will continue to fall on those states that assert domestic jurisdiction over the firms involved.* Graham, Hermann & Marcus, *Section 7 of the Clayton Act and Mergers Involving Foreign Interests,* 23 STAN. L. REV. 205 (1971); *See* Stockmann, *Reflections on Recent OECD Activities: Regulation of Multinational Corporate Conduct and Structure, post;* Kurek, *Supranational Regulation of Transnational Corporations: The UNCTAD and CTC Efforts, post.*

37. Scott & Yablonski, *Transnational Mergers and Joint Ventures Affecting American Exports* 14 ANTITRUST BULL. 1 (1969).

38. *The whole economic structure of other countries may be dependent on cartel or joint efforts—as in vital industries where the foreign government is reluctant to allow prices and*

profits to fluctuate through the forces of competition. [*Id.* at 7.]

39. *See, e.g.,* Baker, *Antitrust and World Trade: Tempest in an International Teapot,* 8 CORNELL INT'L L.J. 16, 27 (1974).

40. *Cf.* ANTITRUST DIVISION, U.S. DEP'T OF JUSTICE, ANTITRUST GUIDE FOR INTERNATIONAL OPERATIONS 15 (1977), *with* Griffin, *A Critique of the Justice Department's Antitrust Guide for International Operations,* 11 CORNELL INT'L L.J. 215, 230–33 (1978).

41. This possibility is becoming a reality with increasing frequency: [A] *growing merger trend within Western Europe's own business organizations may be preempting the investment opportunities available to United States firms desirous of establishing or enlarging beachheads overseas.* Scott & Yablonski, *supra* note 37, at 2.

42. United States v. Gillette Co., 406 F. Supp. 713 (D. Mass. 1975) (consent decree).

43. When the antitrust laws are applied to foreign transactions, two distinct domestic concerns must be considered: The first is American industries' interest in competitive access to world markets. The second is the American consumer's interest in having access to foreign goods and the competitive forces they engender. Both of these interests would be jeopardized if enforcement authorities in the United States ignored this possibility.

44. A case-by-case approach may help ensure fairness in individual cases, *see* note 30, *supra*, but codification of easily understood standards affords certainty to business transactions and reduces problems of enforcement.

ANNEX 1: SENATE BILL S. 600

96TH CONGRESS
1ST SESSION

S. 600

To preserve the diversity and independence of American business.

IN THE SENATE OF THE UNITED STATES

March 8 (legislative day, February 22), 1979

Mr. Kennedy (for himself, Mr. Metzenbaum, Mr. Pressler, Mr. Melcher, and Mr. McGovern) introduced the following bill; which was read twice and referred to the Committee on the Judiciary

A BILL

To preserve the diversity and independence of American business.

Be it enacted by the Senate and House of Representatives of the United States of America in Congress assembled, That this Act may be cited as the "Small and Independent Business Protection Act of 1979".

SEC. 2. Notwithstanding any other provision of law, no person shall merge or consolidate with any other person engaged in commerce, or acquire, directly or indirectly, such amount of the stock or other share capital of such other person as to enable such person to control such other person, or acquire, directly or indirectly, a majority of the assets of such other person, if—

(a) each person has assets or sales exceeding $2,000,000,000;

(b) each person has assets or sales exceeding $350,000,000; or

(c) one person has assets or sales exceeding $350,000,000 and the other person has 20 per centum or more of the sales during the calendar year immediately preceding the acquisition in any significant market.

SEC. 3. (a) Except as provided in subsection (b), it shall be an affirmative defense to an offense under sections 2(b) and 2(c) that—

(1) the transaction will have the preponderant effect of substantially enhancing competition;

(2) the transaction will result in substantial efficiencies; or

(3) within one year before or after the consummation of the transaction, the parties thereto shall have divested one or more viable business units, the assets and revenues of which are equal to or greater than the assets and revenues of the smaller party to the transaction.

(b) Such affirmative defense shall not be available if one of the parties to the transaction has within one year previous to the transaction been a party to a prior transaction coming within the provisions of section 2(b) or 2(c).

SEC. 4. (a) Authority to enforce compliance with section 2 is vested in the Attorney General of the United States and the Federal Trade Commission.

(b) The Attorney General and the Federal Trade Commission shall adopt procedures by which parties to a transaction within the terms of sections 2(b) and 2(c) can ascertain the determination of the Attorney General or the Federal Trade Commission as to whether or not the transaction is within the terms of any of the affirmative defenses set forth in section 3. If the Attorney General or Commission, pursuant to such procedures, advises a party that a transaction is within the terms of any of the affirmative defenses set forth in section 3, the Attorney General and the Federal Trade Commission shall be barred by such advice in the absence of proof that the determination was based in whole or substantial part on an intentional misstatement by the party requesting such advice.

SEC. 5. Injunctive relief for private parties may be granted under the same terms and conditions as prescribed by section 16 of the Clayton Act.

Definitions

SEC. 6. (a) As used herein, "efficiencies" shall include economies of scale in manufacturing, marketing, distribution, and research and development.

(b) As used herein, "significant market" means any line of commerce in any section of the country which has annual sales of more than $100,000,000.

SEC. 7. (a) The provisions of this Act are in addition to and not in lieu of other provisions of the antitrust laws and nothing in this Act shall be deemed to authorize or make lawful anything heretofore prohibited or made illegal by other antitrust laws.

(b) This Act shall apply to all mergers or consolidations occurring after March 11, 1979.

ANNEX 2: SHENEFIELD LETTER RE INTERNATIONAL IMPLICATIONS OF
SENATE BILL S. 1246

September 18, 1979; letter from John H. Shenefield, assistant attorney general, Antitrust Division, Department of Justice to Senator Edward M. Kennedy, chairman, U.S. Senate Judiciary Committee, re: International Implications of S. 1246, the Energy Antimonopoly Act of 1979.

Honorable Edward M. Kennedy
Chairman
Committee on the Judiciary
United States Senate
Washington, D. C. 20510

Dear Mr. Chairman:

As you know, the Administration has indicated its support for S. 1246, the Energy Antimonopoly Act of 1979, as it would be amended by proposals forwarded to the Committee under cover of my letter to you of July 31, 1979. As thus amended, S. 1246 would restrict large acquisitions by major American petroleum producers and their "affiliates", the latter being defined to include all companies controlling, controlled by, or under common control with, major producers. Restrictions on acquisitions by affiliates are intended to eliminate the possibility that revenues of major producers might be channeled through such companies to make acquisitions, resulting in evasion of the purposes of the statute. Channeling major producers' revenues away from acquisitions of unrelated firms toward investment in energy production and development is a major goal of the bill.

Concern has arisen, however, over the possible international ramifications of legislation that at least on its face would restrict acquisitions by all foreign companies affiliated in some way with major American producers. This concern is amplified by the fact that the bill as amended by the Administration's proposals would restrict acquisitions by major producers and their affiliates of foreign, as well as domestic, companies. It is argued that national jurisdictional limits would be exceeded by such legislation, principles of international comity would be violated, and foreign sovereigns offended, perhaps resulting in retaliatory action to the detriment of energy production abroad. While these concerns might be somewhat ameliorated by clear legislative history to the effect that invocation of the statute would be tempered by jurisdictional and comity considerations, we believe that further amendments clarifying its proper scope would be desirable.

The "foreign affiliate" question may be divided into two issues: (1) coverage of acquisitions by foreign firms that control major American producers, and the other subsidiaries of such foreign firms, and (2) coverage of acquisitions by foreign firms which are themselves controlled by major American producers.

(1) Acquisitions by Foreign Firms Controlling Major American Producers And Other Subsidiaries of Such Foreign Firms

Applying the restrictions of S. 1246 to foreign firms that control major American producers, and the other subsidiaries of those foreign firms, appears to raise the more difficult issues. The problems are not merely theoretical; two of the 18 major American producers covered by S. 1246 as it would be amended by the Administration's proposals, Standard Oil of Ohio and Shell, are controlled by foreign firms. Asserting jurisdiction over foreign firms involves considerations not encountered in wholly domestic contexts. Differing national interests and policies must be accommodated in both legislative and judicial processes, and connections with American interests identified. Here, covering acquisitions by foreign parents and sister subsidiaries would not appear to be appropriate if acquisitions by such firms would not be likely as a general matter to adversely affect legitimate American interests that the bill is designed to protect. We are unable to conclude—with the confidence desirable to assert jurisdiction over foreign firms—that foreign parents would be likely to use major producers' revenues to make acquistions to such an extent as to seriously undercut a major goal of the bill. Thus, from both the jurisdictional and comity standpoints, coverage of such foreign company acquisitions is of doubtful propriety, and the Administration's proposal was not intended to be applied in such situations.

Foreign parents and sister subsidiaries of major American producers (as well as foreign governments) may, however, reasonably argue that technical coverage of their acquisitions by S. 1246 is objectionable. They may argue that international jurisdictional or comity precedent is not adequate to protect against assertion of U.S. jurisdiction in excess of its proper bounds. They may also fear the development of a cloud on the legality of proposed acquisitions despite general assurances to the contrary in legislative history or from enforcement authorities.

These considerations have led us to conclude that it probably would be wise to further amend S. 1246 to eliminate coverage of foreign firms that control major American producers, and the other subsidiaries of such foreign firms. Practically speaking, eliminating coverage of such firms would not appear to interfere with the goals of the legislation. Wholesale transfer of funds to foreign parents (other than transfers in the ordinary course of business such as normal dividend and interest payments) seems unlikely in view of the fact that only two of the producers covered by the bill presently have foreign parents and there is significant minority ownership of the American producer in each instance. Evasion through such use of a foreign parent as an acquiring medium seems unlikely; should a foreign parent acquire a firm that could not be acquired by a major American producer, and then attempt to convey such firm to the American producer—perhaps arguing the applicability of the intraenterprise exception in the bill—the entire series of transactions would rightly be viewed as an indirect acquisition by the American producer. Creation of whole cloth foreign parents by other American producers to evade the statute also would be unavailing; acquisitions through such schemes clearly would be indirect acquisitions by the producer, and fully subject to the new law.

In light of these considerations, we are submitting herewith minor modifications to the Administration's proposed amendments to S. 1246 that would eliminate coverage of foreign firms that control major American producers, and the other subsidiaries of such firms. The definition of "affiliate" would be altered to include only firms that are "controlled by" such major producers. Attached is an appropriately altered draft of S. 1246 as it would be amended by the Administration's proposals.

(2) Acquisitions by Foreign Firms Controlled by American Producers

With perhaps less force, it has been argued that acquisitions by domiciliaries of other countries should not be covered by the proposed legislation regardless of their control by major American producers. The argument is most forcefully advanced in hypothetical contexts in which foreign law or policy arguably prompts, if not mandates, acquisitions otherwise within the technical proscriptions of the bill.

Wholesale exemption of acquisitions by foreign subsidiaries of major American producers clearly appears inappropriate. First, a broad statutory exemption could seriously undercut the goals of the legislation by opening avenues of foreign acquisition opportunities which could divert significant major producer revenues from increased energy production. A direct connection between acquisitions by foreign subsidiaries of major American producers and the legitimate interests of this country is thus reasonably likely, and supports the exercise of jurisdiction over the activities of such foreign firms in many circumstances.*

Second, a broad statutory exemption is unnecessary, since principles of international law and comity may lead to the conclusion that a particular acquisition by a foreign firm which is controlled by a major American producer is not proscribed, notwithstanding its technical coverage by the bill. Foreign laws and policies would be taken into full account in applying the statute, as would the extent to which the particular acquisition in question would be inconsistent with the purposes of the legislation. For example, where an acquisition by a foreign subsidiary of a major producer of another

* It should be noted here that under the terms of the draft statute, challenges to acquisitions by foreign subsidiaries of major American producers may be made through suit against the foreign firm itself, where grounds for the exercise of jurisdiction over the foreign firm exist, or through suit against the major American producer which is making the acquisition indirectly, or both. Effective enforcement of the bill will not necessarily require naming as a defendant a foreign affiliate through which an acquisition is being made.

foreign firm is in full accord with expressed public interests of the foreign nation (perhaps including interests in increased energy producton), even though the acquisition is not mandated in the strict legal sense, comity may compel deference to those interests. By way of further example, it may be possible in some circumstances to be confident that a merger of a foreign subsidiary of a major producer with another foreign firm does not entail any drain on the producer's revenues, is instead supported entirely by the resources of the foreign firms involved, and would enhance the competitiveness of the resulting firm to the clear benefit of foreign public policies. Since application of the statute in the international context depends in part on the extent to which an acqustion would interfere with the goals of the bill, here too, principles of international law and comity—that will be applied by the courts and in the exercise of prosecutorial discretion as well—may render application of the new statute inappropriate. If further assurance is needed that the principles of international law and comity are to be applied by the courts and prosecutors alike, we would have no objection to the statute, on its face, providing that "This section's applicability to foreign acquisitions shall be interpreted in accordance with the principles of international law and comity."

Thus, there does not appear to be sufficient reason to create any broad statutory exemption for acquisitions by foreign subsidiaries of major American producers. Reasoned decision-making with regard to application of the statute to such acquisitions should provide safeguards against international friction on the one hand and evasion of the statute's goals on the other. . . .

Sincerely yours,

John H. Shenefield
Assistant Attorney General
Antitrust Division

Proposed Amendment to S. 1246, Acquisitions by Major Oil Companies—
Proposed New Section 7B of the Clayton Act

(a) No major producer engaged in commerce, or affiliate thereof, shall, directly or indirectly, through merger, consolidation or acquisition, acquire control or a majority of the assets of any other person if

(1) such other person has total assets of $100 million or more, and

(2) in the case of an acquisition of a majority of the assets, $100 million or more of assets would be acquired.

(b) No acquisition shall be prohibited by this section if the likely effect of the acquisition would be substantially to enhance competition in the domestic or foreign commerce of the United States.

(c) For purposes of this section—

(1) A "major producer" is any person incorporated in the United States who, together with the persons it controls, produced an average of 150,000 barrels or more per day world-wide of crude oil and natural gas liquids in the immediately preceding calendar year. Production of crude oil and natural gas liquids shall include interests in such production.

(2) An "affiliate" of a major producer is a person who ~~controls,~~ is controlled by, ~~or is under common control with,~~ such major producer.

(3) The total assets of a person shall include those of all persons controlled by such person.

(4) Assets acquired within a period of three years shall be presumed to be the subject of a single acquisition.

(5) Control means having the power, directly or indirectly, to direct or cause the direction of the management and policies of a person through the ownership of voting securities or otherwise; provided, however, that control shall not arise solely out of a bona fide credit transaction. Ownership of, or the power to vote, 15 percent or more of the outstanding voting securities of a person creates a rebuttable presumption of control. Ownership of, or the power to vote, less than 15 percent of the outstanding voting securities of a person does not create a presumption of control or lack of control.

(6) "United States" includes the several States, the territories, possessions and commonwealths of the United States and the District of Columbia.

(7) (A) Except as provided in subparagraph (B) of this paragraph, the value of assets is the amount at which such assets are carried on the books used as the basis for reports filed by a person pursuant to Section 13 or Section 15(d) of the Securities Exchange Act of 1934 or which would be used if Section 13 or Section 15(d) of the Securities Exchange Act of 1934 were applicable to require reporting by such person.

(B) In the case of acquisition of less than all of the assets of a person, in determining whether a majority of person's assets would be acquired, the value of assets is the fair market value.

(d) (1) Nothing contained herein shall be construed to prohibit any acquisition involving solely persons controlling, controlled by, or under common control with one another.

(2) Nothing contained herein shall be construed to render unlawful any acquisition on the basis of increases in production or assets after consummation.

(e) (1) For purposes of sections 4 and 16 of this Act, this section shall not be considered part of the antitrust laws.

(2) In any action to enforce this section, whenever a challenged acquisition has been or may be consummated, the court shall, upon petition, issue an order appropriate to ensure that the assets and operations of the parties to the acquisition are kept intact and held separate and that the parties do not interfere with or participate in the management or internal affairs of one another pending final adjudication. This paragraph shall not be construed to affect in any way any determination as to the need for or propriety of a temporary restraining order or preliminary injunction enjoining consummation of any acquisition which may be prohibited by the section.

(f) Nothing contained herein shall be construed to provide any defense or immunity to any acquisition which would violate Section 7 of this Act or otherwise be unlawful.

(g) This section shall apply to acquisitions consummated after June 1, 1979 and prior to January 1, 1991.

The "Economic" Analysis of Transnational Mergers

WILLIAM JAMES ADAMS

No congregation of lawyers can be considered complete without a token economist. The role of the economist consists of describing the *economic* mode of analyzing the legal problem under consideration. Unfortunately from the standpoint of the token, economists rarely agree on criteria appropriate for the appraisal of economic phenomena. With respect to transnational corporate mergers, four modes of analysis may be described legitimately as economic.

Two of the modes of analysis should be familiar to all members of the antitrust bar. The first of these might be called "competition as a quasi goal of society." It is based on this argument: In a market economy, it is impossible to achieve economic efficiency in the absense of competition in relevant markets. Moreover, competition is compatible with, perhaps even conducive to, the realization of other social goals such as decentralization of political, economic, and social power. Given the difficulty of measuring directly the true elements of social performance, the state of competition in relevant markets can safely be considered a proxy for them.

Reasoning of this sort appears frequently in U.S. judicial opinions discussing the antitrust laws. Such reasoning would lead the student of transnational mergers to investigate the effects of such mergers on the state of competition in relevant markets—principally those found in the countries of the acquiring and acquired firms.

A great deal of research of this sort has been performed—at least on the theoretical plane.[1] Unsurprisingly, transnational mergers are seen to have both desirable and undesirable effects on the state of competition. To understand why, imagine an industry in country A organized as a tightly knit oligopoly comprised exclusively of mononational firms. Now imagine acquisition of one of the oligopolists by a large firm domiciled in country B and engaged in the same line of business. On the one hand, the transnational merger might destabilize comfortable oligopolistic agreements in country A.

This article is adapted from a presentation made by Professor Adams at the Symposium on Transnational Corporate Concentration held at the University of Michigan Law School on November 9 and 10, 1979. Professor Adams is associate professor of economics and law at the University of Michigan.

The multinational firm has wider horizons than do its mononational counterparts. As a result, the kinds of behavior which it finds desirable may be anathema to the mononationals. Even if the two types of firms have the same goals, cognitive differences between firms heterogeneous in nationality may render collusion less successful than it might otherwise be. On the other hand, this transnational merger might elevate barriers to new competition in both countries. If the multinational firm is large in relation to the mononational firms in country A, it might operate as a giant among pygmies—making entry into that market distinctly less attractive than it would have been otherwise. If the multinational firm's rivals in country B perceive a need to match the initiated integration pattern,[2] then potential entrants into market B may feel the ante necessary to enter the industry there has been elevated. For these reasons, among others, the net effect of the transnational merger on the state of competition is ambiguous.

Not all economists embrace the view that competition should always be treated as a desideratum. The dissenters frequently reason that although competition is needed to guarantee efficiency in the allocation of resources among industries, competition can be incompatible with efficiency in the production of particular goods. If technology exhibits increasing returns to scale over wide ranges of output, then large market shares may be needed to produce at low unit-cost. Moreover, market power may be conducive to rapid technological change. In such situations, the gains in efficiency associated with competition must be compared with the losses in efficiency—static and dynamic—associated with competition. Competition itself is desirable only when the benefits exceed the costs.[3]

This view may be called the competition for the sake of efficiency mode of analysis. It pervades the decisions rendered in European antitrust proceedings. Such a view suggests that transnational mergers should be evaluated on the basis of direct evidence regarding their impact on economic efficiency. Evidence of this type can be found in the literature on multinational corporations. Some such evidence bears on whether multinational or mononational corporations should be considered the better managed. Other such evidence bears on the extent to which multinational corporations facilitate the international diffusion of advanced technology and labor skills.[4] Still other evidence bears on the extent to which efficient scales of operation are attained more often by multinational than by mononational companies.

If we confine our attention to the written decisions of antitrust authorities, these are the two types of economic analysis we find. However, the written decisions fail to convey an accurate impression of the kinds of economic issues on which many decisions turn. The discerning reader will find two other types of analysis lurking in the shadows; the concealed arguments weigh more heavily in the outcomes than do their more obvious counterparts. As a result, it would be a mistake to characterize the difference between U.S. and European views on mergers in general, and transnational mergers in particular, as being the treatment of competition as an end versus the treatment of competition as a means for achieving economic efficiency. Certain economic doctrines motivate European antitrust policy.

The first of these focuses on questions of distribution. In one form or another, the argument comes down to this: direct foreign investment changes the international distribution of income. To the extent that national governments care only about incomes accruing to their own citizens, they should favor or oppose transnational mergers on the basis of whether their own citizens are likely to gain or lose income from the transaction.

Among the key economic questions associated with this position are where does the acquiring company obtain the funds needed to finance the transnational merger, what do the sellers of the acquired firm do with the money they receive from the buyers, and what will the acquiring company do with the cash flow of the acquired company? These questions cannot be answered satisfactorily until particular transnational mergers have been studied in great detail.

The fourth economic framework for analyzing transnational mergers, like the third, does not focus on the impact of such mergers on economic efficiency. Rather it focuses on the ability of national governments to implement national economic policies. The argument runs like this: national governments are responsible for the welfare of their constituents; they devise and attempt to implement economic policies accordingly. Inevitably, at some point during the process of implementation, governments must rely on the business community. The business community must exhibit two characteristics—admittedly, characteristics difficult to realize simultaneously—if it is to be helpful to government. On the one hand, some firms in each industrial sector should possess market power sufficient to ensure the capability of accomplishing governmental goals. On the other hand, despite their power, such firms should remain sufficiently dependent on governmental favors to ensure that they will act in the public interest.

This may be designated the *dirigiste* approach to the evaluation of mergers. I believe that it, and, to a lesser extent, the distributional mode of analysis, are used extensively in European antitrust affairs. How else can one explain the attempts of several European governments to create national champions—domestic firms large enough to fight their governments' battles in various market arenas?[5] Surely the desire to ensure productive efficiency cannot be considered a plausible answer. Such a policy would prompt attempts to merge small- and medium-size enterprises—not the largest of oligopolists.

If distributional and *dirigiste* modes of analysis prevail in Europe, then the following three observations are in order. First, no amount of evidence regarding economic efficiency in general, or economies of scale in particular, will suffice to determine how a European government will choose to treat particular mergers. If economists wish to influence such treatment, they will have to investigate more fully the effects of transnational mergers on the ability of national governments to implement national economic policies. Studies of the following types of questions would be needed: What kinds of industrial structures permit firms to execute governmental economic policies successfully? In particular, is great seller concentration necessary? If so, is it sufficient? Second, what kinds of policy instruments must the government wield in order to insure that it can induce firms to behave in the public interest? For example, is the creation of governmental enterprises in key sectors of the economy helpful? Is it necessary? What are the key sectors of the economy in this context?

In effect, what economists must do is assess the cost-effectiveness of *dirigiste* economic policy. My own feeling is that *dirigiste* governments, for example, the French, have paid a high price for reliance on large firms to execute their economic policies.[6] In the first place, I suspect that the price has been high in pecuniary terms. Great market power is often accompanied by great political power. As a result, the firm most able to satisfy governmental desires is the firm most able to extract a handsome *quid pro quo*. In breeding firms resistant to the powers of competition, governments may well have been breeding firms resistant to governmental control. In the second place, I fear that the political price of the *dirigiste* strategy may be even larger than the pecuniary price. As the formulators of economic policy begin to rely heavily on large business corporations, they begin to rely less heavily on the organs of government. To the extent that governmental institutions are responsible de facto to all citizens, and to the extent that business enterprises are not so responsible, *dirigiste* economic policy saps the strength of political democracy. In this connection, it is ominous to note that many of the original proponents of indicative planning now consider it to be excessively elitist in practice.[7]

My second observation relates to the question of whether or not transnational mergers are likely to be controlled soon by some transnational authority. As much as ever, national governments see the need for national economic policies. In no small measure, this need may be attributed to the rapidity and force with which macroeconomic disturbances are transmitted across national frontiers.[8] Until supranational institutions succeed in creating a stable economic order for the world, national governments are unlikely to surrender their most potent methods of controlling their economies. There is some reason to believe that, rightly or wrongly, many governments consider the control of mergers to be one such method. The unwillingness of the Council of the European Communities to grant broad authority to control mergers to the European Commission is certainly consistent with such a view. In any event, those who would control multinational corporations via supranational authorities should be concerned more with an international macroeconomic policy than with international antitrust laws or codes of conduct for transnational corporations, for only through a consideration of a nation's macroeconomic concerns can supranational institutions deal effectively with problems of transnational corporate concentration.

Finally, it is obvious that different modes of economic analysis can lead to different conclusions regarding the desirability of particular transnational mergers. It is important, therefore, that governments choose wisely among the economic criteria already discussed. Unfortunately, until government officials declare openly that factors other than economic efficiency and competition affect the desirability of mergers, economists—prone as they are to take official pronouncements at face value—will not conduct the relevant empirical research. And policy makers, observing no evidence to contradict the wisdom of their decisions regarding transnational mergers, may unwittingly tread a path which does not serve the public interest.

NOTES

1. *See e.g.*, R. CAVES, INTERNATIONAL TRADE, INTERNATIONAL INVESTMENT, AND IMPERFECT MARKETS (Princeton Special Papers in International Economics No. 10, 1974).

2. *See*, F. KNICKERBOCKER, OLIGOPOLISTIC REACTION AND MULTINATIONAL ENTERPRISE (1973).

3. *See*, Williamson, *Economies as an Antitrust Defense: The Welfare Tradeoffs*, 58 AM. ECON. REV. 18 (1968).

4. *See, e.g.*, Dunning and Steuer, *The Effect of United States Direct Foreign Investment in Britain on British Technology*, MOORGATE AND WALL STREET, (Autumn 1969), 5–33.

5. Industrial policies favorable to the creation of national champions are advocated in L. STOLERU, L'IMPERATIF INDUSTRIEL (1969).

6. *See* S. COHEN, MODERN CAPITALIST PLANNING: THE FRENCH MODEL (2d ed. 1977): J. ZYSMAN, POLITICAL STRATEGIES FOR INDUSTRIAL ORDER: STATE, MARKET, AND INDUSTRY IN FRANCE (1977).

7. Indicative planning consists of establishing voluntary output, input, and price targets for particular industries.

8. *See* R. COOPER, THE ECONOMICS OF INTERDEPENDENCE: ECONOMIC POLICY IN THE ATLANTIC COMMUNITY (1968).

Sherman Act Applications to Predation by Controlled Economy Enterprises Marketing in the United States: Departures from Mechanical Formulae

DEBORAH M. LEVY

In a reproachful dissent in *United States v. Columbia Steel*,[1] the late Justice Douglas sought to remind his brethren what the antitrust laws of the United States are all about:

> [A]ll power tends to develop into a government in itself. Power that controls the economy should be in the hands of elected representatives of the people, not in the hands of an industrial oligarchy. Industrial power should be decentralized. . . . That is the philosophy and the command of the Sherman Act.

It is no small irony that the same distrust of industrial concentration in private hands that animates the Sherman Act[2] also underlies the organization of the state-controlled economy. In the words of Justice Douglas, this distrust amounts to "a theory of hostility to the concentration in private hands of power so great that only a government of the people should have it."[3] In the United States, the Sherman Act and other antitrust laws resulted from this distrust of industrial concentration. Other nations, fearing the excesses of private power, have created state-controlled economies, making industry part of government. As economic barriers between relatively free market economies and controlled economies fall, their component commercial and industrial enterprises face competitors who are as alien in their business practices and economic origins as in their nationality.

The official foreign trade monopolies of a state-controlled economy must conduct business within the constraints of a central economic, political, and social plan. Trade with market economies is potentially disruptive, because Western[4] pricing policies, delivery schedules, and financing arrangements

Deborah M. Levy is a member of the class of 1981, University of Michigan Law School.

may not dovetail with the internal goals of the planned economy.[5] These same goals, and the centralization required to pursue them, can be equally unsettling to market economies and their unordered constellations of businesses. In free market economies, controlled economy enterprises (CEEs) threaten to upset uncontrolled markets that function on the premise that businesses operate for private profit. When goods from a planned economy are marketed in an unplanned economy, there is a potential for intentional or unwitting disruption of the market when foreign government planners change production priorities or pricing policies. In the late 1950s, for example, Soviet planners decided to dispose of surplus aluminum and tin. Using contracts with deescalation clauses, the Soviets were able to undercut the international price whenever it fell. In this manner, they disposed of their surplus, causing the world aluminum and tin prices to collapse. The difficulty of characterizing such behavior was raised by a witness at a 1974 Senate hearing on East-West trade and the antitrust laws: "Is it dumping? Is it competition? We are on a very fine line here. If it's dumping it should be curbed. If it's competition, it should be encouraged."[6]

Any such line drawn to mark out areas of behavior by CEEs should not stop at the difference between "dumping" and "competition," for the absence of a statutory dumping violation does not necessarily indicate competition. Indeed, competition, a difficult enough standard to use in evaluating the behavior of free market firms, is a concept encountering even greater difficulty in discussions and evaluations of behavior by firms from controlled economies.

In a market economy, some goods may enjoy a "natural competitive advantage"[7] stemming from lower costs of capital, labor, or materials, for example, or from efficient business practices. Firms with such advantages can undersell their competitors, if they choose, or make other business decisions exploiting their competitive advantages and successes. The greatest "natural competitive advantage" enjoyed by a market firm, however, does not release that firm from the exigency of showing a profit. By contrast, a CEE need not turn a profit to survive. Any disparity between a low price and the higher value of the resources that go into a particular good produced or marketed by a CEE is compensated for by other components of the state economic plan. To characterize this central allocation of resources in the same manner as cheap labor or efficient private management seems inappropriate. The market economy notion of a "natural competitive advantage" is not easily applied to goods from a planned economy, where government planners set a low price in accordance with national objectives. Firms from planned economies, as instrumentalities of their governments, enjoy a variety of other advantages *vis-à-vis* their free market counterparts. Governments may be willing, through state enterprises, to enter new product markets or geographic markets, when private companies would be deterred by the lack of private returns. Governments and their enterprises, seeking social returns and buttressed by other sectors of the economy, may forge ahead despite the absence of profits. State enterprises may establish coordinated marketing for exports and may take advantage of territorial monopolies of materials—in both instances bringing substantial power to the markets they enter.[8]

In short, "free marketers" in the United States face a competitor unrestrained by the unruly "rules" of competition. Traditionally, the disruption wrought by CEEs has been addressed in the United States as a problem of international trade regulation.[9] But the threat to competition posed by the trading activities of state monopolies in United States markets makes a Sherman Act response one that ought to be explored.[10] The first reason for such a response has already been suggested: the absence of a dumping or other statutory international trade regulation offense does not necessarily indicate that all is well in the market. Controlled economy enterprises, as government-supported monopolies, bring concentrated power to bear in United States markets, and engage in trading practices susceptible of predatory manipulation. Such power is of a dimension that the Sherman Act (the Act) was meant to control; such practices, used to capture markets, are the sort the Act condemns. A state trader can use its monopoly position at home to gain monopoly power in other markets, without violating the letter of the international trade regulation statutes. If, however, the Sherman Act is meant to protect U.S. markets from the evils of monopolies, and if monopoly is what a state trader is all about, a trade regulation response might miss the point. Moreover, statutory international trade regulation remedies by nature emphasize governmental or international trade interests, rather than the interests and complaints of the individual domestic businesses affected by state monopoly power. While courts like to remind litigants that the antitrust laws protect competition rather than competitors,[11] antitrust laws do in fact protect individual firms, affording relief in the form of treble damages to harmed "competitors." Relief of that sort is not generally available through the trade regulation statutes. A treble damage private action for dumping is authorized by § 801 of the Revenue Act of 1916, but the action does not encompass cases where there is no home market and no other countries to which the product in question is exported from which to calculate a price floor for the purpose of identifying dumping. A § 801 violation is predicated on imports priced below prices "in the principal markets of the country of their production, or other foreign countries to which they are commonly exported." But a dumping case against a CEE is likely to require constructed or substituted price or value to establish dumping, given the absence of sales (and thus comparable prices) of the product in the home country, or the artificiality of those prices that are established, or the lack of other countries of export. Such a cause of action against single-market export activity, with the price of the allegedly dumped goods measured against a constructed or substituted value, was cognizable under the Antidumping Act of 1921 and remains so under the Tariff Act of 1930, § 773(c) (as amended by the Trade Agreements Act of 1979, § 101), but neither statute authorizes a private suit.[12]

Quite apart from the private remedy gap in existing international trade law is a more fundamental problem. There is a reluctance to characterize marketing techniques of foreign government exporters as trade regulation offenses. It has been argued by two Department of Justice officials that the antitrust laws "provide adequate remedies if true predation can be proved."[13] Yet the Department of Justice has indicated in its *Guide for International Operations* that predatory or unfair marketing by CEEs is within the province of the international trade laws.[14] While it would be premature to conclude that predatory practices by CEEs marketing in the United States will slip unnoticed or unabated through the cracks between U.S. antitrust and international trade laws, and that the power of CEEs in U.S. markets will grow to alarming magnitudes, it is not too early to examine the relevance and possible application of the Sherman Act to the power and practices of CEEs. In the first case to present these issues, *Outboard Marine Corp. v. Pezetel*,[15] the court did not face up to the challenges posed to the free market by CEEs, denying that the Sherman Act could be used to meet those challenges. But although Sherman Act analysis must take account of the special problems posed by the CEEs, the policies underlying the Act are indeed relevant to the practices and power, including the potential power, of these firms.

THE CASE OF THE POLISH GOLF CARTS: ONE COURT'S RESPONSE TO THE CONTROLLED ECONOMY ENTERPRISE

Pezetel Foreign Trade Enterprise of the Aviation Industry, an agency of the People's Republic of Poland, began in 1970 to manufacture "Melex" (named for Mielec, Poland, site of Pezetel's factory) electric golf carts solely for export to the United States, under an agreement with a U.S. company providing the specifications for the carts.[16] From eight carts in that year, the imports burgeoned to 8,040 by 1974, amounting to 19 percent of the U.S. electric golf cart market. Figures for the first few months of 1975 indicated a 35 percent market share. As the market share of Melex carts increased, sales of Cushman golf carts, manufactured by Outboard Marine Corporation (OMC), dwindled. OMC could not meet Pezetel's low price. Together with other U.S. manufacturers, OMC brought charges against Pezetel under the Antidumping Act of 1921,[17] but by the end of 1975 it was forced to cease production of its Cushman line. In 1977, OMC filed suit in federal district court in Delaware, where Pezetel had incorporated a subsidiary, also known as Melex, advancing, *inter alia,* several Sherman Act claims, supported in part by theories of liability based on practices and advantages of Pezetel inherent in its organization as a Communist state monopoly.

Count 1 of the complaint alleged that Pezetel, Melex, and the defendant distributors of Melex carts violated Section 1 of the Sherman Act by conspiring to restrain interstate and foreign trade; Count 2 alleged a Section 2 violation consisting of monopolization or attempted monopolization of the manufacture, sale, and distribution of carts. Counts 3 and 4 were Wilson Tariff Act[18] and Antidumping Act of 1916[19] claims, respectively.[20]

OMC claimed that Pezetel's pricing practices were predatory and, as such, actionable under Section 1 as elements of a plan to restrain trade, and under Section 2 as culpable behavior leading to attempted or actual monopolization. The plaintiff did not allege below-cost pricing, arguing that this standard had no meaning in a suit against an enterprise from a state-controlled economy, where "the costs of materials, labor and capital even if shown in books and records, reflect the value judgments not of the marketplace, but of central government planners."[21] Predatory pricing was demonstrated, according to OMC, by Pezetel's practice of setting the price of Melex golf carts "far below the floor of the marketplace" in an exercise of "raw economic power."[22]

OMC also urged the court, for purposes of the monopolization charge, to look beyond a mathematical calculation of market share in determining whether Pezetel had achieved monopoly power. In calculating monopoly power, OMC argued, the court should take into account the support afforded Pezetel by the Polish government. The state monopoly could maintain its prices because it was backed by vast—nationally-scaled—financial resources far greater than those available to free market competitors. Unconstrained by the need to show a profit, Pezetel was said to enjoy market power not measurable by a concentration ratio. Finally, OMC argued that Pezetel had forced the five largest firms in the industry into a loss position, thereby demonstrating its monopoly position in the U.S. market.[23]

Ruling on a motion to dismiss for failure to state a claim, Judge Schwartz was sensitive to OMC's quandary. He noted that its grave injury was undisputed, but questioned whether the loss was cognizable under the Sherman Act.[24] His answer, in large part, was negative. All that survived of the Sherman Act claims was a count of attempted monopolization predicated on Pezetel's alleged 35 percent market share and the alleged use of territorial restraints among its distributors to perpetuate that share[25]—a claim that did not rest on Pezetel's state-controlled characteristics, but that could have arisen against any species of business enterprise.[26]

THE SECTION 1 COMPLAINT: PREDATION IN RESTRAINT OF TRADE AND THE BELOW-COST PRICE TEST

Although the court found the concerted action element of Section 1 of the Sherman Act satisfied by OMC's allegations regarding agreements between Pezetel and Melex distributors, it rejected the allegation that the Melex pricing strategy was predatory and thus an unlawful restraint of trade. Predatory pricing, the court said, is an offense "generally manifested by selling below one's own cost for the purpose of effectuating long term domination of the market."[27] By this standard, OMC's allegations of "predatory and unfair" prices were deficient: "Notably absent are allegations that the prices are below cost or that any of the defendants are foregoing a profit."[28] The court held that the below-cost predatory pricing standard was not subject to variations; to devise a new test or to allow OMC to prove the predatoriness of Pezetel's pricing by evidence other than that bearing on costs and profits of the defendant would "usurp Congress" and amount to nothing less than "a perversion of both the judicial function and the antitrust laws."[29] In Judge Schwartz's view, OMC was attempting to set up the antitrust laws as a "sanctuary for those who cannot compete against lower prices be they the result of simple efficiency, economies of scale, cheap labor, technological expertise or anything other than commercially mischievous conduct."[30] With respect to pricing policies, commercially mischievous conduct can apparently take just one form: namely, setting prices below costs.

THE SECTION 2 COMPLAINT

Judge Schwartz swiftly disposed of the allegation of monopolization, in a sentence and a footnote. Relying solely on market concentration to the exclusion of all other indicators of monopoly power, he determined that under *United States v. Aluminum Company of America,*[31] Pezetel's 35 percent market share failed, as a matter of law, to establish monopolization. Acknowledging that the ability to control prices in the market was another usual test of monopoly power, the court nonetheless held that market share alone was the proper test for gauging the power of a CEE in a U.S. market.

> In measuring the market power of a more conventional competitor—one not benefited by a government subsidy—ability to control price would be the focal point of the analysis. . . . Here, the presence of a controlled economy conferred upon the defendants power over price that another competitor might have achieved only through unlawful anticompetitive conduct.[32]

The court accepted the allegation that Pezetel's 35 percent market share constituted a "reasonable probability of success" of monopolization sufficient to show an attempt to monopolize if the "critical element" of specific intent were shown.[33] But in another narrow interpretation, Judge Schwartz held that he could not infer the requisite specific intent from Pezetel's pricing practices. The plaintiff, Judge Schwartz stated, must allege conduct that is not a "normal, industrial response to market opportunities," but rather that is intended to limit the opportunities of competitors to drive them out of the market.[34] OMC's complaint regarding the low prices offered by Pezetel to

Melex dealers did not meet this test, according to Judge Schwartz: "As earlier emphasized, the low prices offered to Melex dealers by defendant manufacturer or defendant importer are not alleged to be below Pezetel's costs or
otherwise predatory."[35] Of course, OMC did allege that the prices were
predatory, and earlier in the opinion Judge Schwartz noted that they were
described by the plaintiff as "predatory and unfair."[36] The point was not that
OMC failed to allege either below-cost pricing or pricing practices that were
"otherwise predatory," but that the court failed to accept a theory of predatory
pricing that departed from the "below-cost" test.

Judge Schwartz based his rejection on *United States v. Grinnell Corp.*,[37]
where the Supreme Court had identified the hallmark of monopolization as
"the willful acquisition or maintenance" of monopoly power in contradistinc-
tion to growth or development resulting from a superior product, business
acumen, or historic accident. *Grinnell* was not an attempted monopolization
case, but rather a case of monopolization. To find it controlling of the case
before him, Judge Schwartz must have assumed that the distinction between
willfulness of acquisition and innocent acquisition of power was instructive
of the distinction between behavior from which one could infer an intent to
acquire monopoly power, and behavior implying only innocent motives. Defendants in *Grinnell,* with 87 percent of the accredited central station service
business (involving the sales of burglar alarms, fire alarms, and sprinkler
systems) were deemed to hold monopoly power. "Willful acquisition" was
hardly in question, given the defendants' participation in restrictive agreements, pricing practices, and takeovers. The question before the Supreme
Court was one of the relevant market for the purpose of the antitrust offense.
Nevertheless, Judge Schwartz adopted "the language of *Grinnell*" as his
own:

> That Pezetel's competitive advantage results from a government sub-
> sidy by a controlled economy that permits defendant to offer virtually
> identical products at a cheaper price is not actionable under Sherman
> Act § 2. Employing the language of *Grinnell,* such a product may be
> considered superior to another comparable product available only at a
> higher price. Certainly a firm that exploits the opportunity through
> technology, cheap labor or a government subsidy to offer the same
> product at a reduced price can be said to be responding normally to
> market opportunities. As such, defendants [sic] use of low prices ap-
> pears to fall with the *Grinnell* exception and therefore is not considered
> mischievous conduct from which § 2 intent can be inferred.[38]

In effect, the court fused a cost-based predatory pricing standard with the
Grinnell statement to conclude that a CEE which exploited its government
subsidy and management to offer the same product as its free market enterprise counterparts at a reduced price was no different from any competitor
exploiting the advantages with which it was blessed.

PREDATION AND POWER: SHERMAN ACT APPLICATIONS TO THE
CONTROLLED ECONOMY ENTERPRISE

The Sherman Act is flexible enough to take notice of the special problems posed to U.S. markets by East-West trade. Judge Schwartz's narrow reading of the Sherman Act in this context may have resulted from a concern that the plaintiff was seeking to convert the antitrust laws into a powerful instrument of protectionism. Such protectionism, which would afford particularized benefits in the form of treble damages to complaining U.S. firms, would plainly be offensive to a system of international trade in a way that the usual international trade regulation remedies are not. The latter, after all, are admittedly protective of U.S. industry. Their use against practices deemed unfair engenders none of the apparent hypocrisy that would attach to similar use of the Sherman Act, with its philosophy of invigorating competition and safeguarding for consumers a diverse market. Moreover, international trade regulations, insofar as they are premised on price adjustments through tariff levies, reflect a willingness to accommodate the disparate national economic values of both the importing and exporting governments. This method of economic regulation appears more palatable to foreign sovereigns than does antitrust regulation that, through its treble damage provision, necessarily conveys a punitive message as well as an indictment of foreign national economic views. Conceding the risk that the Sherman Act might serve as a disguised form of protectionism, the fact remains that the policies underlying the Act are decidedly relevant to the challenges CEEs may present in the U.S. market. More importantly, these policies, if thoughtfully wielded, are susceptible of fair and nonprotectionist applications to state-controlled firms.

PREDATION: ASSIMILATING INTERNATIONAL RULES IN A SHERMAN
ACT ANALYSIS

Under Section 1, predatory pricing is a substantive offense, complete in itself if joined by the required complicity, rather than, as in Section 2, conduct from which inferences may be drawn about an intent to monopolize. If the offense were defined exclusively in terms of below-cost pricing, judicial refinements might indeed pervert the statute. But the statute's concern is not, in fact, so narrow. In analyzing a challenged pricing policy,

It is . . . important to determine whether the price-cutter possesses an adventitious or meretricious advantage, unrelated to competitive merits, either by reason of doing business in a multiterritorial market, where the local price-cutting can be recouped by monopolistic profits elsewhere, or by reason of being able to subsidize a losing operation by the profits from a different line of business. . . .[39]

This unrestrictive characterization of predatory pricing in restraint of trade avoids stressing the exact mechanism and mathematics behind price-cutting. Even the *Pezetel* court used a subjective concept, "commercially mischievous conduct," to describe the Section 1 evil. But the court simply refused to find mischief in any pricing policy other than one involving the setting of prices below marginal costs. Given the advantages it enjoys, a CEE may well be able to set prices that are predatory in a meaningful sense, and in restraint of trade, even if the prices are not measurably below costs. By insisting on an allegation of below-cost pricing—an allegation that OMC was evidently unable to make against a CEE, whose costs of production are arguably as artificial as its product prices—the court cut off the inquiry without giving the plaintiff an opportunity to prove that Pezetel's pricing policies involved the very sort of mischief at which Section 1 is directed.

In like fashion the court's refusal to entertain OMC's argument that Pezetel's intent to monopolize could be inferred from the defendant's prices circumvented a thorough examination of the nature and purpose of the pricing policies, giving short shrift the underlying principle of *Swift & Co. v. United States*,[40] that the character of actions and plans are crucial in Sherman Act analysis. Specifically, by shrinking from the task of assaying Pezetel's admixture of business and government, the court gave voice to a contradictory judgment: that a CEE can be said to respond normally to the "market" opportunity of its government-planned and government-proffered subsidy monopoly.

The formula of normal behavior originated in the *Standard Oil* case,[41] where Justice White contrasted legitimate market ascendancy by "normal methods of industrial development" with unlawful "new means of combination which were resorted to in order that greater power might be added than would otherwise have arisen had normal methods been followed."[42] The usefulness and meaning of this distinction diminish when transposed into a case involving a CEE. Even its reformulation in *Grinnell*, where "historic accident" had a place among the nonactionable sources of monopoly power, is of limited relevance to a CEE case. Surely the Court was not there delivering an opinion on the "historic accident" of centrally run economies. The Sherman Act accountabilities of enterprises that benefit from the economic organization of their home states were not before the Court, not even by analogy.

Despite the inappositeness of the "below-cost" and "market opportunity" tests, Section 2 case law provides some insight into the problem of reconciling antimonopolization policy with CEE practices. Monopolization is an offense involving the possession of monopoly power acquired by unlawful conduct. The conduct is either evaluated independently, against some standard of unlawful activity, or examined as the basis from which an unlawful monopolistic intent can be inferred. If a firm does not achieve monopoly power, it may nonetheless be guilty of an attempt to monopolize, if it acts with the intent to garner that power and comes within a "dangerous probability" of success.[43] A firm may unlawfully exploit otherwise lawful advantages under

Section 2: intent, modes of operation, and market preeminence may combine to create culpability.[44]

In *Times-Picayune Publishing Co. v. United States*[45] the Supreme Court elaborated on the type of proof required in an attempt case. While subjective intent to injure competition is required, evidence about the defendant's state of mind is not. The unlawful intent can be inferred from various evidentiary sources—most importantly, from conduct.[46] Whatever the difficulties of formulating definitions of monopolistic conduct or intent, the fact that such conduct and intent are the focal points of a Section 2 inquiry is crucial to the problem of how the pricing practices of CEEs might fit into the framework of law.

These focal points should not be obfuscated by tests and formulae that may not reveal anything about monopolization or attempted monopolization. The purpose of identifying predatory practices and setting them up as tools of analysis is to identify a broader offense—the intentional and unreasonable control of competition. Unbending adherence to inflexible tests such as a "cost-based predatory pricing analysis" may arrest the judicial function in Section 2 of discerning unlawful conduct and intent. As Professor Lawrence Sullivan has insisted in response to a sophisticated economic analysis identifying instances of predatory pricing,[47] functional and objective standards are useful, but are not "*the* way . . . to get at predatoriness."[48]

Flexibility in ferreting out predation by state traders carries costs and risks. If U.S. courts were to develop standards of predation that would transform the Sherman Act into an amorphous international "fair trade" regime activated at the suggestion of market predominance by a state trader and aimed directly at practices likely to be commonplace to CEEs, international trading relations, as well as general U.S. foreign relations, would be imperiled. Other "flexible" remedies that might be achieved through modifications to existing import regulations would run the same risks. It might be possible to expand the 1916 Antidumping Act[49] to allow treble damage actions against the type of single market export activity at issue in *Pezetel,* where there is neither a home market, nor any other export market from which to calculate a price floor for the purpose of identifying dumping. Alternatively, a private antidumping remedy might be added to the Tariff Act of 1930,[50] which authorizes only government action against single-market trading situations, with the prices of the allegedly dumped goods measured against a constructed or substituted value. A private recovery remedy could be built into the market disruption provisions of the Trade Act of 1974,[51] or selected international trade regulation laws could be incorporated into the "antitrust laws" covered by the private action provision of the Clayton Act.[52]

Such revisions would certainly cheapen the antitrust laws and contribute nothing substantial to the meaning of predation or monopoly power. If tacked onto the body of traditional antitrust law, these amendments would graft a policy having little to do with monopoly onto statutes having everything to do with monopoly. The resultant legal structure of "antitrust" law would be hobbled by an anomalous appendage that could strike against foreign marketers who have nowhere near a monopoly position, although they may indeed have violated rules of fair trade. If patterned after antitrust laws, but kept statutorily separate from them, these modifications of international trade regulation laws would mark significant departures from the tendency to treat international trade regulation at the governmental level, departures that would transform protectionist laws into offensive weapons in the hand of private U.S. firms.

The more realistic and difficult task is to adhere to standards of predation that will preserve the economic environment mandated by the Sherman Act without interfering with international trade or political relations. To be avoided are condemnations of a CEE's home organization, which could stir up international animosities; unfair presumptive tests applied exclusively to CEEs; and impossible requirements demanded of controlled economies regarding the way they conduct their foreign trade. To devise standards in keeping with considerations of international relations, judges should turn to international referents. They must identify conduct that is internationally recognized as predatory and that is also of the same quality or that effects the same evils as traditional Sherman Act predatory practices.

The General Agreement on Trade and Tariffs,[53] for example, grapples with state trading in a general manner, with respect to all the state parties, and in a specific way, with provisions formulated for centrally planned states. The antisubsidies provisions address a variant of the price advantage issue seen in *Pezetel,* Article XVI prohibiting government subsidies that produce lower export than domestic prices of goods, and Article VI allowing the importing state to assess a countervailing duty if injury to a potential or established industry is threatened or caused. Article XVII treats state trading specifically, admonishing state enterprises to make purchases and sales

> . . . solely in accordance with commercial considerations, including price, quality, availability, marketability, transportation and other conditions of purchases or sales, and . . . [to] afford the enterprises of the other contracting parties adequate opportunities, in accordance with customary business practice, to compete for participation in such purchases or sales.[54]

The accession agreements of Poland, Romania, and Hungary, in acknowledgment of the special problems posed regarding freer international trade by planned economies, commit those states to affirmative action to increase imports, provide for special valuation treatment of their exports, and devise safeguards for importing states against the three countries' export prices.[55] While all these directives and declarations are subject to varied interpretations, and while they have not bound the acceding states to a regime of completely fair, free, and competitive international trade, they do indicate common, if somewhat fuzzy, agreement about proper trade behavior.

Norms of conduct have been established; material deviations are unfair and predatory.

The Treaty of Rome[56] also deals with state enterprises established by the contracting parties, recognizing, like GATT, their obstructionist potential. Unlike GATT's Article XVII rule of conduct, the Treaty of Rome's Article 37 required an adjustment of state trading monopolies "so as to ensure that, when the transitional period expires, no discrimination exists between the nationals of Member States as regards the supply or marketing of goods."[57] This adjustment was part of the more fundamental task of the EEC, that of establishing a unified system of undistorted competition for public and private enterprises, with both types of enterprise subject to the rules of competition.[58] Again, a standard of commercial conduct has been established among nations. Agreement can also be reached bilaterally: when the United States extends nondiscriminatory tariff treatment to a Communist country, it includes in the bilateral agreement "safeguard arrangements" providing for consultation when prospective or actual imports threaten or produce market disruption.[59] The 1974 Trade Act also authorizes import restrictions to prevent such disruption.[60] Even if not indicating consensus on norms, the bilateral agreements indicate commitments to adhere to certain modes of behavior or to submit to remedial consequences.

Agreements to preserve competition in East-West or public-private trade have been framed consonant with sovereign interests and national goals. There has been no effort to write state trading out of existence; there have been varied and experimental efforts aimed at integrating state trading into the international system. Poland was not asked to rid herself of her trade monopoly before joining GATT; similarly, the state enterprises of the EEC countries, though "adjusted" for competition's sake, are accorded deference for the sake of politics. Article 90 of the Treaty of Rome qualifies the general rule that public enterprises are subject to antitrust, antidumping, and anti-subsidies rules with the statement that public undertakings "entrusted with the operation of services of general economic interest or having the character of a revenue-producing monopoly" are subject to the trade rules only to the extent the application does not interfere with their functions.[61] In sum, there has evolved an amalgam of deference to the political impulses animating state enterprises and submission by these enterprises to standards of fair trade and competition.

Of course, rules or standards of international law are rarely universally agreed upon. Further, rules or standards to which a state binds itself in a multilateral agreement such as GATT, or in a bilateral agreement, such as one entered into under the Trade Act of 1974 extending nondiscriminatory tariff treatment to a state-controlled economy, are not necessarily transferable to other legal contexts such as the Sherman Act. To make more difficult the question for "international" standards applicable to the type of transaction at issue in *Pezetel*, only six Communist or Socialist countries are members of GATT and thus bound to its rules on export sales;[62] moreover, U.S. bilateral treaties, with rules against predatory export practices, do not span the controlled economy globe.[63] Therefore, even if one agreed that the standards regarding market disruption and unremunerative pricing expressed in these international documents help identify predatory practices in the context of the Sherman Act, a great many nations would remain uncovered by any such standards. This limited coverage would be politically unpalatable, as nations with which the United States has come to a trading *modus vivendi* through negotiations and treaties would be at a comparative disadvantage to those nations without this status and its attendant obligations.

The discrepancy could be avoided by applying the relevant standards without discrimination. Such uniform application seems unobjectionable for the same reasons that transferring international standards contained in conventions should not be seen as violating principles of treaty law and interpretation: the courts would not be spuriously creating or expanding international responsibilities or liabilities out of arbitrarily selected conventional provisions. Their use of international behavioral criteria would in fact manifest a sensitivity to foreign interests, while at the same time this use would serve legitimate domestic competition policy. Nothing in international law constrains U.S. courts from finding predation and attaching liability under domestic laws to any number of practices engaged in by foreign firms, whether free market or state-controlled. What this flexible (and necessarily imprecise) transfer of international standards would signify is the recognition that while state trading might present myriad instances of practices that seem vaguely unfair, and fewer examples of practices that seem undesirable (and thus possibly actionable under the Sherman Act if present in conjunction with other elements proscribed by the law), U.S. judges will not depend on parochial notions of commercial mischief. Neither, however, will they close their eyes to all predation that stems from state planning by woodenly adhering to tests for predation that could never be applied to CEEs. Such rigidity would ignore the possibilities of law and accommodation. As John Zysman mused, looking to the future,

> These state traders confront the advanced capitalist countries with new conditions of trade competition. The question is whether this layer of trade surrounding the core of the principal OECD countries is cut off from private trade, incorporated within present arrangements for conducting private trade, or has altered the system of private trade itself.[64]

The Sherman Act need not be irrelevant to the marketing practices in this country of commercial enterprises from controlled economies, and international rules of trade, however imperfectly formulated and incompletely adopted, need not be irrelevant to antitrust analysis. The former can find useful and fair standards in the latter, and the latter can find expression and advancement within a domestic legal framework constructed to keep intact a social and economic environment to which the United States is committed.[65]

ASSESSING THE MONOPOLY POWER OF CONTROLLED ECONOMY
ENTERPRISES

In ascertaining the power an enterprise holds in a market and in determining whether that power amounts to monopoly power, courts would find little guidance in rules and standards set out in international trade agreements. Rules of conduct do not speak to de facto states of affairs, however carefully the rules may be designed to promote or deter certain future balances and distributions. Yet the characterization of market power is as much a part of Section 2 of the Sherman Act analysis as the characterization of behavior, and the state trader may bring to a free market very great power by virtue of its government-sanctioned monopoly and national deep pocket.

The *Alcoa* 30-60-90 test is not the last word on monopoly power, and it was probably not intended to be. Indeed, given the circumstances in which it was formulated, the argument can be made that it is particularly inappropriate for generalized use. Judge Hand did not arrive at the ratios in a deductive manner; rather, the fractions were presented to him as operative facts of the case and he analyzed them in that context. To adopt these ratios—which, as the difference between the lower court's and Judge Hand's calculations indicates, were highly susceptible to manipulation—as generally significant overlooks the historical setting and binds post-*Alcoa* cases to an amalgamation of market statistics and corporate behavior that happened to emerge in that case. Unquestioning adoption of the *Alcoa* test rests the determination of monopoly power on market share analysis which fortuitously occupied Judge Hand's opinion.

Closer scrutiny of *Alcoa* reveals that Judge Hand himself did not rely solely on the concentration ratio in determining whether Alcoa held monopoly power. He emphasized that the reason Alcoa's proportion of the market was significant was that it gave the company virtually complete control in the market.[66] While he acknowledged his focus on the concentration of producing power, he reiterated that a root evil was the "possession of unchallenged economic power." If that power existed, it was "irrelevant" that the possessor reaped only a fair profit.[67]

In *United States v. United Shoe Machinery Corp.*,[68] Judge Wyzanski brought to "exfoliation," as he later put it,[69] the inherencies in the seeds of *Alcoa*. These inherencies, according to Judge Wyzanski, who was Judge Hand's law clerk when the latter handed down the *Alcoa* decision, amounted to a market structure analysis for Section 2 monopolization. In estimating a defendant's strength under such an analysis, Judge Wyzanski gave some weight to its percentage of the market, but he also felt it proper to examine its pricing policies, to compare the defendant and its competitors in terms of financial resources, facilities, accumulated experience, and variety of products offered, and to take note of the market barriers erected by the defendant.[70]

The list of monopoly power indicia can be amended as new market situations arise. If a firm acts as though it has preponderant market power, a tentative inference of monopoly power can be drawn. If a firm performs as if it has dominant market power, a similar inference can be drawn. Although one usually thinks of exorbitant profits as the main act of a monopolist performance, the performance may entail whatever activities the monopolist wishes to pursue and is able to pursue thanks to its release from the worries of competition: maximization of sales volume, maximization of cash flow, or even the achievement of a favorable image.[71] While not determinative, "size is itself an earmark of monopoly power,"[72] and cannot be ignored as a red flag marking monopoly power. Where "market power" may appear absent by market concentration standards, "monopoly power" may nonetheless exist in terms of vast aggregations of wealth that can underwrite a ruthless ascent to market predominance. One might test for this monopoly power by surveying the financial resources available to the firm under scrutiny.[73]

Distinguishing the particularized finding in the *Alcoa* case from the general theory underlying those finding leads one to a rather broad lesson that has been largely ignored in Section 2 cases. Judge Hand recognized that a finder of fact would come out differently in the case if he began with a different opinion regarding what goods and productive capacity were competing in the market. The inquiry central to identifying monopoly power concerns what a firm brings to the market and whether what it brings can crush its competitors. The power that a CEE brings to the market in question— assets, state management, longevity while maintaining unremunerative prices—is not reflected in a concentration ratio. It should, however, factor heavily in a realistic evaluation of its power in the market.

In this area, as in that of predatory practices, judges may subject the Sherman Act to hostile criticism by applying novel tests to CEEs when commonplace standards yield no useful information. Here again, however, as in the predation field, the inquiry suggested is consistent with (and in fact no departure from) that which is normally undertaken in Section 2 analysis. Courts generally determine the existence of monopoly power by employing a flexible calculus embodying a wide spectrum of indicia. It happens that when judges deal (as they always have) with free market firms, a large percentage of sales that a firm is able to capture in the market is particularly persuasive evidence of monopoly power. When dealing with CEEs, the other indicia should gain in significance. A court has a duty under the Sherman Act to discern monopoly power. It can do little with tests that measure the concern of the statute incompletely, if not misleadingly.

However consistent with Sherman Act policy (and even necessary for Sherman Act enforcement) one considers this means of discerning monopoly power, the problems attendant to its actual application cannot be wished away or muffled by good intentions. Courts may come dangerously close to banning CEEs from the U.S. market for the concomitants of their very nature: size and freedom of action in formulating market strategies. The suggestion has been made that smallness is a virtue in industrial organization, and that the antitrust laws exist in part as tools to prevent the absolute size of a firm from reaching gargantuan proportions.[74] Whether this belief or commitment is truly part of Sherman Act policy, it should have no voice in proceedings against CEEs. These enterprises embody the economic and social policy of another sovereign, and the requirement to comply with U.S. law should not grow into an insistence that the foreign sovereign revamp its internal organization. The doctrine of comity cautions against judicial zealousness when a controversy reaches deeply into the interests of a foreign sovereign. There are also political limits to what the adversary process can accomplish with respect to monopoly power, domestic or foreign, and the evils it wreaks on consumers and on social and economic structures.

CONCLUSION

One should recall the irony presented at the beginning of this article, that U.S. antitrust laws and centrally planned economies have addressed the same problem and come up with widely differing solutions: a system of maximum competition among private actors and a regime of public monopolies. If the issue of monopoly power were merely one of economic power, a CEE would have no unique cause for complaint upon being told by a U.S. court that its power in a U.S. market was at an unacceptable level. But the issue is more fundamental, reaching into general questions of power; a centrally planned government might perceive any U.S. court judgment against the strength of its foreign trade organizations as an attack upon its vital economic and political interests. Power is quintessentially politics. The danger faced by courts in considering allegations of predatory practices by CEEs is one of purposefully or inadvertently honoring protectionist protestations having nothing to do with Sherman Act policy. The danger posed at this juncture with respect to monopoly power is that judges will make determinations having too much to do with the essence of the Sherman Act—that is, U.S. judges may intrude into the arena of core governmental concerns. The judicial function in domestic antitrust cases naturally enough includes the enforcement of antitrust claims against privately owned corporations. Inevitably, this involves an acceptable, albeit significant, judicial intrusion into the behavior and structure of U.S. enterprises. The acceptability of this function diminishes when judges assume a similar role in policing the activities and structure of CEEs, necessarily implicating foreign sovereign interests and decision making.

But the difficulties should not deter judges who are presented with monopolization cases against CEEs from fulfilling the purposes of the Sherman Act by seeking out monopoly power, just as the fine line that separates predation from competition in the range of CEE marketing practices should not discourage judges from uncovering truly predatory activities in Section 1 and 2 cases. As the tests already outlined suggest, courts can apply the Sherman Act with meaning to both the practices and power of CEEs, provided they unchain themselves from formulae that are largely irrelevant to CEEs. Courts can couple enforcement with fair-mindedness and tolerance of international diversity if they tailor their new test of CEE predation to international standards and if they observe the political limits on the judicial process in their evaluations of the power the state traders bring to U.S. markets.

NOTES

1. 334 U.S. 495, 536 (1948).
2. 15 U.S.C. §§ 1–2 (1976).
3. 334 U.S. at 536 (1948).
4. Although controlled economies or Socialist states are not confined to Eastern Europe, and free market economies are not inevitably "Western," "East-West trade" is convenient shorthand for free market/controlled economy trade.
5. The disruptions are dealt with in part through contract terms and conditions. For example, Soviet Foreign Trade Organizations are directed to purchase at the lowest world price and to sell Soviet goods at prevailing world prices, or, if none are discernible, at some minimum figure. In so-called compensation or buy-back agreements, that price is calculated to ensure that exports will cover the cost of Western-supplied technology or equipment used to produce those exports. If the Western seller has no need for the product, it may often assign the purchase contract to another party satisfactory to the Eastern party. Another mechanism by which the state-controlled economy avoids unsettling effects is the license agreement. The Eastern licensee of Western technology must earn convertible currency in order to pay the licensor, and that need often translates into a license provision that a licensor might wish to avoid: the licensee gets the right to sell output from the licensed technology in Western (convertible currency) markets. For an overview of the adaptive mechanisms of Eastern European countries to East-West trade problems, *see* J. CONNOR, JR., LEGAL ASPECTS OF DOING BUSINESS WITH THE USSR AND EASTERN EUROPE (1977).
6. *International Aspects of Antitrust Laws: Hearings before the Subcomm. on Antitrust and Monopoly of the Senate Judiciary Comm.* 93d Cong., 1st and 2d Sess. 114 (1973–74) (statement of Samuel Pisar).
7. Parsons, *Recent Developments in East-West Trade: The U.S. Perspective,* EAST WEST TRADE 165 (1973).
8. For a catalogue of state trading advantages, *see* Kostecki, *State Trading in Industrialized and Developing Countries,* 12 J. WORLD TRADE L. 187 (1978).
9. *See, e.g.,* Revenue Act of 1916 § 801, 15 U.S.C. § 72 (1976) (antidumping); Tariff Act of 1930 § 303, 19 U.S.C. § 1303 (Supp. III 1979) (countervailing duties); Trade Act of 1974 § 337, 19 U.S.C. § 1337 (1976) (unfair import trade practices); Trade Act of 1974 § 406, 19 U.S.C. § 2436 (Supp. III 1979) (disruption of markets by Communist imports); Tariff Act of 1930, tit. VII, *as amended by* Trade Agreements Act of 1979, §101, 19 U.S.C. §§1671–77g (Supp. III 1979) (countervailing and antidumping duties); Antidumping Act of 1921, 19 U.S.C. § 160 *et seq.* (1976) (repealed by the

Trade Agreements Act of 1979 § 106(a), 93 stat. 193).
See also Grzybowski, *East-West Trade Regulation in the United States: The 1974 U.S. Trade Act, Title IV*, 11 J. WORLD TRADE L. 501 (1977). A recent symposium integrated international trade regulation with antitrust analysis in examining § 337 of the Trade Act of 1974, a provision that is a cross between an antitrust and a trade regulation statute. *See Symposium, Section 337 of the Trade Act of 1974*, 8 GA. J. INT'L & COMP. L. 27 (1978).

10. "State monopolies" or "state trading" can denote anything from trading units maintained by governments acting as entrepreneurs to trading units distinct from governments but owned by them. It can exist in industrialized free market Western economies as well as in Communist and Socialist systems. *See generally* Kostecki, *supra* note 8. *See also* Baban, *State Trading and the GATT*, 11 J. WORLD TRADE L. 334 (1977); Reuland, *GATT and State-Trading Countries*, 9 J. WORLD TRADE L. 318 (1975); Zysman, *The State as Trader*, 54 INT'L AFF. 264 (1978).

Kostecki has predicted that "the existence of state trading may considerably eliminate the role of competition in international markets and consequently call for a new analytical framework to explain the patterns of state-traded imports and exports." *Supra*, note 8, at 207. This forecast was prompted by an observation of the effects of state trading on the international market and how those effects are achieved. States engage in state trading to achieve a variety of objectives. Domestic objectives include price and distribution policy, the integration of foreign trade into a central economic and/or social plan, revenue-raising for the

government, and health and strategic control. External objectives include the desire for international bargaining power, export expansion, the fulfillment of international obligations, and the linkage of trade with politics.

The following discussion will center on state trading by centrally planned economies only—but it is just this category that embraces the broadest descriptions of the ways, means, ends, and effects of state trading.

11. *See, e.g.,* Outboard Marine Corp. v. Pezetel, 461 F. Supp. 384, 400 (D. Del. 1978) discussed *infra*.

12. *See* Revenue Act of 1916 § 801, 15 U.S.C. § 72 (1976); Tariff Act of 1930 § 773(c), 19 U.S.C. § 1677b(c) (Supp. III 1979).

13. Rosenthal & Sheldon, *Section 337: A View From Two Within the Department of Justice*, 8 GA. J. INT'L & COMP. L. 47, 51 (1978).

14. Justice believes that an American licenser of a CEE is adequately protected against any "unfair advantage" the CEE may enjoy in the licenser's domestic markets by international trade laws. *See* ANTITRUST DIVISION U.S. DEP'T OF JUSTICE, GUIDE FOR INTERNATIONAL OPERATIONS 40–41 (1977).

15. 461 F. Supp. 384 (D. Del. 1978).

16. Pezetel's predecessor, Elektrim Foreign Trade Company for Electrical Equipment, Ltd., made the initial agreement with Products International, which acted as importer of the Melex carts until 1973. At that time, Pezetel succeeded Elektrim as the Polish manufacturer, and purchased Products International's inventory and existing contracts with U.S. distributors. It formed Melex USA, Inc., a wholly owned Delaware corporation, and entered directly into exclusive sales and distributorship agreements

with several concerns, which became codefendants in the case. *See* 461 F. Supp. at 389; Defendant Melex USA, Inc.'s Brief in Support of its Motion to Dismiss at 1–3, Outboard Marine Corp. v. Pezetel.

17. 19 U.S.C. § 160 *et seq.* (1976) (repealed in 1979). The Department of the Treasury found that Melex sales in 1973–74 were at "less than fair value," and the International Trade Commission found that these sales resulted in injury to domestic producers. Treasury arrived at "foreign market value" by determining the prices charged for carts in Canada. The practice of using as a guideline prices charged for similar goods in a free market third country or of arriving at a constructed value was subsequently codified in § 205(c) of the Trade Act of 1974, 19 U.S.C. § 164(c) (1976), repealed by the Trade Agreements Act of 1979 § 106(a) and reenacted by the Trade Agreements Act of 1979 § 101. *See* Tariff Act of 1930, § 773(c), 19 U.S.C. § 1677b(c) (Supp. III 1979). *See generally* 43 Fed. Reg. 35,263 (1978); 19 C.F.R. § 153.7. The antidumping proceeding has a complicated history, with much of the argument centered on the question of valuation. *See also* 461 F. Supp. at 390; *Oversight of the Antidumping Act of 1921: Hearings on the Adequacy and the Administration of the Antidumping Act of 1921 Before the Subcomm. on Trade of the House Comm. on Ways and Means,* 95th Cong. 2d Sess. 106 (1977) (statement of Donald A. Webster).

18. 15 U.S.C. § 8 (1976).
19. 15 U.S.C. § 72 (1976).
20. 461 F. Supp. at 390.
21. Brief of Plaintiff Outboard Marine Corp. in Opposition to Defendants' Motions to Dismiss Complaint at 43.
22. *Id.* at 48. As the defendants' consolidated reply emphasized, OMC complained only that Pezetel's prices were below the costs of "most" U.S. manufacturers. Defendants Pezetel and Melex's Consolidated Reply to Outboard Marine Corporation's Brief at 5–6.

23. Brief of OMC, *supra* note 21, at 33–42, 46–47.
24. 461 F. Supp. at 388, 391.
25. *Id.* at 405–6, 410.
26. Although this Note will not discuss it, the most frequently debated issue regarding suits, antitrust or otherwise, against CEEs is that of sovereign immunity. *See, e.g.,* P. Shephard, Sovereignty and State-Owned Commercial Entities (1951); S. Sucharitkul, State Immunities and Trading Activities in International Law (1950); Baker, *Antitrust Remedies Against Government-Inspired Boycotts, Shortages, and Squeezes: Wanderings On The Road to Mecca,* 61 Cornell L. Rev. 11 (1976); Brower, Bistline, and Loomis, *The Foreign Sovereign Immunities Act of 1976 in Practice,* 73 Am. J. Int'l L. 200 (1979); Joelson and Griffin, *The Legal Status of Nation-State Cartels Under United States Antitrust and Public International Law,* 9 Int'l Law. 617 (1975); Note, *American Antitrust Liability of Foreign State Instrumentalities: A New Application of the Parker Doctrine,* 11 Cornell Int'l L.J. 305 (1978).

The Foreign Sovereign Immunities Act of 1976 (28 U.S.C. §§ 1330, 1332, 1391, 1441, and 1602–11 (1976)) (FSIA), has not put to rest discussion about what entity qualifies as a foreign state or instrumentality; what activity qualifies as political (and immune) and what is commercial; and what the relationship is between the so-called *Parker* doctrine (from Parker v. Brown, 317

U.S. 341 (1943), an antitrust exemption for certain state action or state-induced action) and the FSIA in antitrust suits against state enterprises. Regarding refinements in the *Parker* doctrine, *see* City of Lafayette v. La. Power & Light Co., 98 S. Ct. 1123 (1978); Bates v. State Bar of Arizona, 433 U.S. 350 (1977); Cantor v. Detroit Edison Co., 428 U.S. 579 (1976); Goldfarb v. Virginia State Bar, 421 U.S. 773 (1975).

For an example of a court displacing the FSIA's political-commercial test of immunity in an antitrust suit by the *Parker* doctrine immunity test, *see* New Mexico v. Amer. Petrofina, 501 F.2d 363 (9th Cir. 1974).

For his part, Judge Schwartz had little difficulty finding Pezetel amenable to suit under the FSIA and Section 4 of the Clayton Act. 15 U.S.C. § 15. Regarding the *Parker* doctrine exemption, he noted, 461 F. Supp. at 397, that the exemption depends on a full consideration of all facts and circumstances, and thus was not appropriately addressed in a motion to dismiss. This inconclusiveness suggests that in a given antitrust suit a given CEE may well be deemed subject to the jurisdiction of the court. While the questions and problems of suing state enterprises for antitrust violations are unsettled and for that reason interesting, they ought not preclude examination of further issues that arise once a CEE is brought under a court's jurisdiction.

27. 461 F. Supp. at 400.
28. *Id.*
29. *Id.*
30. *Id.*
31. 148 F.2d 416 (2d Cir. 1945). Judge Hand pointed to Alcoa's 90 percent share of the relevant market as evidence of the possession of monopoly power; he then went on to speculate that two-thirds of the market would indicate a doubtful case of monopoly power, while one-third would fall short of monopoly power. *Id.* at 424.
32. 461 F. Supp. at 404 n. 38.
33. 461 F. Supp. at 404.
34. *Id.*, citing L. Sullivan, Handbook of the Law of Antitrust 99 (1977).
35. 461 F. Supp. at 404.
36. 461 F. Supp. at 400.
37. 384 U.S. 563 (1966).
38. 461 F. Supp. at 405.
39. Mt. Lebanon Motors, Inc. v. Chrysler Corp., 283 F. Supp. 453, 459 (W.D. Pa. 1968), *aff'd per curiam*, 417 F.2d 622 (2d Cir. 1969). In theory, a restraint of trade is not lessened by the fact that consumers reap an initial benefit of low prices, but, "[p]erhaps the greatest problem with winning even true predation cases is that judges and juries are reluctant to find that low prices today may injure the ultimate consumer tomorrow." Rosenthal & Sheldon, *supra* note 13, at 51.
40. 196 U.S. 375 (1905).
41. Standard Oil Co. of N.J. v. United States, 221 U.S. 1 (1911).
42. *Id.* at 75.
43. 196 U.S. at 396.
44. *Id.*
45. 345 U.S. 594 (1953).
46. *See* Independent Iron Works, Inc. v. United States Steel Corp., 322 F.2d 656, 656–57 (9thCir.), *cert. denied*, 375 U.S. 922 (1963); United States v. American Oil Co., 249 F. Supp. 599, 809 (D.N.H. 1966); L. Sullivan, *supra* note 34, at 135.
47. Areeda & Turner, *Predatory Pricing and Related Practices Under Section 2 of the Sherman Act*, 88 Harv. L. Rev. 697 (1975).
48. L. Sullivan, *supra* note 31, at 110. *If there is one task that judges and juries, informed through the adversary system, may really be good at, it is identifying the pernicious in*

human affairs. To contend that the conventional formulation which looks, in a sense, for evil, ought to be amended to one which looks solely to an effect validated by economic studies is to assume too much about the precision of applied economics and to assume too little about the value of the more humanistic modes of inquiry.

. . . .

The best course . . . is to leave the avenues of inquiry as open as may be. Objective data, such as that stressed by Areeda and Turner, could then be used either to attack or defend, but also could any other evidence indicative of predatory intent.

49. 15 U.S.C. § 72 (1976).
50. Tariff Act of 1930 § 731 *et seq.*, 19 U.S.C. § 1673 *et seq.* (Supp. III 1979).
51. 19 U.S.C. § 2436 (Supp. III 1979).
52. 15 U.S.C. § 12 (1976).
53. General Agreement on Tariffs and Trade, Basic Instruments and Selected Documents (BISD), "Text of the General Agreement," 55 U.N.T.S. 174.
54. *Id.* at 252.
55. See GATT, "Protocol for the Accession of Hungary to the GATT," BISD (20th Supplement, 1974) at 3–8; GATT, "Protocol for the Accession of Romania to the GATT," BISD (18th Supplement, 1972), at 5–10; GATT, "Protocol for the Accession of Poland," BISD (15th Supplement, 1968), at 46–52.
56. Treaty Establishing the European Economic Community, 298 U.N.T.S. 4300 (1958) (EEC Treaty).
57. *Id.* at art. 37.
58. Mestmäcker, *State Trading Monopolies in the European Economic Community,* 20 Vand. L. Rev. 321, 325, 353 (1967).
59. 19 U.S.C. § 2435 (1976).

60. 19 U.S.C. § 2435(b)(3) (1976).
61. EEC Treaty, *supra* note 56; at art. 90.
62. Czechoslovakia, Cuba (original members), Hungary, Poland, Romania, and Yugoslavia.
63. General headnote 3(e) of the Tariff Schedules of the United States, 19 U.S.C § 1202 (West Supp. 1980) identifies Communist countries not entitled to most-favored-nation customs rates: Albania, Bulgaria, Cuba, Czechoslovakia, Estonia, East Germany (and East Berlin), Hungary, Communist Indochina, Communist Korea, Kurile Islands, Latvia, Lithuania, Outer Mongolia, Southern Sakhalin, Tanna Tuva, Tibet, and the USSR.
64. Zysman, *supra* note 10, at 267.
65. As one of the U.S. negotiators at the Tokyo Round of Multilateral Trade Negotiations wrote,

    Systems of international rules such as the GATT may encourage compliance . . . [U]nless the system is a dead letter, its mere existence influences the policy decisions of member governments, who would be reluctant to violate the system's rules openly . . . [O]ne of the primary but unspoken purposes of the many parts of the MTN [multilateral trade negotiations] is to assure the system's conformity with the norms of its members so that it can again exercise a degree of moral authority.

    Graham, *Reforming the International Trading System: The Tokyo Round Trade Negotiations in the Final Stage,* 12 Cornell Int'l L.J. 1, 28 (1979).
66. 148 F.2d at 424.
67. *Id.* at 427.
68. 110 F. Supp. 295 (D. Mass. 1953), *aff'd per curiam,* 347 U.S. 521 (1954).
69. Wyzanski, *Closing Remarks, Antitrust Symposium: Section 2 of the*

Sherman Act, 10 Sw. U.L. Rev. 131, 133 (1978).

70. 110 F. Supp. at 343.

71. Sullivan, *supra* note 34, at 80–87.

72. United States v. Paramount Pictures, 334 U.S. 131, 174 (1948).

73. Cooper, *Attempts and Monopolization: A Mildly Expansionary Answer* to the Prophylactic Riddle of Section Two, 72 Mich. L. Rev. 373, 380 n. 20 (1974).

74. 148 F.2d at 428–29; W. Letwin, Law and Economic Policy in America 85–95 (1965); H. Thorelli, The Federal Antitrust Policy 180–229 (1955).

Foreign Approaches

United Kingdom Regulation of Transnational Corporate Concentration

J. DENYS GRIBBIN

This article begins by describing the United Kingdom's policy toward outward and inward direct investment and then sets out the essentials of the competition laws that are among the major, nondiscriminatory regulatory mechanisms that affect corporate behavior and planning. The article also analyzes the development of competition policy as a microeconomic instrument along with its application to monopoly, oligopoly, and cartels involving transnational corporations. Competition policy, except for cartels, is shown to be relatively benign toward mergers until recently, and with respect to monopoly and oligopoly has sought remedies in regulation of prices and behavior rather than through structural change. Recent proposals, including a new Competition Act, are described. The analysis will show that although transnational corporations have been prominent in competition policy enforcement, substantial detriments arising from their transnational nature have not yet been identified, despite the presence of adverse effects on the public interest. Traditional fears associated with foreign investment in the United Kingdom do not, therefore, seem to be justified, insofar as the abuse of market power is concerned. In practice, the United Kingdom has relied principally on an effective tax system and competitive markets to ensure an equitable distribution of the gains from foreign direct investment, and there has been relatively little interference with inward flows of capital.

This article does not enter into the complexities of defining a *transnational* corporation. As its purpose is to report on the U.K. government regulation of companies simultaneously controlling and operating wealth-producing assets in more than one country, it concentrates on those businesses which fall within the framework of regulation. This means outward and inward direct investment, the greater part of which is still in the manufacturing industry.

J. Denys Gribbin is a staff member, Monopolies & Mergers Commission, The United Kingdom. The views expressed in this article are those of its author only.

U.K. POLICY TOWARD FOREIGN INVESTMENT

Since the Industrial Revolution of the nineteenth century, outward and inward direct investment have been important components of U.K. economic
activity, and after World War II they assumed even greater significance.
Outward investment has traditionally been greater than inward; by 1974 the
value of the former was £ 10,000 million, and the latter was £ 6,900 million.
However, the pattern of outward investment has changed in recent decades.
Before World War II and for some time thereafter the Commonwealth and
former colonies were the major recipients; now these have been replaced by
North America and Western Europe. The latter are also the most important
sources of inward flows, with the United States normally providing well over
50 percent. Inward investment was concentrated in manufacturing industry,
but there is now considerable entry into banking with U.S. banks acquiring a
major share. In 1971 the United Kingdom held 15 percent of the stock of
direct foreign investment in developed economies compared with the 52
percent for the United States. Given such a commitment it is not surprising
that U.K. regulatory policies toward national and transnational corporate concentration are liberal and nondiscriminatory.

Until November 1979 both forms of investment—inward and outward—
required permission from the Bank of England under the Exchange Control
Act of 1947.[1] The principal objectives were threefold: (1) to protect the U.K.
balance of payments, (2) to ensure that inward investment made an appropriate contribution to the foreign exchange reserves relative to the degree of
acquired control, and (3) to ensure that the price of assets purchased reflected their fair market value. There were no cases of importance during this
period in which government authorities refused permission for inward investment. Since the U.K.'s balance of payments has been strengthened by sales
of North Sea oil the need to protect the exchange rate has diminished and
exchange control has ceased since November 1979. Part II of the 1975
Industry Act[2] introduced an additional control on inward investment which
empowered the government to prohibit takeovers of important manufacturing firms where these would be against the national interest. Also, for certain
takeovers consummated after 1975, the secretary of state could acquire the
assets, subject to safeguards, and vest them in the National Enterprise
Board.[3] This provision has not been used.

There is one notable exception to present policy which relates to the
North Sea oil reserves. Here, the government has imposed special rules on
exploration, trading, as well as a Petroleum Revenue Tax.[4] These controls are
nondiscriminatory even though a major share of the exploration investment
is held by foreign controlled companies.

Successive U.K. governments have traditionally welcomed direct foreign
investment. The secretary of state of the former Labour administration issued
the most recent policy statement, which appears in the foreword to the 1976

U.K. publication of the OECD *Guidelines for Multinational Enterprises*. In welcoming the guidelines and the intergovernmental consultative machinery, he stated:

> The U.K. has a special interest in this package in view of its major stake in international investment. Inward investment has made a substantial contribution to our economy notably in terms of increased productive capacity and employment, and the Government continues to welcome foreign investment which contributes to our future development. Investment overseas by U.K. companies brings us a substantial return and enables us to develop markets overseas for U.K. exports and to secure supplies of raw materials.[5]

The present government has made no policy statement, but there is no reason to believe it will change this position, particularly in view of the relaxation of exchange control in November 1979.

SOME ECONOMIC EVIDENCE AND POLICY ISSUES

As a response to the growing debate about multinationals in the late 1960s, the U.K. Board of Trade commissioned an independent study to examine some of the major implications of direct foreign investment. This study was published in 1973 under the title "The Impact of Foreign Direct Investment on the United Kingdom."[6] It was not intended to form a basis for U.K. policy, but provided valuable insights into some of the critical issues. The authors identified three areas for examination:

1. the possibility that there is a loss of national control over the economy attributable to foreign investment,
2. the possibility that there may be a loss of national autonomy because of the influence of the government of the foreign parent company; and
3. the economic effects of foreign investment on the U.K. balance of payments, technological development, industrial relations, and competition, as well as locational effects within industrial regions.

The report found little evidence of detriment to national control and autonomy, although some potential disadvantages accruing from foreign ownership were identified.[7] However, these problems were not likely to arise unless the U.K. subsidiary was part of a multinational network based on the international division of labor and subject to strong central control. Even then the incidence of such arrangements was relatively rare. The conclusion on economic effects was that on balance direct investment had brought material gains from increased investment, improved balance of payments, access to technology, and, tentatively, increased competition. The report found a tendency for foreign investment to locate itself in oligopolistic industries (their degree of concentration being higher), but the authors cautioned that in the absence of foreign firms, competition might not be enhanced; there were also several large national firms in the concentrated industries. Indeed, foreign entry may be a strong deterrent to domestic firms wishing to exploit market power. The authors also suggested that oligopoly did not necessarily indicate an absence of competition and a concomitant failure of firms to share real income gains in the form of lower product prices and higher factor incomes.[8]

The study's findings on the association between inward investment and oligopoly highlighted the importance of market structure and its influence on competition. Some have questioned the validity of these findings since the data which was relied on came from the 1963 Census of Production, and there have been substantial subsequent changes in the sources and amounts of investment. A less rigorous but more recent analysis by this author confirms the earlier findings. Data from the 1971 Census of Production at the three digit (SIC) level of aggregation show that for 104 industries the average share of sales coming from foreign-owned firms was 15 percent; there was a noticeable, but weak, positive relationship between the degree of concentration of sales and foreign ownership. Table 1 contains the sales concentration data, grouped by foreign ownership and share held by the five largest firms. However, these statistics understate the relationship. There are another 41 industries where the degree of ownership is not disclosed for reasons of confidentiality. These industries are, on the average, more concentrated than the 104, so it is highly likely that their inclusion would strengthen the statistical result. Nevertheless, the relationship as found is not strong, and this points to one conclusion: foreign ownership is unlikely to be a major cause of high concentration in the U.K. manufacturing industry. There is also a policy implication—there are several sufficiently concentrated industries with above-average foreign ownership shares so as to cause legitimate concern with the state of competition within these industries, and to question whether foreign ownership in these circumstances results in forms of conduct and standards of performance which are against the U.K. public interest yet not readily susceptible to national antitrust remedies. The remainder of this article will examine these concerns.

THE COMPETITION LAWS AND THEIR APPLICATION TO CORPORATE CONCENTRATION

United Kingdom competition policy has its origins in the wartime planning for postwar full employment and trade liberalization. At home it was accepted that the aims of competition policy were to promote industrial efficiency and

Table 1.
Sales Concentration and Foreign Ownership in U.K.,
Three-Digit Manufacturing Industry, 1971

Foreign-Owned Share (in percentage)	Top Five Firms' Share of Sales[a]					Total
	1–20%	21–40%	41–60%	61–80%	81–100%	
0	5	5	2	6	3	21
1–20	9	17	17	5	6	54
21 40	—	6	8	4	3	21
41–60	—	1	2	1	1	5
61–80	—	—	1	1	1	3
81–100	14	29	30	17	14	104

Source: Census of Production and Business Statistics Office.

a. In some industries this may be four or six.

help restrain price increases.[9] As a result of U.S. wartime initiatives to promote trade liberalization in order to secure international full employment it was agreed that safeguards should also be implemented to permit investigation and control of U.K. firms participating in national and international export cartels.

Postwar policy can be conveniently divided into two periods, demarcated on the basis of the predominant forms of industrial structure and behavior. In the first, from 1948 to the early 1960s, the prewar and immediate postwar inheritance of cartels was the primary policy target; in the second, which followed and continues today, the concern is with the growth of industrial and aggregate concentration.

The legislative landmarks of the earlier period are the Monopolies and Restrictive Practices (Enquiry and Control) Act of 1948,[10] and the Restrictive Trade Practices Act of 1956;[11] these provide, by contrast, a fair illustration of the pragmatic nature of economic regulatory policy and its development. However, as this policy was hardly concerned with dominant firms, and did not examine issues which might have been raised by the transnational corporate activities, it will only be briefly described.

The 1948 Act was neutral toward industrial structure and behavior, there being no presumption that cartels or high concentration were detrimental. Its purpose was, as stated in the title, to enquire into, and, if necessary, control monopolies and restrictive corporate practices. This it did successfully in the eight years prior to 1956.[12] A Monopolies and Restrictive Practices Commission (Commission) was established to investigate, upon reference from the Board of Trade, situations where competition was restricted, and to make public interest judgments pertaining to the structure, behavior, and performance of the industries or firms concerned. The "public interest" test was very broad, but in practice the Commission interpreted it in economic terms consistent with the purpose of achieving greater industrial efficiency.[13] As there was no legislative presumption against restrictions or competition it was for the Commission to decide that the performance of a cartel or dominant firm was better promoted by limiting competition rather than encouraging it.

During the first eight years, the Commission investigated a representative sample of eighteen cartels, two dominant firms, and examined a wide range of practices coming within the general description of collective discrimination. Although it found, in some special and limited circumstances, that certain collective limitations on competition had encouraged technical efficiency and rapid diffusion of new technology, its conclusions on cartels were overwhelmingly unfavorable.[14] Generally it found that cartels kept inefficient high cost capacity in existence, froze industry structures, retarded innovation, and caused costs and prices to be higher than they would be if there was greater competition.[15] The cumulative effect of this evidence, together with the Commission's strong condemnation of collective restrictions such as exclusive dealing, aggregated rebates, refusal to supply, and the collective enforcement and maintenance of prices (resale price maintenance), was to swing public opinion to the view that cartels should be prohibited on the presumption that they caused substantial detriment to the economy.

Before discussing the implementation of these conclusions in the 1956 Restrictive Trade Practices Act[16] it is useful to note three facets of the 1948 Act which have been of long term significance. The first is the robustness of the public interest criteria;[17] these were adequate to deal with the consequences of cartels, dominant firms, and mergers until 1973. By 1973 experience suggested that these criteria should relate more precisely to the newer policy goal of controlling concentration. Second, the wording of the sections dealing with collective behavior had been sufficiently flexible to bring both implicit and explicit collusion with their reach.[18] Third, and most important for this article, the 1948 Act established the limit of U.K. jurisdiction, which has remained unchanged. References by the Board of Trade to the Monopolies Commission could only be made where goods were supplied in the United Kingdom, or when the manufacturing process under investigation was performed within the United Kingdom. Moreover, application of the order-making power extended only to British subjects, corporate bodies incorporated in the United Kingdom, or persons carrying on business there; however, the power also extended to acts performed outside the United Kingdom by those entities listed above.

The second policy stage relevant to cartels was implemented through the Restrictive Trade Practices Act of 1956.[19] Henceforth collective restrictions on competition were presumed to be against the public interest; firms wishing to continue to participate in or to form cartels were required to disclose full details to a new enforcement agency, the Office of the Registrar of Restrictive Trading Arrangements, which then placed them in a public register. If the restrictions were not abandoned or modified, the registrar brought the infringing cartel before the newly created Restrictive Practices Court for a condemnatory judgment and prohibition on continuance. To rebut the presumption the participants could plead specified benefits, but few succeeded in doing so.[20]

The registration requirement revealed for the first time the extent to which the manufacturing industry and its distributors were subject to private collective regulation. By the end of 1963, 2,430 agreements were on the register, over 80 percent of those that were eventually disclosed. It is estimated that about 50 percent of manufacturing output was regulated in this way.[21]

Through a combination of public disclosure, determined action by the registrar, and Restrictive Practices Court decisions, the 1956 Act had a dramatic effect. Only eleven agreements received the approval of the court, the remainder being abandoned by the parties or modified to eliminate their restrictive effects. As a consequence of this vigorous policy there has been little effort by industry since the early 1960s to form legal cartels;[22] although new agreements are registered, they deal only with minor matters and are judged to have no significant effects on competition. British cartel legislation has been extremely effective in abolishing them and has thereby contributed substantially to improved industrial efficiency.[23]

THE CONTROL OF CORPORATE CONCENTRATION

The second period of U.K. competition policy begins in the late 1950s, naturally enough, after the successful and speedy abolition of cartels, and addresses the structural problems of concentration which arose out of postwar growth and trade liberalization. During this second period, the adaptability of earlier legislation was explored. Subsequently, the earlier statutes were refined and strengthened with the infusion of merger control and greater powers to deal with existing monopoly and oligopoly.[24]

Notwithstanding the earlier extensive cartelization of the manufacturing industry, structural change in the form of increasing concentration occurred in the U.K. economy. There are several reasons for this trend toward increased concentration. Technical change in many industries led to new opportunities for scale economies; economic growth at home and abroad created larger markets; developments in communications and innovations in management techniques made it easier for multiplant firms to be controlled efficiently; and successive government administrations promoted mergers in some industries as a means of achieving greater industrial efficiency. By the late 1950s, therefore, it was possible to see increasing concentration, and an important vehicle for this was merger.[25] Interestingly, the success in abolishing cartels added fuel to the developing merger boom.

The evidence on growing concentration has recently been reviewed in

Table 2.
Share of the One Hundred Largest Enterprises in U.K.—
Manufacturing Net Output 1909–72

	1909	1924	1935	1940	1953	1958	1963	1968	1970[a]	1972[a]
Share (in percentage)	16	22	24	22	27	32	37	41	39	41

Sources: S. J. PRAIS, THE EVOLUTION OF GIANT FIRMS IN BRITAIN (1976); DE-PARTMENT OF PRICES AND CONSUMER PROTECTION, A REVIEW OF MONOPOLIES AND MERGERS, Green Paper, Cmnd. No. 7198 (1978).
a. A change in statistics slightly reduces comparability with earlier years.

a consultative document (Green Paper) of the previous government, *A Review of Monopolies and Mergers Policy*.[26] This review indicated that both aggregate concentration and market concentration had grown more rapidly in the United Kingdom than in the United States and other European economies, so that by the 1970s levels of concentration were substantially higher.[27] Before describing the legislative response to this structural change it will be useful to set out some of the data which illustrate the growth of concentration.

Aggregate concentration in the United Kingdom is usually indicated by the share of net output or employment held by the 100 largest enterprises in the private manufacturing industry; these indicia provide the most convenient measure for the twentieth century. As they also reflect the growth of market concentration they are a useful index of change.

Table 2 illustrates the growth of aggregate concentration in the twentieth century. The conclusion from this series is that the U.K. post–World War II rate of growth has been double that of the prewar period, although the U.S. pre- and postwar growth rates are approximately the same.

Growing market concentration can be shown through a further analysis of the relative importance of the 100 largest firms in the major industry groups (table 3). The 100 largest enterprises increased their share of manufacturing output by 9 percentage points over the fourteen years, even though in two major industries, metal manufacture and vehicles, it fell. This can only be regarded as a significant change in industrial structure.

The rise in concentration must be seen in the context of greater competition from imports; for example, in 1955 imports were 4.5 percent of home sales of manufactured goods whereas by 1977 they had grown to 15.9 percent.[28] To the extent that the imports are not made by the largest firms in each industry this rising import share may reduce the market power consequences of a higher concentration of U.K. production.

Mergers have played a major role in the growth of concentration. British statistics provide a reasonably accurate description of the prolonged merger

Table 3.
Estimated Share of the One Hundred Largest Enterprises by Industrial Order
(percentage of employment)

Industrial order	1958	1972
Food, drink, and tobacco	28	53
Chemicals and allied industries	34	42
Metal manufactures	55	22
Engineering and electrical goods	32	37
Shipbuilding and marine engineering	18	28
Vehicles	69	61
Metal goods	4	19
Textiles	9	29
Leather, leather goods, and fur	—	9
Clothing and footwear	6	
Bricks, pottery, glass, cement, etc.	11	28
Timber and furniture	—	5
Paper, printing, and publishing	16	29
Other manufacturing	24	29
Total manufacturing	27	36

Source: DEPARTMENT OF PRICES AND CONSUMER PROTECTION, A REVIEW OF MONO-
POLIES AND MERGERS, Green Paper, Cmnd. No. 7198 (1978), annex A.

Table 4.
Mergers between Industrial and Commercial Companies 1954–78

Period	Companies Acquired (annual average)	Average Amount paid £m
1954–58	291	0.4
1959–63	693	0.6
1964–68	891	0.9
1969–73[a]	988	1.4
1974–78	373	1.7

Source: Business Monitor M7.

a. Data after 1968 are on a slightly different basis, but this does not distort the picture shown here.

boom which began in the late 1940s and early 1950s. Table 4 gives relevant data for five year periods from 1954 to 1978. The long and upward swing in activity is readily apparent. Peak years were 1972 and 1973 when there were 1,210 and 1,205 mergers respectively. An earlier peak was 1965 with 1,000 mergers. (These coincide with peaks in economic activity and share values on the Stock Exchange). The steadily rising trend in the average value of

Table 5.
Inward Investment Mergers 1969–78

Period	Companies Acquired (annual average)	Average Amount Paid £m	Share of All Mergers	
			Number	Value
1969–73	19	2.6	2.0	3.6
1974–78	11	8.1	2.4	13.4

Source: Business Monitor M7.
Note: This table does not include acquisitions by foreign-owned companies already operating in the United Kingdom.

acquired firms is also noted; some part is, of course, due to the inflation of asset values.

Most mergers result in the disappearance of relatively small firms; between 1962 and 1969 only 3 percent of acquired companies were valued at over £ 5m. While the pattern changed in the 1970s, large company acquisitions still only represented 7 percent of the total number of acquisitions, but 62 percent of the assets acquired.

Reliable data on inward investment mergers has only been available since 1969.[29] Table 5 shows the flow and some relevant comparisons. The flow of inward mergers indicates a similar pattern of decline in the 1974–78 period, although the fall is less pronounced possibly because the number of mergers made by firms in the EEC doubled between the periods which, in turn, substantially reduced the importance of U.S. firm activity. These mergers differ in one major respect from U.K. activity—on the average they are substantially larger in terms of the assets acquired.

Table 6 gives some perspective to the data on the postwar merger boom and shows how it has contributed to the growth of concentration.

THE POLICY ISSUES OF CONCENTRATION

The immediately preceding section has examined the evidence on the growth of concentration in the United Kingdom. Concern over this development led in 1978 to a further review of the competition laws by an official committee composed of civil servants, known as the Leisner Committee. Its report was published as the Green Paper,[30] which in paragraph 3.40 succinctly stated the relevant policy concerns:

It was noted in paragraphs 3.20 to 3.23 that increased concentration could be detrimental to consumers. This might arise from the emergence of a single dominant firm which exerted its market power to

Table 6.
Estimates of the Contribution of Mergers to the Growth of Concentration

Study	Hart, Utton & Walshe (1973)	Utton (1971)	Aaronovitch & Sawyer (1975)	Hannah & Kay (1977)	Prais (1976)
Time period	1958–63	1954–65	1958–67	1957–69 1969–73	1958–70
Change in concentration attributable to mergers	33%	43%	62%	116%ᵃ 95	50%

Source: Department of Prices and Consumer Protection, a Review of Monopolies and Mergers, Green Paper, Cmnd. No. 7198 (1978).
a. *I.e.*, concentration would have fallen in the absence of mergers.

obtain monopoly profits. Much more common, given the structure of British industry, is the situation where several large firms dominate a market. Under oligopoly it is possible for firms to forego price competition in favour of competition in other areas. Companies tend to be conscious of the interdependence of their activities and this may lead to collusion in formulating decisions making them less responsive to the needs of consumers. The various forms of non-price competition involve, to a greater or lesser extent, resource costs and these in turn can mean higher prices to the consumer. The creation and defence of a position of market dominance can also involve resource costs which do not necessarily yield a social gain. Thus the accretion of market power through greater concentration can result in a range of practices which are unique to markets characterised by dominant firms and which are potentially against the public interest.

THE LEGISLATION ON CORPORATE CONCENTRATION

The Monopolies and Restrictive Practices Act of 1948

Although used primarily to explore the economic consequence of cartels, the Monopolies and Restrictive Practices Act of 1948[31] was also designed to test monopoly and oligopoly against the same public interest criteria. The 1948 Act permitted the Board of Trade to make references to the Monopolies Commission either where one firm held a one-third share of the market for goods (or process of manufacture), or where two or more firms met the same share test and acted jointly to restrict competition, whether or not they formally agreed to do so.[32] Between 1948 and 1956 only two references of dominant firms were made—those of matches and matchmaking machinery[33] and industrial and medical gases[34]—so the 1948 Act was little used against large firms in concentrated industries.

In the period following the 1956 Restrictive Practices Act the Monopolies Commission explored some of the consequences of growing concentration, although the policy response to it was slow, there being only an average of 1.3 references a year between 1956 and 1966. The investigations began to examine the causes and consequences of significant market power, and thereby laid a foundation for future work, as well as drawing attention to the consequences for the public interest when such power was exercised. Practices found to be against the public interest included agreements with foreign suppliers that eliminated competition in the United Kingdom, open and concealed acquisitions of competitors, price discrimination, resale price maintenance, and exclusive dealing with full-line forcing.[35] Two industries included foreign-owned companies of substantial size, subsidiaries of large multinationals; however, the investigations did not link any adverse impact from market power solely to the multinational nature of the enterprises involved. Although the references were few in number, the industries investigated were large and important and the impact of the findings was greater than might be thought;[36] these findings contributed to the next stage of policy development—a legislative response to the rising wave of mergers.

The Monopolies and Mergers Act of 1965

Public debate about merger control began in the early 1960s, fueled in part by a number of spectacular and hard-fought takeover battles. In 1964 the Conservative government issued a White Paper[37] containing proposals for strengthening the competition legislation. Among other things it proposed the introduction of merger control. The White Paper welcomed the growing merger wave because of the potential economic gains—better use of resources, economies of scale, increased research and development, and greater strength for competing in international trade. Only a small minority of mergers were thought potentially detrimental, and therefore appropriate targets for a regulatory scheme tailored to deal only with them. Thus, the White Paper recommended a highly discriminating regulatory system that applied to few mergers and avoided a per se prohibition. This philosophy was to shape policy and its implementation until more serious scrutiny of the potential gains from concentration occurred in the 1970s.

The 1965 Act[38] substantially strengthened the competition laws. Services became subject to investigation by the Monopolies Commission; merger control was instituted, with an automatic reference of certain pending newspaper mergers; the Monopolies Commission was increased in size to cope with a greater workload; and the order-making powers of the Board of Trade were extended to prices, price discrimination, display of prices, and most importantly, prohibition of mergers, dissolution, and conditions on business activity where a merger could not be dissolved. Moreover, the power to dissolve applied to any monopoly the Commission found to be against the public interest.[39]

For the purpose of this paper the most important innovation of the 1965 Act was the power conferred on the Board of Trade to make references of actual or proposed mergers to the Monopolies Commission for a judgment on their public interest consequences. This was the first attempt at a clear antitrust remedy for mergers and the regulation of concentration which arises through merger. The underlying philosophy was that each merger should be treated on its merits, there being no general presumption that an increase in concentration would decrease competition, or that even if concentration did lessen competition that this was necessarily detrimental.[40] As this was the same approach as to monopoly and oligopoly, the public interest criteria were not altered; mergers had to face the same test.

In keeping with the 1964 White Paper view that only a small proportion of mergers merited further scrutiny, the 1965 Act laid down two criteria which narrowed the scope of governmental concern. To be within the scope of control, a merger either had to create or intensify a monopoly as defined in the 1948 Act,[41] or the gross assets to be acquired had to be £5 million or more. *Merger* is not precisely defined; it may occur when two enterprises cease to be distinct, or where one enterprise has the ability to control or materially influence the policy of another.[42] Therefore, *merger* was not definitionally limited to a rigid concept of corporate restructuring or actual asset acquisition; the term could be extended to activities that did not involve a formal mixing of corporate assets or identities.

The 1948 Act did not impose upon enterprises a requirement to notify the Board of Trade of an intended merger; however, government action had to be initiated within six months after a merger became publicly known.[43] In practice, governmental control soon resulted in de facto prenotification because there was a risk that the merger might be dissolved after it had taken place. To assist in reaching decisions the Board of Trade set up an interdepartmental Mergers Panel which processed the relevant information and made recommendations to the president of the Board of Trade who alone had power to refer to the Monopolies Commission.

Upon receipt of a merger reference, the Commission must reach a conclusion within six months, but the minister can grant a three-month extension. If the Commission decides that a merger would be against the public interest, it may propose a remedy or recommend prohibition or dissolution. The minister may decline to act on such recommendations. However, if the Commission does not initially find against a particular merger, the minister has no independent power of prohibition or dissolution.[44]

The Fair Trading Act of 1973

Like its predecessors, the 1973 Act[45] made major innovations in competition policy that, building upon the accumulated experience of earlier enforcement, strengthened the regulatory mechanism and emphasized the promotion of competition. In particular, the legal and organizational changes have created a more effective means of controlling corporate concentration.

The 1973 Act derives directly from the experience of using earlier legislation to deal with issues raised by the growth of concentration. The deeper analysis of structural change that had come from the Commission's investigations suggested that in the presence of generally higher industrial concentration in the 1970s, the emphasis of regulatory policy should be placed more on oligopoly and its consequences. Moreover, the long-term implementation of policy had illustrated that, except for the continuing political sensitiveness of some mergers, monopoly, oligopoly, and restrictive practices did not raise issues which needed to be settled by ministers. Accordingly, policy implementation could be removed from direct ministerial control and placed with an independent body, a view reinforced by the need for an expanded program of enforcement to grapple with oligopoly.

The new legislation expressed these conclusions by reducing the market share definition of monopoly from 33 to 25 percent, and by creating the Office of Fair Trading (OFT), which was responsible only to Parliament.[46] The director general of the OFT was given the power to make his own monopoly and oligopoly references to the Monopolies Commission, subject to a ministerial veto publicly exercised. This veto provision indicates that the power to refer remained under political control, thus reflecting the continuing view that mergers may raise social and political problems not usually associated with settled monopoly.

The 1973 Act instituted another important change. Since the Monopolies Commission had found restrictive service agreements to be similar in effect to those for goods, the same procedures were applied to both. Agreements were presumed to be against the public interest and had to be registered.

THE IMPLEMENTATION OF POLICY REGARDING CORPORATE CONCENTRATION

The authoritative source of information on the public interest consequences of concentration are the reports of the Monopolies Commission. Table 7 sets out a brief description of the workload. Of particular importance are the reports on monopoly and oligopoly in the supply of goods, and those on mergers, except newspapers.[47] The general references reported on refusal to supply, parallel pricing, recommended prices, and professional services.

Table 7.
Investigations by the Monopolies Commission, 1957–September 1979[a]

Investigation	Number
Supply of goods	39
Supply of services	17
Mergers	
General	31
Newspapers	8
General references	4
	99

Source: J.D. GRIBBIN, THE POSTWAR REVIVAL OF COMPETITION AS INDUSTRIAL POLICY (Government Economic Service Working Paper No. 19, 1978).

a. Excludes a follow-up study on imported timber.

THE INVESTIGATIONS INTO MONOPOLY AND OLIGOPOLY

These references demonstrate the growing concern of policy with oligopoly. Of thirty-nine references only fourteen were of single-firm monopoly, and the emphasis on oligopoly in recent years is becoming more pronounced. The Commission's findings on the public interest consequences of monopolies and oligopolies have created a substantial body of evidence about behavior and performance in concentrated industries. Under the legislation, the Commission may find either structure, behavior, or performance to be against the public interest; it has rarely made such decisions about structure, there being only four cases in which it concluded that the monopoly or oligopoly itself was detrimental. Table 8 summarizes the relevant findings. The practices have been divided into the two groups. Those in the second are more likely to be unequivocally judged detrimental when associated with oligopoly or monopoly since they directly restrict competition by erecting artificial entry barriers. The practices in the first group are less easily assessed and the evidence suggests that their consequences must be examined on a case-by-case basis in the context of particular markets. For example, numerous instances of technical price discrimination were examined, but the Commission concluded they had no significant effect on competition. The same point may also be made about recommended prices.

TRANSNATIONAL CORPORATIONS AND THE MONOPOLY REFERENCES

Transnational corporations are prominent in the thirty-nine industries which have been investigated for monopoly or oligopoly conditions. This is not surprising, there being in the United Kingdom a strong correlation between

Table 8.
Practices Found Against the Public Interest

Practice	Number of Cases in which Practice Occurred
Group 1	
Monopoly pricing/monopoly profit	9
Discriminatory pricing	8
Vertical integration	3
Acquisition of competitors	2
Recommended or imposed resale prices	6
Patent-licensing policy	1
Delivered-pricing system	2
Financial interest in competitors	1
Failure to disclose ownership of subsidiary	1
Group 2	
Restriction of supply to certain outlets	3
Restrictions on sale of competitors' goods	13
Restrictions on the supply of inputs to competitors	1
Full-line forcing	2
Rental-only contracts	1
Tie-in sales	4

Source: DEPARTMENT OF PRICES AND CONSUMER PROTECTION, A REVIEW OF MONOP-OLIES AND MERGERS, Green Paper, Cmnd. No. 7198 (1978). Updated by author.

company size, the market structure in which it operates, and the extent to which the company engages in foreign trade and investment.[48] For the purpose of this article transnational corporations have been divided into those that are owned and have their main base in the United Kingdom (national companies that have expanded abroad), and foreign-owned companies that entered U.K. markets either by direct investment or acquisition. Over 90 percent of the U.K.-owned companies which were among the leading suppliers considered in the thirty-nine references were transnational in that they had one or more subsidiaries abroad. However, because of limited U.K. jurisdiction, these references were limited to imports into or exports from the United Kingdom; hence, the Commission was precluded from examining the actual overseas operations of these transnational corporations. These reports do not indicate that the transnational links have reinforced the market power of the U.K. parent.[49]

The incidence of foreign-owned companies among the leading suppliers in the thirty-nine references is shown in Table 9.

Before discussing the implications for competition in the United Kingdom it is worth noting that the reports which cover these twenty references

Table 9.
Foreign-Owned Companies in Monopoly References, 1957–79

Report	Company	Country of Parent	Adverse Finding
1. Chemical Fertilizers. 1959	Potash Ltd.	France/Germany	Yes
2. Electrical Equipment for vehicles. 1963	Champion	U.S.	Yes
3. Petrol to retailers. 1965	Esso, Regent,	U.S.	Yes
	Mobil,	U.S.	Yes
	Petrofina	Belgium	Yes
4. Color film. 1966	Kodak	U.S.	Yes
5. Detergents. 1966	Proctor & Gamble	U.S.	Yes
6. Aluminum semi-manufacture. 1966	Alcan	Canada	Collusive agreement revealed
7. Electric lamps. 1968.	Philips	Holland	Yes
8. Starch, glucose. 1971	Brown & Polson (CPC),	U.S.	No
	Tunnel Refineries,	U.S.	No
	Albion Sugar	Holland	No
9. Breakfast cereals. 1973	Kellogg's,	U.S.	No
	Nabisco	U.S.	—
10. Chlordiazepoxide, Diazepain. 1973	Roche Products	Switzerland	Yes
11. Footwear machinery. 1973	British United Shoe Machinery	U.S.	Yes
12. Primary Batteries. 1974	Mallory	U.S.	Yes
13. Frozen Food. 1976	Findus	Switzerland	—
14. Indirect Electrostatic Repro. Equipment. 1976	Rank/Xerox	U.S./U.K.	Yes
15. Diazo materials	General Aniline and Film (GAF),	U.S.	—
	Addressograph Multigraph	U.S.	Restrictive agreements revealed
16. Cat and Dog Foods. 1977	Pedigree Petfoods	U.S.	No

Table 9—Continued

Report	Company	Country of Parent	Adverse Finding
17. Ceramic sanitary-ware. 1978	Doulton,	France	No
	Ideal Standard	U.S.	No
18. Wholesale supply of petrol. 1979	Esso, Texaco,	U.S.	No
	Mobil, Conoco,	U.S.	No
	Gulf, Amoco,	U.S.	No
	Chevron,	U.S.	No
	Total,	France	No
	Petrofina	Belgium	No
19. Electric cables.	Pirelli,	Italy/U.K.	No
	Standard Telephones and Cables	U.S.	No
20. Electric meters. 1979	Landis and Gyr,	Switzerland	No
	Sangamo Weston	U.S./Netherlands Antilles	No

provide insight into the motivation for, and economic consequences of, direct foreign investment. They also lend empirical support to the industrial organization theories which stress the importance of the foreign firm's competitive advantage derived from product differentiation, new processes, and research and development.

Typically, new foreign investment followed a period of market exploration through exports.[50] In general, the investments involved new plant construction rather than acquisitions. A large proportion of these new firms were established in the United Kingdom during the interwar period, with some originating in the first decade of the twentieth century.[51]

This process has not stopped as entry continues to exploit new market opportunities.[52] Recent decades reveal a greater tendency to enter by acquiring a U.K. company already in the market, as for example the acquisitions of Findus (frozen food) by Nestlé,[53] and those of GAF and Addressograph Multigraph in the diazo market.[54] A number of these foreign-owned firms have subsequently developed into substantial transnational corporations in their own right, mainly because entry to the United Kingdom was often regarded as a method of avoiding tariff barriers protecting former Commonwealth markets and the European Economic Community. Prime examples of this development are British United Shoe Machinery, Kodak, and Rank Xerox.[55]

In addition to illustrating the process of foreign entry into U.K. markets, these twenty reports also provide a valuable framework for examining the impact of transnational corporate entry on competition in the United Kingdom. This relatively high incidence of foreign ownership in concentrated industries raises three questions:

1. Do the links with the parent contribute to market power in the United Kingdom?
2. If so, has that market power been used against the public interest?
3. Are existing U.K. antitrust remedies sufficient to regulate the market power of such foreign-owned companies, and what problems do they bring in enforcement?

The information in table 9 lists the foreign-owned companies which are among the leading suppliers. In some cases these did not possess either 33 percent or, later, 25 percent of the market share; therefore, unless they formed part of a complex monopoly (oligopoly) the Commission could not make public interest judgments against them. However, these enterprises were examined since they were leading suppliers.

The relevant cases are Nabisco,[56] Findus,[57] and GAF and Addressograph.[58] In the diazo market, the Commission discovered a restrictive agreement. Both GAF and Addressograph Multigraph acquired U.K. companies in 1966; the dominant supplier was U.K.-owned and played an important part in organizing the collusion which began before the U.S. entry. A restrictive agreement also was discovered in the aluminium semimanufacture market, but the investigation was abandoned since the agreement was subject to the restrictive practices legislation.

Apart from these references, foreign-owned companies were substantial suppliers in eleven of the references in which the Monopolies Commission made adverse public interest findings. These may be divided into three groups: those in which the company was the dominant supplier (Champion, Kodak, Kellogg's, Roche Products, BUSM, and Rank Xerox); those in which the company was either dominant in a subsector of the market, or where a duopoly existed (Potash Ltd. and Mallory Ltd. operated in subsectors, while Proctor and Gamble was a duopolist); and those in which the company participated in an oligopoly (the oil companies and Philips).[59]

The fact that in eleven references there were adverse findings where foreign-owned companies were involved would not, in and of itself, prove the hypotheses that foreign ownership caused or contributed to the detriment. However, the references do provide some evidence that may be used to determine to what extent the parent-subsidiary linkage contributed to the dominant position and behavior of the company in the United Kingdom.

Some background information is necessary for validating any conclusions on the effects of foreign linkages on U.K. market structure. First, in none of the references did the Commission find the dominant position itself was against the public interest, so even in those instances where strong links were important, foreign ownership per se could not be considered detrimental.[60] Second, as the adverse findings were about behavior, these must be viewed in the context of the structure and history of each market. In the oligopolistic petrol retail market, such activities as exclusive dealing, tie-in arrangements, and preemptive purchase rights to premises, were judged to be against the public interest, but these forms of behavior were not imported; rather, they were practiced by the U.K. suppliers—Shell Mex and BP—and were common in other industries where there were strong forward vertical links into distribution. In the electric lamp market, Philips was the second largest supplier among five.[61] Philips entered the United Kingdom shortly after World War I, and conformed to established patterns of restrictive behavior. Mallory had a large share in a small but growing sector, but it was subject to some influence from the overall dominant supplier EverReady (ER), (U.K.-owned) both because of ER's share, over 70 percent, and its 25 percent holding of Mallory's equity.

There is evidence that foreign entry can have beneficial effects upon the competitiveness of market structure. Proctor and Gamble had entered the U.K. market in 1930 by acquisition of a failing company, and effectively transformed an almost complete monopoly held by Unilever into a duopoly. Although the Commission considered whether Proctor and Gamble and Unilever were using adverse advertising and pricing policies, the Commission did not find that these detriments resulted from the control exercised by the U.S. parent.[62]

The conclusion suggested by this group of investigations is that where the market is shared with a U.K. firm, either by oligopoly or segmentation, the links with the parent apparently do not strongly influence behavior. Of more importance seems to be the relative position of the foreign-owned firm vis-à-vis its U.K. competitors, and the length of time the foreign-owned firm has been present in the United Kingdom. In all these cases the firms had been trading for so long that they ceased to be regarded as foreign and conformed substantially to patterns of behavior established by wholly owned U.K. firms.

Links with foreign parents appear more important in those investigations where the foreign-owned firm was dominant. Table 10 summarizes relevant data about five such investigations, and indicates what appear to be the critical links with the parent that contribute to the subsidiary's dominant position in the United Kingdom.[63]

It should be noted that except for the joint venture between Rank and Xerox, the foreign investments are longstanding; this had a considerable influence on the Commission's views as to whether the subsidiary's market dominance could be linked with the parent. In the cases of Champion, Kodak, and BUSM, the Commission found that their initial impact on the market stemmed from the parents' economic advantages, but that these were not crucial for long term success.[64] The U.K. subsidiary of Champion was able to establish itself in the market in part because of the parent's trading relationship with Ford, which also had a subsidiary in the United Kingdom. However, the Com-

Table 10.
Monopolies Commission Reports on Foreign-owned Dominant Firms

Company	Entered U.K.	Market Share Percentage	Adverse Findings	Links with Parent
Champion	1922	71 (1960)	a) price discrimination, original, replacement equipment;	a) assisted entry through sales to U.S. subsidiaries of parent's customers in U.S.;
			b) prices & profits	b) supply of components;
			c) RPM	c) production techniques know-how, R&D;
				d) close consultation on major policies
Kodak	1898	75 (1964)	a) prices & profits;	a) patents;
			b) exclusive dealing;	b) pricing policies coordinated;
			c) tie-in sales.	c) consultation on major policies;
				d) day-to-day management in U.K.
Roche Products (limited to prices)	1908	99 (1972)	a) pricing policy & profits;	a) patents;
			b) price discrimination.	b) purchase of active ingredients (transfer pricing contributed to adverse finding);
				c) access to group R&D;
				d) close control of parent.
British United Shoe Machinery	1899	44 (1971)	a) cancellation charges	a) on capital expenditures, appointment of directors, acquisitions disposals;
				b) free access to R&D, patents of parent;
				c) exports through parent's other subsidiaries

Table 10—Continued

Company	Entered U.K.	Market Share Percentage	Adverse Findings	Links with Parent
Rank/Xerox (joint venture)	1956	89 (1975)	a) restrictive patent licensing; b) rental-only policy; c) group-pricing plan; d) tie-in of toner	a) patents; b) voting control exercised by Xerox; c) profit-sharing agreement; d) Xerox controls long-range plans, major policies, pricing, sales, patents, trademarks; e) RX is principal exporter for group.

Source: The Monopolies and Merger Commission.

mission decided that Champion's market dominance was attributable to price discrimination between original and replacement equipment—a common feature it noted in the automobile parts industry of several countries.[65] In addition, World War II had strengthened Champion's market position since a number of competitors seriously weakened by the war effort were unable subsequently to reestablish themselves.

As for Kodak, the Commission stated:

> We think the bulk of the color film trade in this country was likely, for economic reasons, to fall into the hands of not more than two or three suppliers in any event; that the emergence of Kodak as the leading supplier is due primarily to the strength of its already established position in the photographic industry which was reinforced in the years during and after the war, to the support of its American parent and to the technical and commercial skills with which it has exploited these advantages; but that it has attained a high [*sic*] degree of dominance in the color film market than might have been the case if stronger British-based competition had been forthcoming and if other suppliers whose products are subject to import duty had been able to compete on equal terms.[66]

One of the important advantages of the link with the parent was access to patents and R&D, but the Commission concluded that Kodak had not abused its strength in these areas. Thus, although the U.S. parent contributed to Kodak's high share in the U.K. market, the foreign parent's technological and economic assets were found to be the major cause of dominant market power in the United Kingdom.

British United Shoe Machinery (BUSM) was somewhat different from Champion and Kodak in that it was the largest subsidiary of the three, responsible for the greater part of group exports, and its R&D effort was similar in magnitude to its parent. While USM's early advantages in the U.S. market had contributed to BUSM's position, BUSM's market strength in the United Kingdom resulted from subsequent independent developments.[67] The Commission was more concerned about BUSM's links with the parent's subsidiary DVSG in Germany since patents and know-how were pooled with all USM's companies. The practice which the Commission found objectionable—varying cancellation charges according to whether a new contract was made—did not appear to be a consequence of foreign parent influence.

Rank Xerox and Roche Products differ to a considerable extent from the three companies discussed earlier, as well as from each other. Rank Xerox is a special case that began as an equal joint venture between Xerox, the innovator, and Rank, the partner providing financial, management, and organizational expertise. Success, therefore, was the result of both parties' contributions. Subsequently Xerox became the majority shareholder, with responsibility for long-term planning, pricing policy, patents and licensing, major sales development, and other issues not immediately relevant to U.K. market dominance. Rank Xerox retained responsibility for day-to-day management, but was subject to strong central control from the parent. The practices found to be adverse were the result of the two companies' joint efforts, even though in a formal sense effective control passed to Xerox.[68] The problem for the Commission was that of finding an effective antitrust remedy to the patent licensing practice rather than the existence of foreign ownership.

Roche Products was also a special case in that it arose from the failure of the price control mechanism operated by the Department of Health and Social Security for drug purchases.[69] The investigation was confined to Roche's pricing policies and profit level, but the Commission also examined the patent behavior of the parent and the transfer prices for active ingredients sold to the U.K. company as well as other aspects of foreign-parent influence.[70] While the Commission could not express an opinion on these issues because of the form of the references,[71] it was reasonably clear that Roche Products was subject to very strong central direction from a foreign parent whose policies did not take the U.K. public interest into account. Specifically, the transfer prices and charges for group overheads resulted in excessive prices and profits with no tax payments, although a precise determination of how excessive was not possible because of the unwillingness of the parent to supply relevant data.[72] Therefore, while the Commission could not comment on the control exercised by the parent, it had serious doubts about the balance of advantage derived from the foreign ownership of the U.K. subsidiary.

The purpose in analyzing these cases was to see whether they provided evidence that foreign ownership contributed toward the market dominance of the subsidiary and hence, its ability to follow policies contrary to the U.K. public interest. Except for Roche Products, the Commission's reports seem to suggest that where the subsidiary has been long established the initial advantages accruing from a foreign parent are no longer crucial; instead dominance appears to be related to the U.K. subsidiary's ability to survive over a long period. This ability derives from skills developed in the U.K. market. There are, of course, continuing links with parent companies from which the subsidiaries obtain advantages, but these do not appear to be the most important factor. Thus, these cases do not raise a strong presumption that foreign ownership is itself detrimental. However, the Roche case, along with the others, shows that the potential for detriment exists because of the nature of the parent-subsidiary relationship, for example in patent licensing, transfer pricing, or direction of export activity. This then raises the question whether existing U.K. antitrust remedies are adequate to deal with actual problems that exist or may arise in the future.

Before discussing the three references which illustrate the areas where antitrust enforcement loses its bite, it is useful to state that insofar as structure and behavior in the United Kingdom are concerned, the government's remedial powers, with the exception of the control of advertising, are quite strong. A monopoly may be dissolved, or prices and most other aspects of conduct can be regulated by order if necessary. Examples of successful remedial action are Kodak, where the practices ceased, and Proctor and Gamble, whose prices for detergents were regulated.[73]

The three references that raise enforcement problems are Potash Ltd., Roche Products, and Rank Xerox. In the first, the U.K. company was virtually a sales agency for overseas owners of potash supplies (a commodity that is not naturally available in the United Kingdom), and there was no direct way of influencing their policies since the power to regulate price was not instituted until 1965. The remedial recommendation was that U.K. firms should seek and develop other sources of supply and U.K. aggregate buying power should be used to improve bargaining. Aggregation of buying power did occur and, subsequently, other sources of supply became available. Nevertheless, this case illustrated the difficulty of influencing the policies of companies operating outside U.K. territorial jurisdiction.

In the Rank Xerox case the Commission found that the company's patent licensing policy was against the public interest. According to the 1949 Patent Act,[74] an adverse finding could lead to granting a compulsory patent license. However, this remedy would not have extended to the U.S. parent of Xerox. The Commission was content to rely on a 1975 consent order issued by the U.S. Federal Trade Commission;[75] however, this order contains a potential flaw in that Xerox is not obliged to provide know-how for uses outside the United States. It remains to be seen whether this is a serious barrier to a potential entrant.

The *Roche Products* case[76] raised the problem of obtaining information and cooperation from companies outside the U.K. jurisdiction. In this instance, the reluctance of Hoffmann La Roche, the parent, to cooperate did not prevent the Commission from discovering enough information to reach valid conclusions about the company's prices and profits. However, if this information had not been available or of no consequence, the Commission may not have been able to assess the reasonableness of prices and profits.[77]

CONCLUSIONS ON TRANSNATIONAL CORPORATIONS AND THE
MONOPOLIES REFERENCES

At the beginning of this section three questions were posed: (1) whether foreign ownership increased the market power of U.K. subsidiaries, (2) whether foreign ownership had operated to the detriment of the U.K. public interest, and (3) whether existing antitrust remedies were adequate to deal with this type of market power. Analysis of the references suggests the following conclusions:

1. There is a relatively high incidence of foreign-owned companies in the concentrated industries which were investigated by the Monopolies Commission;
2. Direct foreign investment was a method of transferring a product, technology, or other advantages possessed by the parent to the U.K. subsidiary and initially these were crucial for making successful entry;
3. The activity of the subsidiary after entry, however, (particularly its responses to existing structure and behavior) were major factors in developing market power—in the long run these became more important influences than the links with the parent; and
4. There is no compelling evidence that foreign ownership has resulted in detriments to the public interest through abuse of market power. However there are cases where such detriment may occur, and U.K. remedial powers are limited because of jurisdictional limitations.

MERGERS POLICY AND TRANSNATIONAL CORPORATIONS

When merger control was introduced in the United Kingdom in 1965 it was intended only to apply to a relatively small proportion of corporate acquisitions which had a potential for detriment to the public interest. The reasons for this have been outlined earlier;[78] these continued to determine enforcement of policy until 1973. Mr. Antony Crosland, then president of the Board of Trade in the Labour administration, expressed what was a widely held view in a speech on monopolies and mergers policy in June 1969: "I believe that in Britain, at this moment in time, the trend to mergers has been on balance beneficial. . . ."[79] The same attitude was expressed, but in different

Table 11.
Mergers Subject to Control 1965–78 (excluding newspapers)

Period	No.	Assets Acq. £ Billion	Type of Merger Percent, Assets			Market Share Created in Horizontal Mergers	
			Horiz.	Vert.	Div.		
1965–69	466	16.6	88	5	7	25–50	45
1970–73	438	12.8	65	4	31	51–80	28
1974–78	887	34.2	66	7	27	81–100	15
						NA	12
Total	1791	63.6	72	6	22		100

Source: Graham, *Trends in U.K. Merger Control,* 14 TRADE AND INDUSTRY 525 (1979).

words, by the Conservative secretary of state and president of the Board of Trade, Mr. John Davies, in the House of Commons in December 1970. Explaining how he intended to implement policy he said, "I would make a reference of a merger only if I considered that competition in the relevant market would be restricted to a damaging degree as a result of that merger."[80]

A change came, however, in the early 1970s as the evidence of concentration accumulated and questions began to be raised as to when, or whether, the economic benefits of the merger wave would appear. Reviewing policy in November 1973 the minister for trade and consumer affairs, Sir Geoffrey Howe, said "no Government could be expected to see the process of concentration continue unquestioned indefinitely at the sort of pace which we have seen over the last decade . . . so I believe the facts already justify a more active use of our merger powers than has previously been the norm. . . ."[81]

Table 11 provides a historical depiction of enforcement policy by giving data on the mergers subject to the legislation from August 1965 to 1978. Notable features are the continuing rise in the annual number of mergers and their size, the absolute (although diminished) importance of horizontal merger, and the substantial increase in concentration which resulted. Until 1973 inward investment accounted for about 10 percent of all mergers, but in recent years the proportion has risen to 15 percent.[82]

The benign attitude towards mergers which shaped policy from 1965 to 1973 is illustrated by the rate of reference to the Monopolies Commission. Up to the end of 1973, 904 mergers were considered by the Mergers Panel and 25, or 2.8 percent, were referred for investigation.[83] From 1973 to 1978, the number of references increased to 28, a rate of 3.2 percent. Some characteristics of those, and the Commission's findings, are set out in table 12. The body of evidence that has now been accumulated, although limited in some respects, suggests some tentative conclusions. It appears that an adverse

Table 12.
References to the Monopolies Commission and Its Conclusions 1965–78.
Number (excluding newspapers)

| Type | Public Interest | | | Total | Referral Rate Percent |
	Against	Not Against	Abandoned		
Horizontal	12	9	9	30	2.3
Vertical	3	3	—	6	5.1
Diversified	3	6	8	17	4.3

Source: Graham, Trends in U.K. Merger Control, 14 TRADE AND INDUSTRY 525 (1979).

finding is more likely for a horizontal merger than for a vertical or diversified merger. Indeed, for diversified mergers the likelihood seems to be against an adverse judgment.[84]

THE MONOPOLIES COMMISSION'S FINDINGS ON INWARD INVESTMENT MERGERS

Although there have been only six references of mergers which were substantial acts of inward investment, the Commission's findings are a valuable supplement to the evidence derived from the monopoly investigations. All six were horizontal mergers. Table 13 contains relevant details.

Although the sample is limited, it suggests that substantial detriment to the U.K. public interest was not identified with such inward investment, with one exception. A brief description of the Commission's frame of analysis and how it was applied in the cases of Dentsply Int. Inc./AD International, and Eurocanadian Ship-holding/Furness Withy and Manchester Liners illustrates this more clearly. In order to evaluate the effect of foreign ownership of U.K. firms, the Commission developed an analytical framework that took into account the major issues raised by inward investment. Certain elements were assigned a specific weight or degree of importance depending on the facts in each case. These are the effects: on competition in the U.K. market, on supply and service to consumers or customers, on research and development, on the management and efficiency of the U.K. company and its employees, on the location of manufacturing, and on the balance of payments.[85] The Commission is required to assess advantages and disadvantages under each heading and reach a conclusion. It does not regard foreign ownership as a per se detriment; as it said of Dentsply "we see no reason to think that the fact that Dentsply is a multinational foreign based company will in itself be contrary to the public interest."[86]

In the proposed merger of Dentsply and AD International, the two companies had a trading relationship extending back to 1900 when ADI's prede-

Table 13.
Inward Investment Mergers Considered by the Monopolies Commission[a]

Name	Date of Report	Foreign bidder	Finding
1. Dental Manufacturing/ Dentists Supply of New York/Amalgamated Dental	September 1966	U.S.	Not adverse (did not take place)
2. Dentsply Int. Inc./ AD International	June 1975	U.S.	Not adverse
3. H. Weidman/BS	August 1975	Switzerland	Not adverse
4. Eurocanadian Ship-holding/Furness Withy and Manchester Liners	October 1976	Bermuda	Adverse
5. Fruehauf Corp.; Crane Fruehauf	August 1977	U.S.	Not adverse
6. FMC/Merck/ Aliginate Industries	July 1979	U.S.	Not adverse

a. There is some duplication as the first and second references involved the same two companies, Dentsply Int. Inc. (formerly Dentists Supply of New York) and AD International, the U.K. company which changed its name from Amalgamated Dental.

cessors obtained from Dentsply an exclusive franchise for teeth and other dental products for Europe and other territories. According to renewed agreements, ADI was prohibited from manufacturing teeth.[87]

To determine the public interest consequences, the Commission collected evidence under each of the above headings from customers, the dental profession, government departments, and other sources. The Commission's concluding remarks indicate how an inward investment merger is assessed:

> The only potential detriment to the public interest that we found in the proposed merger is the possibility that Dentsply might use its substantial market power to adopt unacceptable pricing policies in the United Kingdom. However, we do not consider any such detriment can be regarded as an over-riding argument against the merger bearing in mind the characteristics of Dentsply and the restraints on such policies, including potential competition from abroad. In our view the possibility is outweighed by the advantages likely to arise under several heads. These include the following:
>
> *a*) benefit to ADI's research and development in the United Kingdom;
> *b*) improvement of the management, general efficiency and productivity of ADI;

c) gain to the United Kingdom balance of payments through imports and increased exports.

Moreover, we think there would be some detriment to the public interest if the merger did not take place in that there would be an adverse effect on ADI's overseas business and on the United Kingdom balance of payments.[88]

Substantially the same framework was used for the merger of Eurocanadian Shipholding, Furness Withy and Manchester Liners.[89] The latter companies were prominent in liner operations and voyage charters, with Manchester Liners carrying a substantial proportion of U.K. and Canadian trade. Manchester Liners was also the subsidiary of Furness Withy and was the main user of the port of Manchester and the Manchester Ship Canal. Both participated in the shipping conferences which regulated freight rates on their routes.

Eurocanadian was a Bermuda-based company, but was originally of Canadian registration. It operated in the Europe/Canada trade and was linked in a complex grouping named Cast which provided shipping and other services on other routes. It did not participate in shipping conferences.

In these mergers the consequences of foreign ownership were given more weight because of the international nature of Eurocanadian and its parent Cast, and the possibility that their commercial interests might not always coincide with the U.K. public interest. The Commission issued its judgment on the merger with Manchester Liners (ML), saying:

ML gives a first class service to British exporters and shippers generally. Transfer of control to ECS would be likely to impair this service. It might well deprive the British shipper of his present choice between a conference and nonconference service. ML's operations would become closely integrated with those of the Cast group and, because of the widely differing nature and objectives of the two groups as they are at present, ML would suffer substantial disruption and damage. The economies that might be obtained by the Cast group from a merged North Atlantic container operation would compensate neither for this nor for the shift in the centre of control abroad. The effects of the merger on the balance of payments and on employment would be more likely to be unfavorable than favorable. ECS's proposals to use larger container ships would be likely at least to accelerate any substitution of Liverpool for Manchester as the base port for ML's North Atlantic operations and we think this would be harmful to regional interests.[90]

CONCLUSIONS ON INWARD INVESTMENT MERGERS

To date there have been relatively few references of foreign-initiated mergers to the Monopolies Commission; one could conclude that most of these did not appear to involve the potential for substantial detriment. The Commission's findings support this conclusion; in only one out of six such mergers did the Commission conclude that foreign ownership would be adverse to the U.K. interest. In the other mergers the potential for benefits was considered favorable, thus lending further support to the generally benign policy stance toward mergers.

RECENT DEVELOPMENTS

Earlier in this article mention was made of the Green Paper, *A Review of Monopolies and Mergers Policy.*[91] This report was the result of an internal committee of officials set up by the previous government to appraise the competition laws in the light of the growth of corporate concentration and the United Kingdom's entry into the EEC. The committee made recommendations on mergers, monopolies, and uncompetitive practices. Its main suggestion regarding mergers was that U.K. policy should move away from a benign attitude toward one of neutrality under which mergers likely to have a "significant effect" on competition would be subject to much more critical scrutiny. Nonstatutory guidelines would define *significant effect* in a manner similar to the following. Horizontal mergers that resulted in a market share of at least 25 percent of sales or production in a U.K. market of £4 million or greater or where the assets to be acquired were £1 million or greater, would be subject to increased scrutiny. Similar guidelines would apply to vertical mergers where the acquirer or acquired company had a market share of at least 25 percent and the acquirer was taking over a significant supplier or customer. Conglomerate mergers would also be considered to have a significant effect on competition where the acquired company had a market share of at least 25 percent, or the worldwide turnover of the combined enterprise was £350 million or more of which a significant proportion arose in the United Kingdom and where the gross assets to be acquired were £16 million or more.[92] When applied to recent experience these guidelines suggest that the effect would be to increase the existing rate of merger references from 3 percent to 12 percent. If implemented, these changes would represent a very considerable shift in emphasis and would effectively mark the end of the previous policy that presumed mergers to be beneficial to the U.K. economy.

The main policy proposals on monopoly were that there should be a continuing program of references to the Commission and that oligopoly be defined in terms of market share held by the largest four or five firms.[93]

The committee identified another problem area—uncompetitive practices by dominant firms. Investigations by the Monopolies Commission had shown consistent adverse effects from behavior which created or strengthened entry barriers, so it was proposed that further consideration be given to devising effective remedies, particularly where such practices occurred in small and local markets.

This proposal has been taken up by the new government in its Competition Act, now before the House of Commons, and which is a first stage in a longer term development of policy.[94] Under the Act, the director general of fair trading, after investigating complaints of uncompetitive practices and publishing a report, would have power to allow undertakings on the condition that firms will change their behavior.[95] If they fail to give satisfactory assurance, he may then refer the practice to the Monopolies Commission for a judgment whether such practices are against the public interest.[96]

The Act also provides for new power to investigate nationalized industries and certain other publicly owned bodies.[97] This would strengthen the review procedures and enables the Monopolies Commission to examine and report on their efficiency, costs, and services to consumers, as well as determine whether a monopoly has been abused. The secretary of state would have power to make remedial orders. Another provision would give the Office of Fair Trading the power to investigate prices or charges of major public concerns.[98]

CONCLUSION

This article has reviewed U.K. legislation that may be used to control the development of corporate concentration, and in particular how it has been applied to transnational corporations investing in the United Kingdom. The foreign ownership of industry arouses fears in developed and developing countries alike. There is concern that national sovereignty and independence may be undermined, economic growth restricted or distorted, and consumers, workers, and national entrepreneurs exploited by the alleged superior market power of the foreign investor. The United Kingdom as a highly developed economy has been both a major recipient and provider of foreign investment and thus has a considerable body of accumulated experience with it. As regards foreign investment in the domestic market the available evidence does not suggest that the United Kingdom economy has been significantly exploited. Direct foreign investment has been taking place throughout the twentieth century and has brought substantial economic gains in the form of new products, new technologies, greater per capita investment (particularly in the less-favored regions), and gains to the balance of payments. Although direct foreign investment tends to locate itself in concentrated industries, U.K. firms also share the positions of dominance so that it is likely these industries would also be concentrated in the absence of foreign investment. To ensure that the undoubted gains from foreign investment are equitably shared, the United Kingdom has traditionally relied on exchange control (now abandoned), an effective tax system, and competitive markets as the main regulating mechanism. The evidence from Monopolies Commission investigations of dominant positions, mergers, and foreign ownership does not suggest that transnational concentration results in substantial and frequent failures in competition. Thus, this part of the regulatory mechanism appears to operate effectively. Nevertheless, problems arise, and legislation evolves to deal with those which are capable of remedy by national action.

NOTES

1. Exchange Control Act, 1947, 10 & 11 Geo. VI, c. 14.
2. Industry Act, 1975, c. 68.
3. Industry Act, 1975, c. 68, Part II, Powers in Relation to Transfers of Control of Important Manufacturing Undertakings to Non-Residents.
4. Oil Taxation Act, 1975, c. 22.
5. SECRETARY OF STATE FOR INDUSTRY, *Foreword,* DEPARTMENT OF INDUSTRY, INTERNATIONAL INVESTMENT, GUIDELINES FOR MULTINATIONAL ENTERPRISES, Cmnd. No. 6525 at iv (1976).
6. M.D. STEUER, P. ABELL, J. GENNARD, M. PERLMAN, R. REES, B. SCOTT & K. WALLIS, THE IMPACT OF FOREIGN DIRECT INVESTMENT ON THE UNITED KINGDOM (1973).
7. *Id.* at ¶¶ 1.44–1.51.
8. *Id.* at ¶¶ 5.32–5.49.
9. EMPLOYMENT POLICY Cmnd. No. 6257 (1944).
10. Monopolies and Restrictive Practices (Enquiry and Control) Act, 1948, 11 & 13 Geo. VI, c. 66.
11. Restrictive Trade Practices Act, 1956, 4 & 5 Eliz. II, c. 68.
12. J. D. GRIBBIN, THE POSTWAR REVIVAL OF COMPETITION AS INDUSTRIAL POLICY (Government Economic Service Working Paper No. 19, 1978).
13. *Id.*
14. *Id.*
15. *Id.*
16. Restrictive Trade Practices Act, 1956, 4 & 5 Eliz. II, c. 68.
17. Monopolies and Restrictive Practices Act, 1948, § 14. This required the Commission to judge whether the industry or the firm's arrangement secured the efficient production and distribution of goods, enabled markets to work efficiently, encouraged technical improvements and new enterprise, promoted a balanced regional distribution of resources, and promoted exports.
18. *E.g.,* pre-1956 cartel reports, and post-1956 dominant firm reports, as in The Monopolies Commission, *Wire and Fibre Ropes,* H.C. 2 (1973).
19. Restrictive Trade Practices Act, 1956, c. 68.
20. Section 21 of the 1956 Act provided for seven beneficial effects which could be pleaded. A further description together with cases is given in R.B. STEVENS and B.S. YAMEY, THE RESTRICTIVE PRACTICES COURT (1956).
21. *See* Elliott and Gribbin, *The Abolition of Cartels and Structural Change,* in 2 WELFARE ASPECTS OF INDUSTRIAL MARKETS, STUDIES IN ECONOMICS (A.P. Jaquemin & H.W. DeJong ed. 1977).
22. *See Reports of the Registrar of Restrictive Trading Agreements* (1973).
23. *See* D. SWANN, D. O'BRIAN, W. MAUNDER & W. HOWE, COMPETITION IN BRITISH INDUSTRY (1973).
24. *See* text accompanying notes 31–36 *infra.*
25. *See* table 6, *infra.*
26. DEPARTMENT OF PRICES AND CONSUMER PROTECTION, A REVIEW OF MONOPOLIES AND MERGERS

Policy, Green Paper, Cmnd. No. 7198 (1978).

27. The policy recommendations will be reported later.

28. *Supra* note 26, at 11, table 4.

29. *I.e.,* mergers by which a foreign-owned company enters the U.K. market, illustratively by acquiring a U.K.-owned firm.

30. *Supra* note 26.

31. Monopolies and Restrictive Practices (Enquiry and Control) Act, 1948, 11 & 13 Geo. VI, c. 66.

32. Section 3 of the Monopolies and Restrictive Practices Act of 1948 permits the market to be defined in terms of sales or production.

33. The Monopolies Commission, *Supply and Export of Matches and Match-Making Machinery,* H.C. 161 (1953).

34. The Monopolies Commission, *Supply of Certain Industrial and Medical Gases,* H.C. 13 (1956).

35. *See* table 8, *infra.*

36. *E.g.,* chemical fertilizers, electrical equipment for motor vehicles, and wholesale petroleum.

37. Board of Trade, Monopolies, Mergers and Restrictive Practices, Cmnd. No. 2299 (1964).

38. Monopolies and Mergers Act, 1965, c. 50.

39. *Id.* at § 3(6).

40. Under § 6(2) of the 1965 Act, the Monopolies Commission was required to satisfy itself that a merger subject to the legislation had taken place, and decide whether it "operates or may be expected to operate against the public interest. . . ." *See also* note 17, *supra.*

41. Section 3 of the Monopolies and Restrictive Practices (Enquiry and Control) Act of 1948 laid down the requirement of one-third share of the market. This applied to monopolies and mergers until reduced to one quarter in the Fair Trading Act of 1973.

42. *See* Monopolies and Mergers Act, 1965, c. 50, § 7.

43. *Id.* at § 6(9).

44. Section 6(10), of the Monopolies and Mergers Act of 1965, establishes that the remedial powers apply only if the Commission has found the merger or proposed merger to be against the public interest. It should be noted that Parliament has the ultimate authority to grant relief by enacting legislation.

45. Fair Trading Act, 1973, c. 41.

46. *Id.* at § 1.

47. References of newspaper mergers is automatic if the continued circulation will total 500,000 or more copies per day; so far the Commission has not judged any to be detrimental.

48. This is because companies in concentrated industries are larger than those in less concentrated industries, and because there is a considerable concentration of exports and foreign investment; *i.e.,* the twenty largest manufacturing concerns account for 25 percent of U.K. exports.

49. *E.g.,* through control of raw materials or technology. In only one case, asbestos, was the raw material supply controlled from abroad by a subsidiary.

50. *See, e.g.,* the activities of those multinationals exporting Champion spark-plugs, Kellogg's breakfast cereals, and Kodak products.

51. *E.g.,* Kodak and United Shoe Machinery entered at the end of the nineteenth century; Nabisco, as the Shredded Wheat Company, in 1908.

52. *See, e.g.,* the joint ventures of Xerox and Rank to develop the plain paper copier market, and Mallory with its battery technology.

53. *See* The Monopolies and Mergers Commission, *Supply in the United Kingdom of Frozen Foodstuffs for Human Consumption* H.C. 674 (1976). Paragraphs 186–89 set out

the facts on the entry of Findus and its acquisition by Nestlé.

54. *See* The Monopolies and Mergers Commission, *Supply in the United Kingdom of Copying Materials Sensitized with One or More Diazonium Compounds* H.C. 165 (1977). Paragraphs 83–85 describe the acquisition of Hall Harding by GAF, and ¶¶ 103–6, the acquisition of Admel International by Addressograph Multigraph.

55. *See* The Monopolies and Merger Commission, *Supply and Exports of Machinery for the Manufacture of Footwear* ¶¶ 72, 103, and 104, H.C. 215 (1973); The Monopolies Commission, *Supply and Processing of Color Film* ¶ 43, H.C. 1 (1966); The Monopolies and Mergers Commission, *Supply of Indirect Electrostatic Reprographic Equipment* ¶ 51 H.C. 47 (1976).

56. *See* The Monopolies and Mergers Commission, *Supply of Ready Cooked Breakfast Cereals* H.C. 2 (1973).

57. *Frozen Foodstuffs, supra* note 53.

58. *Diazo Copying Materials, supra* note 54.

59. *See* table 9 *supra*. In the case of Kellogg's, the Commission thought that while profits were not then excessive they could become so in the future.

60. However, the reference of Roche Products was limited to an examination of prices, so there could be no finding about the monopoly. This case is discussed more fully *infra*.

61. A U.K. company, British Lighting Industries, had the highest share. Its market behavior was conditioned by a history of restrictions with occasional competition.

62. In the U.K., Proctor and Gamble undoubtedly obtained substantial advantage from the parent with respect to product development, management, and marketing techniques. *See*

The Monopolies Commission, *Supply of Household Detergents* ¶ 10 H.C. 105 (1966).

63. Kellogg's is excluded because the Commission did not examine the parent subsidiary relationship, and, in any case, no practices were found to be against the public interest.

64. The Monopolies Commission, *Supply of Electrical Equipment for Mechanically Propelled Land Vehicles* H.C. 21 (1963); *Color Film, supra* note 55; and *Machinery for the Manufacture of Footwear, supra* note 55.

65. *Electrical Equipment, supra* note 64.

66. *Color Film, supra* note 55, at ¶ 252 *(footnote omitted)*.

67. *Machinery for the Manufacture of Footwear, supra* note 55, at ¶¶ 66–104.

68. *Supply of Indirect Electrostatic Reprographic Equipment, supra* note 55, at ¶¶432–47. Practices against the public interest were restrictive patent-licensing, rental-only policy, group-pricing plan, and the tie-in of toner.

69. The Monopolies Commission, *Supply of Chlordiazepoxide and Diazepain* ¶¶ 18, 19, 172–81, H.C. 197 (1973).

70. *Id.* at ¶¶ 48–52, 206–17.

71. Under § 6(1) (a) of the 1948 Act, a reference could be limited to specific aspects of conduct. This meant that the Commission had only to consider those questions contained in the reference. In the case of Roche it was only required to decide on the public interest consequences of the level of prices.

72. *Supply of Chlordiazepoxide and Diazepain, supra* note 69, at ¶¶ 125–70, 208.

73. Undertakings were given by both companies to the Board of Trade to achieve the necessary remedies.

74. Patents and Designs Act, 1949, 12 & 13 Geo. VI, c. 62.

75. *Supply of Indirect Electrostatic Re-prographic Equipment, supra* note 55, at ¶¶ 148–61.

76. *Supply of Chlordiazepoxide and Diazepain, supra* note 69.

77. Once it had reached a conclusion, the order-making powers were sufficient to enforce the recommendation that prices of Librium be reduced to 40 percent of their previous level and Valium to no more than 25 percent.

78. *See* text accompanying note 37 *supra*.

79. Green Paper, *supra* note 26, at 153–55 (annex H. "Extracts from Ministerial Statements on Mergers Policy").

80. *Id.* at 155.

81. *Id.* at 156–61. *See also* J.D. GRIBBIN, *supra* note 12, and Green Paper, *supra* note 26, for a more detailed review of the change in merger policy, and the economic evidence thereof.

82. *See* Graham, *Trends in U.K. Merger Control,* 14 TRADE AND INDUSTRY 525 (1979).

83. *See* Gribbin, *The Operation of the Mergers Panel since 1965,* 14 TRADE AND INDUSTRY 70 (1974).

84. *See* table 12, *supra*. This conclusion, however, is tentative because a high proportion of such mergers were abandoned by the parties once a reference was made.

85. *See, e.g.,* The Monopolies and Mergers Commission, *Dentsply In-ternational Inc. and A D International Ltd.* ¶ 193 H.C. 394 (1975).

86. *Id.*

87. *Id.* at ¶ 52.

88. *Id.* at ¶¶222–23.

89. The Mergers and Monopolies Commission, *Eurocanadian Shipholdings Ltd. and Furness, Withy and Co. Ltd. and Manchester Linen Ltd.* H.C. 639 (1976).

90. *Id.* at ¶ 424. Because FW was the parent of ML the judgment influenced the Commission conclusions on that merger. It thought that the possibilities of conflict of interest between FW and Cast would be likely to lower the efficiency of FW. As Eurocanadian had acquired sufficient shares in FW to materially influence its policy, the remedy was that the shareholding be reduced over a two year period to not more than ten percent and in the meanwhile Eurocanadian should not exercise its voting rights in respect to the excess over 10 percent. This recommendation was accepted.

91. Green Paper, *supra* note 26.

92. *Id.* at ¶ 5.20.

93. *Id.* at ¶¶ 5.24–5.31.

94. Competition Act, 1980, c. 21.

95. *Id.* at §§ 2, 3, and 4.

96. *Id.* at § 5.

97. *Id.* at §§ 11 and 12.

98. *Id.* at § 13.

Regulation of Concentration Through Merger Control: Germany's Continuing Efforts

KURT STOCKMANN

The Federal Republic of Germany's Law Against Restraints on Competition (the ARC),[1] establishes an extensive regime for regulating market-dominating enterprises. Therefore, large corporations, both national and multinational, are the subject of particular scrutiny in the Federal Republic. Rather than identify and address all the provisions pertinent to corporate concentration (a task whose tedium would be matched only by its enormity), this analysis will undertake three tasks: (1) briefly describe the general scope of West German merger law, (2) discuss the application of the law to cases of transnational concentration, and (3) explain the proposed Fourth Amendment to the ARC as it affects merger control.

The German merger control law was introduced in 1973,[2] sixteen years after the basic antitrust statute—the ARC—had been enacted. At the outset, it should be noted that corporate concentration itself is not prohibited; rather, by framing the 1973 law in terms of "merger control," the German government premised the regulatory policy on corporate activities that created concentration—that is, mergers, acquisitions, and other actions or corporate arrangements.[3]

The merger control amendments to the ARC provide, in general, for two methods of enterprise concentration regulation—a notification procedure and a control procedure.[4] The notification procedure was formulated with the intent that it be used as an instrument for collecting comprehensive data on trends of corporate concentration. However, it is also used in conjunction with the techniques for preventing concentration.

The participating corporate enterprises in either a proposed or consum-

This article is adapted from a presentation made by Mr. Stockmann at the Symposium on Transnational Corporate Concentration held at the University of Michigan Law School on November 9 and 10, 1979. Mr. Stockmann is chief, International Section of the Bundeskartellamt of the Federal Republic of Germany. Mr. Stockmann would like to thank Ms. Florence R. Keenan for her efforts in preparing this written contribution.

mated merger are obliged to notify the Federal Cartel Office (FCO) of the merger if the participating parties meet certain market share or absolute size criteria.[5] Under the "market share" criteria, all completed mergers must be reported to the FCO if, within the relevant geographic region (that is, either the national territory or a substantial part thereof, *e.g.*, the Saarland), the merger creates or augments a combined market share of 20 percent or more, or if one of the participating enterprises already possesses a 20 percent share in another market.[6] Thus, the reporting obligation extends not only to horizontal mergers, but to vertical and conglomerate mergers that involve a participant with a significant market share (20 percent or more) in another geographic or product market.[7] Failure to meet the notification requirements may lead to the imposition of fines.[8]

As a rule, the notification of a merger is required only after consummation of the merger. There is an exception, however, for particularly large mergers. Prior notification is required if the proposed merger involves at least two enterprises recording individual sales of at least one billion DM in the preceding fiscal year.[9]

Each enterprise participating in the merger must file a report with the FCO, specifying basic descriptive information such as the form of the merger, as well as the name, location, and business activity of the participating enterprises. More complex information is also required, including market share data and the basis for the market share computation, the number of employees and sales, and any details of relationships with other enterprises (for example, affiliation relationships, percentage holdings, and other forms of corporate control).[10]

The second step to the regulatory scheme—the merger control procedure—applies if a merger is likely to create or strengthen a market-dominating position.[11] If a merger is likely to create or strengthen a market-dominating position, the FCO has the authority to prohibit the merger.[12] If the merger has been consummated prior to the FCO's determination, it may be dissolved.[13] There is an important threshold level—500 million DM of combined sales between the merging enterprises—which, if not met, precludes the application of merger control.[14]

Moreover, the threshold of market dominance is very high, definitely higher than the threshold the U.S. antitrust law provides in Section 7 of the Clayton Act under the "lessening of competition" test.[15] The concept of a market-dominating position is defined in Section 22 of the ARC. Under this definition, an enterprise is market-dominating if it has either no competitor or is not exposed to substantial competition or occupies a paramount market position in relation to its competitors. As a matter of practice, the most important criterion for establishing market domination is market share.[16] The law creates a rebuttable presumption of market domination if an enterprise has a market share of one-third or more and annual sales of at least 250 million DM; or in the case of oligopoly, if three or less enterprises have a combined market share of one-half or more, or five or less enterprises have combined market shares of two-thirds or more, and each of the enterprises has annual sales of at least 100 million DM.[17]

However, the concept of paramount market position—encompassing a rather fluid or broad spectrum of competitive circumstances—is of particular importance in coping with vertically integrated enterprises and conglomerates where strict reliance on market share criteria is of limited value for determining market domination.[18] Factors for determining paramount market position include market share, financial strength, access to supply or sales markets, links with other enterprises and the existence of legal or factual barriers to market entry.[19]

Turning the focus to the interests of the participating parties to a merger, the ARC provides several avenues for obtaining merger approval. If the FCO finds that the merger creates or strengthens a market-dominating position, the merger may still be approved if the participating parties can show: (1) that the merger will improve competitive conditions, and (2) that these improvements outweigh the detrimental effects of the market domination.[20]

In the event that the FCO has prohibited a merger, the participating enterprises may apply for authorization of the merger to the federal minister of economics. The minister will authorize the merger if the restraint on competition is balanced by the overall economic advantages of the merger, or if the merger is justified by an overriding public interest. In authorizing the merger, the minister can impose restrictions and requirements in order to preserve overall economic advantages or to protect the public interest. However, such conditions may not subject the participating enterprises to a continuous control of conduct.[21]

An appeal against the Federal Cartel Office's prohibition may also be taken to the Berlin Court of Appeals, and may be taken at the same time the enterprises apply for authorization from the federal minister of economics. The minister's decision may also be appealed. The appeals may be based on new facts and evidence, and the Federal Cartel Office's findings do not have *res judicata* effect in the Berlin Court of Appeals. Points of law are subject to further review on appeal by the Federal Supreme Court.[22]

In applying this law to cases of transnational concentration, it should be noted that the law does not distinguish between entirely domestic mergers and mergers involving foreign firms or even mergers realized exclusively between foreign firms. The jurisdictional test for the application of the law is whether there are effects in the German territory.[23] This is a very clear and unlimited adoption of the so-called effects principle as opposed to the conduct principle, which requires that at least part of the conduct causing relevant anticompetitive effects has taken place on the territory of the country assuming jurisdiction.

The exact scope and content of the "effects" test is a matter not yet resolved. In a number of earlier decisions, the Federal Supreme Court held that there was no general notion of effects for jurisdictional purposes; rather the existence or absence of effects has to be judged in connection with the rule of substantive law invoked in any particular case. Otherwise the ARC provisions could be extended to a point which was not intended by the legislature.[24] For instance, if the legality of an export cartel is the question, whether there are effects in the Federal Republic of Germany for purposes of exerting jurisdiction has to be decided by interpreting the rule on export cartels.[25] Consequently, the applicability of ARC's notification and prohibition procedures depends on the interpretation of the substantive rule of law, *i.e.*, ARC §§23 and 24, and not only on § 98(2)'s effects doctrine.

A recent Supreme Court decision examining the relationship between the notification and control procedures may have potentially major ramifications for the application of the German merger control law to multinational corporations operating both within and without German territory. The case involved an acquisition completed in the United States of a New Jersey corporation, Allied Chemical Corporation (ACC) by another New Jersey corporation, Harmon Colors Corporation (HCC). HCC was wholly owned by Rhinechem Corporation (New York), which was wholly owned by Bayer International Finance N.V. (Dutch Antilles), which, in turn, was wholly owned by the appellant Bayer AG, a German producer and distributor of organic pigments. ACC also produced organic pigments and had developed a great expertise in the field although without achieving a substantial share of the market. Bayer AG and ACC together accounted for less than 4 percent of the organic pigments market in Germany in the year prior to the acquisition and slightly more than 4 percent in this year.

The FCO considered Bayer a party to this merger because its affiliate HCC (twice removed) was dependent on it as defined in Section 17(2) of the Joint Stock Companies Act. The FCO considered that Bayer AG was obliged to notify it of the acquisition by Bayer's affiliate HCC, regardless of the fact that the acquisition was completed abroad; it was sufficient that the German market is affected.[26]

The appellant argued that the decisive criterion for requiring notification of the merger under ARC Section 23(1) was whether a market dominating position was likely to be created or strengthened, *i.e.*, the criterion for merger prohibition under ARC Section 24(1). In essence, the appellants asserted that the need to comply with the ARC notification requirement was circumscribed by the jurisdictional elements for substantive merger control.

The FCO and the Berlin Court of Appeals had held that the notification procedure played an independent role in merger control, apart from the actual control provisions. The Supreme Court affirmed the government's position and rejected appellant's argument. The Supreme Court held that the notification of a merger can be required if it has a perceptible immediate effect on the conditions of competition in the relevant domestic market regardless of whether these effects are substantial or whether the merger will create or strengthen a position of market domination.[27] The Supreme

Court found perceptible direct effects on the domestic market in spite of the low market share of the parties because, as a result of the merger, ACC ceased to be a competitor, and Bayer, in addition to increasing its sales turnover, gained access to ACC's know-how from which Bayer hoped to derive an improved competitive position in relation to the leading competitor. That this could promote competition is irrelevant to the application of the notification requirement; it is relevant only in the context of merger prohibition.[28]

The consequences of this dramatic decision could be quite sweeping if the FCO enforces the notification requirement to the extent allowed by this decision. However, with the exception of the *Bayer* case, the FCO typically has been generous toward foreign participants in a merger, particularly with regard to notification requirements.[29] The FCO's policy of limiting the enforcement of the notification requirement is supported by three considerations. First, extraterritorial application of the ARC notification requirement does not necessarily promote the procedure's fundamental purposes of providing information on concentration developments within Germany and establishing a trigger mechanism for prohibition control where warranted. As the Supreme Court stated, the ARC's jurisdictional effects doctrine is not aimed at the situation found abroad as such, but at the domestic effect emerging as a result of a merger.[30] Second, strict enforcement of the limits allowed by the Supreme Court's decision would probably incur the international criticism of the sort precipitated by the extraterritorial application of U.S. antitrust law. Third, the restricted enforcement policy serves administrative convenience by alleviating the FCO's burden of data collection and analysis which would be onerous if the Supreme Court's decision was applied to its fullest extent.

The German legislature is also aware of this potential for broad enforcement of the notification requirements. At present it is contemplating how far considerations of international comity and the desire to avoid international conflicts might warrant a retrenchment of the Supreme Court's sweeping doctrine.

This leads to the final topic—the proposed Fourth Amendment to the ARC which embraces a tougher approach to corporate concentration. This draft amendment is now being discussed in the Bundestag's Committee on Economic Policy.[31] The government draft amendment, prepared by the Ministry for Economic Affairs, embraces two primary considerations: First, the draft evinces a concern to make merger control more effective with respect to vertical and conglomerate mergers. Although the experience since the enactment of a merger control law is relatively satisfactory with regard to horizontal concentrations, it is less satisfactory in regard to vertical and, in particular, conglomerate concentration. Historically, the entry of large enterprises into markets characterized by small- and medium-sized enterprises has tended to destroy or deteriorate the structure of these markets in a relatively short time.

The second consideration evinced in the amendment is a desire to close loopholes used by large, market-dominating enterprises to circumvent government control; this evasion has, to a large extent, disadvantaged small businesses. Large enterprises have abused the "affiliation clause" of ARC § 24(8)2 which exempts from control those mergers involving an enterprise with sales of less than 50 million DM in the preceding year. Of 260 mergers exempted in 1977, 230 fell within this affiliation clause. A great number of these mergers involved large enterprises acquiring medium-sized companies that fell below the 50 million DM threshold.[32] Some enterprises also have abused the intent of ARC § 23(2)2 (which defines mergers subject to control as those involving acquisitions of 25 percent of voting capital) by acquiring less than 25 percent voting capital yet simultaneously entering into arrangements to gain excessive influence within the acquired enterprise. Thus, in theory, these enterprises can escape merger control although, in fact, the FCO has considered such acquisitions evasions of the merger definition if the acquirer obtains the same legal position as if he had acquired a 25 percent share.[33]

To address these concerns, the Fourth Amendment proposes a number of changes to the law with respect to market dominating enterprises. Among the improvements proposed by the draft amendment are:

1. The inclusion of a provision to prevent the evasion of merger control by particular forms of voting rights and shareholdings;
2. The adoption of additional presumptions of market domination allowing better coverage of conglomerate and vertical mergers characterized by: (a) the penetration of large enterprises into markets characterized by small- and medium-sized firms, (b) the acquisition by a large firm of a market-dominating but smaller firm, and (c) the merger of several very large enterprises;
3. Better coverage of cases where oligopoly positions in important sectors of the economy are further strengthened as a result of a merger;
4. Modification of the affiliation clause so as to subject most mergers of large enterprises with small- and medium-sized firms to the merger control requirement;
5. Filling the legislative gap in the supervision of abuses by market-dominating enterprises by skimming off of pecuniary benefits earned as a result of an abuse, and rendering abuse decisions more immediately enforceable.[34]

The first of the above improvements expands the definition of merger and widens the range of mergers subject to the notification requirements. This would rectify the evasion from merger control by enterprises acquiring effective control of another enterprise although less than the 25 percent of the voting capital which defines *merger* under the current provision.[35]

The second recommended improvement creates presumptions with respect to market domination that can be more easily applied to vertical and conglomerate mergers. The current presumptions of paramount market position have had practical effect in controlling primarily horizontal mergers. In practice, presumptions of paramount market position have been based on market shares and readily applied to horizontal mergers. In cases of vertical and conglomerate mergers, a merger does not result in a homogenous, aggregated market share since the relevant markets of each participating enterprise remain separate and distinct. The market share analysis used in horizontal concentration cases has not been easily adopted to these variegated market concentrations, thereby impeding effective control.[36] The amendment provides three presumptions that ease the burden of proof in the case of vertical and conglomerate mergers in establishing a paramount market position. The first presumption of paramount market position applies if an enterprise recording sales of at least two billion DM in the preceding year merges with an enterprise doing business in a market in which at least two-thirds of the market is attributable to small and medium enterprises. The second presumption exists if an enterprise recording sales of at least two billion DM in the preceding year merges with an enterprise recording sales of at least 100 million DM and is in a market-dominating position in one or more markets. The final presumption applies if the participating enterprises recorded a combined turnover of at least ten billion DM in the preceding year and at least two of the participating enterprises recorded individual turnovers of at least one billion DM. These presumptions serve as guidelines for enterprises contemplating a merger as well as standards for the FCO's prohibition control. The presumptions reach only large enterprises, thus maintaining the primary aim of merger control—to prohibit only mergers that threaten economic or social detriment.[37]

The oligopoly amendments would change the law's current market approach—based on competition within the oligopoly group—to one which considers whether a merger in an oligopolistic market creates or strengthens a market-dominating position. The Fourth Amendment's new criterion is restricted to merger control of important, closely knit oligopolies having a paramount market position in relation to other competitors. The proposed criterion should effectuate control of horizontal concentration trends in tight oligopolistic markets.[38]

The fourth recommended improvement addresses the affiliation clause exemption of certain mergers from control. As noted earlier, an unintended result of the affiliation clause (ARC § 24(8)2) has been that some large enterprises have penetrated into markets with primarily small- and medium-sized companies, thereby seriously deteriorating competitive structures. The exemption's sales turnover limit of fifty million DM would be lowered to two million DM, effectively eliminating this exemption. This amendment and the new presumptions regarding paramount market position together might to some extent improve conglomerate concentration control.

The fifth recommendation for improving ARC's control of market-dominating enterprises is aimed at quickening the abuse proceedings and enlarging the sanctions against abuses by market-dominating enterprises. The amendment provides for the immediate enforceability of abuse decisions under § 22(5), eliminating the suspension effect the present law allows if an appeal is lodged. The cartel authority would still be able to forego the immediate enforcement of the decision, if the general public interest in early discontinuation of the abuse is outweighed by the possible hardship for the enterprise and the legal considerations associated with the particular circumstances. This fifth recommendation also provides for the payment of damages for the period between issuance of the decision and conclusion of the final appeal. It also provides for the skimming off of profits obtained by abuses after the decision is issued that are not offset by the payment of damages.[39] No more hidden gains from antitrust violations will be theoretically possible.

In summary, the Federal Republic of Germany has tried to adopt a flexible yet vigilant approach to regulating corporate concentration. Experience has shown that certain improvements would result in even more government involvement in, and control of, industrial structure and intercorporate activity in Germany. If the Fourth Amendment is enacted into law, the legislature will have evidenced its willingness to increase government involvement in structuring the Federal Republic's economy.[40]

As for the ARC and multinational corporations, the courts appear amenable to the extension of antitrust regulation, and specifically merger control, to foreign corporations whose activities affect the German economy and internal level of competition. To be certain, data on levels of transnational corporate concentration and merger activity will be gathered through the application of the merger notification requirement to foreign corporations. Inasmuch as this data can be a valuable first step toward actual control, a trend toward extraterritorial substantive regulation may develop with time. Moreover, enactment of the Fourth Amendment would probably generate additional momentum for increased extraterritorial scrutiny. However, awareness of the U.S. experience in extraterritorial antitrust enforcement, as well as the existent EEC antitrust regime that could be applied to transnational corporate activity, warrants a cautious approach in this area.

NOTES

1. Gesetz gegen Wettbewerbsbeschränkungen (Act Against Restraints of Competition) of July 27, 1957, BGBL. Teil I, 1081 (1957). (ARC).
2. Statute Amending the Act Against Restraints on Competition of August 3, 1973, BGBL., Teil I, 917 (1973).
3. ARC § 23(2) enumerates several transactions and arrangements that

are deemed to be mergers within the meaning of the law. These include certain acquisitions, takeovers, certain contractual arrangements, executive board appointments, and "any other relationship between or among enterprises on the basis of which one or several enterprises may exercise directly or indirectly a controlling influence over another enterprise." ARC § 23(2)5.

4. ARC §§ 23, 24, 24a.

5. ARC §§ 23(1), 24(a)(1).

6. ARC § 23(1)1.

7. *See*, A. RIESENKAMPFF, GESETZ GEGEN WETTBEWERBS-BESCHRÄNKUNGEN 85 (1977).

8. ARC § 39.

9. ARC § 24a(1).

10. ARC § 23(5).

11. ARC § 24(1).

12. ARC § 24(2).

13. ARC § 24(2).

14. ARC § 24(8)1.

15. A number of antitrust experts have suggested that Germany move in the direction of the lower United States standard for restraints on competition in order to better effectuate control action.

16. Court rulings indicate that the relevant product market includes all products so closely related by attribute, function, or price that an educated consumer regards these as interchangeably able to fulfill his need. *See* WuW/E BGH 990(991) "Papier-filtertüten II" E/BGH 1435 (1440) "Vitamin B$_{12}$" and WuW/E BGH 1445 (1449) "Valium." Foreign markets are not considered by the Federal Cartel Office. However, the minister of economic affairs may do so under ARC § 24(3). He did, in fact authorize the acquisition of one of the largest German-owned oil companies, finding that the merger did not threaten the market economy since, on a worldwide scale, the resulting German enterprise was only medium in size. *See* WuW/E BMW 147 "Veba/Gelsenberg."

17. ARC § 22(3)2.

18. However, it should be noted that in administrative practice, the market share criterion has been given decisive weight in assessing these other factors and whether they demonstrate the existence of a market-dominating position. *See, Explanatory Memorandum to the Fourth Bill to Amend the Act Against Restraints of Competition of September 27, 1978*, German Bundestag, 8th Term, Document 8/2136, 27 (1978).

19. ARC § 22(1)2.

20. ARC § 24(1).

21. ARC § 24(3). The Federal Cartel Office cannot take such criteria into account; it assesses the merger exclusively on the basis of its competitive aspects.

22. ARC §§ 62–72; §§ 73–75.

23. ARC § 98(2) which states:
   This law applies to all restraints of competition which have effects within the territory in which this law applies, even if such effects are caused by actions taken outside such territory.

24. Judgment of 12 July 1973, Federal Supreme Court, W. Germany, BGH St 24, 208, 212; WuW/E BGH 1276 ff., 1279 (1973)—"Ölfeldröhre."

25. Judgment of 12 July 1973, Federal Supreme Court, WuW/E BGH 1276; FEDERAL REPUBLIC OF GERMANY, B5, WORLD LAW OF COMPETITION, pt. 9, § 3.04(3)(j) (re application of the ARC to export cartels).

26. Judgment of 29 May 1979, Federal Supreme Court, WuW/E BGH 1613 ff. (1979) "Organische Pigmente."

27. *Id.* at 1615. The court held that the main rationale underlying Section 23 was not whether competition is or would be actually impaired, but that such an effect is likely due to the size of the parties to the merger and the competitive situation in the relevant market, and that the Federal Cartel Office must be allowed to observe economic concentration. The court did not address the issue of whether the ARC would apply to the participation of a German enterprise in a merger completed abroad when the acquired foreign enterprise is not

carrying on business within the Federal Republic. Also unanswered is whether the ARC would apply to a merger that involved a foreign corporation that was not engaged in any type of commerce in the German economy, but could still be considered a "potential entrant" for the future. As applied by U.S. antitrust authorities in international merger cases, the potential entrant doctrine has been severely criticized. *See* Fugate, *The Department of Justice's Antitrust Guide for International Operations*, 17 Va. J. Int'l L. 645, 661 (1977).

28. *Id.* at 1615.
29. The FCO has promulgated its own standards for enforcing merger control. The detailed standards are difficult to understand for someone not familiar with German antitrust law, but it is safe to say that they are far from the limits drawn by the Federal Supreme Court. With regard to foreign mergers involving foreign participants, the FCO scrutinizes only mergers in which at least one German company participates (thus disregarding all mergers involving only foreign participants). The standards also significantly narrow the qualifying range for notification by distinguishing between joint ventures and other forms of concentration.

The FCO summarized its interpretation of the ARC with regard to mergers involving foreign corporations as follows:

A.
Effects on national territory are therefore present in any case, if a merger is realized within the area of application of the GWB [the ARC] (e.g. by the acquisition of the assets or shares of a domestic enterprise, establishment of a joint venture on national territory—even if the acquiring enterprises resp. [sic] the es-

tablishing enterprises are foreign enterprises). A merger realized abroad is in regard to domestic subsidiaries of the participants assumed to be a merger realized on national territory (Section 23(3) sentence 4 GWB).
B.
Mergers realized abroad have domestic effects, if the merger influences the structural conditions for domestic competition and if at least one domestic enterprise (also subsidiaries or other connected enterprises) is participating.
(1) If mergers are realized abroad between only two directly participating enterprises (all categories of mergers except joint ventures— e.g. the acquisition of the assets or the shares of a foreign enterprise by a domestic enterprise—)
(a) domestic effects are present, if both enterprises had been doing business on the national territory already before the merger, either directly or via subsidiaries, branch offices, or importers,
(b) domestic effects may be present, if before the merger only one enterprise was doing business on national territory, but e.g.
(i) after the merger, supplies of a foreign participant into the national territory are likely because of reasons of production techniques (on higher or lower production levels) or because of relations to the domestic participant in regard to the range of products. Whether such future supplies are likely depends normally on whether such or similar products are already traded between the countries involved and such suppliers are not hindered by technical or administrative obstacles to trade;
(ii) by the merger the know-

how of a domestic enterprise is perceptibly increased resp. [sic] commercial property rights are transferred on this enterprise.

(2) In cases of joint ventures established abroad, domestic effects depend primarily on the productive and geographic activity of the joint venture. Whether there are domestic effects in such cases is to be assessed in regard to the activity of the joint venture by observing the principles described under B.1. whereby the relationship in regard to production techniques and/or product range depends on the relationship between the joint venture and the domestic participant.

A joint venture realized abroad may also have domestic effects if

a) a foreign enterprise participating in the joint venture had been doing business in the field of business of the joint venture on the national territory, or if it is reasonably likely that it would start doing business on the national territory without the merger;

b) the domestic enterprise participating in the joint venture acquires production capacities to such extent that its domestic supply capacity is perceptibly changed (substitution of domestic production for exportation by production export). Precondition for such "perceptibility" is regularly an already powerful market position of the domestic participant.

FEDERAL CARTEL OFFICE, ANNUAL ACTIVITY REPORT for 1975, 45 (1975). For examples of merger cases involving foreign participants cf. FEDERAL CARTEL OFFICE, ANNUAL ACTIVITY REPORTS for 1973, 70 (1973) and for 1974, at 34.

30. "Organische Pigmente" WuW/E BGH at 1615.
31. *See* annex 1 *infra.*
32. OECD, ANNUAL REPORTS ON COMPETITION POLICY IN OECD MEMBER COUNTRIES, 1978/No. 2 at 36.
33. *Id.,* 1977/No. 2 at 35 & 36.
34. Bill to Amend the Act Against Restraints of Competition of September 27, 1978, German Bundestag, 8th Term, Document 8/2136, 1–2, (1978). *See* annex 1 for translation of relevant provisions.
35. *Explanatory Memorandum, supra* note 18, at 30.
36. *Id.* at 26.
37. *Id.* at 25–27.
38. *Id.* at 25.
39. *Id.* at 29–32.
40. Indeed, as the Explanatory Memorandum states:
    Business concentration can impair competition in the same way as cartelisation. It, too, can reduce the encouragement to efficient action and to achieving technical progress. As far as social policy is concerned, excessive concentration of economic power destroys the foundation of an order based on the principle of freedom. Political democracy and market economy are unthinkable without decentralised power.
    See Explanatory Memorandum, supra note 18, at 24.

ANNEX 1: SELECTED EXCERPTS FROM THE "FOURTH BILL TO AMEND THE ACT AGAINST RESTRAINTS OF COMPETITION"

Article 1

The Act Against Restraints of Competition as published on 4 April 1974 (Legal Gazette I, p. 869), as amended by Article 59 of the Act of 14 December 1976 (Legal Gazette I, p. 3341) shall be amended as follows:

1. Section 12 shall be worded as follows:

   "Section 12
   (1) With regard to agreements and decisions of the nature described in Sections 2, 3, 5 (1) and (4), 5a (1) and 5b (1), the cartel authority may take the measures described in subsection (3),
   1. insofar as the agreements and decisions or the manner of their implementation constitute an abuse of the market position obtained as a result of the exemption from Section 1, or
   2. insofar as they violate the principles concerning trade in goods and commercial services accepted by the Federal Republic of Germany in international treaties.
   (2) With regard to agreements and decisions of the nature described in Section 6 (1), the cartel authority may take the measures described in subsection (3), insofar as
   1. the conditions mentioned in subsection (1) No. 2 are present, or
   2. the implementation of the agreements or decisions substantially impairs predominating foreign trade and payments interests of the Federal Republic of Germany.
   (3) The cartel authority may
   1. direct the participating enterprises to discontinue the abuse objected to,
   2. direct the participating enterprises to amend the agreements or decisions, or
   3. declare the agreements and decisions to be of no effect."

2. Section 22 (3) sentence 2 shall be worded as follows:

   "As regards the calculation of the market share and turnover, Section 23 (1) sentences 2 to 10 shall apply, as appropriate".

3. Section 23 shall be amended as follows:
   (a) The following sentences 8, 9 and 10 shall be added to subsection (1):

   "Where all or a substantial part of the assets of another enterprise are acquired, the calculation of the market share, number of employees and turnover of the selling enterprise shall take account of the sold assets only. Sentence 8 shall apply, as appropriate, to the acquisition of shares, insofar as less than 25 per cent of the shares are retained by the seller and the merger does not satisfy the conditions set out in subsection (2) No. 2 sentence 3 and No. 5. If a person or an association of persons not being an enterprise is entitled to the majority interest in an enterprise, he, she or it shall be deemed to be an enterprise."

(b) In subsection (2) No. 2, sentences 4 and 5 shall be substituted for sentence 4:

"The acquisition of shares shall also be deemed a merger, insofar as the acquirer obtains, by means of an agreement, bylaws, articles of association, or a resolution, the legal position held in a joint stock company by a shareholder owning more than 25 per cent of the voting capital. Shares in an enterprise shall be equal to voting rights."

(c) Subsection (6) sentence 3 shall be worded as follows:

3. "Section 46 (2), (5) and (9) shall apply, as appropriate".

4. After Section 23 the following Section 23a shall be inserted:

"Section 23a
(1) Notwithstanding Section 22 (1) to (3), for merger control purposes a paramount market position shall be presumed to be created or strengthened as a result of a merger, if
  1. an enterprise which recorded a turnover of at least DM 2,000 million in the last completed business year preceding the merger merges with another enterprise which
     (a) operates in a market in which small and medium-sized enterprises have a combined market share of at least two thirds and the enterprises participating in the merger have a combined market share of at least 5 per cent, or
     (b) is market-dominating in one or several markets which in the last completed calendar year had a turnover of at least DM 100 million, or
  2. the enterprises participating in the merger recorded a combined turnover of at least DM 10,000 million in the last completed business year preceding the merger and at least two of the participating enterprises recorded individual turnovers of at least DM 1,000 million; this presumption shall not apply, insofar as the merger also satisfies the conditions of Section 23 (2) No. 2 sentence 3 and the joint venture does not operate in a market with a turnover of at least DM 500 million in the last calendar year.
(2) For merger control purposes two or three enterprises shall also be deemed market-dominating, if in one market they obtain the highest market shares and a combined market share of 50 per cent, except when the totality of enterprises have no paramount market position in relation to the other competitors. Sentence 1 shall not apply, if

1. that totality comprise [*sic*] enterprises which recorded turnovers of less than DM 500 million in the last completed business year, or
2. the merger exclusively affects a market which had a turnover of less than DM 100 million in the last calendar year, or
3. the enterprises participating in the merger obtain a combined market share not exceeding 15 per cent.

Section 22 subsections (1) to (3) shall remain unaffected.

(3) Section 23 (1) sentences 2 to 6 and 8 to 10 shall be applied regarding the calculation of the turnovers and market shares."

5. Section 24 subsections (8) and (9) shall be worded as follows:

"(8) Subsections (1) to (7) shall not apply
1. if the participating enterprises recorded a combined turnover of less than DM 500 million in the last completed business year, or
2. if an enterprise which is not a controlled enterprise and in the last completed business year recorded a turnover of less than DM 50 million affiliates itself to another enterprise; except when one enterprise recorded a turnover of at least DM 2 million and the other a turnover of at least DM 1,000 million, or
3. insofar as a market is affected in which goods or commercial services have been supplied for at least five years and which in the last calendar year had a turnover of less than DM 10 million.

Section 23 (1) sentences 2 to 10 shall be applied regarding the calculation of the turnovers.

(9) Subsection (8) sentence 1 No. 2 shall not apply insofar as competition in the publication, production or distribution of newspapers or periodicals or parts of them is restricted within the meaning of subsection (1) as a result of the merger."

6. Section 24a shall be amended as follows:
(a) Subsection (1) sentence 2 shall be worded as follows:

"The project shall be notified to the Federal Cartel Office, if
1. one of the enterprises participating in the merger recorded a turnover of at least DM 2,000 million in the last completed business year, or
2. at least two of the enterprises participating in the merger recorded individual turnovers of DM 1,000 million or over in the last completed business year, or
3. the merger is to be effected under the law of a Land by legislation or any other governmental act."

(b) Subsection (1), sentence 5, shall be worded as follows:

"Section 46 (9) shall apply, as appropriate, to the information and documents obtained in connection with the notification."

(c) Subsection (4) first half sentence shall be worded as follows:

"If a merger project has to be notified under subsection (1), sentence 2, it shall be unlawful either to complete the merger prior to the expiry of the one-month period specified in subsection (2) sentence 1, and, if the Federal Cartel Office has given the information referred to in subsection (2) sentence 1 prior to the expiry of the specified four-month period or the extension of time agreed upon, or to participate in the completion of the merger, except when the Federal Cartel Office, prior to the expiry of the periods mentioned in subsection (2) sentence 1 has given written information to the person who has effected the notification that the merger project does not meet the conditions of prohibition set out in Section 24 (1);"

7. Section 24 b (5) shall be worded as follows:

"(5) The Monopolies Commission shall issue every two years, by June 30, an opinion covering the situation which prevailed during the last two completed calendar years and submit it immediately to the Federal Government, the first opinion being due on June 30, 1976. The opinions pursuant to sentence 1 shall immediately be submitted to the legislative bodies by the Federal Government and at the same time by published by the Monopolies Commission. Within a reasonable period the Federal Government shall present its views and comments on the opinions to the legislative bodies. The Monopolies Commission may give additional opinions as it deems appropriate. The Federal Government may instruct it to give additional opinions. The Monopolies Commission shall submit opinions pursuant to sentences 4 and 5 to the Federal Government and publish them. The Federal Minister for Economic Affairs may also request an opinion from the Monopolies Commission in particular cases which are submitted to him for decision under Section 24 (3)."

8. Section 26 shall be amended as follows:
(a) In subsection (1) the words "certain enterprises" shall be substituted for the words "certain competitors".
(b) The following sentence 3 shall be added to subsection (2):

"For the prohibition procedure pursuant to Section 37a (2) a supplier of a certain type of goods or commercial services shall be presumed to depend on a purchaser within the meaning of sentence 2, if, in addition to the price reductions or other considerations customary in the trade, that purchaser regularly obtains special benefits not granted to similar purchasers".

(c) The following subsection (3) shall be added:

"(3) Market-dominating enterprises and associations of enterprises within the meaning of subsection (2) sentence 1 shall not use their market position to cause other enterprises in business activities to accord them preferential terms in the absence of facts justifying such terms. Sentence

1 shall also apply to enterprises and associations of enterprises within the meaning of subsection (2), sentence 2, in relation to the enterprises depending on them."

9. Section 35 shall be amended as follows:
   (a) Following subsection (1) the following subsection (2) shall be inserted:

   "(2) Any person who wilfully or negligently contravenes any decision issued by the cartel authority or the appellate court within the meaning of subsection (1) shall, if the decision or determination pursuant to Section 70 (3) becomes final, compensate for any damage suffered from the date of service of the decision."

   (b) The former subsection (2) shall become subsection (3).

Regulating Multinational Corporate Concentration—The European Economic Community

JOHN TEMPLE LANG

It is the purpose of this article to discuss the policies and goals of the efforts of the European Communities to regulate multinational corporate concentration. For reasons that will become clear in the course of the article, it is necessary to start by outlining the means available to the European Communities, both presently and potentially, to promote these policies. It is not possible to see what those policies might be or how they are likely to develop without understanding the practical implications of the various legal rules on which the Community might rely in the future.

This article does not deal directly with merger regulation under the European Coal and Steel Community Treaty (ECSC Treaty), or with procedural questions, although both of these are of some interest in connection with the main topic.

SOME BASIC CONCEPTS: DOMINANT MARKET POWER AND OLIGOPOLIES

The basic provisions for antitrust enforcement in the European Community (Community) are found in Articles 85 and 86 of the EEC Treaty. Article 85 prohibits restrictive agreements and enumerates several forms of restriction that fall within the ban. Article 86 prohibits the abuse of a dominant market position by one or more firms. Both articles require some effect on trade between the members of the European Community.

The EEC Treaty makes it clear that dominant positions are not themselves unlawful. It is only the *abuse* of a dominant position, including all kinds of anticompetitive and exclusionary behavior that is prohibited.[1] Therefore, even a monopoly or other clearly dominant corporation does not have to prove that it acquired its position legitimately by "superior skill, foresight and industry."[2] No action can be taken to end the dominance of a corporation as such, no matter how undesirable its market power may appear to be, nor how

John Temple Lang is a solicitor, Republic of Ireland and legal adviser, EEC Commission. This article represents only personal views.

often or how seriously it may have abused it.[3] This explains and justifies a concept of dominance that is broader, and is applicable to corporations with smaller market shares, than the concept of monopoly under U.S. antitrust law.

THE CONTINENTAL CAN JUDGMENT AND ITS LIMITATIONS

In 1973 the Court of Justice rendered its judgment in *Europemballage Corporation and Continental Can Co. Inc. v. Commission.*[4] The Court of Justice held that it is a violation of Article 86 of the EEC Treaty[5] for a corporation already in a dominant position to acquire a competitor, if the acquisition strengthens its position so that the resulting market power "substantially fetters competition."[6] The Court of Justice rejected the argument that a violation of Article 86 could be committed only if existing dominant power was used to carry out the acquisition, and held that structural changes likely to restrict competition indirectly were prohibited by Article 86 as well as behavior likely to restrict it directly. Thus, acquisition of a competitor by a dominant firm is unlawful even if the same acquisition would be lawful in the absence of a dominant position. On the ultimate question of liability, the Court of Justice annulled the EEC Commission's (Commission) decision, holding that the Commission had failed to prove the relevant market; but the principles stated by the Court of Justice still stand. Although the Court of Justice's interpretation of Article 86 had been suggested by the Commission as early as 1966,[7] in 1973 the judgment created some controversy; however, it is not now seriously questioned that it correctly states the law.

The case law since *Continental Can* suggests that the Court of Justice might now accept the notion that any acquisition which substantially increases the market power of an already dominant corporation (or that substantially reduces the amount of competition remaining) would violate Article 86.[8]

As a rule of law regulating, or enabling the EEC Commission to regulate, corporate concentration, the rule in *Continental Can* had two serious limitations. First, the prohibition applies only where at least one of the corporations involved in the concentration or merger was already dominant within the meaning of Article 86. Second, the Commission could take action only after the concentration or acquisition had been carried out and therefore could not act to prevent the concentration beforehand. The limitations call for some comments.

The first limitation is less important now than it appeared to be, since the Court of Justice in *United Brands*[9] held that a corporation with a market share of only 40–45 percent, but facing only much smaller competitors in the relevant market and having considerable competitive advantages, can possess a dominant position. Hence, many more corporations are dominant, and so subject to Article 86, than was believed in 1973.

The second limitation is also less important than it might appear, since a prudent and well-advised corporation is likely to seek informal approval from the Commission before carrying out a merger that it might later be compelled to unwind. Even if it does not seek such approval, merger documents almost always expressly condition the merger on the receipt of all necessary consents including the consents of national antitrust and exchange control authorities as well as that of the EEC Commission. It is true that there are limits on the legal value of an informal approval from the Commission,[10] although a formal negative clearance, which would have more value, could be obtained in due course. Unwinding a merger which has been carried out is an extremely difficult, expensive, and unsatisfactory operation even if it had been previously contemplated that it may be necessary.

Moreover, it is not completely clear that the *Continental Can* rule would apply to the acquisition of a dominant corporation by a smaller competitor, although this would have substantially the same effect on competition as the more familiar scenario of a large company acquiring the smaller.

Another problem relates to the substantive content of the rules as to "abuse" under Article 86. Although the word implies some ethical content, the *Continental Can* judgment is expressed objectively.[11] The question therefore arises: Could an acquisition that undoubtedly had anticompetitive effects but that was thought desirable for other reasons be permitted under Article 86? The question (to which there is no clear answer under existing law) is probably one that would occur more readily to a European antitrust lawyer than to a U.S. antitrust lawyer. It is perhaps a question of more theoretical than practical importance under Article 86.

It might, however, be significant since Article 86 prohibits abuse of a dominant position "in a substantial part" of the Common Market.[12] Such a dominant position might exist now in the EEC, or might exist in the future in one of the new member states, because economic integration had not brought about a free flow of goods from elsewhere in the EEC. (Indeed, the abuse might lie precisely in preventing such a flow from taking place.) An acquisition by a firm which was regionally dominant might have serious anticompetitive effects in the region in question, and so might be prohibited under Article 86, even though it was (or would become) reasonable in the context of the Community as a whole.

A question related to the use of Article 86 in merger cases in practice is whether the Commission has an implied power under the EEC Treaty to adopt an interim decision before a final decision prohibiting a dominant firm from commencing or continuing a course of action which the Commission considers, pending a final decision on the matter, is contrary to Article 86. The Court of Justice held in *National Carbonising*[13] that the Commission had such an implied power under Article 66 of the European Coal and Steel Community Treaty, but the corresponding question under the EEC Treaty did not come before the Court of Justice until 1980, when the court held that this power also exists in both Article 85 and Article 86 cases under the EEC Treaty.[14]

There is no doubt that the *Continental Can* rule would enable the Commission to prohibit many undesirable mergers, without any need for new legislation. Equally, however, it is clear that some mergers which would be undesirable could not be attacked under the rule.

PROPOSED REGULATION FOR THE CONTROL OF MERGERS: CONTENTS AND COMMENTS

Primarily because of the two limitations on the *Continental Can* rule, in 1973 the Commission submitted to the Council of the European Communities (Council) a proposal for a regulation giving the Commission power to control mergers.[15] The draft requires prior approval by the Commission for certain mergers, and applies to mergers even if neither of the corporations involved is dominant.

The discussions on the draft are still continuing in the Council, six years later, despite regular urging from the Commission and from the European Parliament. It is clear that the draft will not be adopted in its original terms, and it is not yet clear what the final terms of the regulation are likely to be. The draft regulation has received extensive commentary, but has not been formally altered since it was published.

The draft regulation declares:

Any transaction which has the direct or indirect effect of bringing about a concentration between undertakings or groups of undertakings, at least one of which is established in the common market, whereby they acquire or enhance the power to hinder effective competition in the common market or in a substantial part thereof, is incompatible with the common market in so far as the concentration may affect trade between Member States.

The power to hinder effective competition shall be appraised by reference in particular to the extent to which suppliers and consumers have a possibility of choice, to the economic and financial power of the undertakings concerned, to the structure of the markets affected, and to supply and demand trends for the relevant goods or services.[16]

In other words, the draft, in broad terms, made it unlawful to create a dominant position by means of a *concentration*.[17] The language is the same as that used in Article 66 of the European Coal and Steel Community (which, however, contains no overriding exemption for *good* mergers).

The draft regulation went on to say:

3. Paragraph 1 may, however, be declared inapplicable to concentrations which are indispensable to the attainment of an objective which is given priority treatment in the common interest of the Community.[18]

It thereby allows the Commission to permit an anticompetitive merger for some unspecified overriding purpose, in language much vaguer than Article 85(3).[19] There is a similar provision in German law.

The draft permits smaller concentrations falling below a specified threshold. A merger would be exempt under the draft regulation if:

(1) the aggregate turnover of the undertakings participating in the concentration is less than 200 million units of account [U.S. $276 million at end August 1979]; and

(2) the goods or services concerned by the concentration do not account in any Member State for more than 25% of the turnover in identical goods or services which, by reason of their characteristics, their price and the use for which they are intended, may be regarded as similar by the consumer.[20]

As can readily be imagined, the level at which this threshold should be drawn has been one of the most controversial aspects of the draft regulation.

The draft also provided an exemption from its prior notification requirements: concentrations where the aggregate turnover of the enterprises concerned is between 200 and 1,000 million units of account (U.S. $276 million and U.S. $1,381 million at the end of August 1979), and also cases where the firm being acquired was small (turnover less than 30 million units of account [U.S. $41.43 million]). Turnover in all cases means group turnover, and includes turnover outside the EEC.

The draft regulation defines *concentration* in terms of a wide definition of *control,* not limited to shareholding or ownership.[21]

1. The concentrations referred to in Article 1 are those whereby a person or an undertaking or a group of persons or undertakings, acquires control of one or several undertakings.

2. Control is constituted by rights or contracts which, either separately or jointly, and having regard to the considerations of fact or law involved, make it possible to determine how an undertaking shall operate, and particularly by:

   (1) Ownership or the right to use all or part of the assets of an undertaking;

   (2) Rights or contracts which confer power to influence the composition, voting or decisions of the organs of an undertaking;

   (3) Rights or contracts which make it possible to manage the business of an undertaking;

   (4) Contracts made with an undertaking concerning the computation or appropriation of its profits;

   (5) Contracts made with an undertaking concerning the whole or an important part of supplies or outlets, where the duration of these

    contracts or the quantities to which they relate exceed what is usual in commercial contracts dealing with those matters.

3. Control is acquired by persons, undertakings or groups of persons or undertakings who:
   (1) Are holders of the rights or entitled to rights under the contracts concerned;
   (2) While not being holders of such rights or entitled to rights under such contracts, have power to exercise the rights deriving therefrom;
   (3) In a fiduciary capacity own assets of an undertaking or shares in an undertaking, and have power to exercise the rights attaching thereto.

4. Control of an undertaking is not constituted where, upon formation of an undertaking or increase of its capital, banks or financial institutions acquire shares in that undertaking with a view to selling them on the market, provided that they do not exercise voting rights in respect of those shares.[22]

Under the draft regulation, the Commission has three months from receipt of notification to commence proceedings. If it does not act within that time, the concentration (even if it is one for which prior approval is needed) may go into effect, but the Commission may make an interim decision requiring suspension of the concentration.[23] It must then reach a final decision within nine months. Regulations 17/62[24] and 1017/68[25] would not apply to concentrations covered by the regulation and Articles 85 and 86 remain applicable to mergers not covered by the draft regulation. Moreover, Article 85 and Article 86 liability would be preempted by the regulation in these cases covered by the regulation. A few comments on this proposed legislation are worthwhile.

First, market share requirements are unavoidable, but not easy to apply in practice. It is not clear whether the *market* concept in the draft regulation above would be interpreted by the Court of Justice in exactly the same way as it has interpreted the concept of the relevant market, as for example, in *United Brands* and *Hoffmann-LaRoche*.[26]

Second, merger control is regarded as filling what seems to be a gap in the Community's antitrust powers, so it is essential that the decision-making body under the regulation should be the same as for other antitrust questions, namely, the Commission. Under the merger regulation, the Commission would have exclusive power in merger cases. In cases under Articles 85–86 its power is not, in theory, exclusive (although in practice national antitrust authorities never enforce Community law).

Third, the basic principle (preventing mergers creating dominant positions) is a much narrower one than the principle of substantially lessening competition found in Section 7 of the Clayton Act.

Fourth, the market share threshold is based on the market in any one member state. This means that smaller mergers come under closer scrutiny in small member states than in large ones since the markets are smaller. Moreover, the regulation does not expressly contemplate a merger whereby the merged firms join a group of oligopolists who together have the power to hinder competition, although Article 86 expressly applies to a dominant position held by more than one firm.

Finally, the draft regulation would apply to some joint ventures, although joint ventures are not mentioned specifically. The Commission would therefore have to ensure that its policy on creation of dominance under the regulation was in line, *mutatis mutandis,* with its policy on otherwise similar joint ventures not falling under the regulation but substantially restricting competition and falling under Article 85(1).

The Commission has stated five main problems related to the draft regulation: (1) the legal basis for the proposed regulation, (2) the principle of premerger control, (3) the scope of the regulation, (4) the possibility of derogations from the concept of incompatibility with the Common Market, and (5) notification of planned mergers and decision-making powers.[27]

First, the legal basis of the proposed regulation is found in Articles 87 and 235 of the EEC Treaty. (Article 235 gives power to adopt appropriate measure to take any action necessary to attain any Community objective, where no other means are provided in the Treaty.) The Legal Affairs Committee of the European Parliament has stated that it considers this sufficient.[28] Second, premerger control avoids the difficulties of undoing a completed merger,[29] and even if it was not obligatory, enterprises would normally seek informal opinions before putting the merger into operation. Premerger control has worked under the ECSC Treaty and in Germany. Third, the threshold above which mergers are *prima facie* unlawful is of course a key issue, and is one of the most controversial clauses in the draft regulation. The higher the threshold, the fewer the number of cases that will warrant examination and the easier it would be for the Commission, with its limited manpower, to handle them.[30]

ARTICLE 85 APPLICATION TO CONCENTRATION

In 1966 the Commission published its Memorandum on Concentrations.[31] It examines whether Article 85 could be used to control concentrations, and sets out the views of certain professors who had been asked by the Commission for their analysis as well as the Commission's comments on these views and related issues.

A majority of the professors believed that Article 85 applied to concentrations when three conditions were fulfilled: (1) that competition is appreciably restricted (*sensiblement restreinte*), (2) that the concentration results from an agreement (and not, for example, from the acquisition of shares on a stock exchange without the agreement of the corporation being acquired), and (3) that "legally distinct enterprises remain in existence after the concentration" is carried out. Whether, according to this interpretation, Article 85 would offer effective control over concentrations depends on the interpretation of the third condition. Whatever its exact meaning, it appears to be a condition which would not be difficult for well-advised corporations to avoid (although there might be tax and other disadvantages of doing so) through "fusions" of the legal entities of the participating corporations or by acquisition of the business of a corporation rather than the shares in the corporation itself (with, if necessary, the liquidation of the selling corporation).

A minority of the professors considered that Article 85 did not apply to concentrations because concentrations do not relate to the behavior of enterprises but rather modify their internal structure which, it was thought, does not necessarily limit competition.

The Commission came to the same conclusions as the minority, but for rather different (and more convincing) reasons. The Commission noted that national antitrust legislation usually treats mergers and restrictive agreements separately, regarding the latter as *prima facie* objectionable and the former as *prima facie* or generally acceptable. The Commission thought that the uniform application of Article 85 to both would prohibit too many mergers or too few restrictive agreements.

Also Article 85(3) was thought inappropriate to mergers since their effects on competition are not easy to foresee. Moreover, it would be difficult to approve a merger under Article 85(3), since an exemption can be granted only if the legally suspect activity is indispensable to obtain the benefits.[32] In addition, Article 85(3) implies temporary exemptions given only as long as the conditions required for them are fulfilled; but mergers would need to be authorized permanently.

And automatic nullity, provided for by Article 85(2), would sometimes be inappropriate for unlawful mergers, since nullification would have consequential effects on related transactions and on stock ownership and so would go further than merely reestablishing the previously existing position. The appropriate way of dealing with an unlawful merger is divestiture.[33]

To sum up, the Commission felt that, in view of the structural consequences of mergers, they should be subject to legal rules different from those applying to agreements. These arguments do not now seem as strong as they did in 1966, and there are contrary arguments to be drawn from court decisions since then. The contrast between official attitudes at the national level toward restrictive agreements and mergers is certainly not now as strong as it once was.[34] To apply Article 85 to both restrictive agreements and mergers does not necessarily mean to apply it uniformly. Granted, it is not always easy to judge the effect of restrictive agreements on competition, but judging the effects of mergers does not seem to be necessarily or inherently more difficult. Indeed in some circumstances it might be easier. The argument that mergers could only be approved under Article 85(3) if they were "indispensable" to achieve the benefits expected of them is of course correct, but it does not by any means follow that this would be an unsatisfactory result. (After all, mergers are always thought to bring some benefits, and the Court of Justice has recognized preservation of employment as a legitimate matter for the Commission to take into account under Article 85(3).[35]

Nor does it follow that Article 85 should be interpreted as not applying to mergers at all. Exemptions under Article 85(3) are indeed given for specified periods, but this is mandated by Regulation 17/62, not Article 85(3) itself. As regards the "nullity" fear, the better view is that Article 85(2) applies to agreements to set up joint ventures and that ownership of a joint venture is never void.[36] If this is true for joint ventures, the same would also be true for mergers.

The argument that mergers involve changes of ownership[37] to which Article 85(2) is inappropriate is certainly not applicable to many of the kinds of mergers covered by the definition of *control* in the draft merger regulation. Many of these would not involve any change of ownership but would involve contracts to which Article 85(2) could reasonably be applied.

More important, the Court of Justice has repeatedly said that Article 3(f) must be used to interpret Articles 85 and 86.[38] Article 3(f) states that it is one of the Community's tasks to institute "a system ensuring that competition in the common market is not distorted." In *Continental Can* the Court stressed that the antitrust Articles of the Treaty must be interpreted so as to avoid a lacuna in the law (as there clearly would be if mergers were permitted freely), and that the distinction between structural changes and behavior is not decisive if both restrict competition.[39]

These arguments all suggest that Article 85 might indeed apply to mergers between firms neither of which was occupying a dominant position. It would also obviously be irrational if a dominant firm having a 60 percent market share was unable to acquire a competitor having a further 30 percent (which is clearly the law under *Continental Can*), but if when all the circumstances other than market shares were similar, two firms each having a 45 percent market share were entirely free to merge. It could of course be argued that such a merger was an abuse by the two firms of a jointly held dominant position, but seems an unsatisfactory approach to the problem since it could apply only when all the evidence needed to prove joint dominance (whatever that evidence may be, exactly as to which, see below) was available. This is an anomaly which has been apparent only since *Continental Can.*

Some of the reasons given by the Commission seem in retrospect to be less important than practical considerations which could have been given in 1966. There are two practical reasons for considering Article 85 as being inapplicable to mergers. First, it was widely believed that most corporations in most sectors of industry in the European Community were too small to be efficient or competitive on an international level, and that mergers would be desirable and should not be inhibited. Indeed the Commission has ensured the adoption of various measures intended to facilitate mergers of small firms. Second, if Article 85 applies to mergers, it would apply to so many mergers that the work of the competition directorate general would be greatly increased. However, the parties to mergers, unlike the parties to most restrictive agreements, wish to know as soon as possible whether an antitrust authority will or will not approve of what they are doing. A given number of merger cases will therefore cause far more pressure from the participants for quick decisions than the same number of cases involving restrictive agreements. These are both respectable arguments, and are legitimate policy considerations for a small and, in 1966, relatively inexperienced antitrust authority.

In retrospect, there was another policy reason for not seeking to apply Article 85 to mergers, whether or not it was in the minds of those responsible at the time. Europe then contained, and still does, many serious and unjustifiable restrictive agreements. It would certainly have been bad enforcement policy to divert the attention of the Commission from its first task of dealing with clearly unlawful agreements and involving it in the much more complex, legally and politically controversial, and time-consuming task of dealing with mergers. Many of the most basic principles of Community law were not yet clearly established in 1966; it was obviously the best policy for the Commission to establish them, and to deal with the most obviously and seriously unlawful arrangements, before launching itself into more difficult and sophisticated problems. If this consideration was in the minds of the Commission in 1966, it was a legitimate and sound reason for the articulated policy on mergers. But, like the other considerations set out above, the passage of time may have seriously eroded its validity.

Theoretically, the question whether Article 85 prohibits mergers could be brought before the Court of Justice at any time by a private litigant, whether a corporation trying to prevent itself being taken over or a competitor fearing the creation of an overwhelming rival.[40] The Court of Justice would consider the question in the light of Article 3(f), and might again hold, as it did in *Continental Can,* that the EEC Treaty should not be interpreted as having an important lacuna. If the Court of Justice were to disagree with the position taken by the Commission in 1966, it could adopt either of two interpretations of Article 85: one position would be that Article 85, in the light of Article 3(f), prohibited mergers creating a corporation or group with a dominant position. This would be essentially the position under the draft merger regulation. Alternatively, it could take the position that Article 85 applied to all mergers on the same conditions as to restrictive agreements; that is, they are prohibited if they appreciably restrict competition (and would have to be justified under Article 85(3). This would correspond more closely to the principle in Section 7 of the Clayton Act. With either approach it would be necessary to prove an effect on trade between member states. Neither interpretation would require prior authorization for mergers, and neither would imply that Article 85 would apply to mergers not resulting from agreements between the merging corporations.

Would the Court of Justice interpret Article 85 to apply to mergers? If Article 3(f) prohibits strengthening of a dominant position by acquisition of a competitor, as the Court of Justice held in *Continental Can,* then it may also prohibit creation of a dominant position by merging of two nondominant competitors. If Article 3(f) prohibits the elimination of competition by merger involving a dominant company, it may prohibit the elimination of competition by mergers involving nondominant companies. Indeed the Court of Justice in *Continental Can* said,

> [O]ne cannot assume that the Treaty which prohibits in Article 85 certain decisions of ordinary associations of undertakings restricting competition *without eliminating it,* permits in Article 86 that undertakings *after* merging into organic unity, should reach such a dominant position that any serious chance of competition is practically rendered impossible. . . .The endeavour of the authors of the Treaty to maintain in the market real or potential competition even in cases in which restraints on competition are permitted, was explicitly laid down in Article 85(3)(b). . . . Articles 85 and 86 cannot be interpreted in such a way that they contradict each other, because they serve to achieve the same aim. . . . (Article 86) is not only aimed at practices which may damage consumers directly, but also at those which are detrimental to them through their impact on an effective competitive structure, *such as is mentioned in Article 3(f)* [emphasis added].[41]

Certainly there are strong arguments for saying that, since *Continental Can,* Article 85 applies to mergers, or at least to mergers which create a dominant firm.

It hardly needs to be stressed that interpreting Article 85 as applying to mergers would eliminate certain anomalies and irrational results. If Article 85 does not prohibit mergers, then close cooperation between two firms with large market shares would be prohibited if it substantially eliminated competition between them, yet a complete merger, which would end all competition between them, would be lawful.

JOINT VENTURES

The view that Article 85 applied to joint ventures with restrictive effects on competition, and to any other arrangements under which economically (and not merely legally) separate enterprises continued to exist after a transaction, was expressed clearly by the Commission in the Concentration Memorandum.

However, the principles upon which Article 85 should be applied to joint ventures have been confused by an argument prompted by, though not found in, the Concentration Memorandum. The argument centered around the question of where the line should be drawn between concentrations and joint ventures. It was based implicitly on the assumption that concentrations were exempt from Article 85; therefore, if it could be shown that a joint venture should be regarded as a concentration, it would not be subject to Article 85 even if it had the effect of restricting competition. Needless to say, this assumption was difficult to justify since it implied that Article 85 would not be applied in situations where it appeared that it should apply fully. The assumption, however, gained respectability from the undoubted fact that in German and U.S. antitrust laws joint ventures are dealt with primarily under the provisions under merger regulation, and not restrictive agreements. It never became clear why this would necessarily be the appropriate approach in a legal system with no express merger control legislation, such as the EEC. The assumption also gained respectability from the habit of describing some joint ventures as partial concentrations, thereby adding a third imprecise basic concept to a field already equipped with two (joint venture and concentration).

Under the view that Article 85 does not apply to complete mergers, two approaches were possible. Article 85 could be interpreted as applying to all agreements except those leading to complete mergers or concentrations, that is, those after which only one economic entity remains. Alternatively, Article 85 could be interpreted as not applying to any agreements leading to partial mergers or concentrations (however exactly these should be defined) or *a fortiori* to complete mergers or concentrations. Obviously, if the first alternative correctly stated the law, it would be important to be able to distinguish between complete mergers and joint venture arrangements. If the second alternative was the law, it would be important to be able to distinguish between joint ventures which are partial concentrations and joint ventures which are not.

Faced with joint venture situations of considerable genuine difficulty and with a situation of considerable intellectual confusion, the Commission, conscious that this was ultimately a question to be decided by the Court of Justice, reacted with caution. In its Sixth Report on competition policy, the Commission limited the practical scope of the putative partial concentration theory by saying what, in its opinion, the theory did *not* mean. In particular, the Commission stated that no joint venture could be regarded as a concentration exempt from Article 85 if the pooling of the areas of business involved weakened competition between the parent companies in other areas, particularly in related areas, where the parent firms remained formally independent of each other.[42] The other requirement, according to the Commission, of these "exceptional cases" is that the parent firms must have irreversibly transferred their business activities in the field in question to the joint venture. This means that a joint venture could never be regarded as a concentration unless both the parent firms previously carried on the activities in question independently. So understood it is indeed relevant only in "exceptional cases."

On the assumption that either the first approach is correct and Article 85 may apply to all joint ventures unless they are really complete mergers, or that cases of "partial concentrations" are rare enough to be ignored in the rest of this article, the next question is how to distinguish between joint ventures and complete mergers. The Commission's Sixth Report makes this clear: "Cases in which the parent companies transfer all their assets to the joint venture and themselves become no more than holding companies . . . will usually be considered to constitute a merger,"[43] that is, a complete merger. Although in the past difficulties caused by company and tax laws of member states have given rise to highly complex arrangements such as those in the Dunlop-Pirelli and Agfa-Gevaert mergers, most people would agree that the distinction between joint ventures and complete mergers is a genuine distinction in theory, even if it may occasionally be difficult to apply in practice.

No discussion of this rather complex area of law would be complete without an examination of the rules applying to joint ventures themselves. These rules are important because the joint ventures prohibited by Article 85 are primarily those that occur in already concentrated markets.

Under the *Continental Can* ruling, Article 86 prohibits the extension of a dominant position through the setting up of a joint venture, or the acquisition of a share in an existing joint venture. No joint venture cases under Articles 85 and 86 have yet come before the Court of Justice. However, the court has laid down several rules which are relevant to joint ventures. Articles 85 and 86 and Article 3(f) are aimed not only at behavior which may cause damage to consumers directly, but also at practices which are detrimental to them through their impact on an effective structure of competition.

> The distinction between measures which concern the structure of the undertaking and practices which may influence the market cannot be decisive, for any structural measure may affect market conditions, if it increases the size and economic power of the undertaking.[44]

Article 85(1) applies to agreements which clearly tend to reduce competition, even if they contain no formal restrictions on the freedom of the enterprises involved.[45] In assessing the economic effects of a given agreement all the surrounding economic circumstances must be taken into account.[46]

The general principle applied by the Commission is that any agreement between two or more enterprises under which a corporation is owned or controlled jointly by them may fall under Article 85 if the agreement has the effect, directly or indirectly, of restricting or reducing competition between the parent enterprises or from third parties.[47]

The effects on competition may result from express contractual clauses or may result naturally from the mere existence and operation of the joint venture and of the relationship of the parent enterprises with it.[48] If such effects are reasonably foreseeable, it is irrelevant that there are no contractual restraints on the freedom of the parties to compete.

Joint ventures may have a variety of different kinds of effects on competition. For example, if the joint venture sells the products of its parents to third parties, it may largely eliminate competition between them. Even if it does not sell all of its parents' products, they will tend to align their prices on the joint venture's prices.[49] If the joint venture sells its products or services to its parent corporations, or does research for them, it may reduce competition between them, especially if its products are end products. Again the parents may tend to align their prices. Even if the joint venture is selling to third parties and is not in competition with either of its parents, the existence of the joint venture may preclude the parents from entering the market independently of one another, as they would otherwise have done in the absence of the joint venture.[50]

In an oligopolistic market a joint venture between two oligopolists may alter the structure of the market, both reducing competition between the parents and making it less likely that other competitors will enter the market.[51] If the joint venture has taken over all the activities of one or both parents in a given sector, this might indicate inability to continue independent operations in the market, or a wish to end competition with a major competitor. Much depends on circumstances. The facts of the only case involving a situation of this kind were unusual, involving vertical relationship between two corporations neither of which were in a position to remain in the market without close links with some other firms already in the market.[52] Alternatively, a joint venture may be a forum for coordinating the parents' policies, but this has never been the sole ground for a finding that the joint venture fell under Article 85(1); rather, it was used as an argument in a case where there was specific evidence that this was the intention of the parents.[53]

Article 85(1) will apply to any of these kinds of effects on competition only if in the circumstances they are significant. Even if Article 85(1) applies, a joint venture can often be justified under Article 85(3). The extent of the effect on competition is often crucial in joint venture cases. Joint ventures where one or both parents, or the joint venture itself, have a large market share, or where the joint venture has the effect of eliminating most of the competition between its parents, are particularly likely to be unjustifiable.

The better view is that joint ventures which are prohibited by Article 85 are not void (though express restrictive clauses in joint venture agreements may be). They are, however, subject to divestiture.[54]

The Commission has so far approved a number of joint ventures under Article 85(3), and has prohibited a joint venture only in one case,[55] in which the agreement offered no advantages and involved parties with large market shares.

In theory and in practice, it is important to ensure as far as possible that an antitrust policy is consistent and uniform across the whole spectrum, from cartels through joint ventures to complete mergers. As the Commission has never claimed power to control complete mergers (except in cases under Article 86), it has limited itself to ensuring that its policies on joint ventures and cartels are consistent with one another, and that firms cannot do by joint venture what they could not do without a joint venture.

ARTICLE 86 APPLICATION TO DOMINANT POSITION, OLIGOPOLY, AND MERGERS

Article 86 expressly prohibits any abuse by more than one undertaking of a dominant position. This makes it clear that there may be a violation of the EEC Treaty by several dominant enterprises in circumstances to which Article 85 does not apply, that is, where there is no collusive or concerted behavior. Oligopoly is not, of course, itself unlawful under EEC law. Thus far, however, there are no decisions involving a dominant position held by more than one firm.

In any market in which a small number of large firms held most or all of the market, the firms in question will be acutely aware of one another's behavior. The market strategy of each must take account of the probable reactions of the others, and they will tend to act similarly, especially if the other oligopolists' behavior can be accurately foreseen.

Several authors[56] have suggested that Article 86 applies to an abuse by a small number of enterprises in an oligopolistic market, even if no one of them has overall dominance and even without any concerned practice between them, at least when all behave in a parallel manner.

For example, if all the members of an oligopoly charge excessive prices for their products, this can occur over a significant period of time only if there is no significant price competition between them (and no significant price competition from outside the oligopoly). Excessive prices and absence of price competition might coexist with competition between the members of the oligopoly in other respects. Article 86 seems to be applicable both when there is no competition between oligopolists and when the only competition between them, for whatever reason, does not have the effect of eliminating the allegedly illegal collective behavior. In other words, if all the oligopolists practice the behavior that is said to be abusive, the fact that there may be competition between the oligopolists in other respects is irrelevant.

Most abuses of dominant power occur because normal competition does not occur or is not sufficient to prevent them. If market power is being used in the same way by a number of enterprises, the fact that the users of it are not a monolithic bloc in other respects does not make the market power any less real, or any less liable to abuse.

But, if it is not necessary for several enterprises to occupy a dominant position in order to eliminate competition between them at all, what are the tests of a collective dominant position? Basically, the tests of market power are the same whether it is held by one or more enterprises. The power to behave independently of outsiders, to exclude competition, to determine prices or to control a significant proportion of total production or distribution, without being subject to the influence of competitors, purchasers, or suppliers, may be exercised collectively. If dominant power is power which is great enough to be abused, then collective dominant power is power which may be abused collectively.

As will be recalled, *Continental Can* held that Article 86 prohibits an anticompetitive merger by a firm occupying, alone, a dominant position. Article 86 clearly prohibits abuse by more than one firm occupying a dominant position. How far can Article 86 be used to control mergers not involving the only dominant firm in the market? Several cases need to be considered:

1. If two firms are shown to hold a dominant position (whatever the precise requirements for such a finding), it seems clear that if they merge with one another, the merger would be under *Continental Can* a violation of Article 86. Similarly, if they set up a joint venture which has, or is likely to have, substantial anticompetitive effects on their behavior, this is unlawful under Article 86 even if Article 85 does not apply;

2. If three firms are shown to hold a dominant position, and two of them merge with one another, a more difficult question arises.

3. Moreover, two firms may jointly hold a dominant position, and one of them may merge with a third, nondominant competitor in the same market, thereby increasing its own market power and the aggregate market power of the two dominant firms. Here again the question arises whether this might be unlawful.

Article 86 speaks of "abuse by one or more undertakings of a dominant position" not of "abuse by an undertaking occupying, alone or with other undertakings, a dominant position." Should it therefore be interpreted as prohibiting only conduct committed by all the undertakings involved? If the answer is yes, the acquisition of a competitor by one of several dominant firms is lawful, and probably the merger of two dominant firms, where a third exists, is also lawful.

On the other hand, Article 86 could also be interpreted as prohibiting abuses committed by one or more, but not necessarily all, dominant firms (provided that competition between the dominant firms does not prevent the putatively unlawful behavior from continuing, or being successful, in which case the firms are not jointly dominant in the relevant respect, according to the theory suggested here).

To illustrate this proposition, suppose a market dominated by two firms each having a 45 percent market share, the remaining 10 percent being held by a few small corporations unable to offer serious competition. Suppose that firm *A*, one of the two dominant firms, begins to offer fidelity rebates and require its customers and distributors to deal exclusively with it by various means. Is this contrary to Article 86?

It is submitted that it is. This behavior would strengthen *A*'s market position vis-à-vis its only serious rival, and its minor competitors. It would make the market shares of the two big firms more static. Competition would be further reduced. Also, if A's behavior is lawful, the absurd result is that it would become unlawful as soon as its chief rival began to practice the same behavior. This result would be not only irrational and contrary to principle, but intolerable, since it would deny to the rival the freedom to compete with its major competitor on equal terms, and would favor the first oligopolist in adopting new anticompetitive practices. One could envision a type of race by each oligopolist to initiate behavior that, but for the fact that it was the only company so behaving, would be unlawful and contrary to competition in the Common Market. The EEC Commission and the Court of Justice, it is suggested, should be particularly ready to insist on the preservation of that degree of competition which can exist between oligopolists jointly holding a dominant position, and should prevent either of them from strengthening its position by anticompetitive means at the expense of anyone else.

It seems to follow that a merger or acquisition by one of several firms together having a dominant position will, if the effect of the merger on competition is sufficiently significant, constitute a violation of existing Community law, whether or not the other firms involved in the merger also occupy the collective dominant position. The practical significance of this result for the Community power to control concentration in already concentrated industries is considerable.

However, it must not be assumed that a merger of one oligopolist with a smaller competitor necessarily has adverse effects on competition. A smaller number of stronger competitors may cause intensified competition[57] and an acquistion by the smallest oligopolist of a smaller firm (or of a large firm outside the relevant market) may strengthen the former's position and promote competition. Similarly, although a merger creating a jointly dominant firm, for example, creating the second firm in a duopoly, might be unlawful, it might also be desirable if on balance it strengthened rather than reduced such competition as existed in the market. If such an affirmative competition-enhancing defense is proved in fact, it apparently would be valid under Community antitrust law. This is because a merger by a jointly dominant firm that increased competition appears to be lawful under the *Continental Can* principle.

Similar questions may be raised under the draft merger regulation, which prohibits any concentration whereby the participants "acquire or enhance the power to hinder effective competition." Does this mean the exclusive power to hinder effective competition, or the power, whether alone or with other firms not involved in the concentration, to hinder effective competition? The interpretation of this is slightly easier than that of Article 86, however, and may not depend on it. Since Article 86 makes it clear that more than one enterprise can occupy a dominant position, that is, can have the power to hinder effective competition, it would follow that a concentration which enhances that power would fall under the regulation. The power of all the holders of a collectively dominant position would be enhanced if two of them merge and the third does not, or if one of two dominant firms acquires a third competitor, but of course only the firms involved in the merger or acquisition would have violated the EEC Treaty.

SUMMARY OF COMMUNITY LAW ON CONCENTRATIONS

In summary, the EEC clearly has power under existing law to prevent mergers and acquisitions involving firms which are already dominant. Under well-established law a considerable number of firms are considered dominant, and are thus subject to all the duties which Article 86 imposes, at least in narrow markets. The EEC also has power to prevent already dominant firms from increasing their market power through anticompetitive practices, and also to prevent oligopolies from behaving in corresponding ways (although in this respect the extent of the law is unclear). In general, however, there is no power to put an end to dominance or oligopoly as such, and until either new legislation or a new interpretation of the EEC Treaty is adopted there is no power to prohibit mergers involving previously nondominant firms even if their effect is to create a clearly dominant firm, or even a monopoly. Under existing law there is no power to approve a merger involving a dominant firm that would have the effect of substantially restricting competition, no matter how desirable the merger might seem on other grounds. Joint ventures can be adequately controlled under existing law. The Community probably already has power to prohibit mergers involving one or more of the members of an oligopoly who together occupy a dominant position.

The Community will have no power to control mergers between corporations which after the merger will not be dominant (either alone or together with other firms) under the proposed merger regulation; such a power could come only from the wider of the two theoretically possible new interpretations of Article 85. This adds up to a position which is not wholly satisfactory, but which provides powers which are by no means insignificant and which so far have been little used.

SPECIAL PROBLEMS OF APPLICATION:
INTERFACE OF NATIONAL AND COMMUNITY LAW

The national authorities of several member states, in particular Belgium, Germany, France, Ireland, and the United Kingdom, have, at least in theory, some powers to control concentrations under existing national laws. Belgium and the Netherlands are considering new legislation on mergers.[58] Also, other national legislation is sometimes used to prevent what are considered to be undesirable concentrations.

National authorities would not seek to prevent mergers of corporations outside their countries, and Community law applies only when trade between member states is affected, so some mergers would be subject only to one set of legal rules or the other. However, a merger between, for example, a German corporation and a British firm may now be subject to three laws, the German and British national merger control legislation and Community law.

If Community law and applicable national laws both prohibit, or both permit, a given merger, no difficulty is likely to arise. If Community law prohibits a merger allowed by national law, Community law prevails. It is not yet clear what the legal position is if Community law permits a merger but national law does not.

In *Walt Wilhelm v. Bundeskartellamt*,[59] an antitrust case (but not a merger case), the Court of Justice said:

> [I]n principle the national cartel authorities may take proceedings also with regard to situations likely to be the subject of a decision by the Commission. However, if the ultimate general aim of the Treaty is to be respected, this parallel application of the national system can only be allowed in so far as it does not prejudice the uniform application throughout the Common Market of the Community rules on cartels and of the full effect of the measures adopted in implementation of those rules. . . .
>
> Article 87(2)(e), in conferring on a Community institution the power to determine the relationship between national laws and the Community rules on competition, confirms the supremacy of Community law. . . .
>
> It would be contrary to the nature of [the EEC] system to allow member states to introduce or retain measures capable of prejudicing the practical effectiveness of the Treaty. The binding force of the Treaty and of measures taken in application of it must not differ from one state to another as a result of internal measures, lest the functioning of the Community system should be impeded and the achievement of the aims of the Treaty placed in peril. Consequently, conflicts between the rules of the Community and national rules in the matter of the law on cartels must be resolved by applying the principle that Community law takes precedence.
>
> . . . .
>
> Consequently, and so long as a regulation adopted pursuant to Article 87(2)(e) of the Treaty has not provided otherwise, national authorities may take action against an agreement in accordance with their national law, even when an examination of the agreement from the point of view of its compatability with Community law is pending before the Commission, subject however to the condition that the application of national law may not prejudice the full and uniform application of Community law or the effects of measures taken or to be taken to implement it.[60]

The Court of Justice is clearly not saying that a national authority may do as it likes, nor apparently is it saying that Community law has wholly occupied the field. Rather, there appears to be a category of cases not clearly defined in which action by national antitrust authorities would be incompatible with Community law. The mere fact that the result might be different under the two systems of law does not mean automatically that national law cannot be applied.

In the area of exemptions from regulation under Article 85(3), there may perhaps be two kinds of cases: (1) those where the Commission has granted an exemption for an agreement of relatively little importance, not because it promotes some very important Community objective but because there is no strong objection to it, and (2) cases where the Commission has granted an exemption for an agreement of great importance for Community policy in the sector in question. If this distinction is valid, it would follow that national law could be applied so as to prohibit an agreement in the first category but not one in the second category. However, the first kind of case may not in fact exist, and if it does not exist the legal position is clear. On the other hand, if indeed the two categories exist, and if the Commission approved a restrictive merger, acting under Article 85, it would have to be determined into which of the two categories the case fell. In practice such cases would normally fall within the second category, if the Commission confined itself to important merger cases.

It seems clear from the wording of the draft merger regulation that if the Commission authorizes a merger under the clause which permits authorization for mergers "indispensable to an objective given priority treatment in the common interest of the Community," it would be contrary to Community law for a national antitrust authority to prohibit the merger.[61]

How likely is a conflict over merger cases between the Commission and a national antitrust authority? Not all the member states have authorities with power to control mergers. It is possible to imagine a situation in which a national authority might want to allow a merger at any cost to preserve jobs, or might want to prevent a takeover by interests outside the member state in question. But national antitrust policies are moving toward harmonization with Community law on other issues, and national authorities might be glad to have the help of the Commission either to prevent or to promote a controversial merger. Though differences of opinion are perhaps more likely to arise over merger policy than about restrictive agreements, the fact that there have been so few differences of opinion in the application of Articles 85 and 86 is encouraging.

Markert[62] has suggested that the situation in relation to mergers could be clarified by providing that all mergers falling under the regulation should be exempt from national merger control laws, provided that the jurisdictional test of an effect on trade between member states was objective and capable of being readily applied, that the Commission's standards were not significantly less strict than those of national authorities, and that the Commission has the administrative facilities necessary to carry out a prompt and thorough investigation of all difficult cases. Meanwhile, practical solutions could be found through cooperation between the Commission and national authorities.

POLICY IMPLICATIONS FOR THE FUTURE

Although a number of merger cases have been dealt with informally by the Commission and are described in the annual competition policy reports of the Commission, *Continental Can* remains the only formal decision on mergers that has so far been adopted by the Commission. It is hardly possible therefore to outline a comprehensive EEC policy on mergers.[63] However, it is possible to note a series of points about such a policy which have been suggested from various sides, although none of them has ever been adopted as the policy of the Commission.

Community merger policy will seek to limit itself to dealing with a small number of truly important cases, initially horizontal mergers between competitors, then vertical mergers, and finally conglomerate mergers much later. It is believed that only a small number of very large mergers are likely to be found to be contrary to the Community interest. Moreover, the small staff in the Competition Directorate General of the Commission would not be in a position to handle a large number of merger cases in addition to their existing work. Thus, this approach would therefore be adopted as a pragmatic enforcement policy, whatever the exact terms of the merger regulation when it is finally adopted. Consequently, businessmen need not anticipate Commission involvement in any but the largest and most obviously anticompetitive mergers. The Commission will of course seek more staff to handle merger cases and may attempt to delegate simple restrictive practices cases to national authorities and courts.

The Commission is likely to avoid articulating general policies, opting instead for a case-by-case approach. This implies an approach adjusted to the circumstances of each industry involved. The Committee on Economic and Monetary Affairs said in 1973, "Probably. . . the Commission is not yet as familiar with the conditions of competition and economic interlinking in the Community as would really be desirable for a European monopoly authority."[64]

Community jurisdiction over mergers will be limited by two requirements. One or more of the corporations or groups of corporations involved must be "established" in the EEC, and the merger must have an effect on trade between member states. A merger affecting only the external trade of the Community would not be subject to Community jurisdiction, because Articles 85 and 86 and the merger regulation only apply when trade between member states is affected. These broad principles would apply even if Community jurisdiction over mergers was based on a new interpretation of Article 85 rather than on the new merger regulation.

It is not clear how far the Commission would seek to exercise jurisdiction over a merger involving holding companies outside the EEC but with subsidiaries established in the Common Market; in clear cases of attempted evasion it would no doubt do so.

In considering the effects of a merger on competition, the Commission will likely take into account actual or potential competition from outside the Common Market as well as from competitors already established in it.[65]

Economic studies carried out by the Commission and summarized in the annual reports on Competition Policy show that concentration has increased in European industry. For the reasons already referred to this is in general probably desirable.

The Commission will tend to favor mergers across frontiers within the Community rather than mergers between corporations or groups in the same member state, because the former kind of mergers promote the economic integration of the Community.[66] This is a policy consideration with no parallel in United States antitrust law.

A law granting an antitrust authority discretion to allow even seriously anticompetitive mergers for overriding policy reasons is likely to be much more difficult and controversial to administer (and much more difficult to foresee) than a simple ban, notwithstanding the experience of the Commission and other European antitrust authorities in operating such "weighing-up" rules. In performing this discretionary function, the Commission is likely to be guided by the principles of Article 85(3) under which the merger must be indispensable to promote an overriding Community objective, consumers must get a fair share of the benefits to be obtained from it, and the merger must not give the firms concerned the opportunity to eliminate competition. Obviously, the benefits obtained from the merger must outweigh the harm resulting from any restriction of competition.[67] The Commission will also refer to the rules laid down in Article 66 of the ECSC Treaty, in particular the prohibition on mergers which evade competition rules by establishing an artificially privileged position involving a substantial advantage in access to supplies or markets.

Economies of scale are easy to allege and hard to prove. The Commission is unlikely to be much impressed by any argument about greater efficiency due to larger size, or increased concentration, unless it is a very well researched argument. There is evidence that these benefits are often not obtained, or that these benefits are outweighed by the difficulties of running large and complex enterprises. In any case, economies of scale can usually be obtained through internal expansion, and the Commission's policy of confining itself to large mergers should mean that no merger justified by economies of scale should come up for consideration.[68]

As a matter of procedure, complaints about mergers can be expected from corporations resisting a take-over bid or from competitors fearing the emergence of more powerful rivals. The Commission will be compelled to decide when it is appropriate to adopt interim (interlocutory) measures. These questions have already arisen in merger cases and others under the

European Coal and Steel Community Treaty and in the *Camera Care* case, a refusal to supply case under the EEC Treaty.[69]

The Commission will not be anti–United States or anti-Japan in its policies. Indeed, it is less likely to be so than the national authorities of some of the member states might be, or might have been in the past. Furthermore, the greater the degree of economic integration achieved within the Common Market, the less difficult it will be for the Commission to have a clearly coherent and consistent policy on mergers, not subject to adjustment to suit special regional circumstances.

In assessing the effect of a proposed merger on competition the Commission is likely to focus primarily on market structure: the number of substantial sellers and buyers on the market, the relative sizes of the market shares of the firms, barriers to entry, the extent to which the Common Market forms a unified market, and the degree of rigidity in distribution systems. The Court of Justice has in several cases under Articles 85 and 86 emphasized the importance of these factors, and one would expect them to be still more important in merger cases.[70]

The effects of a proposed merger must be assessed primarily on structural criteria because a merger is approved on a permanent basis and its long-term effects will not depend, for example, on whether the firms involved have or have not practiced exclusionary behavior in the years before the merger. The criteria written into the draft merger regulation for the absolute prohibition of a merger are "the power to hinder effective competition in the Common Market or in a substantial part thereof" and two quantitative criteria premised on turnover and market share. The phrase quoted is likely to be interpreted in the light of the case law of the Court of Justice on dominance under Article 86, which gives some weight to factors other than market share.[71]

Both the *Continental Can* rule and the draft merger regulation prohibit the acquisition of dominant power through mergers (though the regulation has certain exceptions). Under the Treaty, dominant power legitimately acquired is subject to restraints on behavior under Article 86, but not to divestiture. However, it would not be an argument in favor of a merger that the Commission will in any event retain the power to control the behavior of the new dominant firm.

In horizontal merger cases one would expect the Commission to seek to prevent significant additional concentration and the elimination of important competitors. Market shares would be the principal criterion used, but not the only one. The Commission can also be expected to follow a stricter enforcement policy when the industry concerned is becoming more concentrated than when the merger takes place in an otherwise static situation. Therefore, the Commission will be attentive to trends in market structure as well as market shares. The Commission would probably also tend to favor a merger necessary to keep a firm in business if no less restrictive course of action was available. No figures can be given for the percentage market shares which would trigger Commission intervention, although some indications can perhaps be obtained from the cases under Article 86, notably *United Brands* and *Hoffmann-LaRoche*.

EEC antitrust law does not limit itself to horizontal mergers, and it is clear that the rules also prohibit vertical mergers with substantial anticompetitive effects, such as raising barriers to entry or creating competitive disadvantages for other corporations (as distinct from making the merged firm more efficient) by cutting off their access to customers or suppliers.[72]

Nothing useful at this stage can be said about probable EEC antitrust policy on conglomerate mergers, although no doubt mergers involving potential entrants and mergers making uncompetitive reciprocal buying probable will be looked at carefully.

NOTES

1. On the two categories of abuses *see* C. BELLAMY & G. CHILD, COMMON MARKET LAW OF COMPETITION, 186–7, 196 (2d ed., 1978); Temple Lang, *Monopolisation and the Definition of "Abuse" of a Dominant Position under Article 86 EEC Treaty*, 169 COMMON MARKET L. REV. 345 (1979); Temple Lang, *Abuse of Dominant Positions in European Community Law, Present and Future, Some Aspects*, in INTERNATIONAL ANTITRUST (B. Hawk, ed. 1979).

2. United States v. United Shoe Machinery Corp., 110 F. Supp. 295, 341 (D. Mass. 1953), *aff'd per curiam* 347 U.S. 521 (1954).

3. To this general principle there appears to be one exception, or apparent exception. If it is shown that the dominance of a dominant firm was due primarily or wholly to behavior unlawful under Article 85 or 86 of the Treaty Establishing the European Community, 298 U.N.T.S. No. 4300 (1958), merely prohibiting the firm from continuing the behavior in question is an insufficient remedy, since the firm would still enjoy the results of its past unlawful behavior. In those circumstances the Commis-

sion has the power to order divestiture in order to recreate a competitive situation and take away the privileged position insofar as it had been improperly obtained.

4. Case 6/72, [1973] E.C.R. 215.

5. Article 86 of the EEC Treaty reads, in part:
   Any abuse by one or more undertakings of a dominant position within the common market or in a substantial part of it shall be prohibited as incompatible with the common market in so far as it may affect trade between Member States.

6. Continental Can [1973] E.C.R. 215 at ¶ 26.

7. Memorandum on Concentration, Doc. SEC (65) 3500 of December 1st, 1965; *see* Markert, *Antitrust Aspects of Mergers in the EEC*, 5 TEXAS INT'L L. FORUM 32 (1969).

8. Joined cases 40/73 et al., *in re* European Sugar Cartel [1975] E.C.R. 1663 at ¶¶ 483, 527; Case 27/76, United Brands v. Commission, [1978] E.C.R. 207 at ¶¶ 189, 192; Case 85/76, Hoffmann-LaRoche v. Commission, [1979] E.C.R. 461 at ¶¶ 90, 120.

9. Case 27/76, United Brands v. Commission, [1978] E.C.R. 207.

10. Case 71/74, FRUBO v. Commission, [1975] E.C.R. 563, 582. *See also* Cases 255/78, 1–3/79, Guerlain and others 33/79 and 99/79 judgments dated July 10, 1980 (not yet reported).

11. *See* Case 85/76, Hoffmann-LaRoche v. Commission, [1979] E.C.R. 461, 554–55.

12. *See* Case 13/60, Geitling v. High Authority, [1962] E.C.R. 83 (interpreting the term *substantial part* contained in the ECSC Treaty.

13. Case 109/75R, National Carbonising Co. v. Commission, [1975] E.C.R. 1193.

14. Case 792/79, Camera Care v. Commission, Order of 24 January 1980, [1980] E.C.R. 119.

15. 16 O.J. Eur. Comm. (No. C 92) 1 (1973); *see also Resolution of the European Parliament* 17 O.J. Eur. Comm. (No. C 23) 19 (1974); 17 O.J. Eur. Comm. (No. C 88) 19 (1974); 14 O.J. Eur. Comm. (No C 66) 11 (1971); *Europien Parlement Documents de seance* No. 197, February 2, 1970.

16. Article 1, *Proposal for a Regulation of the Council on the Control of Concentrations Between Undertakings,* 160 O.J. Eur. Comm. (No. C 92) 2 (1973).

17. For definitions of a *dominant position* given by the court since the merger regulation was submitted to the Council, *see* Case 27/76, United Brands v. Commission, [1978] E.C.R. 207 at ¶ 65; Case 85/76, Hoffmann-LaRoche v. Commission, [1979] E.C.R. 461 at ¶ 38–39.

18. *Supra* note 16, at Article 1(3).

19. Article 85(3) of the EEC Treaty permits the nonapplication of Article 85(1) to an otherwise prohibited agreement, decision, or concerted practice *. . . which contributes to improving the production or distribution of goods or to promoting technical or economic progress, while allowing consumers a fair share of the resulting benefit, and which does not:*
    (a) impose on the undertakings concerned restrictions which are not indispensable to the attainment of these objectives;
    (b) afford such undertakings the possibility of eliminating competition in respect of a substantial part of the products in question.

20. *Supra* note 16, at Article 1(2).

21. *See also* the definition of control under the ECSC Treaty, Decision No. 24–54, O.J. Eur. Comm. 345 (1954).

22. Article 2, *Proposal for a Resolution of the Council on the Control of Concentration Between Undertakings,* 16 O.J. Eur. Comm. (No. C 92) 3 (1973).

23. *See also* U.K. Fair Trading Act 1973, c. 41 § 74.

24. O.J. Eur. Comm. (No. L 13) 204 (1962).

25. O.J. Eur. Comm. (No. L 175) 1 (1968).

26. United Brands v. Commission, [1978] E.C.R. 207; Hoffmann-LaRoche v. Commission, [1979] E.C.R. 461.

27. EEC Commission, Seventh Report on Competition Policy 57 (1978).

28. [1972–1973] Eur. Parl. Doc. (No. 263) 73 (1973) (Amer.).

29. OECD, *Fusions et Politique de Concurrence* at 48–49 (1974).

30. Markert, *EEC Competition Policy in Relation to Mergers,* 20 Antitrust Bull. 107, 119 (1975); Lyon-Caen, *Le controle des concentrations: etude de la loi française et de la proposition européenne,* 15 Rev. Trim. Droit Eur. 1 (1979).

31. Doc. SEC (65) 3500 of December 1, 1965.

32. Joined Cases 56 and 58/64, Costen & Grundig v. Commission, [1966] E.C.R. 299, 348.

33. The Commission also said that it would be difficult to draw a clear and complete line of demarcation between concentrations and restrictive agreements. However, Article 85 would apply where two economically independent enterprises continue to exist after the transaction is completed; therefore, in the case of joint ventures, Article 85 would apply.

34. *See, e.g.,* A REVIEW OF MONOPOLIES AND MERGERS POLICY, Cmnd. No. 7198 ¶¶ 1.14, 5.9–5.22 (1978). In recent years Ireland and France have enacted legislation providing for merger control and the U.K. and Germany have strengthened their laws on the subject. For further consideration of these issues, *see* Stockmann, *Reflections on Recent OECD Activities: Regulation of Multinational Corporate Conduct and Structure, post.*

35. Case 26/76, Metro-Grossmarkte v. Commission, [1977] E.C.R. 1875 at ¶ 43.

36. Ritter & Overbury, *An Attempt at a Practical Approach to Joint Ventures under the EEC Rules on Competition,* 14 COMMON MKT. L. REV. 601, 620–21 (1977); Temple Lang, *Joint Ventures under the EEC Treaty Rules on Competition,* 12 IR. JUR. 15, 34–36 (1977).

Article 3 of the draft merger regulation expressly provides that a Commission decision that a concentration or proposed concentration is not permissible under the regulation "shall not automatically render null and void the legal transactions relating to such operation" and gives the Commission power to order divestiture or any other action that may be appropriate in order to restore conditions of effective competition.

37. MESTMÄCKER, EUROPAISCHES WETTBEWERBSRECHT §§ 30 (IV), 33 (1974).

38. Continental Can, [1973] E.C.R. 215 at ¶ 25; Commercial Solvents, [1974] E.C.R. 223 at ¶ 25; United Brands, [1978] E.C.R. 207 at ¶¶ 63–65; Hoffmann-LaRoche, [1979] E.C.R. 461 at ¶¶ 38, 125, 132.

39. Continental Can, [1973] E.C.R. 215 at ¶¶ 25, 21, and 24, respectively.

40. *C.f.* Case 26/76, Metro-Grossmarkte v. Commission, [1977] E.C.R. 1875. *See also* Temple Lang, *The Position of Third Parties in EEC Competition Cases,* 3 EUROP. L. REV. 177 (1978).

41. Continental Can, [1973] E.C.R. 215 at ¶¶ 25–26.

42. EEC COMMISSION, SIXTH REPORT ON COMPETITION POLICY (1977) ¶ 55. *See,* Temple Lang, *Joint Ventures Under the EEC Rules on Competition,* 13 IR. JUR. 132 (1978).

43. EEC COMMISSION, SIXTH REPORT ON COMPETITION POLICY (1977), ¶ 38.

44. Continental Can, [1973] E.C.R. 215 at ¶¶ 21, 26, 27.

45. Case 8/72, Cementhandelaren v. Commission, [1972] E.C.R. 977, 989–90; Case 71/74, FRUBO v. Commission, [1975] E.C.R. 563, 583.

46. Case 5/69, Volk v. Vervaecke, [1969] E.C.R. 295; Case 23/67, Brasserie de Haecht v. Wilkin, [1967] E.C.R. 407.

47. Temple Lang, *supra* note 36, at 19–22.

48. *See* Commission decisions in Bayer-Gist Brocades, 19 O.J. EUR. COMM. (no. L 30) 13 (1976); Kali und Salz, 17 O.J. EUR. COMM. (No. L 19) 24 (1974); IFTRA Aluminum, 18 O.J. EUR. COMM. (No. 228) e, 8 (1975); Henkel Colgate, 15 O.J. EUR. COMM. (No. L 14) 14 (1972); Laval Stork, 20 O.J. EUR. COMM. (No. L 215) 11 (1977); Vacuum Interrupters, 20 O.J. EUR. COMM. (No. L 48) 32 (1977); GEC-Weir Sodium Circulators, 20 O.J. EUR. COMM. (No. L 327) 26 (1977); ICI-Montedison [1977] E.C. BULL. No. 7/8, at 30–32; WANO-ICI Blackpowder, 21 O.J. EUR. COMM.

(No. L 322) 26 (1978); Floral, O.J. Eur. Comm. (No. L 39) 51 (1980).

49. Commission decision in Kali und Salz, 16 O.J. Eur. Comm. (No. L 217) 3 (1973), *reversed on other grounds*, Cases 19 and 20/74, [1975] E.C.R. 499; ICI-Montedison, [1977] E.C. Bull. No. 7/8, at 32.

50. GEC–Weir Sodium Circulators, 20 O.J. Eur. Comm. (No. L 327) 26, 31 (1977). This is the kind of situation discussed in U.S. v. Penn-Olin Chemical Co., 378 U.S. 158 (1964).

51. Vacuum Interrupters, 20 O.J. Eur. Comm. (No. L 48) 32 (1977).

52. SHV-Chevron, 18 O.J. Eur. Comm. (No. L 38) 14 (1975).

53. WANO-ICI Blackpowder, 21 O.J. Eur. Comm. (No. L 322) 26, 31 (1978).

54. Temple Lang, *supra* note 36, at 33–36.

55. WANO-ICI Blackpowder, 21 O.J. Eur. Comm. (No. L 322) 26 (1978).

56. Referred to by Waelbroeck in 4 Megret, Louis, Vignes & Waelbroeck, Le Droit de la Communauté Economique Européenne 73–74 (1970); *see* Schroter, *Le Concept de Position Dominante dans l'Application des Articles 66 Paragraphe 7 du Traité ECEA et 86 du Traité CEE*, in Regulating the Behavior of Monopolies and Dominant Undertakings in Community Law 434, 456 (Van Damme ed. 1977); Kellogg Co., 83 FTC 1756 (1974); *see* G. Bellamy & G. Child, Common Market Law of Competition 183 (2d ed. 1978); Case 13/60, Geitling v. High Authority, [1962] E.C.R. 83.

57. OECD, Market Power and the Law 90 (1970), based on Case 13/60, Geitling v. High Authority, [1962] E.C.R. 83.

58. Developments in national laws are outlined in the annual reports of the EEC Commission on Competition Policy; *see also* OECD, Fusions et Politique de Concurrence (1974).

59. Case 14/68, [1979] E.C.R. 1, 15, 16–17; *see also* Case 154/77, Procureur du Roi v. Dechmann, [1978] E.C.R. 1573 at ¶ 17.

60. Wilhelm v. Bundeskartellant, [1979] E.C.R. 1, 14–15; *see also* cases 255/78, 1–3/79, 37/79, and 99/79, Guerlain and others, judgments dated July 10, 1980.

61. Markert, *supra* note 30, at 136, says that if national law calls for the prohibition of a merger exempted under Article 1(3) of the proposed merger regulation, "the prevailing view is that such a prohibition would be in conflict with EEC law."

It should be noted that because Article 86 requires the abuse of a dominant position "within the common market or in a substantial part of it," a problem arises where a proposed merger would be anticompetitive in a national context, but likely to increase competition, at least in the long run, in the European Community. It is probable that the Commission would approve such a merger, provided there is adequate proof of the procompetitive effects.

62. Markert, *supra* note 30, at 136–38.

63. *See Broad Lines of a Competition Policy on Structures of the Steel Industry*, 13 O.J. Eur. Comm. (No. C 12) 5 (1970).

64. Report of the Committee on Economic & Monetary Affairs, [1973–1974] Eur. Parl. Doc. (No. 362) 73 (1974).

65. *Id.* The Committee on Economic and Monetary Affairs of the European Parliament recommended that this should be said expressly in the regulation.

Any demonstrable procompetitive effects on the world market of mergers within the Community might need to be considered. It is necessary when determining the competitive level of a particular market to take account of potential competition from extra-Community sources. Also, if a merger of two Community corporations would facilitate their joint penetration of, for example, the Japanese market, thus providing a substantial net benefit to the Community, that factor should be considered, even though such a merger might appear to diminish competition looking only in the Community market.

66. This policy consideration would not apply to a merger between a corporation based outside the Community and a corporation based in the Community. Insofar as such a merger might increase the competitive position of the Community-based corporation and thus increase competition (and so perhaps economic integration) within the Community, this might need to be taken into account.

67. Consten & Grundig v. Commission, [1966] E.C.R. 299, 348.

68. *See* Markert, *supra* note 30, at 117.

69. Camera Care v. Commission, Order of 24 January 1980, [1980] E.C.R. 119.

70. *See, e.g.,* the United Brands and Hoffmann-LaRoche cases, *supra* note 17.

71. *See* United Brands v. Commission, [1978] E.C.R. 207, 276–85.

72. *See* ECSC Treaty, Article 66.

Canadian Merger Policy and Its International Implications

ERIC K. GRESSMAN

The implications of Canadian merger policy are of deep concern to U.S. and other foreign investors who have invested or are considering investing in Canada. U.S. interests own 60 percent of Canada's manufacturing industry.[1] In 1978, approximately 250 mergers in Canada involved a foreign-owned or foreign-controlled buyer (usually U.S.).[2] Therefore, it is not surprising that Canada's merger policy is no less important to the decisions of foreign investors in Canada than the Justice Department's policies are to domestic investors in the United States. At the same time, the Canadian government and public are concerned with their merger policy as a means of regulating foreign acquisitions that affect the economic well-being of Canada.

Canadian merger policy is also important to explain the past and future trends of U.S. investment in Canadian industries, the effects of foreign investment in Canada, and the response of Canadian authorities to transnational corporate concentration within their economy.

This article is divided into four sections: (1) the pre-1970 history of Canadian merger policy, (2) the development of Canadian merger policy during the 1970s, (3) the international ramifications of early and recent Canadian merger policy, and (4) the future changes in Canadian merger policy and their probable effects.

THE HISTORY OF CANADIAN MERGER POLICY: 1889–1969

Canadian Anti-merger Legislation

Despite the importance of policies generated by the Crown and the courts, a study of Canadian merger policy must begin with an examination of Canada's antitrust statutes. The statutory language prescribes the limits within which Canadian judges and prosecutors can act. In contrast to the U.S. experience,[3] the impetus for the original antitrust legislation in Canada

Eric K. Gressman is a member of the class of 1981, University of Michigan Law School.

came from small businessmen rather than from the general populace. In the late nineteenth century, Conservatives felt pressure from powerful agricultural interests that were angry over the rising prices of farm implements, which they viewed as a result of the domination of the farm implement industry by a few combines. In response, the Conservatives attempted to show their concern about the inflationary economic conditions brought on by combines.[4] Acting without government support, Clarke Wallace, a Conservative member of Parliament, proposed the creation of a Select Committee to examine the practices of combines. Parliament agreed to the proposal and appointed Wallace to head the "Committee to Investigate and Report upon Alleged Combines in Manufacturers, Trade and Insurance" (the Committee). The Committee found that the evils caused by combines justified some form of legislation,[5] but only mildly condemned the actual combines investigated. The Committee demonstrated more concern over nonmembers of combines than in protecting consumers.[6] Subsequently, Wallace introduced a bill which met opposition from powerful business interests.[7] When the Senate received the bill for approval, it weakened its provisions by inserting the condition that competition be "unduly" limited and prices be "unreasonably" raised.[8] Though Wallace and his followers opposed these changes, they decided that a compromise bill was better than none at all, and although the statute did not specifically mention mergers, it did set the tone for all future merger legislation during this period. Perhaps the provision of S.C. 1889 relating to sanctions is most significant. The 1889 Act provided only for criminal penalties, in part because legislators felt civil penalties might be unconstitutional.[9] Criminal sanctions remain at the core of Canadian antitrust law.

The deterrent value of the legislation's misdemeanor sanctions is inconsiderable when compared to the treble damage sanction found in U.S. antitrust laws. Moreover, Canadian criminal law's burden of proof further depletes the government's arsenal against anticompetitive practices. The Crown must prove beyond a reasonable doubt that the defendant violated the statute. This burden favors the defendant far more than the preponderance of the evidence standard applicable to civil cases.

In addition to the statute's heavy burden of proof, enforcement under the combines laws must meet the requirements of *mens rea* and strict construction. The *mens rea* standard increases the burden placed upon the Crown and renders conviction more difficult.[10] Should the combines laws be reformed, legislation sufficiently specific to meet the standard of strict construction of criminal statutes must be implemented.

Aside from limiting antitrust actions to criminal prosecutions, the statute favors alleged violators by requiring proof that defendants have conspired, combined, agreed or arranged "unlawfully" to restrain trade, limit production, and so forth. The 1889 Act thus implies that corporations could engage in anticompetitive practices lawfully. In this respect, the Canadian statute is in sharp contrast to Section 1 of the Sherman Act, which provides that "[e]very combination in the form of trust or otherwise, in restraint of trade . . . is . . . *illegal* " [emphasis added].[11] The Sherman Act on its face thus leaves corporations less room than the Canadian anticombines act to argue that their anticompetitive practices are somehow legal.

Finally, the defendant is favored by the requirement that a combination must "unduly" limit production or lessen competition to be unlawful. The government must prove substantial detriment to competition. This provision provides the basis for arguments over the effect of a combination.[12]

During the first decade of the twentieth century a merger boom occurred in Canada, and the public and press began to connect mergers with the rising cost of living. In response to public agitation over the perceived economic consequences of mergers, Liberal Prime Minister Laurier and his assistant, MacKenzie King, proposed legislation with primarily investigative and publicity provisions. The 1910 Act was the first attempt to establish the necessary administrative machinery at the federal level to enforce the anticombines laws. Although the government attorneys in the provinces had authority before 1910 to prosecute corporations,[13] these attorneys placed a low priority on prosecuting white-collar crime, and none of the companies responsible for the forty-seven mergers occurring from 1900–1909 were prosecuted.[14]

The statute, known as the Combines Investigation Act of 1910, provided that if six or more Canadian residents made an application, a judge would arrange a meeting between the complainants and the defendants. Following the meeting, the judge could order an investigation, demand more information before proceeding, or refuse to investigate. If the judge decided to investigate, the minister of labor would be informed, and an ad hoc board would be appointed. If an investigation found the defendants guilty of a violation,[15] penalties, set at a maximum fine of $1000 a day and restricted to conduct occurring after the report is filed, were imposed. Moreover, the 1910 Act relied upon publicity as an official sanction of the government. The investigation report, upon which a violation would be founded, could also be published in the *Gazette* for public dissemination.

Although Parliament included mergers within the definition of combines, King emphasized that the 1910 Act was not an attempt to legislate against mergers. Aside from more specific language concerning mergers and the penalty provision, the 1910 Act was similar to that of 1889.[16] In retrospect, the 1910 Act was ineffective in controlling concentration because there was no permanent machinery to enforce the board's decisions and citizens were reluctant to come forward to complain.[17] Attorneys in the provinces were similarly ineffective. Of 160 Canadian mergers occuring from 1910 to 1922, none were prosecuted.[18]

In response to the continued high cost of living after World War I, Parliament passed the Combines and Fair Prices Act as well as the Board of Commerce Act. In doing so it set up the Board of Commerce (Board), and gave it investigatory and judicial powers.[19] In 1921, after the Supreme Court of Canada split upon the question of the Board's constitutionality, the Privy Council declared the statute to be *ultra vires*, characterizing the Board of Commerce Act as emergency economic legislation which was no longer applicable or necessary.[20]

In 1923, MacKenzie King, now prime minister, helped pass the new Combines Investigation Act (Combines Act). This act essentially continued the policies of the 1910 legislation, but imposed new penalties and simplified administrative procedures. Under this legislation the process of forming a combine became an offense if it "operate[d] to the detriment or against the interest of the public."[21] However, the prime minister and most of Parliament maintained the view that mergers normally are beneficial to business and public.[22] By 1934, the newly elected Conservative government could not ignore pressure for further legislation against corporate combinations. The Dominion Trade and Industry Act established a commission to administer the Combines Investigation Act. The Combines Act also permitted the government to control prices and production of all industries, but gave the Commission power to veto such control.[23]

What may ultimately be the most important amendment to the merger provisions of the Combines Act, one that has been retained in present Canadian merger law, occurred in 1935.[24] Parliament declared a merger to be illegal where it " . . . has operated or is likely to operate to the detriment or against the interest of the public, whether consumers, producers or others."[25] The 1935 amendment created a heavy burden of proof upon the government and has recently been interpreted as affording a defense to the charge of illegal merger.[26] In 1946, Parliament added an amendment to the Combines Act that "restored . . . a provision enabling the commissioner to proceed on his own initiative with an inquiry to determine whether a combine exists or is being formed."[27]

This series of legislative enactments succeeded in establishing an administrative machinery for investigation; however, prior to World War II the Commission was greatly weakened by the lack of sufficient staff. The commissioner never had more than one or two professional assistants and some clerical staff during the prewar periods. Expenditures were at a maximum of $62,000 in 1940; however, $38,000 was used for legal fees and only $24,000 to cover the activities of the commissioner.[28] From 1923 to 1940, only twenty reports were made, and only sixteen were published—an average of one per year.[29] None of these reports concerned mergers. Only one merging corporation was prosecuted during this period, and it was not convicted.[30]

From 1940 to 1949, thirteen reports were published. Expenditures reached a high of $169,000 in 1949 of which $65,000 went to legal fees and $86,000 to salaries.[31] Of the reports, four concerned distribution of goods, two covered contractors' activities, and seven reported on combines among manufacturers.[32] After the war, a study of international cartels in manufacturing was published. Large manufacturing firms thus became much more conspicuous among those investigated than before World War II.

The Combines Act was further amended to provide for appointment of deputy commissioners and to give such commissioners the power to gather information and produce studies on monopolistic .conditions in Canada. Other amendments designed to facilitate prosecutions provided that in combines prosecutions, corporations would not have the option of trial by jury.

During the 1940s, the commissioner of the Combines Branch had authority to enter premises, search for documents, subpoena witnesses, and issue a report with or without government support. Businessmen claimed that the commissioner acted as detective, prosecutor, judge, and sentencer by publishing the report.[33] The fact remains, however, the commissioner was hampered by a lack of funds and staff. No Ph.D. economists were Combines Branch employees until 1949.

Because of the complaints about inadequate administration of the anti-combines act, the government appointed the MacQuarrie Committee (Committee). The Committee recommended division of the functions of the commissioner into investigation and research agencies. The Committee also called for more use of empirical studies.[34] Enacting only some of the Mac-Quarrie Committee's recommendations, the Parliament in 1952 divided the Combines Branch into the Director of Investigation and Research and the Restrictive Trade Practices Commission (RTPC).

The role of the Commission was to examine evidence presented to it by the head of the Director of Investigation and Research and by the parties injured by an alleged violation. The director of the Commission would then issue a report. Legislators felt that mere publication of this report would provide a deterrent effect and that the Commission could appraise the effect of the practices (for example, heavy conglomerate merger activity in a certain industry) upon the public interest.[35] In practice, the director's inquiries were mainly the result of informal complaints or newspaper reports. During the 1950s, the Combines Branch examined 815 complaints and submitted thirty-one reports to the minister. Unlike the U.S.'s FTC, there was no requirement that all cases be disposed of by written ruling, and the director and minister had great discretion in dropping cases.[36]

The 1951–52 amendments added the judicial remedy of dissolution to the merger and monopoly provisions. An order of dissolution could be issued even without a formal conviction, if the court found that an act constituting or leading to an offense was likely to occur.[37] Despite the detailed procedures for investigation of combines that was established under the 1950s legislative enactments, the Commission remained handicapped in several ways. Until 1959 the Commission's permanent staff consisted only of clerical personnel. Its reports were often ignored by the Canadian press. Until 1957, the Commission sent a summary of published reports to the press, libraries, and both houses of Parliament. Only five summary reports were published, charging corporations in various industries with merging and monopolizing illegally. Though no action was taken by the minister on these charges, the government at least signalled businessmen that it now regarded illegal mergers as worthy of investigation as price-fixing or resale price maintenance.[38] However, since 1957, the Commission has only released a notice that a report has been published.

Moreover, under the established procedures, issuance of the report ended the job of the RTPC. The decision whether or not to prosecute a corporation became a political or policy decision residing with the minister of justice. After consulting an outside attorney, the minister could decide to prosecute, normally appointing the lawyer that recommended prosecution to try the case. However, if the corporation terminated its practice after the minister's decision to prosecute, the case was usually dropped. The threat of prosecution thus became an important deterrent to the continued existence of an anticompetitive merger.[39]

The government in 1960 appeased business by enacting legislation which separated mergers and monopolies from the rest of the Combines Act. The 1960 amendments were perceived as weakening " . . . the chances of proceeding against mergers . . ."[40] From 1960 to 1969, nine charges of illegal merger were leveled at companies of various industries. Some of the investigations into these mergers were dropped because corporations decided to forego the merger rather than face prosecution. In 1965, however, the government issued an order of prohibition against a merger in the weed killer industry.[41] In addition, corporations were fined $40,000 in 1966 for a merger in the chemicals industry, and in 1967 a merger was prohibited in the iron industry.[42] Although many commentators accused the government of practicing a weak policy toward mergers, [43] the Combines Branch did demonstrate, considering its limited resources, that prohibition of illegal mergers was a top priority. During the 1960s, the number of investigations into charges of merger was greater than the number of price discrimination investigations, and almost as great as the number of resale price maintenance investigations.[44] In retrospect, although Canada was one of the first to legislate against combines, until the 1970s investigation and enforcement under the statutes have been minimal.

The Policies of the Courts: 1889–1960

In the first eighty years of judicial interpretation, the courts developed important statutory and constitutional doctrines applicable to the Combines Act. These doctrines were to provide the basis for the startling case law developments concerning mergers during the 1970s.

The British North American (B.N.A.) Act, originally passed by England's Parliament, established the Canadian constitution and distributed powers between the federal and provincial governments. Three grants of powers could conceivably support federal anticombines legislation. The B.N.A. Act provided the federal government with the general power to "make laws for the peace, good order and good government of Canada."[45] In addition, the power to regulate trade and commerce could provide authority for passage of a federal merger law. Finally, the federal government had authority over criminal law which earlier was used to justify all Canadian merger law. The primary areas of provincial sovereignty are property, civil rights, and matters of a local or private nature.[46]

Since 1889, the courts have consistently upheld the federal combines law solely on the basis of criminal law powers. In cases as early as 1881 the courts restricted the general trade and commerce power to international and interprovincial trade and general trade affecting the entire country.[47] Each time Parliament tried to move away from purely criminal restrictions in the antitrust field, its actions were nullified by the courts. In 1921 the Privy Council held in *In Re the Board of Commerce Act, 1919 and the Combines and Fair Prices Act, 1919*[48] that the Board of Commerce Act, which empowered a board analogous to the U.S. FTC to investigate the restraint of monopolies and mergers, fell beyond the constitutional authority of the federal government.

The Privy Council reiterated its opposition to any development of Canadian administrative remedies to combines violations in 1934, in *O'Connor v. Walden*.[49] The Judicial Committee of the Privy Council emphasized that the Commission at the Combines Branch had no constitutional authority to determine the legal rights of parties involved before it. The Privy Council regarded the Commission as a purely administrative tribunal whose reports had no legal significance. More recently, Justice Judson of Canada's Supreme Court in *Canadian Fishing Co. v. Smith*[50] emphasized in a dissenting opinion that the holding of *O'Connor* was still valid.

Thus, in the constitutional area at least, the courts were a reactionary force during this early period. Whenever a Canadian court confronted the prospect of the development of an administrative tribunal similar to the FTC, it severely limited the tribunal's powers. Legislators did not propose extension of a private right of action in merger legislation fearing such amendments would be held unconstitutional.[51] Therefore, the legislative enactments over this period only added more administrative machinery and penalties, but did not expand the scope of enforcement.

In the period prior to 1960, the courts increased the Crown's burden of proof in merger cases beyond that which appeared on the face of the statute. What emerged from the government's losses in the courts was the unstated rule that the government had to prove the existence of a virtual monopoly in order to win a merger case. In *Rex v. Canadian Import Company*,[52] the government prosecuted a dealer of coal and coke in Quebec who had acquired all other such dealers in the area. The court acquitted the defendants of the charges, finding that the government had not proved sufficient detriment to competition. In *Rex v. Staples*,[53] the court found that control of 50 percent of an industry was insufficient to establish control detrimental to the public.

The government's only successful case during this period came in 1953 in *Rex v. Eddy Match Co.*[54] In *Eddy Match*, the government coupled its merger charges with charges of monopolization and monopoly. From 1927 to

1950 Eddy had a monopoly maintained by predatory practices, followed by acquisition of new entrants. The court held that in a case with such a long history of monopoly, merger with new entrants was detrimental to the public.

Eddy Match did not lead to rulings favorable to the government in merger cases involving concentrated industries. In *Regina v. Canadian Breweries Ltd.*,[55] the Ontario Supreme Court reviewed the legality of a merger which substantially increased the concentration of the beer industry. The defendant brewery had gained control of thirty-seven other breweries in Ontario over a 30-year period. Though the defendant held 61 percent of the market, while Molson and Labatts together held 34 percent, the court failed to consider whether or not the high concentration of the industry operated to the public's detriment. Ruling for the defendant, Chief Justice McRuer noted that he was bound to favor the defendant in criminal cases because of the reasonable doubt standard, the circumstantial evidence rule, and the rule favoring the defendant in the construction of penal statutes. Thus, in *Canadian Breweries,* the court found that a merger which substantially increased concentration in an already oligopolistic market was not sufficient to convict a defendant of a criminal combines offense.[56]

Aside from requiring proof of a virtual monopoly in merger cases, Canadian cases showed signs of changing the meaning of *public detriment*. Early decisions analyzed a combines case solely in terms of whether the activity reduced competition. The courts assumed that a reduction of competition was *prima facie* detrimental to the public. As early as 1912 the Canadian Supreme Court emphasized that an alleged breach of a combines provision should be analyzed from the point of view of harm to free competition.[57] The Supreme Court, in *Container Materials Ltd. v. The King,*[58] reiterated that the anticombines provisions were enacted for the specific public interest in free competition.

The view that Canadian merger law should be analyzed solely from the perspective of the effect on free competition began to lose some of its force in 1958 when the Supreme Court decided *Howard Smith Paper Mills Ltd. v. The Queen.*[59] In that case the appellants argued that their admittedly anticompetitive actions were designed to preserve a dying industry. The majority held that the public had a right to free competition and appellants would not be heard to argue that anticompetitive acts promote the public interests. However, in an important dissent, Justice Cartwright indicated that if the appellants had proved the alleged benefit to the public, he would have had some difficulty affirming the conviction.[60]

Fearing that Justice Cartwright's view would gain majority support in the Supreme Court, Parliament deleted the portions of the conspiracy provision of the anticombines statute that required a showing of detriment to the public. However, Parliament retained the *detriment* language in the merger and monopoly provisions.[61] This apparent oversight allowed the Supreme Court in the 1970s to utilize Cartwright's position to destroy much of the merger provision's force.[62]

RECENT DEVELOPMENTS IN CANADIAN MERGER POLICY

Legislative Developments in the 1970s

Both the proposed and enacted statutes of the 1970s concerning Canadian antitrust law in general, and merger law in particular, were radically different from those enacted in the previous eight years. From 1889 to 1969, Parliament's amendments to the anticombines law were only moderate adjustments.[63] On the other hand, the reforms of the 1970s, resulting in the passage of Foreign Investment Review Act of 1974 (FIRA), constituted fundamental changes in the justifications for, and the approach of, the combines law.

In 1966, responding to the concern of the populace over the increasing concentration of Canadian industries, the government requested that the Economic Council (Council) prepare a report on competition policy.[64] The Council's *Interim Report on Competition Policy*, published in 1969, stated that the prime purpose of competition law was the promotion of economic efficiency. The Council felt that some practices, such as price-fixing, market-sharing, and resale price maintenance, were inimical to the public interest, and should invariably be prohibited. The Council also believed that mergers and monopolies should not be dealt with as criminal offenses. The report's rationale was that criminal law set up too onerous a burden of proof upon a government attempting to prevent a harmful merger. The report went so far as to declare that courts were improper forums for deciding whether to prohibit a merger. Instead, the Council recommended the formation of an expert tribunal. Such a tribunal would allow mergers bringing about cost savings, but would prohibit mergers increasing the market power of the defendants to the disadvantage of the consumer. The feeling was that an expert tribunal could weigh the economic costs and benefits of a merger better than a criminal court. The Council thus adopted Justice Cartwright's position in *Howard Smith Paper Mills* that mergers should not be analyzed solely for their effect on free competition.[65] At the same time, the Council went beyond the Justice's opinion by conferring jurisdiction upon a quasi-judicial tribunal to make these economic judgments.

The report's concept of splitting combines cases into criminal and economic tribunals according to the nature of the offense became the cornerstone of the government's proposals to Parliament in the 1970s. Agreeing with the report, the government perceived the purpose of competition law as a means of achieving efficiency.[66] The government also stood to gain the political support of small businessmen for any reform that lessened the market power of the large foreign and domestic conglomerates.[67]

Despite the report's theoretical soundness, the government realized that it stood on shaky constitutional grounds. To create an expert tribunal to oversee monopolies and mergers, the federal government of Canada had two options. It could seek to change the constitution to expand the trade

and commerce power. However, changing the constitution is always difficult because provincial authorities, fearful of an assault on their sovereignty, are likely to oppose any expansion of federal power. The other option
was to refer the legislation to the Supreme Court to see whether the establishment of such a tribunal fell within the federal powers specified in the
B.N.A. Act. Some recent cases indicated that the Supreme Court might
uphold the constitutionality of a quasi-judicial tribunal,[68] but the possibility
that the Court would reach the opposite result in this instance could not be
disregarded.

In spite of these constitutional problems, the federal government in 1971
sought, without success, passage of a bill that would have adopted the Council's recommendations.[69] The bill provided that criminal procedures were
applicable only to per se offenses such as price-fixing. It also required registration with a competitive practices tribunal for all mergers involving gross
assets greater than $5 million or a foreign acquiring firm. The tribunal was
empowered to prohibit or dissolve a merger when it would engender significantly less competition.

In evaluating a foreign takeover, the tribunal was instructed to examine
whether the merger was likely to (1) extend the market power of the merged
firm in Canada, (2) extend the influence of an international cartel or oligopoly into Canada, or (3) restrict production or exports from Canada.

In the face of intense criticism of the 1971 proposed bill, especially from
large business interests, the government decided to redraft and resubmit it in
two phases. A revised version comprising the first phase became law at the
end of 1975.[70]

The new legislation abandoned the concept that certain anticompetitive
practices were per se offenses. It further pleased big business by retaining
the language of "undueness" and "unreasonableness" in proscribing trade
restraints. However, the bill stated that an agreement can be undue even if
the parties do not control virtually the entire relevant market.

Two major reforms instituted by the 1975 legislation signalled a commitment to more vigorous enforcement of anticombines laws. The act included
provisions for a private right of action for damages resulting from a violation
of the combines laws, although this was not extended to merger or monopoly
violations. Another fundamental reform was the provision that the breach of
an order issued by the Restrictive Trade Practices Commission constituted a
violation of the 1975 Act. Any person injured by the breach was given a
private right of action against the violator.[71]

Some of the most controversial provisions of the government's legislation
were reserved for the second phase of the legislation.[72] Big business zealously
opposed governmental regulation of mergers, monopolization, and volume
discounts, and, as a result, the second bill was not passed. Whether a new
version of that bill is reintroduced will depend upon political developments.[73]
Nevertheless, an examination of the contents of the proposed 1977 legislation is worthwhile, not only because it ultimately may be enacted, but also

because it reflects the new attitudes of the government and much of the Parliament toward changes in the merger laws.

Under the proposed amendments, the Competition Board (Board) is substituted for the Restrictive Trade Practices Commission. Consisting of five to seven permanent members, the Board has as its main objective the examination of trade practices referred to it. The Board can examine mergers and monopolies as well as trade practices specified in the Stage I amendments. Mergers and monopolies under the bill are not criminal offenses, but a court can impose criminal sanctions for violation of the Board's remedial orders.[74]

The proposed legislation would also replace the previous director of investigation and research with the competition policy advocate. The Canadian cabinet appoints the advocate and the deputy competition policy advocates. The advocate's functions are essentially the same as those of the director,[75] but his quasi-judicial responsibilities include investigation of a greater number of practices that are reviewable by the Competition Board. The advocate also has a more active role in presenting the government's position before various administrative bodies.[76]

Violation of the merger provisions of the 1975 Act would no longer be considered a criminal offense under the proposed law. Instead of requiring proof beyond a reasonable doubt of detriment to the public, a burden of proof never overcome by the Crown in contested prosecutions, the bill substitutes the Board's review on the "preponderance of the evidence" standard. The Board can, if the advocate meets this standard, prohibit or dissolve a merger if it substantially lessens competition.[77]

The proposed legislation also addresses the coordination of review of mergers under the combines statute with review of mergers under the Foreign Investment Review Act, enacted in 1974.[78] To understand this portion of the bill's provisions, one must first comprehend the details of the Foreign Investment Review Act.

In response to public concern about the control of Canadian industries by foreign firms, the Canadian government sponsored a study of foreign investments. As a result of this study, Herb Gray, the minister of revenue, wrote a report entitled *Foreign Direct Investment in Canada*.[79] The Gray Report, although noting the advantages of importing capital and technology, warned against the dangers of increasing dependence on the United States. The report recommended the establishment of a screening agency to review the operations and investment of foreign-owned firms. The Gray Report led the government to introduce a bill in Parliament to control foreign direct investments and new takeovers by foreign-owned firms. Following the election of the Trudeau government, Parliament enacted the Foreign Investment Review Act on April 9, 1974.

In general, the FIRA provides that no foreign person or foreign enterprise can "take over an existing Canadian business, or . . . establish a new Canadian business unrelated to any of its existing Canadian businesses, without first receiving the approval of the government of Canada."[80] The criteria used by the cabinet to decide whether to allow a foreign takeover or direct investment is whether the investment "is or is likely to be of significant benefit to Canada."[81] This criterion is a significant switch from that used by the old combines laws, which disallow mergers by a foreign or domestic acquirer only if they are "of significant detriment to the public."

Section 2(2) of the Foreign Investment Review Act enumerates five factors the cabinet should consider in deciding whether the merger or investment is "of significant benefit to Canada." These are:

(a) the effect of the acquisition or establishment on the level and nature of economic activity in Canada, including, without limiting the generality of the foregoing, the effect on employment, on resource processing, on the utilization of parts, components and services produced in Canada, and on exports from Canada;

(b) the degree and significance of participation by Canadians in the business enterprise or new business and in any industry or industries in Canada of which the business enterprise or new business forms or would form a part;

(c) the effect of the acquisition or establishment on productivity, industrial efficiency, technological development, product innovation and product variety in Canada;

(d) the effect of the acquisition or establishment on competition within any industry or industries in Canada; and

(e) the compatibility of the acquisition or establishment with national industrial and economic policies, taking into consideration industrial and economic policy objectives enunciated by the government or legislature of any province likely to be significantly affected by the acquisition or establishment.[82]

The FIRA also designates a procedure for choosing a minister as the administrator of the FIRA, and establishes the Foreign Investment Review Agency (Agency) to "advise and assist the Minister in connection with the administration of the Act."[83] The agency is purely an advisory body. Decisions as to whether to allow an acquisition by a foreign corporation or person remains with the cabinet.

Section 20 of the FIRA contains provisions for enforcement. The government can seek a court order to "render nugatory" a foreign direct investment or acquisition contravening the act. The court can prohibit a shareholder's exercise of voting rights, or require the divestiture of property or shares.[84]

Prior to the passage of FIRA, the federal and provincial governments intervened ad hoc to prevent foreign acquisition of a greater control of Canadian markets. The federal government prevented the foreign acquisition of Denison Mines Ltd. in 1972 and the proposed foreign takeover of Home Oil Company Ltd. in 1972. Occasionally, the provincial governments during the early seventies took steps to prevent foreign acquisitions.[85]

Since the passage of FIRA, the cabinet has approved most of the pro-posed takeovers but has rejected some undesirable acquisitions. In the first year of FIRA's operation, the cabinet allowed thirty-six Canadian-controlled companies to be acquired; three of these companies had assets exceeding $5 million. The primary reason given for disallowing a merger was that it decreased Canadian ownership without sufficient offsetting benefit to Canada.[86]

The inconvenience foreign investors suffer as a result of FIRA may deter some acquirors. Approval by the cabinet of a proposed foreign acquisition rarely occurs within three months of registration with the Agency. Foreign corporations' officers must frequently attend Agency hearings and seek local legal advice. Recently, the Agency has begun to monitor the performance of undertakings by applicants whose investments were allowed. Naturally, some foreign investors would prefer that the government did not scrutinize their activities.[87]

The federal government's commitment to opposing mergers was under-scored by its efforts in the courts. The government secured two convictions of corporations that violated the merger provisions of the combines law in the cases of *Regina v. Electric Reduction Co. of Canada* (the ERCO case)[88] and *Regina v. K. C. Irving Ltd.*,[89] although the decision of the trial court was later overturned by the Supreme Court in *K. C. Irving*.[90] Thus, the government during the 1970s evinced a vigorous opposition to corporate concentration caused by mergers.

The 1977 proposed legislation had attempted to coordinate the efforts of the proposed Competition Board and the Foreign Investment Review Agency. Under the bill, when an acquisition is referred to the Agency for clearance, the Agency must advise the advocate of such application, after which the advocate has fifty days to proceed against the merger in question.[91]

The Courts' Policies During the 1970s

Although the courts have not directly ruled on the constitutionality of the new legislation, there are indications that they would uphold the use of the trade and commerce power to justify the establishment of federal quasi-judicial tribunals and agencies to review the legality of mergers. Courts dur-ing this era broadly interpreted the federal government's authority over inter-provincial and international trade. In *Burns Foods Ltd. v. Attorney General*,[92] the court upheld federal government direct regulation of commerce that affected interprovincial trade. In 1972, the year before *Burns Foods*, Chief Justice Jackett of the Federal Court of Appeals broadly interpreted the gen-eral trade and commerce power to uphold federal regulation of general busi-ness standards in *Vapor Canada Ltd. v. McDonald*.[93]

Aside from enunciating a liberal interpretation of federal powers under the British North American Act, the lower courts have accepted federal power to enforce the merger cases. The dispositions of *Regina v. Electric*

Reduction Co. of Canada[94] and *Regina v. K. C. Irving Ltd.*[95] indicate that the government can win merger cases in the lower courts.

In the *ERCO* case, the corporate defendant pleaded guilty to a merger charge, even though no company had ever before been convicted of a merger offense when the charge was contested. From 1956 to 1966, ERCO was the sole producer of industrial phosphates in Canada. In May 1959, ERCO purchased Dominion Fertilizers, a new entrant into the industrial phosphate market. ERCO also entered into reciprocal agreements with C.I.L. and Cyanimid under which both firms agreed not to enter the industrial phosphates market. ERCO apparently decided that the government could obtain convictions for these offenses if a trial were held, and therefore pleaded guilty.

In *K. C. Irving*, the government convinced a trial court that a company had violated the merger provisions of the Combines Act. K. C. Irving, over a period of several years, acquired all five English-language dailies in New Brunswick. Though the conviction was later overturned,[96] the legitimacy of the government's commitment to preventing mergers it considered illegal, and the perceived competence of the Combines Branch attorneys, was substantially enhanced by the trial court's decision.

The two cases may also have inaugurated a new approach to remedies for violations of the merger laws. This approach emphasizes the use of orders of prohibition rather than fines. Although ERCO was fined a total of $30,000, it was also subjected to an order prohibiting its anticompetitive practices. Realizing the failure of criminal fines as remedies, the court in *ERCO* resorted to a prohibitive order to prevent abuses likely to occur as a result of the merger. Some commentators believe that *ERCO* inaugurated a new conduct-oriented approach to the problem of corporate concentration.[97] If this view is correct, the courts have decided that the criminal remedies are inadequate when applied to merger cases, and that a dissolution of the merger or a prohibitory order preventing abuses of the merger is necessary. This view is consistent with the trial court ruling in *K. C. Irving*, since the court found it necessary to order K. C. Irving to sell both of its Mocton Papers as well as pay a $150,000 fine.

Perhaps the most important ruling of the 1970s was that of the Canadian Supreme Court in *K. C. Irving*, in which the court reinterpreted the "*public detriment*" language of the merger and monopoly provisions. In a unanimous decision, the Supreme Court concluded that, to prevail on a charge of creating an illegal merger or monopoly, the Crown must do more than show that the accused extinguished all independent competition. Referring to cases citing Justice Cartwright's opinion in *Howard Smith Paper Mills Ltd.*,[98] the Canadian Supreme Court held that the Crown must also show that the extinction of competition was, or was likely to be, to the detriment of, or against the interest of, the public. Since there was no finding of fact supporting this part of the merger and monopoly offenses, the Supreme Court dismissed the charges.

Professor Roberts of the University of Western Ontario law faculty asserts that prior to the Supreme Court's ruling in *K. C. Irving,* Parliament, the Economic Council of Canada, the minister of consumer and corporate affairs, economists, and legal scholars all regarded the public detriment elements of the merger and monopoly provisions as relevant only to the extent of injury to the competitive process.[99] According to Roberts, the law before *K. C. Irving* contemplated just one public interest: the public interest in maintaining and encouraging competition. A detriment to the public interest occurs when there exists a real or threatened injury to the competitive process.

Roberts believes that the Supreme Court came to its surprising conclusion because it felt that two premises of the competition laws were inconsistent without the newly established rule in *K. C. Irving.* The merger and monopoly provisions did not contemplate the prohibition of all monopolies. Yet, the prime purpose of competition law is to promote competition. Logically, all monopolies fail to promote competition and should therefore be prohibited. Because the Supreme Court could not square the two premises without invalidating all monopolies and mergers, the Canadian Supreme Court reinterpreted the detriment standard to conform to Justice Cartwright's opinion and thus avoid the logical inconsistencies of the Act.[100]

Roberts labels the *K. C. Irving* decision a disaster to the enforcement of merger laws, because it asks trial courts to act as economists and social scientists. Trial courts under *K. C. Irving* must decide whether the merger or monopoly constitutes an injury to the public interest and whether the injury, if it exists, is outweighed by the social benefits of the merger or monopoly. This would require trial judges to identify and rank countless public policies and then derive and apply the same kind of standards as are applied to detailed public regulation of industry. To be meaningfully applied, the criteria implicit in the *K. C. Irving* decision require continuous supervision of industry.[101]

Though Roberts is probably correct in his assessment of *K. C. Irving* as a blow to the reforms of the merger laws, he overstates his argument by concluding that *K. C. Irving* renders the merger and monopoly laws unenforceable. The *K. C. Irving* ruling would be enforceable if Parliament passed a bill establishing a specialized tribunal capable of analyzing a merger case according to the *K. C. Irving* criteria.[102] In addition, Roberts neglects to analyze the impact of the FIRA. FIRA is not subject to the *K. C. Irving* decision and could in the future constitute a major deterrent to foreign acquisitions.

THE INTERNATIONAL RAMIFICATIONS OF
CANADIAN MERGER POLICIES: 1889–1979

The most discernible effect of Canadian merger policy has been upon the number of foreign acquisitions. A regression analysis would provide a quantitative measure of the effect of weak and strong merger policies on the number of foreign acquisitions. There are difficulties with determining the effect of merger policy through the use of regression analysis. It would be difficult to subject the merger policy variable to regression analysis, since policy is a nebulous notion. One also encounters difficulties determining when a policy begins to become effective. Moreover, policies can be contradictory when one branch of government pursues a course of conduct different from another.

Regressing Canadian merger policies on the number of foreign mergers is thus difficult, though not impossible.[103] The difficulty in this process, however, does not mean that some conclusions concerning the effect of Canadian policies are totally speculative. Policies of one branch are often consistent with those of another. The effect of coordinated policy is easier to perceive since one could connect a weak or strong policy to a change in the number of foreign mergers when all branches adopt the same rather than different policies. Moreover, observers of U.S. merger policy have generally agreed that antitrust laws do have demonstrable effects on business activity. The growth of conglomerates in the United States during the 1960s is often attributed to the application of more per se rules against vertical and horizontal acquisitions.[104] In addition, many cite the Burger Court decisions against the government in antitrust cases as contributing to the merger boom of the mid-1970s.[105]

From 1889 to 1969, the three branches of Canadian government generally followed a consistent policy toward mergers. Thus, one need not worry about evaluating conflicting influences of the courts, legislature, and agencies during the early period. From an examination of the three merger-boom periods, the effect of policy is evident. The greatest expansion of the number of foreign mergers occurred at four times: 1900 to 1913; the 1920s; the late 1950s to the late 1960s; and 1975 to 1978.[106]

In analyzing the merger booms, there is some indication that the number of foreign acquisitions in Canada depended upon the relative development of Canadian and U.S. merger law. The early 1900s witnessed increases in the number of total and foreign mergers in Canada,[107] with the British accounting for most of the foreign acquisitions.

Apparently British investors compared the merger policy positions of the United States and Canada and often found Canada preferable. During this period, merger policy seems to have had an influence. The 1889 Act was still very new and uncertain in application. Moreover, the Canadian government brought no prosecutions against mergers and hence there was no case law on mergers in Canada. In contrast, the United States did have an established antitrust case law. From 1904 to 1911, the Sherman Act was interpreted as prohibiting every contract in restraint of trade.[108] Although the Sherman Act was not directly applied to mergers, it is conceivable that businessmen hesitated to merge in the United States because courts might find the acquisition to be in restraint of trade.

The United States did not experience a merger boom from 1900 to 1913. During this period, the number of U.S. mergers declined significantly.[109] United States and foreign businessmen contemplating a merger may have found Canada a safer legal environment, and this phenomenon fueled the merger boom in Canada. It is interesting to note that the subsequent decline in merger activity coincides with Parliament's passage of the 1910 Act, which included mergers within the definition of combines.[110]

Merger booms occurred in both the United States and Canada during the 1920s. During the 1920s, U.S. investment continued to erode the dominance of British investment in Canada. The high correlation between U.S. and Canadian mergers indicates that decisions to merge in Canada were based on the economic conditions in the United States rather than merger policies. However, Canadian law probably encouraged U.S. firms to merge with companies in Canada. During the 1920s, Canadian antitrust law was in a state of chaos. The temporary nullification of all merger policy by the Canadian Supreme Court in 1921 coincides with the beginning of the merger boom.[111] Americans may have perceived that new legislation on mergers in the 1920s would take time to implement and would be similar to the 1910 Act under which the prosecutors took no action against mergers.[112]

Statistics reveal that the growth of foreign mergers in Canada was more sustained than the increase in mergers in the United States during the 1960s. Canadian merger law probably appeared relatively more attractive than U.S. acquisition law to U.S. and other foreign investors. In the United States, the Warren Court almost always ruled against the defendant in merger cases.[113] The law on mergers was far less developed in Canada than in the United States. The Cellar-Kefauver Amendment to the Clayton Act in the United States strengthened the Justice Department's position against mergers by expanding the jurisdictional reach of Section 7.[114] In contrast, the 1960 amendments to Canadian antitrust law ensured that corporations could merge unmolested by Canadian regulation. Though there was much public debate during the 1960s over the problem of transnational corporate concentration, major reforms did not occur until the 1970s.

The number of foreign acquisitions in Canada grew at an unprecedented rate from 1975 to 1978, though at a slower rate from 1977 to 1978. This occurred in spite of a decline in the number of domestic mergers.

One can devise a number of theories explaining these trends by focusing upon the reaction of foreign investors to the reforms of the 1970s. Perhaps foreigners believed, as did Professor Roberts, that the Canadian Supreme Court in 1975 announced the death of merger policy in *K. C. Irving*.[115] Foreign businessmen may have reasoned that Canadian criminal courts did not have the capacity to convict a corporation of a merger offense using the complex economic criteria specified in *K. C. Irving*. Moreover, the foreign corporations may have decided that the Phase II amendments, which would have set up machinery that could enforce the merger laws according to economic criteria, had no chance of passage since the big business lobby in Canada was vehemently opposed to them. According to this theory, the foreign corporations decided that they could take over Canadian firms without molestation from government authorities.

The above theory ignores the effect of the FIRA on the decision making of foreign corporations. Professor Douglas F. Lamont demonstrates that the anticipation of FIRA and ad hoc intervention of the Crown and provincial governments to prevent foreign acquisitions led to a decline in foreign investment.[116] The decline of foreign mergers in Canada in the early 1970s is consistent with a theory that the first year of FIRA and the ad hoc intervention of Canadian governments induced foreign corporations to look elsewhere. Professor Lamont asserts that U.S. firms from 1970 to 1973 did not choose Canadian firms for acquisitions because of radical change in the investment climate. During this three-year period, the U.S. share of total foreign investment in Canada decreased from 82 percent to 78 percent.[117] The Germans apparently perceived in like manner the new Canadian attitudes toward foreign investment. From 1970 to 1973, the percentage of total foreign investment decreased from 36 percent to 34 percent.[118] According to Lamont, the rate of increase in U.S. foreign investment in Canada slowed during the early 1970s because U.S. corporations decided better opportunities could be found elsewhere.[119]

It was possible that the impact of FIRA would lead to less foreign investment. Certainly the power granted the cabinet under the FIRA could have provided a deterrent to foreign investment. However, the increase in the number of foreign mergers in Canada during the late 1970s indicates that foreign investment via acquisition did not decrease. This phenomenon cannot be explained by comparison with the state of U.S. merger law. The Burger Court during this period almost inevitably held for the defendant in antitrust cases.[120] Firms would probably find the United States a more conducive legal environment for mergers, at least with respect to conglomerate mergers.

There are a number of theories which could explain the recent increase in foreign acquisitions. Foreign corporations may have developed expertise in dealing with the FIRA. In anticipation of FIRA, multinational corporations may have reduced their acquisitions for fear that obtaining government approval would be difficult and costly. As soon as it was clear that the Foreign Investment Review Agency would approve the majority of applications for acquisitions, foreign firms may have decided to apply for as many acquisitions as possible before the Agency became more suspect of foreign takeovers.

A contributing factor to the increase in foreign acquisitions may have been that many of these acquisitions were in service industries outside the jurisdiction of the Agency. The legislature apparently was of the belief that the national interest was threatened less by foreign acquisitions outside the manufacturing and resource industries; moreover, such acquisitions usually involved a small amount of assets. This attitude reflects a Canadian sensitivity to foreign takeover of their natural resources.[121]

Moreover, since coal and rubber industries were already heavily concentrated in foreign hands,[122] much of the foreign investment in the 1970s occurred in other areas. In addition, during the 1970s the Agency demon-

Table 1.
Percentage Distribution of Types of Mergers, Canada and the United States[124]

Country	Type of Merger	Percentage of Total Mergers			
		1945—61	1972	1973	1974
Canada	Broad horizontal	68.25	66.9	68.9	67.7
	Horizontal	40.23			
	Geographic market extension	12.71			
	Product extension	9.71			
	Other	5.60			
	Vertical	22.43	12.3	12.5	9.2
	Conglomerate	9.31	18.8	18.6	23.1
United States		1948–63			
	Broad horizontal	67.02	58.6	56.2	62.9
	Horizontal	23.21			
	Geographic market extension	5.64			
	Product extension	38.17			
	Vertical	19.89	17.2	11.0	4.8
	Conglomerate	12.74	24.1	32.8	32.3

strated a tendency to allow foreign mergers which did not involve a great deal of assets.[123]

Another radical change that occurred in Canada during the 1970s was an increase in the number of conglomerate acquisitions. Table 1 shows the changes in percentages distribution of types of mergers in Canada and the United States.

From table 1, it is apparent that the percentage of broad horizontal mergers has not changed in Canada from the immediate postwar years through the early 1970s. Meanwhile, broad horizontal mergers have declined over the same period in the United States. One of the reasons for the decline in U.S. horizontal mergers is the Supreme Court's application of more stringent rules of illegality to horizontal and vertical mergers.[125] In Canada, the courts did not develop any per se rule against horizontal mergers. Thus, Canada became a safe area for merging with a competitor, and the steady percentage of horizontal mergers throughout these years is not surprising.

In both the U.S. and Canada, vertical mergers decreased throughout the 1970s. The decrease in the United States can be attributed to the per se rules of illegality applied by the Supreme Court to many vertical acquisitions. The decrease in the Canadian percentage may be attributable to the exhaustion of foreign investment opportunities in the mining and natural resource industries. In the earlier period, foreign interests sought control of the natural resources of the industry. By the 1970s foreign manufacturers may have exploited all the possibilities of gaining control of Canada's natural resources and may have sought to expand their markets by merging with a firm in an unrelated industry.

At the same time, FIRA and ad hoc government interaction may have reduced the number of vertical mergers. Foreign manufacturers arguably desire to gain control of the natural resources necessary for the production of their products. If the foreign manufacturers could not merge vertically in their own countries, Canada would be a logical alternative location for such a merger during the immediate postwar era, since the Canadian government was not prohibiting such acquisitions. This theory accounts for the high percentage of vertical mergers from 1945 to 1961. The change in the government's attitude toward foreign acquisitions of natural resources may have triggered a drop in the percentage of vertical mergers during the 1970s.

Finally, conglomerate mergers have been on the rise in both countries. A contributing reason for the increase in percentage of conglomerate mergers in the United States could be that the Supreme Court has not been able to apply traditional market acquisition analysis to conglomerate acquisitions.[126] Merger policy may also have contributed to the rise in conglomerates in Canada. There is no Canadian case law on conglomerate mergers. Furthermore, it is very difficult to prove a lessening of competition from a conglomerate merger. Conglomerate mergers do not alter the number of firms in an industry. One must therefore resort to theories of potential competition to prove a violation. Since Canadian courts have not enunciated a potential competition theory, proof of a violation of the law as a result of a conglomerate merger is exceedingly difficult. This difficulty may have contributed to the increase in the number of foreign conglomerates in Canada.

Aside from altering the number and type of foreign acquisitions in Canada, merger policy or lack of it has not impeded foreign ownership of Canadian industries. As a result of mergers and direct investments, foreign interests in Canada own 95.5 percent of petroleum and coal industries; 93.1 percent of rubber products; 86 percent of the transportation equipment including automobiles; 84 percent of tobacco products; 81 percent of the chemicals industry; and over 50 percent of the machinery and electrical industries.[127] Despite reforms, the merger laws have not prevented this high level of foreign ownership. Such ownership has several important impacts.

Many Canadians of the 1970s view U.S. control as detrimental to their international trade. Many argue that multinational firms use factors of production that are extrememly mobile; such firms would therefore not make decisions solely on the grounds of the most efficient use of Canadian resources.[128] Canadian observers emphasize that foreign firms are ethnocentric and that the host country will tend to end up with fewer economic benefits from the foreign investor. The net result of concentration of industrial control in foreign hands is seen as a less favorable trade balance and fewer collateral benefits such as research and development and management training.[129]

This line of argument is not unassailable. Much of Canada's production must be exported because the home country itself consumes less than half of its products. Canada exports over 50 percent of the goods it produces, whereas large industrial countries consume 80–85 percent of their domestic production.[130] Furthermore, Canada benefits from exposure to the more sophisticated techniques of research and development and management training practiced by some large U.S. firms.

Even if Canadians have a less than fully realistic view of the impact of transnational corporate concentration, their perceptions may be the most important result of such concentration. Canadian scholars have written many volumes concerning their fears of domination by such U.S. firms as Exxon and General Motors.[131] Some fear the rejuvenation of the discredited continental thesis, which asserts that Canada and the United States will merge their respective economies to form one North American market.[132]

These fears can be explained by the recent increase in foreign acquisitions and control of markets. During the 1950s and 1960s, Canadians openly admired the United States, and some called for continentalism.[133] However, throughout the 1970s Canadians became disillusioned with the U.S. presence. Opposition to U.S. investment in Canada was directly correlated with U.S. control of Canadian industry.[134]

Since high foreign investment and acquisition led to discontent among the more densely populated provinces, the federal government became convinced that something had to be done to counter the economic power of U.S. firms in Canada. This conviction led to the passage of FIRA and to various investments undertaken by the government of Canada to prevent foreign acquisitions.[135] Discontent in areas like Ontario led to several investments by provincial governments to counter U.S. acquisitions of Canadian firms.[136]

Because of foreign domination, Canada's economy is subject to some extent to changes in the economies of other countries. On the other hand, Canada benefits in several ways from U.S. domination of industry, such as the advantages of economies of scale achieved by big U.S. firms and cultural exchanges inherent in transnational investment.

PROBABLE FUTURE CHANGES IN CANADA'S MERGER POLICY
AND THEIR EFFECTS

Canadian merger law in the 1980s will in all probability be more aggressive than in the past toward preventing foreign acquisitions. Parliament is unlikely to pass all of what was contained in the proposed 1977 legislation because of the intense business lobby against any regulation of mergers. However, some form of civil legislation dealing with mergers will probably emerge. The government now realizes that application of criminal law to merger violations is inappropriate, particularly in light of the unrealistic standards of review imposed upon criminal courts by *K. C. Irving*. Furthermore, Parliament should feel confident of its constitutional authority to enact such provisions since recent Supreme Court decisions have expanded the federal government's general trade and commerce power.

The federal government in the 1980s will probably seek to enforce anti-merger laws more vigorously, especially against foreign firms. Even if Parliament makes no changes in the merger law, the government has the power under FIRA to prevent most foreign acquisitions. Since nationalism is growing within Canada, the government may feel political pressure to demonstrate its opposition to U.S. domination of Canada's industries, particularly if the increase in foreign acquisitions continues. The government also seems convinced that foreign control of key industries must be curtailed in order to promote economic efficiency.

The courts are probably the only branch of government in Canada that will lack vigor in their policy against mergers in the 1980s. As *K.C. Irving* demonstrated, the Supreme Court is not overly concerned with ensuring that the merger laws are efficiently enforced, because it established standards of review for mergers which could not possibly be applied by lower courts. However, it is unlikely that the Supreme Court, using the recent expansive interpretations of federal powers, would declare a civil law covering mergers unconstitutional.

If Canada does institute a more vigorous policy against foreign acquisitions, the overall number of foreign mergers should decline. But assuming that foreign investors maintain interest in the Canadian market, the number of foreign conglomerate mergers should increase, since foreign corporations would perceive that the Crown has the greatest difficulty proving a lessening of competition in cases involving conglomerate acquisitions. The percentage of horizontal mergers should remain about the same unless the Canadian courts or quasi-judicial tribunals develop per se rules against such mergers, and foreign vertical mergers will probably decline because Canadians fear the control of their natural resources by foreign manufacturers and are likely to enforce vigorously their antitrust laws in this area.

The decline in the level of foreign investment may ultimately lead to a demand for reform of the merger laws to encourage such investment. As stated above, the rise of nationalism and opposition to foreign investment is directly related to the amount of foreign investment. If vigorous merger laws result in a drastic reduction in foreign investment, antagonism toward such investment will wane considerably. Foreign investment in urban areas may become as negligible as it is in rural areas of Canada. In areas of low foreign investment, the people and laws favor foreign investment in order to stimulate their local economy. Eventually, the Canadian populace in urban areas will demand that greater foreign investment be allowed. Thus, ironically, vigorous foreign merger laws may ultimately lead to a call for merger policies favoring foreign investment and acquisitions.

NOTES

1. *Canada's Merger Muddle*, 270 ECONOMIST 80 (1979).
2. *Id.*
3. In the late nineteenth century, the populist and Granger movement in the United States agitated for public control over price-fixing, railroad rebates, and other harmful business practices. In response, Congress created the Interstate Commerce Commission in 1887 to control railroad power and the Sherman Act in 1890 to condemn trade restraints and monopolies. Some observers assert that Congress passed the original antitrust statutes only to appease the reform movement, and therefore purposely left the Sherman Act vague and seemingly innocuous to please powerful business interests. *See* P. AREEDA, ANTITRUST ANALYSIS 43–44 (2d ed., 1974) (discussing the political background of the Sherman Act).
4. C. GOFF & C. REASONS, CORPORATE CRIME IN CANADA: A CRITICAL ANALYSIS OF ANTI-COMBINES LEGISLATION 42 (1978).
5. *Id.* at 43.
6. L. REYNOLDS, THE CONTROL OF COMPETITION IN CANADA 132–33 (1940).
7. For example, an effort was made to weaken Wallace's bill by deleting the provision that a combines conviction would result in a corporation losing its charter. Wallace asserted that these changes were the result of " . . . those men who have formed those illegal combinations and who came down . . . with a great array of lawyers from Montreal and Toronto and with amendments carefully considered, to legislate the bill out of existence." H. C. DEB. 1889, quoted in L. REYNOLDS, *supra* note 6, at 134 n. 5.
8. C. GOFF & C. REASONS, *supra* note 4, at 45. The Act, S. C. 1889, as finally enacted, read:
   1. *Every person who conspires, combines, agrees or arranges with any other person, or with any railway, steamship, steamboat, or transportation company,* unlawfully,
   (a) *To* unduly *limit the facilities for transporting, producing, manufacturing, supplying, storing or dealing in any article or commodity which may be a subject of trade or commerce; or—*
   (b) *To restrain or injure trade or commerce in relation to any such article or commodity; or—*
   (c) *To* unduly *prevent, limit, or lessen the manufacture or production of any such article or commodity, or to* unreasonably *enhance the price thereof; or—*
   (d) *To* unduly *prevent or lessen competition in the production, manufacture, purchase, barter, sale, transportation or supply of any such article or commodity, or in the price of insurance upon person or property;*
   Is guilty of a misdemeanor and liable, on conviction, to a penalty not exceeding four thousand dollars and not less than two hundred dollars, or to imprisonment for any term not exceeding two years; and if a corporation, is liable on conviction to a penalty not exceeding ten thousand dollars and not less than one thousand dollars. [Emphasis added.]
   An Act for the Protection and Suppression of Combinations Formed in Restraint of Trade, Can. Stat. c. 41 § 1 (1899).
9. *See* text accompanying notes 45–51 *infra* which discuss the constitu-

tional issues raised by Canada's competition laws. This is in sharp contrast to American antitrust statutes which provide both civil and criminal penalties.

10. *See* Bertrand, *The Combines Investigation Act,* 44 ANTITRUST L.J. 465, 467 (1975).

11. 15 U.S.C. § 1 (1976).

12. Despite all of the 1889 Act's pitfalls, it did enunciate a statutory philosophy of free competition. One might have hypothesized that Parliament would develop more vigorous provisions over the course of eighty years. However, the true reforms have come only very recently in the history of Canadian merger legislation.

13. Can. Stat. c. 41 § 3 (1889).

14. C. GOFF & C. REASONS, *supra* note 4, at 105.

15. The substantive provisions of the 1910 Combines Act were similar to those of the 1889 Act.

16. C. GOFF & C. REASONS, *supra* note 4, at 53–55.

17. *See* G. ROSENBLUTH & H. THORBURN, CANADIAN ANTI-COMBINES ADMINISTRATION 1952–1960 5 (1963).

18. C. GOFF & C. REASONS, *supra* note 4, at 105.

19. Can. Stat. c. 1 (1919).

20. *In Re* the Board of Commerce Act, 1919 and the Combines and Fair Prices Act 1919 [1922] A.C. 191 (P.C. 1921) (Can.). *See also* R. GROSSE, THE LAW ON COMPETITION IN CANADA 226 n. 2 (1962).

21. The Combines Investigation Act 1923, Can. Stat. c. 9 (1923).

22. C. GOFF & C. REASONS, *supra* note 4, at 59.

23. The Dominion Trade and Industry Act, Can. Stat. c. 9 (1935).

24. *See* Roberts, *The Death of Competition Policy: Monopoly, Merger and Regina v. K. C. Irving Ltd.,* 16

U.W. ONT. L. REV. 215 (1977) and text accompanying notes 99–101 *infra.*

25. Can. Stat. c. 54 § 2(1)(F) (1935).

26. *See* text accompanying notes 99–101 *infra.*

27. *Annual Report of Proceedings under the Combines Investigation Act 3 (1947)* quoted in G. ROSENBLUTH & H. THORBURN, *supra* note 17, at 7.

28. *See* G. ROSENBLUTH & H. THORBURN, *supra* note 17, at 6.

29. *Id.*

30. C. GOFF & C. REASONS, *supra* note 4, at 105.

31. *See* G. ROSENBLUTH & H. THORBURN, *supra* note 17, at 7.

32. *Id.*

33. *Id.* at 8.

34. *Id.* at 17–26.

35. C. GOFF & C. REASONS, *supra* note 4, at 70; *see also* Quinland, *The RTPC: Its Function and Duties,* 44 ABA ANTITRUST L.J. 492 (1975).

36. This process begins when a combines investigation officer conducts the preliminary investigation into an alleged merger or other antitrust violation. If the officer finds conflicting or inconclusive evidence, the director usually drops the matter. If the director decides to continue the investigation, he is ordinarily reasonably confident that the law is being broken. The director has authority to search the records of a company without prior notice, to require the officers of a corporation to testify, and to subpoena a company's records. Unless the director reaches the stage of taking the testimony of corporate officers, he may drop his investigation without reference to the RTPC. C. GOFF & C. REASONS, *supra* note 4, at 33–37; *see also* Quinlan, *supra* note 35.

If the Director continues, he will submit to the RTPC a statement of evidence explaining the nature of the industry investigated, as well as the director's allegations and supporting evidence. In an *in camera* proceeding before the RTPC, combines officers usually represent the director, while lawyers present the firm's position. After the evidence is presented, the director states his conclusions, the opposing counsel replies, and the director then has a chance for rebuttal. Use of empirical economic as well as legal evidence is permitted.

The RTPC's Report to the Minister describes the industry involved, the events leading up to the director's allegations and the remedies deemed advisable. Normally, the report will give no advice as to whether prosecutions are necessary. G. Rosenbluth & H. Thorburn, *supra* note 17, at 38.

37. This standard is comparable to the American "incipiency test" found in Section 7 of the Clayton Act, 15 U.S.C. §18 (1976), which prohibits acquistions or mergers whose effects "may be substantially to lessen competition. . . ." Arguably, the Canadian amendments could be interpreted more broadly than the Clayton Act since, under Canadian law, even the likelihood of events leading to an offense can result in remedial enforcement action.

38. Prior to 1952, no reports had been issued concerning charges of illegal mergers. C. Goff & C. Reasons, *supra* note 4, at 94–97.

39. G. Rosenbluth & H. Thorburn, *supra* note 17, at 40.

40. *Id.* at 93. By separating mergers and monopolies from the rest of the act, Parliament effectively confined the reform efforts to anticompetitive practices other than monopolies and mergers. The 1960 amendments specified that disputes over the existence of combines offenses other than mergers and monopolies are confined to proof of the effect of such practices on competition. Parliament made no such specification in the merger and monopoly provisions and thus allowed the Canadian Supreme Court in *Regina v. K. C. Irving Ltd.*, 72 D.L.R.3d 82 (1976), to hold that defendants could introduce evidence of the effect of an anticompetitive merger and monopoly on the public interest such as increasing returns to scale or efficiency.

41. C. Goff & C. Reasons, *supra* note 4, at 98.

42. *Id.* at 99.

43. *See* Borgsdorf, *Virtually Unconstrained Legal Environment for Mergers in Canada*, 18 Antitrust Bull. 809 (1973); *Canada's Merger Muddle*, *supra* note 1.

44. *See* C. Goff & C. Reasons, *supra* note 4, at 97–100.

45. The British North American Act, 1867, 30–31 Vict., c. 3.

46. *See* Bertrand, *supra* note 10, at 466.

47. Citizens Insurance Co. of Canada v. Parsons, 7 App. Cas. 96 (1881).

48. [1922] A.C. 191 (P.C. 1921) (Can.).

49. [1935] A.C. 76 (P.C. 1934) (Can.).

50. 32 D.L.R.2d 641, 658 (1962).

51. *See* notes 45–46 and accompanying text *supra* for an explication of Canada's constitution; *see also* Hartfield, *The Constitutionality of Canada's New Competition Law*, 26 U. New Brunswick L.J. 3 (1977).

52. 61 C.C.C. 114 (1933).

53. 4 D.L.R. 699 (1940).

54. [1952] 13 C.R. 217 (Que. Ct. K.B. 1951) *aff'd.* 18 Crim. 357 (1954) (Que. Ct. K.B. App. Side 1953).

55. [1960] O.R. 601.

56. Professor Borgsdorf believed that by requiring proof of monopolistic conditions to convict a corporation of a

merger offense the Canadian courts in effect eliminated the merger provision of the Combines Act. According to Borgsdorf, a government intent upon prosecuting a merger offense had to examine whether the monopoly provisions of the Combines Act had been violated. If the government could not prove the defendant had violated any provision related to monopoly, then it could not gain a conviction for a merger offense. Borgsdorf, *supra* note 43.

57. Weidman v. Shragge, 46 S.C.R. 1, 4 (1912).
58. [1942] S.C.R. 147, 151.
59. [1958] 29 C.P.R. 6 (S.C.C.).
60. Professor R. J. Roberts labels Justice Cartwright's position as unrealistic because it attempts to convert judges into economists. Judges do not have the expertise to analyze whether anticompetitive acts harm the public interest more than the alleged beneficial economic consequences of such acts promote the public interest. Roberts points out that, to be truly workable, Justice Cartwright's position would require establishing a public agency with extensive regulatory power over industries to ensure that the public interest is truly promoted by an anticompetitive merger or other act. Parliament specifically rejected public regulation of industry in the 1889 Act, and thus the Justice's position is inconsistent with Parliament's original intent. Roberts, *supra* note 24, at 219–20.
61. *Id.* at 221; see Combines Investigation Act, CAN. REV. STAT. c. 23 §§ 2, 33 (1970).
62. *See* Roberts, *supra* note 24, at 221–26.
63. *See* text accompanying notes 3–44 *supra* for an explanation of pre-1970 amendments to the merger laws.

64. *See* C. FLAVELL, CANADIAN COMPETITION LAW : A BUSINESS GUIDE 6 (1979).
65. *Id.* at 6–8.
66. *Id.* at 7.
67. *Id.* at 8.
68. *See* text accompanying notes 92–95 *infra* for a discussion of recent constitutional holdings of Canadian courts.
69. C-256, 28th Parliament, 3d Sess. (1970–71).
70. The Combines Investigation Act, Can. Stat. c. 76 (1975) (amending CAN. REV. STAT. c. 23 (1970)).
71. Id. at § 12 (amending CAN. REV. STAT. c. 23 § 31.1 (1) (1970)).
72. Realizing the possibility of controversy concerning the proposals, the government commissioned a group of nongovernment experts to gain support for their position. The recommendations of the government-sponsored Skeoch-McDonald Report were similar to those of the Economic Council. The new report recommended a case-by-case approach to mergers. Not having to conform to criminal procedures, the tribunal in the Skeoch-McDonald conception would have great flexibility in choosing decisional criteria for each case. The report left the impression that certain mergers should be encouraged.

The government first presented the Stage II amendments to Parliament as Bill C-42 on March 16, 1977. This bill received considerable criticism in the Senate and had to be withdrawn. The government then resubmitted the amendments as Bill C-13 on November 18, 1977, without substantial change from the provisions of Bill C-42. L. SKEOCH , DYNAMIC CHANGE AND ACCOUNTABILITY IN A CANADIAN MARKET ECONOMY (1976).

73. C. FLAVELL, *supra* note 64, at 12.
74. C. 13, 30th Parliament, 3d Sess. §§ 34, 41 (1977).
75. *Id.* at § 6.
76. *Id.*
77. *Id.* at § 29. A merger is defined broadly as "any acquisition or establishment by one or more persons . . . of any control over or interest in the whole or any part of the business of a competitor. . . ." *Id.* A joint venture is included within the definition of a merger if it is effected by the creation of a new corporation.

    The provisions of the proposed law are applicable to all conglomerate and vertical mergers. Horizontal mergers are subject to review only if they result in control of more than 20 percent of the market. Subsection 4 of the proposed Section 31.71 specifies the factors that the Board should use in analyzing a merger case. The most important of these are:

    (1) the size differential between the businesses of the parties to the merger and those remaining;
    (2) the barriers to entry into the market in question and the effect the merger might have on them;
    (3) any history of growth by merger by any party to the merger;
    (4) any history of anticompetitive behavior by any party;
    (5) any likelihood of removal of a vigorous or effective competitor; and
    (6) any likelihood that a firm is about to fail or has failed. [Id.]
    The use of "any" in many of these factors indicates that the Board can even consider marginal factors.

    The companies involved could also defend the propriety of their merger on grounds of an increase in efficiency of the Canadian economy. If the Board is satisfied that a merger brought about or will probably bring about a substantial increase in efficiency through savings of resources, it cannot issue an order. However, even where the merger generates efficiency gains, the Board must rule against the merger if it would reduce the relevant market to a virtual monopoly. *Id.*

78. *Id.*; *see* Foreign Investment Review Act, Can. Stat. c. 46 (1973).
79. GOVERNMENT OF CANADA, FOREIGN DIRECT INVESTMENT IN CANADA (1972).
80. Spence, *The Foreign Investment Review Act of Canada*, 4 SYR. J. INT'L L. & COM. 303, 308 (1977).
81. Can. Stat. c. 46 § 2(2) (1973).
82. *Id.*; Spence, *supra* note 80, at 308–9.
83. Can. Stat. c. 46 §§ 3, 7(1) (1973).
84. *Id.*
85. Donaldson & Jackson, *The Foreign Investment Review Act* 53 CAN. BAR REV . 171, 175 (1975).
86. *See* Spence, *supra* note 80, at 312–14, *quoting* [1974–75] FOREIGN INVESTMENT REV. AGENCY ANN. REPORT (1975).
87. *Id.* at 309–11.
88. 61 C.P.R. 235 (1970).
89. 16 C.C.C.2d 49; 45 D.L.R.3d 45 (1974).
90. 72 D.L.R.3d 82 (1976); *see* text accompanying notes 94–102 *infra* for an analysis of *ERCO* and *K. C. Irving.*
91. C. FLAVELL, *supra* note 64, at 395.
92. [1974] 40 D.L.R.3d 731, 737 (1973).
93. [1973] 33 C.L.R.3d 434 (Fed. Ct. App. 1972); *see* Bertrand, *supra* note 10, at 468–69.
94. 61 C.P.R. 235 (1970).
95. 16 C.C.C.2d 49; 45 D.L.R.3d 45 (1974).
96. 72 D.L.R.3d 82 (1976).
97. McFetridge, *The Emergence of a Canadian Merger Policy: The*

ERCO Case, 19 ANTITRUST BULL. 1
(1974).

98. 29 C.P.R. (S.C.C.) (1958); *see* text
accompanying notes 59–62 *supra*
for an analysis of Justice Cartwright's opinion in Howard Smith
Paper Mills.

99. *See* Roberts, *supra* note 24, at 222.

100. *Id* at 223.

101. *Id.* at 226.

102. *See* text accompanying notes 74–78
supra.

103. Such a regression could be performed by using dummy variables.
One could set the years in which
more effective policies were instituted equal to one and those years in
which no or ineffective policies were
instituted equal to zero. Various variables, such as fluctuations in stock
market prices, could be controlled
for. Also, certain adjustments could
be made to account for lag time between passage of legislation and institution of the policy. Thus, the regression of the dummy and control
variables on the number of foreign
mergers would generate a crude
measure of the effect of merger policies on U.S. and other foreign
merger activity in Canada.

104. In his concurring opinion in the
case of FTC v. Proctor & Gamble
Co., 386 U.S. 568, 581 (1967), Justice Harlan emphasized that the
rules that have evolved in connection with mergers of the horizontal
or vertical varieties are often not
appropriate when applied to market
extension and conglomerate
mergers. He suggested that the
courts should attempt to formulate
separate standards for judging the
legality of conglomerates, rather
than applying the *more mechanical
per se rules used in horizontal and
vertical cases.* [Emphasis added.]

105. *See* R. POSNER, ANTITRUST LAW:
AN ECONOMIC PERSPECTIVE 227–32

(1976) (contrasting the Supreme
Court of the 1960s that "wrote antitrust enforcement virtually a blank
check" with today's Supreme Court
which is more conservative in antitrust cases).

106. C. GOFF & C. REASONS, *supra* note
4, at 104.

107. For these early years statistics did
not divide mergers into domestic
and foreign categories, but the
number of foreign mergers is probably highly correlated with the
number of total mergers in Canada.

108. In 1911, Chief Justice White, in
Standard Oil Co. v. United States,
221 U.S. 1, 60, 65 (1911), first applied a "rule of reason" construction to Section 1 of the Sherman
Act. The standard is further discussed in United States v. American Tobacco Co., 221 U.S. 106,
179 (1911).

109. *See* U.S. DEPARTMENT OF
COMMERCE: BUREAU OF THE
CENSUS, HISTORICAL STATISTICS OF
THE UNITED STATES: COLONIAL
TIMES TO 1970 PART 2, 914 (1976).

110. C. GOFF & C. REASONS, *supra* note
4, at 104.

111. *See* text accompanying note 20,
supra.

112. *See* C. GOFF & C. REASONS, *supra*
note 4, at 104.

113. *See* R. POSNER, *supra* note 105.

114. Anti-Merger Act of 1950, Pub. L.
No. 81–1184, § 64 Stat. 1125
(codified at 15 U.S.C. § 18 (1976)).

115. *See* Roberts, *supra* note 24.

116. Lamont, *Emerging Neo-Mercantil-
ism in Canadian Policy Toward
State Enterprises and Foreign Direct Investment,* 8 VAND. J. OF
TRANSNAT'L L. 121, 143–44 (Fall
1974).

117. *Id.*

118. *Id.*

119. *Id.*

120. *See* R. POSNER, *supra* note 105.

121. *See* Lamont, *supra* note 116.
122. *See* Dickey, *The Americanization Syndrome in United States-Canadian Relations*, 6 Cas. W. Res. J. of Int'l Law 82, 85–86 (1973).
123. *See* Spence, *supra* note 80.
124. Royal Commission on Corporate Concentration, Report on Corporate Concentration 147.
125. *See, e.g.*, F.T.C. v. Proctor & Gamble Co., 386 U.S. 568 (1967).
126. *Id.*
127. Dickey, *supra* note 122, at 84.
128. Hudec, *Possible Trade Consequences of Canadian Foreign Investment Policy*, 6 Cas. W. Res. J. of Int'l Law 74, 75 (1973).
129. *Id.* at 74–75.
130. Coutts, *Factors Influencing Canadian-American Trade: A Canadian View*, 6 Cas. W. Res. J. of Int'l Law 56, 58 (1973).
131. Lamont, *supra* note 116, at 121.
132. *Id.*
133. *Id.* at 122.
134. Citizens are most discontented with U.S. investment and most nationalistic in Ontario and other urban centers, the heartland of U.S. investment. In contrast, Canadians in the Atlantic and Prairie provinces, where American investment is low, welcome foreign acquisitions and tend to be less nationalistic. Dickey, *supra* note 122, at 86–87.
135. *See* Lamont, *supra* note 116.
136. *Id.* There are several other consequences of the foreign corporate presence in Canada which exceed the scope of this study. One of the more important of these consequences is the extraterritorial application of foreign laws to much of Canadian industry. The United States and the EEC assert that their antitrust laws apply to their corporations in Canada so long as the effect of the U.S. or European company's transaction in Canada affects competition in the United States or Europe, respectively. United States tax and other corporate laws apply to U.S. firms investing in Canada. Canada has attempted to legislate against the extraterritorial application of such laws but the validity of the Canadian Legislation is in doubt. Sutherland, *Rio-Tinto Zinc Corporation v. Westinghouse Electric Corporation: Extra-territorial Jurisdiction in Antitrust Matters*, 5 Monash L. Rev. 76 (1978).

Structural Aspects of Multinational Corporate Trade with the Nonmarket Economies of Eastern Europe: An MNC Perspective on Domestic and Foreign Regulation

JOHN G. SCRIVEN

In considering the structural aspects of multinational corporate trade relationships with the nonmarket economies of Eastern Europe, it is important, as a preliminary matter, to acknowledge certain intractable features of that trade. Only through a continuing awareness of the interplay of these factors can one hope to understand the role of law or regulation in trade with these states.

Foremost is the recognition that the multinational corporation (MNC), in dealing with a nonmarket economy, is entering an economic environment with assumptions antithetical to its own. To the extent that the MNC hopes to satisfy the trade demand of the nonmarket state, the MNC must allow for a margin of compromise and deviation from its normal modes of doing business. Such an approach, however, is necessarily mutual; the nonmarket economy government, to the extent it seeks to engage in international trading relationships with the Western market economies, must do so in partnership with the latter's evolutionary modality of international trade, the MNC. In so doing, it must also compromise somewhat in its ideological and practical requirements.

This need for pragmatism and compromise is being recognized to varying extents by the nonmarket economies of the Council for Mutual Economic Assistance (CMEA).[1] Their economic imperatives have led to a blossoming of trade with MNCs, especially from the United States and the Federal German Republic, as well as from the other Western democracies. Their Marxist principles have been compromised within their domestic economies to meet the requirements of foreign investment. For example, the Soviet Union and

Mr. Scriven is a member of the legal department of Dow Chemical Company, and until 1979 had particular responsibility for Eastern Europe, Yugoslavia, the Mideast, and Africa. He is a solicitor of the Supreme Court of the United Kingdom.

Poland have recently indicated their willingness to work with capitalist resources in the form of leased equipment.[2] A number of organizations from the CMEA states have established themselves in the market economies[3] and for a number of years the Soviet Union has been operating a bank in Switzerland.[4]

Without such flexibility on the part of these regimes, the complicated commercial arrangements which exist today between the CMEA members and the Western MNCs could never have developed. Although these developments have opened up a large market for U.S., Western, European, and Japanese business, it can be argued that this trade has been equally important over the past decade for the political stability of the Eastern bloc, particularly some of the satellite states, in that it has contributed to a move toward consumerism.[5]

The practical difficulty that arises for purposes of this inquiry, then, is how to produce regulations which are representative of the various economic systems at play in the world, since any regulation which lacks the mutuality necessary for cooperation between such competing philosophies may tend to stultify the natural evolution of international industrial cooperation.

The second important factor which affects the current structure of MNC-CMEA trade relationships is the serious economic problems which the CMEA states are experiencing.[6] Over the last few years these countries have financed their growing demands for Western goods and technology by borrowing in the Western convertible currency market. At the same time they have run up a trade deficit with the Western democracies of U.S. $3.3 billion.[7] This means today that many of the CMEA countries have exhausted their convertible currency reserves and have little or no such currency left, either to buy goods and technology, or even to service their outstanding loan obligations.

With an outstanding convertible currency debt at the end of 1978 of U.S. $15 billion out of total CMEA indebtedness of U.S. $38.8 billion, Poland seems to be in the most perilous condition. At the present time many European bankers view this situation with deep concern. However, this concern is not shared by their North American colleagues who anticipate an increase in convertible currency exposure which will hopefully be funded by the planned increase in exports by the Eastern bloc.

This convertible currency problem which in fact emanates from the failures of the CMEA economies to achieve their planned goals, affects both the satellite CMEA states and the Soviet Union. In 1978 the Soviet deficit in trade with the West increased dramatically, partly due to increased grain purchases which it was forced to cover in part by selling its entire annual production of gold. In 1979 it was projected that the grain harvest would be even worse, the U.S. Department of Agriculture expecting a 50 million ton shortfall. The consequent purchases of grain in convertible currency will put an additional strain on the Soviet Union's ability to purchase Western technology and equipment over the next year.[8]

Such economic developments dominate all aspects of East-West trade today and in particular have led to a vast barter system between the Western industrialized democracies and the CMEA bloc. The impact on MNCs of this trading pattern, commonly called *countertrade,* will be discussed later.

The final factor in the relationships between MNCs and CMEA states which cannot be underestimated is the impact of wholly independent political decisions. Though this factor is not limited to trade with the nonmarket economy states, the monopolistic organizational structure of foreign trade in the socialist countries renders it peculiarly and immediately susceptible to variations in the political climate between the two national trading partners involved.

Bearing in mind these critical factors, this article will discuss the following particular aspects of MNC trade with CMEA states: (1) the organizational structure, in general, of foreign trade with nonmarket economies, (2) the impact of domestic antitrust law on MNC trade with CMEA states, and (3) recent developments in CMEA regulation which affect the structure of trade with MNCs.

THE GENERAL ORGANIZATIONAL STRUCTURE OF MNC TRADE WITH CMEA STATES

In dealing with nonmarket economies, the MNC enters an economic environment inimical to its own. Thus it is worthwhile to reconsider certain basic aspects of socialist trading and economic concepts.

The long-term consequences for the socialist states of the penetration of their domestic markets by capitalist enterprises provides one of the most interesting perspectives on the growing East-West trade relationships. Many in the West feel that such developments are essential for world stability and may lead to some relaxation in those states both in terms of the flexibility of their economic concepts and also in human freedoms.[9] In fact, there are signs that this is already happening. Moreover, the Soviet Union appears to be equally enthusiastic. Professor Maximova, of the Institute for World Economy and International Relations in Moscow, said recently: "We are not going to demand that Western countries should give up their traditional system of economic management, although as Marxists we consider it to be a transitional stage giving way in the future to a more progressive form—a planning system of economic management."[10] Whether in fact this position can be supported in the light of recent trends, such as the move toward leasing aforementioned and the approaches contained in new foreign investment legislation to be discussed, is perhaps open to question.

MNCs, in their relations with CMEA members, must deal with a number of monopolies. The state has a monopoly in all economic activities, both internal and external. Article 14(h) of the *Constitution of the Soviet Union* states: "The competence of the Union of Soviet Socialist Republics, as represented by its highest agencies of state power and agencies of state administration shall embrace . . . foreign trade on the basis of a state monopoly." Within the statewide economic monopoly operate lesser monopolies.[11] The state delegates to its specific agencies specific monopolies, somewhat as the Crown in England granted monopolies in the Middle Ages, the vestigial remains of which are the patent monopoly. Of course, the Ministry of Foreign Trade has a monopoly in all aspects of foreign trade.[12]

These lesser monopolies are further diluted. Under the aegis of the Ministry of Foreign Trade state agencies are established and granted a monopoly in certain aspects of foreign trade. These agencies are denominated foreign trade organizations (FTOs).[13]

These state companies are founded by a ministry of state or other organ of national authority, and under the laws of the respective socialist states are considered independent legal indentities. The state provides them with certain assets which they may use independently. They are liable for the discharge of their obligations up to the amount of the assets entrusted to them and these assets cannot, generally speaking, be removed from their control.[14]

The juridical independence of these state foreign trade organizations has been recognized judicially in a number of Western countries.[15] Nonetheless FTOs, in fact, work under the close supervision of their founding agency.[16] Moreover, the power of the executive in the socialist countries to issue regulations and instructions and to informally govern all activities within the state is vastly greater than is the case in the Western democracies.

This actual and implict interrelationship between the FTO and the state through the Ministry of Foreign Trade is the inevitable consequence of the socialist concept of a planned economy.[17] The activities of the FTO are governed by its annual and five-year plans, which are a part of the annual and five-year plans of the Ministry of Foreign Trade, which are in turn a part of the overall state annual and five-year plans. These plans are a synthesis of the plans of all the component parts of the state apparatus; once accepted by the Communist Party and, in the case of the Soviet Union, by the Supreme Soviet, they have the force of law.[18]

The concepts of state monopoly and the planned economy are maintained in pristine purity only in the fountainhead of communism, the Soviet Union, and its more conservative allies, the German Democratic Republic (GDR), and the Czechoslovak Socialist Republic (CSSR). Other CMEA members have modified their economies to allow for the play of some market forces. For example, since the Economic Reform in Hungary (1967–69) the monopoly of the FTOs has been broken or at least extended so that industrial enterprises could engage directly in foreign trade.[19] So far, more than 100 Hungarian enterprises have been authorized to deal directly with foreign companies. Some prices are also "free," *i.e.*, subject to market forces.[20] And three countries—Hungary, Poland, and Romania—permit, at least theoretically, direct foreign investment.

The organization of the nonmarket economy is a predominant factor for

MNCs in East-West trade, and its bureaucratic rigidity is a continuing frustration for many Western businessmen. On the other hand the socialist planners, particularly at the present time, are frustrated by the "unstable, crisis-inclined nature of the world capitalist market," as they perceive it. There have been calls for a "symbiosis of the planned and market systems." [21]

In fact many of the transactions in East-West trade have been uniquely structured in a legal format that in practice has allowed each partner to achieve its specific goals.[22] The structure of these transactions has substantially mitigated the concern of many Western firms about their inability to participate in what may be a substantial investment through the traditional means of a corporate entity with the equivalent of a board of directors and dividend payments.[23] The forms that have been employed in this trade will sometimes give an advantage to the MNC over smaller companies in dealing with the nonmarket economies. The Soviet Union, particularly, because of its need for very large-scale projects, prefers to deal with large multinational corporations rather than a group of smaller companies.[24] Finally, all of the CMEA states desire to have their trade relationships encompassed within the umbrella of bilateral intergovernmental relationships, a factor which increases the impact of political decisions upon trading relationships.

DOMESTIC REGULATION: IMPACT OF THE U.S. ANTITRUST LAWS ON MNC TRADE WITH CMEA STATES

It is appropriate now to consider how far these imperatives have been recognized by domestic regulation in the United States, and to examine in particular the impact of domestic antitrust law on MNC trade with nonmarket economies. Since the *Alcoa* case in 1945, the U.S. courts have exercised jurisdiction to decide upon the activities of legal entities operating outside the territorial jurisdiction of the United States.[25] This doctrine of extraterritoriality, felt by many to be a form of judicial imperialism, has been extended over the years beyond the antitrust area.[26] Of course, the extraterritorial application of U.S. laws also reaches the activities of the foreign subsidiaries of U.S. MNCs.

With the growth of trade and industrial cooperation between U.S. MNCs and the CMEA countries, the U.S. Justice Department has been forced to take a position on the potential antitrust aspects of such relationships. The most recent and enlightening statements on this subject are contained in the *Antitrust Guide for International Operations* issued by the Justice Department on January 26, 1977. These have been supplemented by comments made by Joel Davidow before the Advisory Committee on East-West Trade of the U.S. Department of Commerce on March 10, 1976, which in turn were amplified in an article published in 1978.[27]

It is unnecessary to consider all aspects of the *Guide for International Operations*, but it is appropriate to highlight some concerns of the Justice

Department in respect of East-West trade. Four potential areas of concern have been discussed: (1) exchange of information, (2) selling cooperation, (3) buying cooperation, and (4) patent and know-how licensing with reexport restrictions.[28]

Of course, the general rule is that U.S. antitrust law is applicable to any concerted restraint on competition which occurs abroad only if the intended and actual effect is to injure U.S. trade. In this context one is compelled by experience to agree with the conclusion set out in the Justice Department's guide "that a very large proportion of international business transactions involving American firms and/or American markets usually will not involve violations of U.S. antitrust law because such transactions will not adversely affect U.S. consumers or competitors."[29] In the case of East-West trade this position is emphasized by the extreme paucity of judicial precedent.[30]

Exchanges of information among competitors involved in East-West trade seem to be acceptable, if made for the sake of gaining experience or learning. Even if there is an intention to achieve a united front in buying or selling, it is unlikely that such an exchange would be illegal under the U.S. antitrust laws.

The Webb-Pomerene Act[31] permits U.S. exporters to join together in associations for the sale of goods abroad at uniform prices and it is felt by Mr. Davidow, for one, that joint selling abroad will not be illegal so long as it produces no adverse effects on U.S. consumers or competitors. The same is true for joint buying arrangements which are entered into by U.S. companies solely for the purpose of securing a lower price for U.S. consumers. However, the Justice Department recommends that "U.S. firms should avoid secret collusive arrangements in selling abroad, even when dealing with a monopolistic state buying agency, since such a buyer, like any other, is entitled to a fair nondeceptive treatment."[32] Such an attitude, whose premises merit serious and challenging consideration, reflects the general support of the U.S. Justice Department for the direction being taken by United Nations organs in respect of the regulation of restrictive business practices in international trade.

Nevertheless, joint ventures and consortia for major commercial projects in nonmarket economies, although almost always involving selling and buying, are normally acceptable so long as weaker firms are not unfairly excluded.[33] Fortunately this view coincides with practical realities. As previously mentioned the Soviet Union is mainly interested in extremely large-scale industrial complexes and projects. Many of these (there are now over thirty) are beyond the technological and financial resources of a single partner. To this extent current demands of East-West trade tend to significantly favor concentration of assets. The need for some sort of joint venture arrangement is almost inevitable except where one of the largest MNCs is involved. This becomes further complicated by the Soviet Union's desire to have buy-back compensation arrangements to finance its convertible currency obligations under these projects.

The Justice Department's greatest concern in East-West trade is the imposition of export restrictions in licensing arrangements with state-owned enterprises in nonmarket economies. These export prohibitions are intended by the licensing company to forestall the export of goods by such state monopolies at unreasonably low prices into Western markets. The department's position is that prohibitions on exports back to the United States may be illegal if they relate to products not produced by the licensed technology or last longer than a reasonable estimate of the life of the know-how involved. Moreover, the Justice Department believes that the U.S. corporations' fears can be adequately addressed under the U.S. antidumping laws.[34] Further, in the view of the department, prohibition of exports to Western Europe is not violative of U.S. antitrust laws since it does not affect U.S. commerce.[35] In fact, many MNCs conduct their East-West trade from Vienna and therefore remain effectively outside the jurisdiction of the EEC authorities as well.[36]

The present posture of the Justice Department is rather nebulous and unspecific. Its position seems to be based solely on the general principle of intended and actual adverse effect on U.S. commerce. This is very understandable considering both the intense political environment in which East-West trade exists and the lack of specific judicial guidance.

As a general observation, U.S. MNCs seem to be able to deal successfully with the monopolies of the nonmarket states without any modification of their general commitment to competition. This may be accounted for by the fact that the very size of the domestic U.S. economy places U.S. companies in a position of strength when dealing with such state enterprises, a factor considered subsequently in this article. Thus, a substantial concentration of assets and economic power will often present opportunities which would not otherwise exist for U.S firms in their dealings with nonmarket economies.

The biggest concern of U.S. companies seems to be with "whip-sawing" tactics sometimes employed by FTOs, whereby the later play the offers of potential suppliers off against each other and so utilize their monopolistic position to beat down the price offered.[37] This tactic is not peculiar to the nonmarket economies and may be found among domestic buyers. U.S. corporations experienced in East-West trade can deal with this phenomenon through long-term trading relationships with FTOs in their respective industries and through competent market research.

Another aspect of trade with CMEA states, the increasing use of countertrade arrangements, perhaps has potential ramifications for domestic antitrust liability. Such schemes, which are becoming an essential feature of East-West trade, require that any sale in convertible currency by a Western supplier shall be offset by a purchase in convertible currency of an equivalent amount by that supplier from its CMEA trading partner.[38] The reciprocity implicit in countertrade requirements, even where there is no contractual linkage between the sale and the counterpurchase (which is often the case), seems to chafe against some aspects of U.S. antitrust philosophy. The demands of such arrangements also favor large corporations at the expense of the smaller ones, since the latter will often not have the ability to absorb such counterpurchases within their own raw material requirements or may lack the ability to sell them in their own markets.

To the extent that the effects of countertrade requirements are felt on the U.S. domestic market, some judicial guidance may be developed which will amplify the unresolved antitrust aspects of East-West trade.

In contrast, it is the anticompetitive or protectionist legislation of the United States, the Trade Act of 1974,[39] which has had most influence recently on trade with the CMEA bloc. The use of the market disruption provisions of § 406 of the Act, while not necessarily consistent with the aims of U.S. antitrust policy, provides some indication of the antitrust approach which might be taken with respect to compensation and countertrade agreements.

This legislation has recently been used as an instrument of national policy. It is premised on the existence of a fundamental difference between the market and nonmarket economies which may place U.S. companies at a disadvantage in certain circumstances. For example, some U.S. chemical producers have attacked the famous compensation agreement made in 1973 between Occidental Petroleum and the Soviet Union.[40] This agreement, which is for a period of twenty years, requires *inter alia* an Occidental subsidiary to purchase each year from the Soviets 1.2 million metric tons of anhydrous ammonia. The U.S. producers complained that this arrangement had caused market disruption of the domestic industry within the meaning of the act because U.S. ammonia plants were running at about only 73 percent of capacity, which was below the break-even point, and such imports were causing the domestic producers either to sell at a loss or lose business. The Trade Act considers that market disruption exists "whenever imports of an article, like or directly competitive with an article produced by some domestic industry, are increasing rapidly, either absolutely or relatively, so as to be a significant cause of material injury, or threat thereof, to such domestic industry."[41] It should be noted that this test is intended to be more easily met than the "substantial cause" test of § 201 of the Act (the "escape clause" provision) which provides a more general protection against market disruption by imported products, a recognition, perhaps, of the special problems of trading with nonmarket economies.

The International Trade Commission (ITC), after investigating the complaint, determined by a three-to-two majority that market disruption did exist in the Occidental case. It recommended to the president that a three-year quota be imposed on U.S. imports of such ammonia from the Soviet Union. In fact, on December 11, 1979, the president decided not to follow the recommendation of the ITC and determined that it was not in the national interest to impose the recommended quotas. This decision was based upon economic argumentation.[42] Subsequently, by proclamation on January 21, 1980, the president reversed his decision. Taking emergency action under § 406(c) of the Trade Act, in the aftermath of the Soviet invasion of Afghanistan, he imposed the quotas which he had originally denied.[43] Although formally related to the economics of the situation, the decision was clearly a use of the act as an instrument of national policy in extreme circumstances. As such its impact on future East-West trade relationships may not be so severe.

Although not the first agreement subject to a Trade Act complaint,[44] the anhydrous ammonia complaint is the most significant, because the agreement initially had the blessing of the U.S. Exim Bank and the U.S. Department of Commerce; the State Department also stated that it was in the best interests of the United States. Moreover, since the Occidental deal was made, the CMEA economies have seriously declined to the point where without such compensation and countertrade arrangements the CMEA states are not in a position to purchase Western goods and technology, countertrade being essential to generate the convertible currency necessary to make such purchases.

Furthermore, the complaint and the Trade Act upon which it is based create difficulties in commercial planning, since due to changes in the domestic market situation a long-term arrangement apparently may be challenged much later, and perhaps repeatedly, in the course of its implementation. A success against Occidental may well have deterred other companies from entering into similar arrangements even with governmental support.

Many MNCs are now forced into compensation arrangements in order to maintain even their present level of trading with CMEA FTOs. Some licensers of technology have faced countertrade requirements which are as much as 140 percent of the value of the licensed technology. One MNC, the Pepsi-Cola Company, may be watching Occidental's experience with the ITC. In return for the right to supply two bottling and mixing plants in Bulgaria and to supply those plants with its concentrate it has entered into a 200 percent countertrade commitment which requires it to purchase Bulgarian bottles, confectionaries, mineral waters, furniture, electric and diesel forklift trucks, and wine.[45]

In conclusion (and further confirming the Justice Department's view) one can say that for most operations of large U.S. MNCs the domestic legislation is not a problem. Many of their sales are from their facilities in Western Europe and the countertrade products are usually utilized in these same facilities or sold off to European-based traders for disposal. Thus, domestic jurisdiction would rarely be obtained.

CMEA REGULATION OF MNC TRADE

Recent Developments in CMEA States

Recently, national legislation concerning direct foreign investment in the form of joint ventures has been enacted in three CMEA States; these efforts have considerable impact on the structure of MNC trade relationships with these countries. The problem of permitting a capitalist presence within a socialist economy remains an open issue in these countries. The more conservative states—the Soviet Union, the GDR, and the CSSR—do not permit such activity; only Romania,[46] Hungary,[47] and Poland[48] at present have laws permitting direct foreign investment. The Bulgarian authorities have indicated that a joint-venture law is in preparation.

The most striking feature of these local enactments is that they have chosen, for the implementation of such projects, a familiar capitalist modality—the joint stock company—very often relying on prerevolution legislation to prescribe incorporation details. By their very participation in a joint venture organized under traditional capitalist legal concepts, MNCs in CMEA countries are involved in the internal cultural, social, and political activities of the host country. This is in sharp contrast with the Yugoslavian joint-venture legislation which requires the foreign partner to invest directly in one of the domestic legal entities peculiar to that country's self-management system—the organization of associated labor[49] (such capitalistic forms of business organization as the joint stock company having been totally abolished). Nor is profit a recognized concept; rather the foreign partner shares in the *net income* of the work organization in the way specified in the joint-venture agreement.[50]

In 1977 Hungary followed the Romanian example by permitting the foreign partner to participate directly in the production process;[51] previously the foreign corporation had been represented only in the joint holding company established primarily for marketing the production of the domestic manufacturing unit utilizing the foreign partner's technology. Because this revision did not produce the interest in foreign investment that had been hoped for, in July 1979 Hungary published an explanatory decree which deals with the Western companies' concerns on accounting, taxation, profit transfer, repatriation of capital, and sales restrictions. Poland this year issued a similar decree,[52] foreign investment in Poland having been previously limited to "units of the non-socialized economy."[53]

Joint ventures form part of the domestic economy, operating in local currencies (although this is not always so in Romania) and becoming part of the national plan. Apart from the fact that no foreign investor may have more than 49 percent of the equity of the joint venture, the decrees contain none of the kind of terminology being discussed in the development of supranational codes. There is no reference to the environment, transfer prices, or the evaluation of technology except for some minor provisions in the new Polish regulations.[54] Apart from the organizational aspects of the joint venture, the main concern of the legislation is that sufficient foreign exchange be generated both for the benefit of the domestic economy, and also for the payment of royalties and profits to the foreign partner.[55] The details of the cooperation are determined by the partners during negotiations and embodied in a joint venture agreement.

It is proper to point out that in negotiation some other issues do emerge which touch on sensitive areas. Because of the planned nature of the domestic economy the foreign investor will usually share with its domestic partner a monopolistic position in the domestic market.[56] The opportunity to enjoy such a monopoly is an inevitable consequence of socialist planning. The "closed economies" of the CMEA members are intended to create a self-sufficient system of production. Even in normal trading activities, MNCs, and indeed any prospective seller into a socialist economy, cannot rely on the free enterprise standards of competition to make its sale:

> No matter how much more reasonably priced, or more suitable [this] product may be to the needs of the eastern European consumer than similar goods available locally, a sale will not be consummated unless the decision to buy fits prescribed government objectives. The Western exporter has learned from experience that [it] cannot count on the traditional factors that enter into the determination of consumer choice, (price, quality, utility) in order to secure the share of the market to which it feels entitled by reason of the efficiency of [its] production and the comparative value of [its] product.[57]

Thus in a joint venture the technology of the MNC helps to create local production to replace previously imported production. The planned economy is not competitive or market-oriented. It does not see the need for competition between its own production and foreign imports, or need the exclusion of such imports formalized by tariff managements or quotas. The state plan for a certain product will merely foresee that products previously imported are now supplied from the domestic production of a certain factory (the joint venture).[58]

In the recent Polish foreign investment legislation specific provision is made for the incorporation of such joint ventures within the national socioeconomic plan.[59] Although this inclusion is somewhat tentative, perhaps because the Polish authorities are inexperienced with the impact of capitalist forces on their economy, such joint ventures are clearly included within the monopolistic centrally planned system.

CMEA states are, thus, not concerned with an MNC presence enjoying a local monopoly. Their objective is an improvement in their convertible currency balances, so that the big debate will be over the volume of exports and who will handle them.

Also at the present time the Hungarians are placing particular emphasis in detailed negotiations on the establishment of a research and development capability with the joint venture. The volume of price for supplies of raw materials by either partner to the joint venture will be another fundamental issue.

In summary, the recent national legislation has been very general, allowing the partners a great deal of flexibility to work out their own arrangement. Control against potential exploitation of the domestic partner by the foreign MNC is exercised through the licensing system in which the project will require the consent of various ministries and agencies of the state bureaucracy before its implementation may commence. The legal framework is designed to satisfy certain basic concerns of the foreign investor regarding its capital and the repatriation of profits and other sums due it. Such legislation is a pragmatic solution, avoiding the inhibition of theoretical principles to allow for the realization of tangible benefits to the domestic economy.

CMEA Approaches to MNC Concentration

The planned economies of the CMEA members essentially differ from market economies in that they are not responsive to the forces of supply and demand; that is, as noted earlier, they are not market-oriented. As such their approach to the tendencies toward concentration among MNCs, which appear to be causing concern in some quarters within the Western industrialized democracies, evidences a rather different perspective. Perhaps also the relevant needs of the market economies in trading with the CMEA bloc may be different than in trading with other regions.

One must remember that each of the CMEA economies is "administered by a group of highly centralized, specialized and substantially nationalized industries, each of which has a monopoly in a particular area of the economy. Each of these organizations has certain exclusive rights and functions and no other organization either internally or externally may exercise those rights or functions."[60] Consumer choice, free pricing, size, and competition are not relevant. They are vestiges of an "inferior" (capitalist) system which the planned economy has superseded.[61]

Accordingly, one would not expect to find provisions similar to the antitrust regulations existing in many of the Western democracies.[62] However, at least one small example in this field does exist. When Hungary introduced in 1968 the "New Economic Mechanism," the pricing system was modified from fixed official prices to allow for certain free prices.[63] Although these prices mainly concerned trading by individuals and small groups outside the socialized economy, the majority of imported products came within the free price category. The relevant statute provides that

> it shall be prohibited to enter into agreements on or in connection with the prices of products directed at or resulting in the barring of the emergence of competition, the creation of a monopolistic situation or the obtaining of unlawful financial or marketing advantages. Agreements defined in para (1) shall be null and void.[64]

However, since the price regulations have no extraterritorial effect they do not cover foreign trade contracts made with foreign parties.[65] Thus, even this provision will not be applicable to MNCs either in regular foreign trade activities for the reasons just stated or within the domestic economy, since their joint venture projects will be within the basic economy where free pricing does not apply.

Although the CMEA members are not particularly concerned with MNC concentration, they do seek modifications in their trading relationships with the West. These have been most clearly articulated in the position of Group D (the CMEA bloc) in the discussions on various Codes of Conduct being developed by UNCTAD and the U.N. Commission on Transnational Corporations.

The position of Group D in these discussions is equivocal. The members feel that such Codes should not be applied to their own state enterprises.[66] They emphasize the need to observe the principles of sovereignty, equality, mutual benefits, political and economic independence, and noninterference in the internal affairs of countries,[67] a position consistent with the nature of their nonmarket economies.

However, Group D does postulate the prohibition of some practices, considered restrictive practices, by MNCs. These include the imposition of restrictions after expiration of agreements, exclusive grant-back provisions, restrictions on research and price-fixing, and tying arrangements. On the other hand, Group D governments wish to retain some flexibility in this field and would provide that such "abusive practices" could be deemed nonobjectionable if the competent national authorities of the acquiring party's country consider such a determination to be in the public interest.[68]

In fact, apart from the political need to be seen as supporters of the developing nations, the CMEA bloc may not be interested in the debate over the conduct and role of MNCs in international trading relationships. They see it as a historical problem which is not of their making.[69]

Some commentators in the West also feel that the strict application of antitrust rules on companies dealing with the monopolistic enterprises of the socialist economies put such companies at an unfair disadvantage.[70] Although large MNCs have the economic strength to take care of themselves in dealing with the demands of CMEA trading partners, this is not necessarily true for small companies, particularly in dealing with the Soviet Union. Its predilection for large trading partners has already been mentioned,[71] and the size of its projects is such that a small company will be able to participate in them only by sharing the financial and other burdens.[72] Given the greater logistical problems for U.S. companies in trading with the CMEA members directly from their home production units in the United States, the following perspective of a Soviet minister may be apposite:

> Our projects are enormous. Almost every one one of them is worth a billion dollars. When I deal with European companies they do not have sufficient industrial, credit and management capacity. When I sign them up for a large project, I have five or six contracts, which gives me five or six headaches. When I deal with a large American company, I have only one headache.[73]

This is obviously not true of Fiat, Bayer, Krupp, or ICI. What the comment may mean is that the Soviet Union and its partners prefer the sheer size of the large MNC. After all, even if a particular Western industry became concentrated in the hands of one or a few companies, that would still provide them with a broad and competitive choice of trading partners.

CONCLUSION

The relevance of MNCs' experience with the nonmarket economies seems evident. There has been very little regulation of MNCs in this respect, whether on a national, regional, or supranational level. Yet in the last decade international trading relationships with those economies have grown impressively, surviving even the vagaries of the political relationships between East and West, to the mutual satisfaction of both economies and their respective governments.

The reason for this lies in the enlightened mutual self-interest on both sides. The MNCs have not sought to subvert the CMEA societies or to impose methods of business upon them. Rather they have utilized their entrepreneurial flexibility to develop new forms of business relationships which do not impose strains on the political theories of their partners. The nonmarket economies have taken a pragmatic and nondogmatic approach to trade with MNCs, explicitly recognizing, for example, the profit motivation of their foreign partners, in their foreign investment legislation.

To quote the words of Henri Schamm: "Clearly, business cannot prosper unless the host country itself has a chance to achieve prosperity; thus a responsible MNE will take into consideration, out of self-interest, the economic and social needs of the country in which it operates."[74] Such an approach has characterized much of the relationship between MNCs and the nonmarket economies. Yet perhaps the alien nature of those economies and the subtle encouragement of size which they emanate pose a dilemma which has been stated by Mr. Pisar and acknowledged by Mr. Davidow:

> I am raising a philosophical and a practical question. How are we going to react to what is happening abroad? Are we going to say to ourselves we must change our system in order to be able to meet the new kind of trade and competition problems that arise abroad or are we going to preserve our system intact?[75]

Such a question exaggerates the current circumstances of East-West trade, but it may do more than hint at the direction in which that relationship is evolving. Perhaps it is even more relevant to other aspects of the international trading relationships of the Western industrialized democracies and their market economies. Furthermore, this question is pertinent to U.S. antitrust officials and legislators who are pondering the proper response to corporate concentration both in the United States and abroad. It may be that the possible repercussions of any anticoncentration measures on East-West trade relations should be more fully discussed before concrete action is taken.

NOTES

1. The Council for Mutual Economic Assistance (CMEA) was established on January 30, 1949. One of its main functions was to be the exchange of economic experience, the extension of technical aid to member nations, and the rendering of mutual assistance with respect to raw materials, foostuffs, machines, and equipment. Its offices are in Moscow. Member states are the USSR, Poland, Hungary, Romania, Czechoslovak S.S.R., German Democratic Republic, Bulgaria, North Korea, Outer Mongolia, Vietnam, and Cuba. The CMEA is commonly known in the West as "COMECON."

2. Grishiani, *Prospects and Limits in Cooperation Deals*, 8 Bus. Eastern Europe 89, 133–34; (1979). It should be noted, however, that in the conservative German Democratic Republic, such a transaction is still considered to be contrary to orthodox Marxist principles. *Id.* at 147.

3. The earliest example is the establishment of ARCOS in the United Kingdom just prior to the U.K.-USSR Trade Agreement of March 16, 1921.

4. Navrodne Bank, Zurich.

5. *Capitalistic Troubles for Eastern Europe*, Bus. Week, August 13, 1979, at 44.

6. The financial data used in the following paragraphs is summarized in *Id.* at 40–48.

7. *Id.* at 40.

8. *Id.* at 44. These comments must now, of course, be viewed in the light of the current U.S. grain embargo. It seems probable, however, that the Soviet Union will be able to obtain its requirements elsewhere so that its convertible currency expenditures will remain the same.

9. *E.g.*, S. Pisar, Co-Existence and Commerce: Guidelines for Transactions Between East and West 58–74 (1970).

10. *See* Maximova, *Industrial Cooperation Between Socialist and Capitalist Countries: Forms, Trends, and Problems*, in East-West Cooperation in Business: Inter-Firm Studies, at 15(C.T. Saunders ed. 1977).

11. *See generally* Conner, *The State Trading Monopoly System*, in P.L.I. Legal Aspects of Doing Business with the USSR and Eastern Europe 9–19 (Practical Law Institute, No. 238, ed. 1977), for a description of the state trading monopoly system in the Soviet Union.

12. *See also*, Grundgesetz, art. 9(5) (East Germany 1949), which states that "[t]he external economy, including foreign trade and foreign exchange economy, is a state monopoly."

13. Thus, in Poland Chiech, in Hungary Chemolimpex, and in the Soviet Union Soyuzkhimeksport are FTOs which have a monopoly of foreign trade in the chemical industry.

14. *See, e.g.*, Hungary Act No. IV of 1959; Civ. Code of the Hungarian People's Republic §§ 31–39; and Government Decree No. 11 of 1967 (13.V.) Korm, as quoted in I. Szasz, Hungarian Statutes Concerning Foreign Trade (1970).

15. The latest and probably most famous decision was the *Rolimpex* case in the United Kingdom which held that decisions of the Polish Ministry of Foreign Trade could constitute force majeure excusing the Polish sugar exporting monopoly from the performance of a supply contract. C. Czarnikow Ltd. v. Centrala Handlu Zagranicznoeg Rolimpex, 1978 Q.B. 176; 1977–3 W.L.R. 677; 1978-1 All E.R. 81; 1977-2 Lloyd's Rep. 201,

C.A.; 1978-3 W.L.R. 274; 1978-2 All E.R. 1043, H.L. (E). Although this decision was probably technically correct, it highlights a problem of comparative law in accepting at face value the legislation of the socialist countries.

16. "A state enterprise may be founded by the minister, the head of an organ of national authority and . . . the executive committee of the council." Hungarian Decree No. 11 or 1967, § 1(2). "In appraising the foreign trade activities of enterprises vested with foreign-trading rights the founding organ shall proceed together with the Minister of Foreign Trade." Hungarian Decree No. 11 of 1967, §23(2).

17. *Id.*

18. Giffen, *The Planning Process and its Implications for Your Contract, supra* note 11, cit. 27–28. Finally, the control of the FTO exercised by its Ministry is confirmed by the fact that each foreign trade transaction requires a license from the Ministry of Foreign Trade.

19. Resolution No. 22 of 1967 (7. VI) G8 of the Economic Committee of the Hungarian Government.

20. Recently the Hungarian authorities went so far as to acknowledge the possibility that a Hungarian enterprise might reduce its labor force to improve its economic performance. Lorinczi & Dorian, *U.S.-Hungarian Joint Ventures: Prospects and Problems*, 10 L. POL'Y INT'L BUS. 1205, 1216–17 (1978). Similar trends may be observed in Poland and Romania. *Romania Considers Decentralized Planning*, 8 BUS. EASTERN EUR. 341–42 (1979).

21. Maximova, *supra* note 10, at 23. *See also* J.K. GALBRAITH, THE NEW INDUSTRIAL STATE 98–109 (1971) (suggesting that some devolutions of planning powers in the socialist countries are not a return to the market but

a shift of some planning functions from the state to the enterprise under the imperatives of technology).

22. C. POPE, A SUPRANATIONAL ORDER: PERSPECTIVES AND PERCEPTIONS, 51–54 (1979).

23. Pisar, *The Changing Economic and Legal Environment for East-West Investment*, 10 INT'L LAW. 1, 7 (1976).

24. *See, e.g.*, Maximova, *supra* note 10, at 18; Pisar, *supra* note 23, at 5.

25. United States v. Aluminum Co. of America, 148 F.2d 416, 444 (2d Cir. 1945).

26. This doctrine is currently a matter of great controversy among Western industrialized democracies. A discussion of the issues raised in the uranium cartel cases involving Westinghouse and Rio Tinto Zinc is contained in Merhige, *The Westinghouse Uranium Case: Problems Encountered in Seeking Foreign Discovery and Evidence*, 13 INT'L LAW. 19 (1979). *See also* Rosenthal, Benson, & Chiles, *Doctrines and Problems Relating to U.S. Control of Transnational Corporate Concentrations, ante*. The position of the U.S. Department of Justice, particularly vis-à-vis the U.K. Protection of Trading Interests Bill, is discussed in Flexner "Antitrust Enforcement in United States Foreign Commerce—"Imperialism or Realism?", a speech given before the Antitrust Law Section of the State Bar of Georgia in Atlanta, Georgia, December 6, 1979.

27. Davidow, *U.S. Antitrust, Free Trade and Nonmarket Economies*, 12 J. WORLD TRADE L. 473 (1978).

28. U.S. DEP'T OF COMMERCE, ANTITRUST IN EAST-WEST TRADE: EXCERPTS FROM THE MARCH 10, 1976 MEETING OF THE ADVISORY COMMITTEE ON EAST-WEST TRADE. 2–5 (1976).

29. ANTITRUST DIVISION U.S. DEP'T OF JUSTICE, ANTITRUST GUIDE FOR INT'L OPERATIONS, 5 (1977).

30. *Supra* note 28 at 1.
31. The Webb-Pomerene Act of 1918, 15 U.S.C. §§ 61–65 (1976).
32. Davidow, *supra* note 27 at 480.
33. *Id.* at 479.
34. For a complete analysis of U.S. Anti-dumping law, *see* ANTIDUMPING LAW: POLICY AND IMPLEMENTATION, 1 MICH. Y.B. INT'L LEGAL STUD. (1979).
35. Davidow, *supra* note 27 at 480. *See also,* ANTITRUST IN EAST-WEST TRADE, *supra* note 28 at 4.
36. *Eastern Europe in Brief,* 8 BUS. EASTERN EUR. 198 (1979).
37. ANTITRUST IN EAST-WEST TRADE, *supra* note 28 at 6–12.
38. For an overview of recent trends in "countertrade" developments, *see* 8 BUS. EASTERN EUR. 329–36, 361–76 (1979); 9 BUS. EASTERN EUR. 17–24, 41–48, 65–72 (1980).

Examples of typical countertrade commitments are:

Company X commits itself to buy, or to have bought through a third party, goods worth $_____ from the following FTOs _____ within _____ months following signature of the contract.

or

Company X hereby commits itself to take [e.g.] Hungarian goods described elsewhere in this contract by (date).

In such cases, it is wise for a company to specify with the utmost precision the types of goods it is willing to take. Without such limitation it may be forced to take products of inferior quality, or the products which it envisaged reselling may become unavailable because the FTO itself has found an export opportunity for that product and now wishes to use the countertrade obligation for the export of some other products.

Although many companies are faced with the need to enter into the kind of explicit countertrade undertaking described above, this is not always so. Companies with long-standing trading relationships with particular FTOs have been able to avoid such arrangements by demonstrating an existing balance in their trading relationships. This is likely to be true for MNCs which will have a greater flexibility to absorb raw materials, for example, produced in the CMEA states into their own western European production facilities.

Other complications exist in addition to the reciprocal aspects of countertrade. It is possible that from the FTO perspective, such a deal is a pure barter arrangement, in which no money exchanges are made. This can happen if the Western seller, having found a customer for the countertrade purchase, obtains from the latter a letter or credit that, after having completed a full circle of endorsements, ends up back in the hands of the Western seller as payment for its sale to the FTO.

Another problem for the Western company purchasing CMEA products under countertrade arrangements can be potential product liability claims. The company may in fact never see those products (for example to ensure their quality and compliance with specifications) because they have been resold through a broker and shipped directly to the ultimate purchaser. In the event of damage from defective products the company may be the most attractive defendant for the damaged party, because it may be difficult to make the FTO a party, or the plaintiff otherwise may be reluctant to pursue that course.

39. U.S.C. §§ 2101–487, (1976).
40. *See* Anhydrous Ammonia from the USSR, TA–406–5, USITC Publ. 1006 (1979).

41. 19 U.S.C. § 2436(e)(2) (1976).

42. H.R. Doc. No. 96–241, 96th Cong., 1st Sess. The decision was designed to ensure reasonable fertilizer prices for farmers and because it seemed likely Soviet imports would be replaced by imports from other sources.

43. Temporary Duty Increase on the Importation Into the United States of Certain Anhydrous Ammonia From the Union of Soviet Socialist Republics, 45 Fed. Reg. 3875 (1980) (to be codified in 3 C.F.R. Proclamation 4714).

44. *See* Certain Gloves from the People's Republic of China, TA–406–1, USITC Publ. No. 867 (1978); Clothespins from the People's Republic of China, the Polish People's Republic, and the Socialist Republic of Romania, TA–406–2, TA–406–3 and TA–406–4, USITC Publ. No. 902 (1978).

45. *Pepsi's Bulgarian Strategy: Reciprocal Marketing*, 8 Bus. EASTERN EUR. 201 (1979).

46. Law No. 1, OFFICIAL BULL. in No. 33 of SR of ROUMANIA, March 17, 1971; Decree Nos. 424 and 425 on Constitution, Organization and Operation of Joint Companies in SR of Romania.

47. Decree of the Hungarian Minister of Finance on Economic Associations with Foreign Participation, No. 28 of 1978 *as amended by* No. 7 of 1977 and No. 5 of 1979.

48. Decree of Polish Council of Ministers on Establishing Joint Ventures in Poland and Their Operation, No. 24 of Feb. 7, 1979.

49. Official Gazette of SFRJ, No. 18/78, Art. 2.

50. Official Gazette of SFRJ, No. 18/78, Arts. 2 and 19.

51. Hungarian Decree No 7 of 1977, § 2(1), *supra* note 47.

52. Polish Decree No. 24 of 1979, *supra* note 48.

53. Decree No. 123/1976 of the Polish Council of Ministers, Preamble.

54. *But see* Law on Joint Ventures of the People's Republic of China, July 8, 1979, Article 5 (liability for losses) and Article 7 (tax holiday), relating to the question of advanced technology.

55. "Roumanian officials, point out that, in their view, the principal aim of the joint venture is to develop or increase exports to hard currency markets." Downey, *Joint Cooperation as an Instrument of East-West Trade*, *supra* note 11, at 121, 125.

56. "This motivation [for the foreign partner] may be dictated by a desire to eliminate or reduce the competition of other firms operating in the same geographical area . . ." Downey, *id.* at 125.

57. S. PISAR, *supra* note 9, at 189.

58. "The closed nature of their system permits, much more efficaciously than meets the eye, the implementation of ultraprotectionist commercial policies by means of simple administrative directives." *Id.* at 190.

59. Annex to Decree No. 24, *supra* note 52, Art. 26.

60. J.H. Griffen, *supra* note 18, at 30.

61. S. PISAR, *supra* note 9, at 23–24.

62. By contrast, in the "market socialism" of Yugoslavia, the basis of an antitrust law is found in the Constitution. Art. 255 . . . which states:
Any merger of organizations of associated labour and any other activity or conduct by organizations of state agencies aimed at preventing free movement, labour and resource pooling and free exchange of goods and services, or at establishing monopolistic positions on the unified Yugoslav market through which material and other advantages that are not based on labour are acquired and unequal relations in business created or which disrupt other economic and social relations determined by the constitution shall be prohibited.

This provision is repeated in the Law on Associated Labour (Official Gazette of SFRJ No. 7/76, November 25, 1976) in Article 21(2) and criminal sanctions for such activities are provided in the form of fines in Article 647 of the same law.

However, one must bear in mind that the system of market socialism is also regulated by a system of self-management agreements and social compacts which introduce a strong element of planning into the economy.

63. Szasz, *supra* note 14, at 16.
64. Decree No. 56 of 1967 (19.XII.) Korm. § 18(1) and (2).
65. Szasz, *supra* note 14, at 7; Decree No. 56, *supra* note 64, at § 1(1).
66. Chance, *Codes of Conduct for Multinational Corporations*, 33 Bus. Law. 1808 (1978).
67. Roffe, *UNCTAD: Code of Conduct on Transfer of Technology: A Progress Review*, 12 J. World Trade L. 351, 352 (1978).

68. *Id.* at 353.
69. *Editorial*, 14 J. World Trade L. 1 (1980).
70. Pisar, *Trade, Law and Peace: A Model Code for East/West Transactions*, 10 J. Int'l. Econ. 267, 280 (1975).
71. See text accompanying note 24, *supra*.
72. It should be noted, however, that as of 1973 MNCs were involved in only 46.5 percent of East-West trade agreements. Of this percentage just under one-half were agreements involving small MNCs (sales below $500 million and one to four foreign affiliates). C. H. McMillan, *Forms and Dimensions of East/West Interfirm Cooperation*, in East-West Cooperation in Business, *supra* note 10, at 55.
73. Pisar, *supra* note 32, at 5.
74. Schamm, *The OECD Guidelines for Multinational Enterprises*, 12 J. World Trade L. 342, 348 (1978).
75. *Antitrust in East-West Trade*, *supra* note 28, at 5.

Multinational Efforts

Reflections on Recent OECD Activities: Regulation of Multinational Corporate Conduct and Structure

KURT STOCKMANN

In recent, years, the Organisation for Economic Cooperation and Development (OECD) has repeatedly addressed, in a variety of forms, the problem of transnational corporate concentration. In the field of restrictive business practices, it has made suggestions on specific antitrust problems, issued council recommendations, and promulgated the 1976 Concil Guidelines for multinational enterprises. Not surprisingly for an organisation that adheres to the principle of unanimity and, consequently, is governed by the law of the smallest common denominator, these efforts have thus far focused more on procedure than on substance. Even where quasi-substantive rules have been adopted, such as in competition guideline 1(a),[1] the "rules" tend to be lenient compared with stricter national antitrust laws like those of the United States and Germany. A structural approach to the problem of concentration, similar to Section 7 of the Clayton Act and the German merger law, has not had a great chance of adoption in the OECD. The reason is simply that most member countries still feel that flexible, conduct-oriented solutions are more appropriate.

Still, it would be rash to underestimate the importance of OECD efforts in this field. Particularly noteworthy are such procedural achievements as the 1967 and 1973 Recommendations on international cooperation, both now replaced by the consolidated Recommendation of 1979.[2] Although the 1967 Recommendation was not specifically intended to address transnational corporate concentration, it was highly relevant to the problem since the recommended procedures were, and under the 1979 Recommendation continue to be, applied in transnational merger cases.

To obtain a complete picture of OECD activity in this field, it is not

Kurt Stockmann is the chief of the International Section of the Bundeskartellamt of the Federal Republic of Germany. He has been a member of the FRG delegation to the OECD and UNCTAD, and is a major contributor to the OECD Guidelines on Restrictive Business Practices.

sufficient to concentrate upon competition guideline 1(a) and corresponding section (1)(a) of the 1978 Recommendation concerning multinationals,[3] or the substantive suggestions in the OECD report on mergers.[4] Rather, competition guideline 4, the recommendations on cooperation with multinationals regarding restrictive business pracitices, is also relevant. The following analysis embraces this broader approach.

Before embarking on this analysis, it is helpful to describe briefly the mechanics of OECD activity. Actions of the OECD in the field of competition originate generally in the OECD Committee of Experts on Restrictive Business Practices (Committee) and its working parties. This Committee, in existence almost since the beginning of the OECD itself, has the authority to examine and comment upon particular competition problems and to report and make recommendations as appropriate to the OECD Council (Council) on matters within its competence.[5] Its studies on specific problems often result in published reports providing "suggestions for action" and/or in draft Council recommendations, which when adopted by the OECD Council, are addressed to member countries. Suggestions for action in such reports do not formally involve the Council even though the Council has to approve of reports of the Committee of Experts. Council recommendations are more formal and have a greater political weight in OECD usage. The OECD guidelines for multinational enterprises do engage the OECD Council but are addressed to enterprises, not member countries as with recommendations.

The first instance of a more than passing reference to some aspects of transnational corporate concentration is to be found in the report by the secretary general on inflation of December 1970.[6] This report discusses the issue of multinational corporate market power in the context of an effective competition policy as a method to fight inflation. It exposes multinationals and their market power as one of the more serious problems in the field of inflation, noting that acquisition by corporate merger is one route to such market power. However, the report does not limit its suggestions for action to market power acquired by external growth. Legislative action is advocated not only against undesirable mergers, but also against concentration of market power in general. In consequence of the secretary general's report on inflation, the OECD Council adopted a recommendation concerning action against inflation in the field of competition policy.[7] This nonbinding recommendation addressed to member countries cautiously advised governments, without specific reference to international restraints of competition or legislation, "to examine the advisability of adopting" effective provisions against the harmful practices of monopolies and oligopolies as well as against undesirable mergers and concentrations of enterprises which limit competition unduly. Both the suggestions for action in the secretary general's report and the recommendation seem to have been used in support of the national legislation generally strengthening competition laws.

Subsequently, the OECD Committee of Experts on Restrictive Business

Practices decided to examine more fully the problem of national and international corporate concentration, and thus established a working party on mergers. The working party's effort resulted in an OECD report on mergers, published in 1975.[8] After a careful analysis of the available data, the report concluded that transnational corporate concentration may have both beneficial and detrimental effects on national economic welfare and competition. In its suggestions for action, the report does not distinguish, in principle, between forms of national and transnational concentration;[9] rather, it recommends that as transnational concentrations raise particularly difficult procedural problems, member countries should utilize the OECD procedures on international cooperation, consultation, and conciliation.[10]

The next, and thus far most spectacular, action relevant to transnational corporate concentration occurred in June 1976 when the OECD Council adopted a Declaration on International Investment and Multinational Enterprises. This declaration recommended a set of "Guidelines for Multinational Enterprises" as well as intergovernmental consultation procedures applicable to these guidelines.[11] The guidelines cover, *inter alia,* general business policies, disclosure of information, and competitive practices. Those three (of seven) sections include provisions which touch directly or indirectly upon problems of transnational corporate concentration.

These guidelines are nonbinding standards of conduct or, in the words of the introductory paragraphs, recommendations jointly addressed by member countries to multinational enterprises operating in their territories.[12] Observance of these guidelines "is voluntary and not legally enforceable." Their objective is "to ensure that the operations of these enterprises are in harmony with national policies of the countries where they operate and to strengthen the basis of mutual confidence between enterprises and States." The introduction provides that every state retains the right to prescribe the conditions under which multinational enterprises operate within its national jurisdiction; moreover, the different entities of a multinational enterprise are subject to the laws of the countries within which they transact business.[13]

As with the suggestions for action relating to the fight against inflation and undesirable mergers, the guidelines refrain from introducing specific substantive rules for multinational enterprises. The introduction explicitly states that guidelines "are not aimed at introducing differences of treatment between national and domestic enterprises"; rather, these enterprises "are subject to the same expectations in respect to their conduct wherever the guidelines are relevant to both."[14] In light of this principle of nondiscrimination, the deliberate absence in the introductory statement of a precise legal definition of *multinational enterprise* is workable.[15]

The first and only quasi-substantive guideline directly relevant to transnational corporate concentration reads:

> Enterprises should, while conforming to official competition rules and
> established policies of the countries in which they operate,

    1. refrain from actions which would adversely affect competition in the relevant market by abusing a dominant position of market power, by means of, for example

       a) anticompetitive acquisitions. . . .[16]

The first point requiring interpretation is the word *enterprise*. It means primarily, of course, "multinational enterprise," although, as stated in paragraph nine of the introduction,[17] the guidelines reflect "good practice for all." In the light of paragraph eight of the introduction it seems clear that the nature of the ownership is irrelevant; it may be private, public, mixed, or state ownership.[18] Less clear is whether the multinational enterprise in toto, including its various subsidiaries and branches located in different countries in different legal forms, is the addressee of this guideline, or whether these individually located entities are each addressees. Although somewhat enigmatic,[19] the introductory phrases seem to favor the second alternative:

> [T]he guidelines are addressed to the various entities within the multinational enterprise (parent companies and/or local entities) according to the actual distribution of responsibilities among them as the understanding that they will co-operate and provide assistance to one another as necessary to facilitate observance of the guidelines. The word "enterprise" as used in these guidelines refers to these various entities in accordance with their responsibilities.

Thus, in spite of being addressed in principle to the various entities, the criterion for the applicability of the guideline seems to be business "responsibility." Although the guidelines do not offer a definition of *responsibility*, interpreting this term as being, among other things, similar to the notion of "control" or "independent decision making authority" would lead to acceptable results. A subsidiary whose pricing policies were controlled by a parent would not be responsible for these prices and not an addressee of the competition guidelines on pricing. If this is true, it is difficult to follow Hawk when he states that the guidelines do not adopt the "highly controversial and ill-defined intraenterprise or 'bathtub' conspiracy doctrine."[20] That the guidelines do not distinguish between operations through a branch or division and operations through a separately incorporated subsidiary does not necessarily support his conclusion.[21] The use of the criterion "responsibility" makes an explicit distinction superfluous: branches and divisions are not responsible but subsidiaries may be, according to the circumstances and the degree of control by the parent company. One may conclude that the guidelines, without explicitly deciding this question, may be interpreted along the lines of the "bathtub conspiracy doctrine" and may possibly approximate the "effective working control" standard of the U.S. Department of Justice *Antitrust Guide for International Operations*.[22] The consequences of this interpretation are of no primary importance in the context of transnational corporation concentration, but they may play a decisive role in other areas such as joint ventures, which are treated by certain antitrust laws as restrictive agreements.[23]

The second element of the introductory wording of competition guideline 1 acknowledges the priority of the individual competition rules and policies of the countries in which the enterprises operate.[24] The word *operate* does not mean that the applicability of the guidelines is based on the "conduct principle" as opposed to the "effects doctrine" recognized by the majority of OECD member countries with antitrust laws.[25] This issue, which is highly contested among OECD member countries, was deliberately left open in the guidelines.

The third criterion a multinational corporation must meet in order to be an addressee of competition guideline 1(a) is that of "dominant position of market power." The concept of controlling abuse of market power, although not entirely unknown to U.S. law, is much more familiar to European antitrust laws.[26] European Community practice under Article 86 of the EEC Treaty illustrates the practical elements of this form of antitrust enforcement.[27] The control of market power abuse is in practice similar to antitrust regulation under Section 2 of the Sherman Act. However, there are some basic differences in the scope of regulation between the Sherman Act and OECD competition guideline 1(a). In one respect, Section 2 of the Sherman Act is broader than guideline 1(a) since Section 2 covers attempts to monopolize while the guideline applies only if a dominant position of market power is already present.[28] How this dominant market position is obtained is entirely irrelevant, as for example in the EEC Treaty Article 86 and Section 22 of the German Act Against Restraints of Competition. On the other hand, guideline 1(a) is broader at least in theory, since its applicability does not necessarily turn upon market share criteria.[29] A dominant position of market power may be established even if the enterprise holds only a small market share but commands superior financial or marketing resources, or more factors of protection, particularly if the relevant market is held predominantly by small- or medium-sized firms.

The fourth criterion is that the action in question has to affect competition in the "relevant market." Although the language is not without ambiguity, OECD member countries will probably interpret the term in the sense that the effect has to be in the same relevant market in which the dominating position of market power is held.[30] Otherwise, the words "in the relevant market" would have little meaning; if anticompetitive effects would be sufficient, irrespective of the market in which they occur, these words could have been omitted.

The actions from which enterprises should refrain are such that "would adversely affect competition." The guidelines do not offer any additional explanation of these terms. In spite of divergent interpretations in different OECD countries and the European Community, it is unlikely that this element will create many practical difficulties. Furthermore, it can safely be assumed that effects on competition that were merely theoretical would not be sufficient to find a violation of guideline 1(a); they would have to be at least "perceptible" in the sense of EEC and German antitrust enforcement practice.[31] However, some countries might interpret competition guideline 1 as requiring "substantial" effects.

Any adverse effects on competition must be brought about by an "abuse." Five subparagraphs give examples for types of abuses, this list being explanatory and not exclusive. Hawk has already suggested that European members of the OECD might interpret an abuse of a dominant position as including practices not enumerated in the list;[32] non-European members might obviously do the same. In regard to concentration this means that not only those forms of abuse falling under competition guideline 1(a), namely anticompetitive acquisitions, are subject to the guideline, but also other forms of external or internal growth not mentioned. Thus, it does not make much sense to interpret the term *acquisition* narrowly. Davidow seems to share this view when he deals with guideline 1(a) and assumes that it covers "acquisitions and mergers."[33] Guideline 1(a) certainly covers all forms of external concentration such as horizontal, vertical, and conglomerate mergers and acquisitions.[34]

The qualification "anti-competitive" is not very meaningful if one accepts that the adverse effects on competition required by the introduction of guideline 1 have to appear in the market in which the enterprise holds a dominant position. The consequence of this requirement in the introductory phrase is that vertical or conglomerate mergers having no adverse effects on competition in the market in which the enterprise holds the dominant position, but only in the market into which the acquiring corporation extends its activities, do not fall under competition guideline 1(a) even though such acquisitions or mergers are anticompetitive. In other words, the qualification does not extend the scope of application of guideline 1(a), which covers only such "anticompetitive" acquisitions which adversely affect competition in the market dominated by the enterprise.[35]

As in Section 7 of the Clayton Act, assessment of anticompetitive effects of an acquisition requires a hypothetical analysis. While under the Clayton Act it is sufficient that the merger *may* lessen competition, guideline 1(a) requires that it *would* adversely affect competition.[36] It seems clear that guideline 1(a) requires a far higher degree of certainty of effect, with a concomitant higher burden of proof and sufficiency of evidence. The criteria to be used in this determination, however, are still unclear, that is, whether the effects have to be expected beyond a reasonable doubt or whether a high degree of likelihood would suffice.

An interesting question is whether any defenses can be raised in cases of acquisitions. Davidow and Hawk[37] are probably accurate in stating that the regular defenses are implicit in competition guideline 1. This conclusion, however, should not be made, as Hawk seems to do, from the "anticompetitive" qualification in guideline 1(a) since it is redundant. Rather, this conclusion can be deduced from the "adversely affect competition" requirement in the introductory phrase or perhaps even from the "abuse" criterion. Thus, under the first alternative a valid failing company defense would be premised upon the argument that the acquisition does not adversely affect competition in the dominated market. Under the second alternative, it could be argued that the acquisition of a "failing company"—one which would no longer be a competitor—does not constitute an abuse.

To conclude the discussion of guideline 1(a), it is quite correct to estimate that no direct and important effects are to be expected, particularly in those countries applying stricter and structure-oriented national merger laws.[38] Still, as a policy statement of the OECD the guideline has a certain value, either as a symbol, a model, or as a clear articulation of a perceived problem, especially in those member countries which have not yet introduced merger control.

The second quasi-substantive competition guideline relevant for transnational corporate concentration is guideline 3:

> Enterprises should, while conforming to official competition rules and established policies of the countries in which they operate . . . refrain from participating in or otherwise purposely strengthening the restrictive effects of international or domestic cartels or restrictive agreements which adversely affect or eliminate competition and which are not generally or specifically accepted under applicable national or international legislation.[39]

This guideline dealing with cartels and other restrictive agreements may be of particular interest for those countries, and the European Community, which do not yet have specific merger legislation. One means of attempting some control over external concentration is to interpret prohibitions of restrictive agreements broadly, for example, by regarding joint ventures as such agreements. A practical illustration of this possibility is afforded by the European Community's practice on joint ventures.[40] Increasingly, the European Community administration tends to regard joint ventures as cartels under Article 85 (1) of the EEC Treaty that prohibits restrictive agreements. This has been done in part by extending the procedural application of Article 85 more and more to transactions which were already considered concentrations in other countries. Someone familiar with this practice may find it adequate to deal with joint ventures under competition guideline 3. Other examples can be found in national antitrust laws, such as those of the United States, that apply merger control under certain circumstances to prevent restrictive agreements in joint ventures.[41] In Germany, the relationship between the ban on cartels, Section 1 of the Act against Restraints of Competition (ARC) and merger control Section 23 *et seq.* ARC, is still in debate; one view is that at least as to certain forms of joint ventures, Section 1 ARC applies either simultaneously with Sections 23 ff., or even exclusively.[42] In this context, it does not seem necessary to go into all the delicate problems of interpreting this guideline but rather to concentrate on those aspects which would make it possible for certain forms of transnational corporate concentration such as joint ventures to be measured under diverging standards, depending on whether they are assessed under guideline 1(a) or 3.

A first and quite important difference is that guideline 1(a) applies only when market domination is already present, while guideline 3 has no such requirement. Consequently, under guideline 3, joint ventures may be found objectionable when classical concentrations do not rise to the level of control under guideline 1(a).

A second question arises in connection with the words "or otherwise purposely strengthening the restrictive effects of" as opposed to "participating in" international or domestic cartels. While guideline 1(a) applies clearly only to those participating in a merger, or, more precisely, to those participants which hold a market-dominating position, guideline 3 also applies to third parties. However, the broad wording of guideline 3 must be interpreted narrowly,[43] certainly in regard to concentrations. The drafters of this text did not intend to subject specific forms of concentration to a more rigorous regime of regulation without some showing of general anticompetitive effects beyond those associated with classical forms of concentration. Joint ventures are, in general, no more anticompetitive than takeovers. The wording, however, leaves no choice; any interpretation that prevented application of guideline 3 to those other than the participants would be clearly incompatible with the express wording of the guideline and, therefore, is beyond the limits of interpretation. In order to reconcile guidelines 1(a) and 3 insofar as corporate concentration is concerned, an acceptable solution might be to interpret "purposely strengthening" as referring to the predominant aim of third party conduct. One must show that the *predominant aim* of the third party is to further the restrictive effects of the concentrative agreements; conduct alone which has such an effect, even if foreseen and substantial, is insufficient. In other words, a showing of intent and purpose to foster a restrictive result is necessary.

The difference in wording in regard to the effects test under guideline 1(a)—"which would adversely affect competition," and guideline 3—"which adversely affect or eliminate competition," are of no material significance. The explicit reference to the elimination of competition in guideline 3 does not imply that an acquisition eliminating competition would not also fall within the "adversely affect competition" standard found in guideline 1(a). Moreover, the difference between "would affect" in guideline 1(a) and "affect" in guideline 3 does not constitute a material distinction. It appears that both guidelines require anticompetitive effects either to be present or to be expected beyond a reasonable doubt or certain degree of probability. The required degree of proof to be applied with guideline 3 remains as uncertain as with guideline 1.[44]

Guideline 3, unlike guideline 1(a), contains a reservation exempting from its coverage agreements "which are not generally or specifically accepted under applicable national or international legislation." This qualification referring to the various exemptions granted certain cartels found in national antitrust laws, such as export cartels, import cartels, rationalization cartels, and crisis cartels, is arguably already covered by the introductory sentence "while conforming to official competition rules . . . of the countries in which they operate." Enterprises engaging in a joint venture falling under a specialization exemption are in compliance with national competition rules,[45] and thus are also in compliance with guideline 3. This qualification reemphasizes that member countries remain free to establish as many exemptions from the ban of restrictive agreements as they wish and, therefore, may permit corporate concentration, both national and transnational, in order to effectuate other economic or social policies. It is not clear that the clause should be considered redundant as regards internationally accepted agreements. If the qualification in guideline 3 were to be deleted, however, the OECD member countries that were also members of the European Community would in all likelihood subsume an agreement exempted by Article 85(3) of the EEC Treaty under "official competition rules . . . of the countries in which they operate." Therefore, the qualification found in guideline 3 does not restrict its scope of application beyond the limits already established by the introductory phrase and the general prevalence of national legislation over the OECD guidelines.

Competition guideline 4 reads:

> Enterprises should, while conforming to official competition rules and established policies of the countries in which they operate . . . be ready to consult and cooperate, including the provision of information with competent authorities of countries whose interests are directly affected in regard to competition issues or investigations. Provision of information should be in accordance with safeguards normally applicable in this field.[46]

In contrast to guidelines 1 through 3, competition guideline 4 deals with procedural problems, doing so in a general fashion and not specifically in regard to problems of transnational corporate concentration. Still, this guideline deserves comment, since dealing with transnational concentration at the OECD level will for a long time be a predominantly procedural problem. Even in the European Community, the probability that an enforceable merger control regulation will be adopted is small. In other international organizations, including the OECD, the chances of such action are even smaller.

To a certain extent, guideline 4 adopts language already used in the OECD recommendations of 1967 and 1973 concerning cooperation, consultation, and conciliation in the field of restrictive business practices affecting international trade.[47] In contrast to these recommendations that are addressed to member governments, guideline 4 addresses enterprises.

Guideline 4 contains various complex prerequisites and, to some extent, this complexity decreases the danger of this guideline being continuously invoked by antitrust authorities in their dealings with transnational corporations.[48] The general requirement "to be ready to consult and to co-operate" is no more than an appeal to make life somewhat less difficult for antitrust officials. Similar appeals in the context of national antitrust proceedings may have a different significance, since unlike the OECD guidelines, in such proceedings there are very real sanctions available against obstreperous enterprises and real benefits to be gained through cooperation.

The situation could be somewhat different in regard to the provision of information which guideline 4 mentions as one of the forms of cooperation. That the provision of information is the main issue becomes evident by reading the second sentence of this guideline. First, I agree with Hawk[49] and Davidow,[50] that "to be ready to provide information" goes beyond legal obligations under existing national laws. This was the prevailing view during the discussions in the working party on multinationals.

Guideline 4 requires cooperation with authorities of "countries whose interests are directly affected." As other scholars have correctly pointed out,[51] this covers authorities of countries in which the enterprises concerned have neither a subsidiary nor a branch office. One should not overestimate the impact of this seemingly sweeping provision. If an enterprise has no subsidiary or branch office in the country concerned, there are not many sanctions available to enforce a request for information based solely on competition guideline 4.

Admittedly, sentence 2 of guideline 4 is vague and ambiguous. In spite of this, Hawk seems to overestimate the potential danger of this mandate for affected enterprises. On the contrary, any enumeration of special safeguards such as business secret, professional secret, and others, probably would have been more dangerous. The reference to safeguards "normally applicable" was meant to preclude any loopholes. "Normally applicable" does not mean that there must be a consensus among OECD member countries about the validity and applicability of a special safeguard. Rather, it merely indicates that the safeguards normally applicable under the applicable national laws (that is, the laws of the countries in which the enterprise possessing the information and the authority requesting the information are located) shall also be available without reservation if guideline 4 is invoked.

The OECD guidelines for multinational enterprises contain some further guidelines relevant for competition. The most important in this context is guideline 3 of the "General Policies" chapter[52] which overlaps in part with competition guideline 4, and is simultaneously applicable with competition guideline 4.

General policy guideline 3 is somewhat limited inasmuch as it is concerned only with the provision of information and not with consultation and cooperation. It is also narrow since it deals only with information requested by the authorities of a country in which the addressee enterprise has a subsidiary or branch. However, this guideline contains a broader mandate insofar as it requires that certain information be divulged to interested authorities, as well as to those entities of the enterprise that operate within the particular national jurisdiction. There are a number of ambiguities and uncertainties involved. According to the wording of this guideline it appears that multinationals are expected to go beyond their legal obligations. However, it is unclear whether the particular entity facing the request for information is under the same obligation. Furthermore, the only safeguard explicitly mentioned is business confidentiality; it is not certain that the others which are clearly covered by competition guideline 4 are equally applicable.

The chapter dealing with "disclosure of information" may also become relevant to transnational corporate concentration.[53] Much of the information to be provided by enterprises under this chapter is relevant for merger control, for example information about the structure of an enterprise, ownership percentage, areas of activities, sales, and investments. The information gathered pursuant to this guideline will be published annually. However, in practice, the burden to the enterprises of providing the requested information will be limited by two principal factors—the costs of collection and publication of the information, and the rules on business confidentiality. These guidelines should not create a greater burden for enterprises than disclosure requirements under competition guideline 4. There are other guidelines also relevant for competition issues, but which have no direct significance for transnational corporate concentration, such as guideline 2 on taxation and intraenterprise transfer pricing. It should be noted, of course, that regulation of intraenterprise activities may well foster or hinder concentration.

For matters related to the OECD guidelines for multinational enterprises, in 1976 the OECD Council adopted a decision establishing an intergovernmental consultation procedure.[54] In the field of competition, a question arises immediately as to the relationship of this procedure, administered essentially by the Committee on International Investment and Multinational Enterprises (IME), to the specific cooperation, consultation, and conciliation procedures in the field of restrictive business practices affecting international trade. Today, the question remains the same as in 1976, that is, whether the consultation and other procedural requirements of one set of guidelines preclude the application of requirements pursuant to OECD decisions. The 1967 and 1973 recommendations regulating these procedures have been consolidated by a new recommendation of 1979[55] without changing their substance or administration by the OECD Committee of Experts on Restrictive Business Practices. There is no explicit answer to this question in either procedure. It appears that both procedures may, in principle, be used in the same case; there is no general priority for one or the other. A transnational merger case may thus lead to consultations under the 1979 Recommendation as well as under paragraph four of the 1976 intergovernmental consultation procedure, provided the proposed merger subjects the interested corporate entities to conflicting requirements under national laws. Although the intergovernmental consultation procedure is, as regards competition, more narrowly focused than the 1979 restrictive business practices procedure, it is not exclusive in the sense that issues falling within the guidelines are the exclusive concern of the IME Committee. It is open to argument which procedure would be more practical to utilize in a specific case. Nothing precludes the same case being negotiated and examined by both committees at the same time. Moreover, the theoretical risk of divergent results could probably be avoided by a minimum of coordination within the OECD.

The OECD report on multinational enterprises under competition policy aspects published in 1977[56] contains a number of cautious and balanced suggestions for action, some of which are relevant to transnational corporate concentration. They have been taken into account in the 1978 Council Recommendation on restrictive business practices of multinational enterprises.[57]

The Council Recommendation adopted in 1978, as well as the report upon which it was based was prepared by the Restrictive Business Practices Committee and its Working Group on multinationals. In regard to its quasi-substantive recommendations the Business Practices Committee kept very close to the competition guidelines. Most differences in regard to the two quasi-substantive rules—guidelines 1(a) and 3 on the one hand and recommendations (1)(a) line 1 and (1)(b) on the other hand—can be explained by the simple fact that guidelines are addressed to enterprises while the 1978 Recommendation is addressed to governments. Accordingly, (1)(a), instead of requesting that the governments "refrain from certain actions," recommends that they "adopt new or supplement existing measures" to "prohibit or control effectively such practices." In substance, the requirements suggested in regard to acquisitions are the same as those contained in guideline (1)(a).[58]

With respect to cartels, though the wording of guideline 3 differs more greatly from recommendation 1(b) than do the measures discussed in the preceding paragraph, there is no implication of substantive differences between the two. The recommendation suggests action against "cartels or other restrictive agreements" without any reference to activities of nonparticipants that purposely strengthen the restrictive effect of such agreements; however, this does not limit remedial action to measures that seek to ensure free participation. On the contrary, a measure to effectively control cartels could also be directed against outsiders that purposely strengthen the restrictive agreement or cartel.[59] Furthermore, the term *cartels or other restrictive agreements* encompasses both national and international agreements explicitly enumerated in this guideline.

The more troublesome difference between guideline 3 and recommendation 1(b) pertains to the safeguard clauses in each instrument. Guideline 3 conditions improper agreements on the basis of those "generally or specifically accepted under applicable national or international legislation"; the recommendation refers only to agreements "without justification." Without being familiar with the history of both the guideline and the recommendation, one would be inclined to seek different interpretations. However, the drafters of both texts intended the guideline and recommendation to cover all possible exemptions to general cartel prohibitions afforded by national and international legislation. Both clauses were intended to cover general and specific exceptions that exist in law, as well as those for which enterprises must show good cause before enforcement or judicial authorities can grant an exception.

The following recommendations (2) to (5)[60] are procedural and based on the report on multinationals. Each may play a role when governments deal with the problem of transnational corporate concentration. These recommendations call upon member countries to improve their antitrust procedures, to cooperate in disclosing information, and to lend aid for effective national antitrust enforcement. They suggest that this cooperation can best be achieved through additional bilateral and multilateral agreements as well as through further use of existing OECD procedures.

It should be noted that substantial importance has been attributed to the Working Party's note accompanying the draft on competition submitted to the IME Committee.[61] It has been suggested by Hawk[62] that this note should be kept in mind in interpreting the competition guidelines. This suggestion certainly was proper until the Council adopted the 1978 Recommendation prepared by the same expert groups that had prepared the guidelines. The note, no doubt, remains valid as to its general statements about the limited amount of information on the role of multinationals in national and international competition.

Although competition guidelines 1(a) and 3 are in substance identical to recommendations 1(a) and (b), this does not necessarily indicate that the Working Party has given up its specific caveat in the interpretative note: namely, that "standards of behaviour dealing with difficult legal and economic concepts such as abuse of market power [and] adverse effects on competition . . . do not in themselves provide simple rules for business executives to follow in all circumstances." This reservation remains valid because of the difference in quality between guidelines for enterprises and recommendations for governments. The practical value of guidelines addressed to enterprises may be seriously compromised by the vague and ambiguous nature of the mandate they contain; in contrast, the vagueness of recommendations for governmental action will have less impact upon their practical and political value.

The final OECD instrument to be briefly examined is entirely procedural. In the field of competition, the procedure set forth in the 1979 Council Recommendation Concerning Cooperation between member countries is the most important achievement of OECD.[63] The part of this procedure dealing with cooperation is likely to be successful since it is practically identical to the 1967 Recommendation, under which cooperation took place with respect to a substantial number of transnational mergers. There is no reason why this should change. On the contrary, the consolidation of the 1967 and 1973 procedures may lead to more frequent consultations between antitrust authorities in international merger cases and on problems of transnational corporate concentration. As to the part on conciliation, this result seems to be less likely, because the conciliation part of the 1973 Recommendation has never been applied.

CONCLUSION

It can be seen that OECD activity with respect to competition policy has primarily been in the area of restrictive business practices—indicating the adoption of what is principally a behavioral approach to the control of multinational enterprises. Though aware of the problems of multinational corporate concentration, the OECD has not thus far taken direct measures with a structural approach as such.

In discerning the reasons for this past tendency toward behavioral rather than structural measures, it must be remembered that OECD efforts are significantly influenced by the principle of unanimity,[64] and therefore tend to represent the least common denominator among the member countries. OECD decisions are usually made by mutual agreement. This principle applies a well to the OECD committees and working parties such as the Committee of Experts on Restrictive Business Practices.[65]

Accordingly, it is important to recognize that less than a third of the OECD member countries have adopted any structurally based approach to merger control.[66] Moreover, enforcement in these countries with structural merger control laws does not always appear wholehearted. Until recently, the member nations have evidenced different attitudes toward the relative benefits and liabilities of corporate concentration, and thus have differed considerably in their attitudes toward regulation of industrial structure. Indeed, some European nations, for example the United Kingdom and France, have in the past actively supported the concentration of economic power in large national corporations.

Thus, the adoption of clear, structure-oriented recommendations should not be expected from the OECD within the next few years. However, it would be a mistake to ignore the influence of the OECD activity in this area since national legislators naturally look to OECD activity when contemplating modification of national regulatory mechanisms. Moreover, the changing political climate in the various member countries with respect to corporate concentration and antitrust laws generally portends a substantial impetus for future OECD action in the field. A number of member countries are adopting a more critical attitude toward the concentration phenomenon, and are moving in the direction of more stringent antitrust policy in general. At the same time, no member country has currently evinced a trend in the direction of fostering concentration. A number of member countries are seriously contemplating enactment of merger controls or have recently introduced such control. The most spectacular example is France, which for many years encouraged corporate concentration. Similar controls are being considered in

Sweden, Finland, and Ireland. Another group of countries, including Switzerland and Germany, is taking action to strengthen its antitrust laws in general.

These national trends will surely be reflected by the delegates in the Committee of Experts, and the Committee of Experts will very likely adopt a more critical attitude toward transnational corporation concentration. Of course, the Organisation's unanimity principle theoretically will preclude formal action if one member country opposes such action. Nonetheless, experience shows that if there is a clear majority on a particular issue, absolute opposition is difficult to maintain over time. Compromise solutions are usually found. Even when this is not possible, it is still more likely that an opposing party will abstain rather than veto a recommendation or suggestion for action.[67] The evolution of competition policies in the member countries promises to keep the problem of transnational corporate concentration on the OECD agenda, and increases the possibility that the OECD will adopt a more vocal and critical position toward such concentration.

In addition to the influences of the member countries, the developments in the European Economic Community and the United Nations will tend to influence future OECD efforts in the area. The European Community, with a functioning antitrust law and enforcement practice, stands as an example of a working supranational antitrust regime, and should lend encouragement to OECD member countries in developing greater cooperation on substantive antitrust matters including mergers and concentration. Although the European communities do not yet have a functioning merger control procedure,[68] except in the coal and steel sectors,[69] a draft European Community merger regulation has been under discussion for several years. Even though there is little chance for effective action in the near future, enactment of a European Community merger law would have a substantial impact on OECD initiatives and would generate additional momentum for future OECD efforts.

The influence of United Nations activities on OECD efforts is somewhat different. The United Nations, unlike the European Community, is a most heterogenous organization, and consequently the likelihood of substantive agreement on economic and competition values and objectives is minimal in that forum. Nonetheless, UNCTAD and the UN Centre for Transnational Corporations are considering the establishment of machinery which will be relevant to the issue of transnational corporate concentration. Although there is a marked disparity between the concerns of the industrialized and the developing countries, any consensus which is achieved in the United Nations organizations will undoubtedly encourage further OECD efforts. For example, if UNCTAD were to establish a permanent committee of experts on restrictive business practices, some method to harmonize the position of the industrialized market economy countries will be required. The OECD would be best equipped to effectuate that objective.

In summary, OECD efforts in transnational corporate concentration will continue. As member countries begin informally to adopt similar attitudes toward the problem, the chances increase for formal OECD action. The potential positive impetus of European Community merger control activities, and the possible necessity of reaching a coordinated OECD position in the realm of United Nations activities both would encourage the OECD to begin a more activist role in the area of transnational corporate concentration.

NOTES

1. Declaration on International Investment and Multinational Enterprises (*21st June 1976*); Guidelines for Multinational Enterprises; Decision of the Council on Inter-Governmental Consultation Procedures on the Guidelines for Multinational Enterprises. These instruments are reproduced in annex 3.

3. Recommendation of the Council Concerning Cooperation Between Member Countries on Restrictive Business Practices Affecting International Trade Including those Involving Multinational Enterprises (Adopted by the Council at its 501st Meeting on 25th September 1979), C(79)154(Final). The recommendation is reproduced in annex 6.

3. Recommendation of the Council Concerning Action Against Restrictive Business Practices Affecting International Trade Including those Involving Multinational Enterprises (Adopted by the Council at its 469th Meeting on 20th July 1978), C(78)133(Final). The recommendation is reproduced in annex 5.

4. Mergers and Competition Policy: Report by the Committee of Experts on Restrictive Business Practices (OECD, Paris, 1979). An excerpt of the report is reproduced in annex 2.

5. Resolution of the Council Concerning Action in the Field of Restrictive Business Practices and the Establishment of a Committee of Experts (Adopted by the Council at its 8th Meeting on 5th December 1961), C(61)47(Final).

6. REPORT BY THE SECRETARY GENERAL, OECD INFLATION—THE PRESENT PROBLEM (December 1970), ¶ 137 *et seq.*

7. Recommendation of the Council Concerning Action Against Inflation in the Field of Competition Policy (Adopted by the Council at its 276th Meeting on 14th and 15th December 1971, and derestricted at its 280th Meeting on 26th January 1972), C(71)205(Final). The recommendation is reproduced in annex 1.

8. Annex 2, *supra* note 4.

9. Annex 2, *supra* note 4, at ¶¶ 185–86.

10. Annex 2, *supra* note 4, at ¶ 187.

11. Annex 3, *supra* note 1.

12. Annex 3, *supra* note 1, Guidelines for Multinational Enterprises, at ¶ 6.

13. *Id.* at ¶ 7.

14. *Id.* at ¶ 9.

15. *Id.* at ¶ 8.

16. *Id.* at competition section.

17. *Id.* at ¶ 9.

18. *Id.* at ¶ 8.

19. Hawk, *The OECD Guidelines for Multinational Enterprises: Competition*, 46 FORDHAM L. REV. 241, 250 (1977).

20. *Id.* at 251.

21. Annex 3, *supra* note 1, Guidelines for Multinational Enterprises, at ¶ 8.

22. ANTITRUST DIVISION U.S. DEPT OF JUSTICE, ANTITRUST GUIDE FOR INTERNATIONAL OPERATIONS (1977).

23. *See, e.g.,* EEC B 1, WORLD LAW OF COMPETITION, Pt. 1. §§ 7.03(3) and (4).

24. Annex 3, *supra* note 1, Guidelines for Multinational Enterprises, at ¶ 7.

25. *See, e.g.,* Restrictive Business Practices of Multinational Engerprises: Report of the Committee of Experts on Restrictive Business Practices (OECD, Paris, 1977), ¶ 199 ¶¶ 195–218 are reproduced in annex 4.

26. Hawk, *supra* note 19, at 255.

27. *Id.*

28. *Id.* at 255–57.

29. *Id.* at 256–257.

30. *Id.* at 257.

31. *See* EEC B 1, WORLD LAW OF COMPETITION, Pt. 1, § 3.03 (3)(d); FED. REPUBLIC OF GERMANY, B 5, WORLD LAW OF COMPETITION Pt. 9, § 3.03(2)(d).

32. Hawk, *supra* note 19, at 259.

33. Davidow, *Some Reflections on the OECD Competition Guidelines,* 22 ANTITRUST BULL. 441, 447 (1977).

34. Hawk, *supra* note 19, at 260.

35. Thus, it appears that guideline 1(a) is more limited in scope of application than EEC, U.S., or West German conglomerate merger reguation, since in the latter, the relevant market is not limited to that into which the acquiring corporation enters.

36. Hawk, *supra* note 19, at 260.

37. *Id.;* Davidow, *supra* note 33, at 448.

38. Hawk, *supra* note 19, at 261.

39. Annex 3, *supra* note 1 Guidelines for Multinational Enterprises.

40. *See, e.g.,* EEC B 1, WORLD LAW OF COMPETITION, Pt. 1, §§ 7.03(3)–(4).

41. United States v. Penn-Olin Chemical Co., 378 U.S. 158 (1964).

42. *See* FEDERAL CARTEL OFFICE GERMAN FEDERAL REPUBLIC, ANNUAL ACTIVITY REPORT FOR 1978, 23.

43. Hawk, *supra* note 19, at 272.

44. *See* text accompanying note 31 *supra.*

45. *See* annex 3, *supra* note 1, Guidelines for Multinational Enterprises, at ¶ 7.

46. Annex 3a *supra* note 1 Guidelines for Multinational Enterprises.

47. Annex 6, *supra* note 2.

48. Hawk thinks that multinationals can expect antitrust officials to rely on Competition Guideline 4 when negotiating during investigations and legislation. Hawk, *supra* note 19, at 274.

49. *Id.*

50. Davidow, *supra* note 33, at 455.

51. *Id;* Hawk, *supra* note 19, at 274.

52. Annex 3, *supra* note 1 Guidelines for Multinational Enterprises.

53. *Id.*

54. Annex 3, *supra* note 1 Decision of the Council on Inter-Governmental Consultation Procedures.

55. Annex 6, *supra* note 2.

56. Annex 4, *supra* note 25.

57. Annex 5, *supra* note 3.

58. *See* text accompanying notes 11–38 *supra.*

59. *See* text accompanying note 43 *supra.*

60. Annex 5, *supra* note 3.

61. Hawk, *supra* note 19, at 245–46.

62. *Id.* at 245.

63. Annex 6, *supra* note 2.

64. *Id.* The principle of unanimity is laid down in Article 6 of the Convention on the Organisation of Economic Co-operation and Development. [1961] U.S.T.1728, T.I.A.S. 4891 Rules 18 and 29 of the OECD Rules of Procedure regulating also the procedure of the OECD Committee of Experts on Restrictive Business Practices and its working parties refer to this article.

65. OECD Rules of Procedure, R. 18 and 29.

66. Austria for example has only certain informational filing requirements and an abuse control regulation; in Denmark, there is no special rule for mergers; in Finland, the harmful ef-

fects of concentration may be the subject of negotiations between business interests and the government regulators; neither Switzerland nor the Netherlands has merger regulation.

67. For example, Switzerland abstained from taking a vote on the 1967 Recommendation of the Council Concerning Co-operation Between Member Countries on Restrictive Business Practices Affecting International Trade. In the following years, Swiss policy changed and Switzerland adopted both the 1973 Recommendation of the Council Concerning a Consultation and Conciliation Procedure on Restrictive Business Practices Affecting International Trade and the 1979 Recommendation of the Council Concerning Co-operation Between Member Countries on Restrictive Business Practices Affecting International Trade. *See* annex 6, *supra* note 2.

68. To a very limited extent, Articles 85 and 86 of the Treaty of Rome may be used as instruments of concentration control, especially Article 85 in regard to joint ventures and Article 86 if a market-dominating enterprise is involved. Both possibilities, however, are no substitute for the envisaged specific merger control procedure.

69. *See* Treaty Establishing European Coal and Steel Community, Article 65 [signed April 18, 1951].

ANNEX 1: RECOMMENDATION OF THE COUNCIL CONCERNING ACTION
AGAINST INFLATION IN THE FIELD OF COMPETITION POLICY

(Adopted by the Council at its 276th Meeting on 14th and 15th December
1971, and derestricted at its 280th Meeting on 26th January, 1972)

The Council,

Having regard to Article 5(b) of the Convention on the Organisation for
Economic Co-operation and Develoment of 14th December 1960;

Having regard to the Resolution of the Council of 5th December 1961
concerning Action in the Field of Restrictive Business Practices and the
Establishment of a Committee of Experts [Doc. No. OECD/C(61)47(Final)];

Having regard to the Report of 18th November 1971 on the Present
Problem of Inflation and, in particular, the proposals (16) and (19) contained
therein [Doc. No. C(70)182];

Having regard to the Interim Report of 26th March 1971 submitted by
the Chairman of the Committee of Experts on Restrictive Business Practices
on Competition Policy and Inflation [Doc. No. C(71)49];

Recognising that an effective competition policy is one important factor
in the achievement of optimum economic growth and price stability; and that
measures to increase competition exercise a pressure on costs, prices and
profits and thus contribute to the fight agains inflation, although the impact
of competition policy is usually apparent in the long term and is less immediate than anti-cyclical fiscal and monetary policies;

Recognising the urgency of curbing inflation and the need for a coordinated and global approach by all Member countries in order to bring about a
significant reduction in inflationary pressures in the near future;

Considering therefore that more emphasis should be given to competition policy at the national level and that, from this standpoint, legislation
against restrictive business practices should be applied with great vigilance
in Member countries and that additional measures could be introduced
where necessary;

Considering moreover that consumer policy can contribute to more rational consumer behaviour, which is essential for the effective functioning of
price and quality competition;

I. RECOMMENDS to the Governments of Member countries

1. that they should promptly take steps, within the framework of their existing legislation:
   (i) to apply their restrictive business practices legislation with great vigi-
       lance against the detrimental effects especially
           (a) of price-fixing and market-sharing agreements,
           (b) of monopolistic and oliogopolistic practices affecting prices, and
           (c) of restrictive business practices in the field of patents and patient
           licensing;

(ii) to keep under review the price situation in key sectors of their economies which have a monopolistic or oliogopolistic structure in order to reduce any excessive prices by administrative or legal means at their disposal;

(iii) to examine whether the bodies responsible for the enforcement of the restrictive business practices legislation have adequate means at their disposal to carry out the measures outlined in paragraphs (i) and (ii) above;

(iv) to strengthen their consumer policies in relation to consumer protection, education and information, where they assist competition to function more effectively;

2. that they should examine the advisability of adopting the following longer-term measures, which may require new legislation:

(i) stronger action—by means of prohibition or control—against resale price maintenance, recommended prices when they operate with a similar effect to resale price maintenance, and refusal to sell employed in connection with resale price maintenance or with recommended prices;

(ii) effective provisions against the harmful practices of monopolies and oliogopolies;

(iii) effective provisions against undesirable mergers and concentrations of enterprises which limit competition unduly;

(iv) extension of their legislation to cover restrictive business practices in service industries or in those sectors to which it does not apply or does not fully apply, when these exemptions are insufficiently justified having regard to the public interest.

II. INSTRUCTS the Committee of Experts on Restrictive Business Practices to review, at its session in the autumn of 1972, the progress made, in particular with regard to short-term action in this field, and to report to the Council.

In adopting this Recommendation, the Council:

1. NOTED the Report by the Committee of Experts on Restrictive Business Practices of 19th November 1971 on Action against Inflation in the Field of Competition Policy [Doc. No. C(71)205 and Corrigendum] and the statement made in this connection by the Delegate for Switzerland at the meeting of the Executive Committee held from 8th to 10th December 1971 [Cf. CE/M(71)39 Part III (Final), Item 278];

2. NOTED with satisfaction the efforts of the Committee of Experts on Restrictive Business Practices to further develop international co-operation for the purpose of increasing competition.

ANNEX 2: EXCERPT FROM MERGERS AND COMPETITION POLICY:
REPORT BY THE COMMITTEE OF EXPERTS ON
RESTRICTIVE BUSINESS PRACTICES (OECD, PARIS, 1979)

General Conclusions

158. The effects upon competition of international mergers are analytically similar to those of domestic mergers, although they sometimes present special problems of evaluation at the national level. On the one hand, unlike purely domestic horizontal mergers, international mergers in some circumstances to not have any adverse effect on concentration at the national level, and they can be a means of introducing vigorous new competition, particularly where the company acquired is a small "foothold" company. It is also possible, of course, that the merger may not improve a non-competitive situation, and may even worsen it if the acquired firm has a large market share. The financial and other resources of the acquiring company can then be used to exploit and increase the already large market share of the acquired company. In addition, a merger which has no effect upon concentration in the countries directly involved may nevertheless increase it at the world level or in third countries. Moreover, an international merger may in some cases lead to restrictions on the freedom of the acquired company to compete in certain product lines or export markets. Also, national control over international mergers sometimes presents jurisdictional and informational problems not encountered in purely domestic mergers. Finally, there is the point that excess profits resulting from international mergers are different to an important degree from excess profits resulting from national mergers, in that the latter involve a domestic redistribution of income whereas the former involve a transfer of income between countries.

159. These considerations seem to point to the conclusion that, at the present time, viewed from the standpoint of their competitive effects, international mergers should, like national mergers, be treated on their respective merits, that is whether they are likely to increase competition in production, distribution and research and therefore the competitiveness of a country's economy or whether, on the other hand, they may create undue concentrations of economic power or otherwise injure competition. This judgement can only be made on a case-by-case basis.

160. There are sufficient indications in some Member countries of a continuing trend towards increase aggregate concentration to suggest the need for the adoption or strengthening of control of both national and international mergers. Possible conflicts between Member countries in the field of international mergers arising out of divergent national merger policies could be reduced if Member countries work toward similar standards and approaches for assessing and dealing with mergers. Moreover, another problem not exclusive to international mergers but requiring an international solution

is the extra-territorial application or effect of competition policies. Although the cases mentioned in this report do not lend support to the view that there are frequent conflicts between Member countries in the field of international mergers, in the event that such extra-territorial application or effect possibly creates difficulties, a solution might be achieved under the 1967 OECD Council Recommendation concerning cooperation between Member countries on restrictive business practices affecting international trade [C(67)-53(Final)] or under the 1973 OECD Council Recommendation concerning a consultation and conciliation procedure on restrictive business practices affecting international trade [C(73)(Final)] or perhaps through creation of some sort of new international anti-trust co-ordination arrangement.

International Mergers

182. The data presented in the chapter on international mergers show, for those countries with records, that these may be a major component of all merger activity and therefore they cannot be ignored on the ground of infrequent occurence. International mergers are a form of direct inward investment, and as such raise basically similar problems of efficiency and competition as do domestic mergers. There is evidence to suggest that this type of merger may result from the desire to exploit some differential advantage, whether it be efficiency or product differentiation; and as a consequence their predominant form is horizontal rather than vertical or diversified. This may not, of course, raise concentration levels in host countries but it does so when the world market for the product is considered, and this may have long-term detrimental consequences. In the short-term, on the other hand, it is suggested that international mergers based on differential efficiency may result in increased competition in host country markets because the foreign entrant would wish to exploit this advantage; and will also not have absorbed any prevailing non-competitive behaviour patterns. For these reasons it is not possible to reach any general conclusions about the effect of international mergers; like many domestic mergers they need to be considered as individual cases.

183. In those countries with merger control systems international mergers have only been rarely considered. Canada and Japan have so far not taken action against mergers between foreign entrants and their own national firms, while in the United Kingdom only one such case was considered and this was found unlikely to operate against the public interest. A few cases have occurred in the United States of America and these have been judged in terms of their effects on competition, the predominant consideration being foreclosure of markets and restraint of expansion of actual or potential competitors in concentrated industries. A similar consideration arose with Continental Can case in the European Economic Community. In view of this relative lack of experience it can be tentatively suggested that few interna-

tional mergers have yet raised problems of enhanced market power, but where they have they have been judged strictly in accordance with competition policy considerations.

184. Although there have only been a relatively small number of international mergers which have appeared to raise questions for competition policy so far, it is likely that the continual growth in international investment and the integration of world markets will lead to many more such cases in the future. The evidence does not suggest that jurisdictional and other problems have yet arisen, but as this may well change in the future with an increased number of international mergers there are good grounds for suggesting that it would be valuable for there to be an international exchange of information and, where necessary, consultations about such mergers.

Suggestions for Future Action by Member Countries

185. The accelerating trend towards merger together with the already high level of concentration in a number of economic sectors draws attention to the problems of competition which are created by changing market structures and it seems therefore appropriate at the present time to suggest to Member countries which have not yet done so to consider the adoption of an effective system of merger control.

186. The following characteristics might be taken into account:
 i) a procedure for registering mergers, wherever this is felt necessary;
 ii) a system to facilitate obtaining information about occurence of major mergers, such as requiring their prior notification;
 iii) minimum quantitative criteria below which mergers would not be subject to control;
 iv) objective criteria or presumptions for use in evaluating mergers;
 v) reasonable time limits for deciding initially whether to allow or challenge certain mergers.

187. With respect to the application of national laws to mergers and acquisitions involving foreign enterprises and any conflicts which may arise from such an application, Member countries are invited to have recourse to the OECD Council Recommendation of 1967 concerning cooperation between Member countries in the field of restictive business practices affecting international trade and to the OECD Council Recommendation of 1973 concerning a consultation and conciliation procedure on restrictive business practices affecting international trade.

ANNEX 3: DECLARATION ON INTERNATIONAL INVESTMENT AND
MULTINATIONAL ENTERPRISES (21ST JUNE 1976)

The governments of OECD member countries, considering

that international investment has assumed increased importance in the
world economy and has considerably contributed to the development of
their countries;

that multinational enterprises play an important role in this investment
process;

that co-operation by Member countries can improve the foreign investment climate, encourage the positive contribution which multinational
enterprises can make to economic and social progress, and minimise and
resolve difficulties which may arise from their various operations;

that, while continuing endeavours within the OECD may lead to further
international arrangements and agreements in this field, it seems appropriate at this stage to intensify their co-operation and consultation on
issues relating to international investment and multinational enterprises
through inter-related instruments each of which deals with a different
aspect of the matter and together constitute a framework within which
the OECD will consider these issues:

Declare:

I. Guidelines for Multinational Enterprises
that they jointly recommend to multinational enterprises operating in their
territories the observance of the Guidelines as set forth in the Annex hereto
having regard to the considerations and understandings which introduce the
Guidelines and are an integral part of them;

II. National Treatment
1. that Member countries should, consistent with their needs to maintain
   public order, to protect their essential security interests and to fulfil commitments relating to international peace and security, accord to entre-
   prises operating in their territories and owned or controlled directly or
   indirectly by nationals of another Member country (hereinafter referred to
   as "Foreign-Controlled Enterprises") treatment under their laws, regulations and administrative practices, consistent with international law and
   no less favourable than that accorded in like situations to domestic enterprises (hereinafter referred to as "National Treatment");
2. that Member countries will consider applying "National Treatment" in
   respect of countries other than Member countries;
3. That Member countries will endeavour to ensure that their territorial sub-
   divisions apply "National Treatment";

Note: The Turkish Government did not participate in the Declaration and abstained
from the Decisions.

4. That this Declaration does not deal with the right of Member countries to regulate the entry of foreign investment or the conditions of establishment of foreign enterprises;

III. International Investment Incentives and Disincentives

1. That they recognise the need to strengthen their co-operation in the field of international direct investment;

2. That they thus recognise the need to give due weight to the interests of Member countries affected by specific laws, regulations and administrative practices in this field (hereinafter called "measures") providing official incentives and disincentives to international direct investment;

3. That Member countries will endeavour to make such measures as transparent as possible, so that their importance and purpose can be ascertained and that information on them can be readily available;

IV. Consultation Procedures

that they are prepared to consult one another on the above matters in conformity with the Decisions of the Council relating to Inter-Governmental Consultation Procedures on the Guidelines for Multinational Enterprises, on National Treatment and on International Investment Incentives and Disincentives;

V. Review

that they will review the above matters within three years with a view to improving the effectiveness of international economic cooperation among Member countries on issues relating to international investment and multinational enterprises;

Guidelines for Multinational Enterprises (Annex to the Declaration of 21st June 1976 by Governments of OECD Member Countries on International Investment and Multinational Enterprises

1. Multinational enterprises now play an important part in the economies of Member countries and in international economic relations, which is of increasing interest to governments. Through international direct investment, such enterprises can bring substantial benefits to home and host countries by contributing to the efficient utilisation of capital, technology and human resources between countries and can thus fulfil an important role in the promotion of economic and social welfare. But the advances made by multinational enterprises in organising their operations beyond the national framework may lead to abuse of concentrations of economic power and to conflicts with national policy objectives. In addition, the complexity of these multinational enterprises and the difficulty of clearly perceiving their diverse structures, operations and policies sometimes give rise to concern.

2. The common aim of the Member countries is to encourage the positive contributions which multinational enterprises can make to economic and

social progress and to minimise and resolve the difficulties to which their various operations may give rise. In view of the transnational structure of such enterprises, this aim will be furthered by co-operation among the OECD countries where the headquarters of most of the multinational enterprises are established and which are the location of a substantial part of their operations. The guidelines set out hereafter are designed to assist in the achievement of this common aim and to contribute to improving the foreign investment climate.

3. Since the operations of multinational enterprises extend throughout the world, including countries that are not Members of the Organisation, international co-operation in this field should extend to all States. Member countries will give their full support to efforts undertaken in co-operation with non-member countries, and in particular with developing countries, with a view to improving the welfare and living standards of all people both by encouraging the positive contributions which multinational enterprises can make and by minimising and resolving the problems which may arise in connection with their activities.

4. Within the Organisation, the programme of co-operation to attain these ends will be a continuing, pragmatic and balanced one. It comes within the general aims of the Convention on the Organisation for Economic Cooperation and Development (OECD) and makes full use of the various specialised bodies of the Organisation, whose terms of reference already cover many aspects of the role of multinational enterprises, notably in matters of international trade and payments, competition, taxation, manpower, industrial development, science and technology. In these bodies, work is being carried out on the identification of issues, the improvement of relevant qualitative and statistical information and the elaboration of proposals for action designed to strengthen intergovernmental co-operation. In some of these areas procedures already exist through which issues related to the operations of multinational enterprises can be taken up. This work could result in the conclusions of further and complementary agreements and arrangements between governments.

5. The initial phase of the co-operation programme is composed of a Declaration and three Decisions promulgated simultaneously as they are complementary and inter-connected, in respect of guidelines for multinational enterprises, national treatment for foreign-controlled enterprises and international investment incentives and disincentives.

6. The guidelines set out below are recommendations jointly addressed by Member countries to multinational enterprises operating in their territories. These guidelines, which take into account the problems which can arise because of the international structure of these enterprises, lay down standards for the activities of these enterprises in the different Member countries. Observance of the guidelines is voluntary and not legally enforceable. However, they should help to ensure that the operations of

these enterprises are in harmony with national policies of the countries where they operate and to strengthen the basis of mutual confidence between enterprises and States.

7. Every State has the right to prescribe the conditions under whch multinational enterprises operate within its national jurisdiction, subject to international law and to the international agreements to which it has subscribed. The entities of a multinational enterprise located in various countries are subject to the laws of these countries.

8. A precise legal definition of multinational enterprises is not required for the purposes of the guidelines. These usually comprise companies or other entities whose ownership is private, state or mixed, established in different countries and so linked that one or more of them may be able to exercise a significant influence over the activities of others and, in particular, to share knowledge and resources with the others. The degree of autonomy of each entity in relation to the others varies widely from one multinational enterprise to another, depending on the nature of the links between such entities and the fields of activity concerned. For these reasons, the guidelines are addressed to the various entities within the multinational enterprise (parent companies and/or local entities) according to the actual distribution of responsibilities among them on the understanding that they will cooperate and provide assistance to one another as necessary to facilitate observance of the guidelines. The word "enterprise" as used in these guidelines refers to these various entities in accordance with their responsibilities.

9. The guidelines are not aimed at introducing differences of treatment between multinational and domestic enterprises; wherever relevant they reflect good practice for all. Accordingly, multinational and domestic enterprises are subject to the same expectations in respect of their conduct wherever the guidelines are relevant to both.

10. The use of appropriate international dispute settlement mechanisms, including arbitration, should be encouraged as a means of facilitating the resolution of problems arising between enterprises and Member countries.

11. Member countries have agreed to establish appropriate review and consultation procedures concerning issues arising in respect of the guidelines. When multinational enterprises are made subject to conflicting requirements by Member countries, the governments concerned will cooperate in good faith with a view to resolving such problems either within the Committee on International Investment and Multinational Enterprises established by OECD Council on 21st January 1975 or through other mutually acceptable arrangements.

Having regard to the foregoing considerations, the Member countries set forth the following guidelines for multinational enterprises with the understanding that Member countries will fulfil their responsibilities to treat enterprises equitably and in accordance with international law and international agreements, as well as contractual obligations to which they have subscribed:

General policies

Enterprises should
1. take fully into account established general policy objectives of the Member countries in which they operate;
2. in particular, give due consideration to those countries' aims and priorities with regard to economic and social progress, including industrial and regional development, the protection of the environment, the creation of employment opportunities, the promotion of innovation and the transfer of technology;
3. while observing their legal obligations concerning information, supply their entities with supplementary information the latter may need in order to meet requests by the authorities of the countries in which those entities are located for information relevant to the activities of those entities, taking into account legitimate requirements of business confidentiality;
4. favour close co-operation with the local community and business interests;
5. allow their component entities freedom to develop their activities and to exploit their competitive advantage in domestic and foreign markets, consistent with the need for specialisation and sound commercial practice;
6. when filling responsible posts in each country of operation, take due account of individual qualifications without discrimination as to nationality, subject to particular national requirements in this respect;
7. not render—and they should not be solicited or expected to render—any bribe or other improper benefit, direct or indirect, to any public servant or holder of public office;
8. unless legally permissible, not make contributions to candidates for public office or to political parties or other political organisations;
9. abstain from any improper involvement in local political activities.

Disclosure of information

Enterprises should, having due regard to their nature and relative size in the economic context of their operations and to requirements of business confidentiality and to cost, publish in a form suited to improve public understanding a sufficient body of factual information on the structure, activities and policies of the enterprise as a whole, as a supplement, in so far as necessary for this purpose, to information to be disclosed under the national law of the individual countries in which they operate. To this end, they should publish within reasonable time limits, on a regular basis, but at least annually, financial statements and other pertinent information relating to the enterprise as a whole, comprising in particular:

i. the structure of the enterprise, showing the name and location of the parent company, its main affiliates, its percentage ownership, direct and indirect, in these affiliates, including shareholdings between them;

ii. the geographical areas* where operations are carried out and the principal activities carried on therein by the parent company and the main affiliates;

iii. the operating results and sales by geographical area and the sales in the major lines of business for the enterprise as a whole;

iv. significant new capital investment by geographical area and, as far as practicable, by major lines of business for the enterprise as a whole;

v. a statement of the sources and uses of funds by the enterprise as a whole;

vi. the average number of employees in each geographical area;

vii. research and development expenditure for the enterprise as a whole;

viii. the policies followed in respect of intra-group pricing;

ix. the accounting policies, including those on consolidation, observed in compiling the published information.

Competition

Enterprises should, while conforming to official competition rules and established policies of the countries in which they operate,

1. refrain from actions which would adversely affect competition in the relevant market by abusing a dominant position of market power, by means of, for example,
   a. anti-competitive acquisitions,
   b. predatory behaviour toward competitors,
   c. unreasonable refusal to deal,
   d. anti-competitive abuse of industrial property rights,
   e. discriminatory (i.e. unreasonably differentiated) pricing and using such pricing transactions between affiliated enterprises as a means of affecting adversely competition outside these enterprises;

2. allow purchasers, distributors and licensees freedom to resell, export, purchase and develop their operations consistent with law, trade conditions, the need for specialisation and sound commercial practice;

3. refrain from participating in or otherwise purposely strengthening the restrictive effects of international or domestic cartels or restrictive agree-

---

*For the purposes of the guideline on disclosure of information the term "geographical area" means groups of countries or individual countries as each enterprise determines is appropriate in its particular circumstances. While no single method of grouping is appropriate for all enterprises or for all purposes, the factors to be considered by an enterprise would include the significance of operations carried out in individual countries or areas as well as the effects on its competitiveness, geographic proximity, economic affinity, similarities in business environments and the nature, scale and degree of interrelationship of the enterprises' operations in the various countries.

ments which adversely affect or eliminate competition and which are not generally or specifically accepted under applicable national or international legislation;

4. be ready to consult and co-operate, including the provision of information, with competent authorities of countries whose interests are directly affected in regard to competition issues or investigations. Provision of information should be in accordance with safeguards normally applicable in this field.

Financing

Enterprises should, in managing the financial and commercial operations of their activities, and especially their liquid foreign assets and liabilities, take into consideration the established objectives of the countries in which they operate regarding balance of payments and credit policies.

Taxation

Enterprises should
1. upon request of the taxation authorities of the countries in which they operate, provide, in accordance with the safeguards and relevant procedures of the national laws of these countries, the information necessary to determine correctly the taxes to be assessed in connection with their operations, including relevant information concerning their operations in other countries;
2. refrain from making use of the particular facilities available to them, such as transfer pricing which does not conform to an arm's length standard, for modifying in ways contrary to national laws the tax base on which members of the group are assessed.

Employment and industrial relations

Enterprises should, within the framework of law, regulations and prevailing labour relations and employment practices, in each of the countries in which they operate,
1. respect the right of their employees, to be represented by trade unions and other bona fide organisations of employees, and engage in constructive negotiations, either individually or through employers' associations, with such employee organisations with a view to reaching agreements on employment conditions, which should include provisions for dealing with disputes arising over the interpretation of such agreements, and for ensuring mutually respected rights and responsibilities;
2. a. provide such facilities to representatives of the employees as may be necessary to assist in the development of effective collective agreements,
   b. provide to representatives of employees information which is needed for meaningful negotiations on conditions of employment;

3. provide to representatives of employees where this accords with local law and practice, information which enables them to obtain a true and fair view of the performance of the entity or, where appropriate, the enterprise as a whole;

4. observe standards of employment and industrial relations not less favourable than those observed by comparable employers in the host country;

5. in their operations, to the greatest extent practicable, utilise, train and prepare for upgrading members of the local labour force in co-operation with representatives of their employees and, where appropriate, the relevant governmental authorities;

6. in considering changes in their operations which would have major effects upon the livelihood of their employees, in particular in the case of the closure of an entity involving collective lay-offs or dismissals, provide reasonable notice of such changes to representatives of their employees, and where appropriate to the relevant governmental authorities, and co-operate with the employee representatives and appropriate governmental authorities so as to mitigate to the maximum extent practicable adverse effects;

7. implement their employment policies including hiring, discharge, pay, promotion and training without discrimination unless selectivity in respect of employee characteristics is in furtherance of established governmental policies which specifically promote greater equality of employment opportunity;

8. in the context of bona fide negotiations* with representatives of employees on conditions of employment, or while employees are exercising a right to organise, not threaten to utilise a capacity to transfer the whole or part of an operating unit from the country concerned in order to influence unfairly those negotiations or to hinder the exercise of a right to organise;

9. enable authorised representatives of their employees to conduct negotiations on collective bargaining or labour management relations issues with representatives of management who are authorised to take decisions on the matters under negotiation.

Science and technology

Enterprises should

1. endeavour to ensure that their activities fit satisfactorily into the scientific and technological policies and plans of the countries in which they operate, and contribute to the development of national scientific and technological capacities, including as far as appropriate the establishment and improvement in host countries of their capacity to innovate;

---

*Bona fide negotiations may include labour disputes as part of the process of negotiation. Whether or not labour disputes are so included will be determined by the law and prevailing employment practices of particular countries.

2. to the fullest extent practicable, adopt in the course of their business activities practices which permit the rapid diffusion of technologies with due regard to the protection of industrial and intellectual property rights;
3. when granting licences for the use of industrial property rights or when otherwise transferring technology do so on reasonable terms and conditions.

Decision of the Council on Inter-governmental Consultation Procedures on the Guidelines for Multinational Enterprises

The Council,

Having regard to the Convention on the Organisation for Economic Co-operation and Development of 14th December, 1960 and, in particular, to Articles 2(d), 3 and 5(a) thereof;

Having regard to the Resolution of the Council of 21st January, 1975 establishing a Committee on International Investment and Multinational Enterprises and, in particular, to paragraph 2 thereof [C(74)247(Final)];

Taking note of the Declaration by the Governments of OECD Member countries of 21st June, 1976 in which they jointly recommend to multinational enterprises the observance of guidelines for multinational enterprises;

Recognising the desirability of setting forth procedures by which consultations may take place on matters related to these guidelines;

On the proposal of the Committee on International Investment and Multinational Enterprises;

Decides:

1. The Committee on International Investment and Multinational Enterprises (hereinafter called "the Committee") shall periodically or at the request of a Member country hold an exchange of views on matters related to the guidelines and the experience gained in their application. The Committee shall periodically report to the Council on these matters.
2. The Committee shall periodically invite the Business and Industry Advisory Committee to OECD (BIAC) and the Trade Union Advisory Committee to OECD (TUAC) to express their views on matters related to the guidelines and shall take account of such views in its reports to the Council.
3. On the proposal of a Member country the Committee may decide whether individual enterprises should be given the opportunity, if they so wish, to express their views concerning the application of the guidelines. The Committee shall not reach conclusions on the conduct of individual enterprises.
4. Member countries may request that consultations be held in the Committee on any problem arising from the fact that multinational enterprises are made subject to conflicting requirements. Governments concerned will co-operate in good faith with a view to resolving such problems,

either within the Committee or through other mutually acceptable arrangements.
5. This Decision shall be reviewed within a period of three years. The Committee shall make proposals for this purpose as appropriate.

ANNEX 4: EXCERPT FROM RESTRICTIVE BUSINESS PRACTICES OF
MULTINATIONAL ENTERPRISES: REPORT OF THE COMMITTEE
ON RESTRICTIVE BUSINESS PRACTICES (OECD, PARIS, 1977)

II. Possible remedies

195. The following possible remedies are discussed from two points of view:
whether they are capable of solving or mitigating the problems identified in
this report and whether they are useful and likely to be accepted by Member
countries in the not too distant future. No attempt is made to suggest one
measure to solve all problems, but rather a set of possible remedies is proposed
which, taken together, may lead in this direction. A wide range of proposals is
included, envisaging, among other things, the creation of new procedures to
obtain more information about multinational enterprises at national and international levels, the development of international consultation, conciliation and
arbitration procedures, or of voluntary codes of good conduct, standards of
behaviour or guidelines for enterprises and governments, and even the creation of a binding international antitrust law and an international agency with
powers of enforcement. In discussing such possible remedies, a distinction is
made between possible action by the business community itself and possible
remedies at national and at international levels.

1. By the business community

196. Action by the business community itself would be a first step, and
would be of a voluntary nature. It would consist of avoiding conduct clearly
at variance with competition guidelines[200] particularly in situations where
affected countries may not apply their laws and policies effectively due to the
international character of the enterprise or practices in question. Co-
operation in furnishing information beyond legal obligations seems already to
be taking place in some Member countries. It should be further encouraged,
in particular with regard to relevant information located outside the national
territory and in the possession of corporate entities other than the one doing
business on national territory. To a certain extent, voluntary co-operation
seems also to be possible in relation to the service of documents. Enterprises
could occasionally waive any rights they might have as to methods or place of
service in the interests of a speedy procedure and resolution of legal issues.

2. At the national level

197. Probably the most effective measures to solve or mitigate the problems
identified in this report would consist of national legislative action. At the
present time, there are no institutions in the world with powers comparable
to those of governments. The experience of countries with more sophisticated competition laws and policies shows that the introduction or strengthening of antitrust laws and competition policies could substantially contribute to solving not only a significant number of the problems connected with

the activities of multinational enterprises but also those of national enterprises. As only governments have the power to take such legislative measures, they also have the responsibility for considering such action in the first instance.

198. Legislative action could solve a substantial number of the problems of national and international economic concentration in relevant markets in which multinational enterprises play a significant role. This could be done by introducing or strengthening, if one already exists, a system of merger control utilising an analysis of the competitive effects of mergers, whether involving multinational or domestic enterprises, with, if deemed necessary, appropriate powers of divestiture or dissolution according to the needs of the countries concerned.

199. Legislative action by Member countries could also include the introduction or, if one already exists, the strengthening of a system of abuse control over economically powerful or market dominating enterprises, among which most multinational enterprises are to be found. Experience in those Member countries which already have a workable system of abuse control shows that many substantive problems relating to powerful enterprises, not necessarily excluding those which may be created by arrangements among affiliated enterprises, can be alleviated under such a system.

200. It does not appear that restrictive agreement legislation is directed at purely intra-corporate conduct for the reasons discussed below. Competition laws and policies in the OECD Member nations generally provide that intra-enterprise practices such as allocation of functions among branches or subsidiaries of a single enterprise are not considered in themselves as an unreasonable restraint of trade. Holding such practices unlawful would be likely to discourage internal growth and decrease efficiency. It might also force upon competition authorities the impracticable task of seeking to create and maintain competition within a single enterprise on an ongoing basis. In no case have arrangements within the same legal entity, such as between branches or operating divisions of the same company, been held to be unlawful. Even in cases involving separate legal entities under common control, findings of illegality have been rare and have been based upon exhaustive factual analysis of the particular cases. In certain instances of arrangements between legally separate entities with partial common ownership which eliminated significant pre-exisiting or potential competition among the entities or which injured competition outside the enterprise by means for instance, of agreed refusals to deal, illegality has been found.

201. A third field in which legislative action by governments could help to resolve problems is that of industrial, commercial and intellectual property rights. Legislation or regulatory action might follow the lines suggested in the OECD Recommendation concerning action against restrictive business

practices relating to the use of patents and licences of 22nd January, 1974 referred to in paragraph 100 above (see Annex III).

202. Governmental action introducing or strengthening merger control systems, control over abuses by economically powerful enterprises and competition rules prohibiting the abuse of industrial, commercial and intellectual property rights are not the only measures capable of diminishing the problems identified in this report although they would certainly be among those which might be expected to have the most far-reaching results. Taking into account the great diversity of laws and policies existing in Member countries it seems to be impossible to draw up a complete list of possibilities for legislative action. In those Member countries, however, which do not yet have legislation prohibiting horizontal and vertical restrictive agreements or a workable abuse control system regulating them, serious consideration might be given to introducing such legislation. A number of Member countries have found it effective to apply their legislation to restrictive conduct which has a substantial, direct and foreseeable effect on the country applying its law.

203. A further possibility for action by governments relates more specifically to antitrust procedure. One of the central problems identified in this report is that of collecting relevant information controlled by a mulitnational enterprise which is located outside the national territory, for purposes of an investigation of conduct affecting the jurisdiction. One of the elements contributing to this problem is the very nature of the multinational enterprise with units in various countries. Additional problems may be created by the reluctance of enterprises to co-operate in providing such information. It therefore seems appropriate that countries should consider, in conformity with the established rules of international law and taking into account international comity, the development of national procedures with a view to enhancing their ability to obtain relevant information which is outside of their territory but which is within the control of the multinational enterprise concerned and which is necessary to the enforcement of national antitrust laws and the disclosure of which is not contrary to the law of the place where the information is located. For example, in certain circumstances, it might be appropriate to interpret non-compliance to the disadvantage of the enterprise which cannot justify such non-compliance. An appropriate legal test for demanding such information may be whether the parent or subsidiary outside the jurisdiction and its affiliate in the jurisdiction both participated actively in the transaction being investigated, or whether the foreign parent actively supervised a local affiliate which did participate.

204. Another problem is the existence in some states of legislation or policies which preclude an enterprise from providing business-related information to foreign governments. A possibility for action by governments to solve this problem would be, perhaps in the context of bilateral or multilateral understandings, appropriate modification of national laws preventing disclosure of

relevant information by or concerning multinational enterprises so as to allow disclosure to competition authorities of other jurisdictions under proper procedures and safeguards. However, where these laws are of general application, such modification may raise problems which go beyond issues of competition policy.

3. At international level

205. At the international level, action may mainly be taken by governments and by international organisations. As to the action of governments at the international level, the least complicated possibility seems to be that of bilateral arrangements, agreements or formal treaties. They could cover a wide variety of subjects, ranging from the exchange of generally available information to the creation of a common antitrust law. As to the first possibility, it should be noted that OECD Member countries already have the opportunity to utilise or develop other procedures dealing with the exchange of informaton at the OECD level (cf. paragraph 206 below). However, Member countries might more readily exchange information which is not generally available on a bilateral basis with countries with similar antitrust and competition philosophies. Bilateral agreements relating to the exchange of information, consultation, conciliation or mutual administrative and judicial aid might well be useful and could lead to further developments which would help to overcome the problems identified in this report. Effectively functioning cooperation may lead the participating countries towards further harmonization of their antitrust laws and competition policies or co-ordination of investigations or procedures, a development which is also desirable from the viewpoint of enterprises doing business in these countries, since it would provide more certainty than currently exists. Also, third countries might, if co-operation was effective between the parties to a bilateral treaty, either wish to join the arrangement in order to mitigate their own problems in the field of antitrust and competition policy, or decide to conclude similar agreements with other countries closer to them in terms of their laws and policies.

206. On a more than bilateral and less than global level, a number of international organisations can and do help to reduce the problems identified in this report. The OECD Recommendation of 5th October, 1967 concerning co-operation between Member countries on restrictive business practices affecting international trade (see Annex I) and the OECD Recommendation of 3rd July, 1973 concerning a consultation and conciliation procedure on restrictive business practices affecting international trade (see Annex II) are procedures which, without discriminating between national and multinational enterprises, may help to iron out some of the problems in question here. The 1967 Recommendation established a voluntary procedure for prior notification of antitrust investigations and proceedings by Member countries when important interests of another Member country are involved. It also provided for the co-ordination of antitrust enforcement, co-operation in devel-

oping or applying mutually beneficial methods of dealing with restrictive business practices in international trade and exchanges of information on antitrust matters to the extent possible. Most of the notifications and requests for information which have been made since 1968 related to multinational enterprises. Certain of these notifications have approached being a form of voluntary consultation procedure aimed at achieving mutually agreed adjustments through discussions among the Member countries concerned. Such a development is in line with the 1973 Council Recommendation, although this Recommendation has never been specifically invoked in practice. Member countries may consider making specific use of this Recommendation, altering it or suggesting alternative proposals.

207. At the regional level, the European Communities have adopted a highly sophisticated antitrust law which, once a system of merger control is introduced, will be among the most comprehensive legislations in the world. It is no more difficult for the Commission, which is the regional antitrust authority having its own powers of enforcement, to enforce its legislation than it is for a national authority to enforce national law; it may take action directly within the territory of all Member States and not only in one of them. Although in the European Communities national laws relating to competition may apply simultaneously, implying that there may be parallel procedures, the fact that there is a fairly comprehensive legislation and an effective competition policy in the European Communities has allowed substantial results to be achieved in regard to the restrictive practices of multinational enterprises the scope of which extends beyond purely national territory.

208. At the OECD level, a common antitrust law comparable to that of the European Communities is not realistically achievable. There are, however, a number of ways other than the OECD Recommendations of 1967 and 1973 in which OECD could help to reduce some of the problems identified above. The Committee believes that the OECD voluntary guidelines contained in the Declaration on International Investment and Multinational Enterprises adopted by the OECD Council, meeting at Ministerial level, on 21st June, 1976, relating to competition and the shaping of corporate conduct in a general way (see Annex IV), should serve useful purposes. Of course, to some extent guidelines dealing with difficult legal and economic concepts such as abuse of a dominant position and adverse effects on competition cannot in themselves provide precise rules for business executives to follow in specific circumstances. Under the national law of various countries, these concepts have been given meaning only through interpretation by the competent tribunals. However, the Committee considered that such guidelines could nonetheless provide useful standards for enterprises and could be of value in helping to achieve a common approach towards multinational enterprises as well as acceptable relationships between multinational enterprises and countries whose trade they affect. In addition, they could contribute to the further development of widely accepted standards within OECD and at world level.

209. Even though certain courses of action may be suggested to Member governments this does not mean that the OECD should cease to study multinational enterprises from various antitrust and competition policy viewpoints. Although the development of an international antitrust law and the creation of an international antitrust authority can only be a long-run possibility, this issue is still being discussed at international level. As most parent companies of multinational enterprises are located in OECD Member countries, among which are to be found those with the most developed antitrust laws, it seems appropriate for the OECD to keep in touch through its Committee of Experts on Restrictive Business Practices with endeavours to establish international antitrust principles and institutions. In addition, it seems appropriate for the OECD to study, through the same Committee, other means of coping with the problems identified in the report in connection with its other work and, at the same time, to endeavour to identify the problems still more precisely in order to achieve a better understanding of their importance and a better basis for the consideration of possible remedies.

III. Suggestions for action

210. In accordance with the considerations set forth in paragraph 198, it is suggested that Member countries which have not yet done so consider the introduction of a workable system of merger control or the strengthening of an already introduced but not effectively functioning merger control system. As regards the criteria to be observed, it is sufficient to refer to the Committee's report on mergers, published by OECD in 1975, paragraphs 170 and 186 of which read as follows:

"185. The accelerating trend towards merger together with the already high level of concentration in a number of economic sectors draws attention to the problems of competition which are created by changing market structures and it seems therefore appropriate at the present time to suggest to Member countries which have not yet done so to consider the adoption of an effective system of merger control.

186. The following characteristics might be taken into account:
    i. a procedure for registering mergers, wherever this is felt necessary:
    ii. a system to facilitate obtaining information about occurrence of major mergers, such as requiring their prior notification;
    iii. minimum quantitative criteria below which mergers would not be subject to control;
    iv. objective criteria or presumptions for use in evaluating mergers;
    v. reasonable time limits for deciding initially whether to allow or challenge certain mergers."

211. In accordance with paragraph 199 above, it is suggested that Member countries which have not yet done so consider the creation of a workable abuse control procedure, the strengthening of an already existing abuse con-

trol procedure for market dominating and economically powerful enterprises or the creation or strengthening of legislation against monopolisation or attempts to monopolise.

212. With reference to the matters considered in paragraph 200 above, the Committee has no changes to recommend at this time in relation to the treatment of intra-corporate arrangements.

213. In accordance with paragraph 201 above, it is suggested that Member countries consider legislation or regulatory action against restrictive business practices relating to the use of patents and licences.

214. In accordance with paragraph 203 above, it is suggested that Member countries consider how they could develop appropriate procedures to facilitate investigation and discovery by their antitrust authorities in regard to information located outside their national territory, in conformity with the rules of public international law and taking into account international comity.

215. Also, in accordance with paragraphs 203 and 204 above, it is suggested that Member countries might, where discretion exists, consider whether and, if so, how and under what safeguards to provide or allow disclosure of information relevant to the enforcement of national antitrust laws and to national competition policy purposes but which at present may not be obtainable or transmissible to other Member countries for legal reasons.

216. In accordance with paragraph 205 above, it is suggested that Member countries consider the possibility of concluding bilateral or multilateral treaties on mutual administrative and judicial aid with other Member countries which would be applicable to the enforcement of restrictive business practices laws.

217. In view of the advisability of taking action in regard to the problems identified in this report not only at national and bilateral levels, it is suggested that Member countries make use as far as possible of the OECD Recommendation of 1967 concerning co-operation between Member countries on restrictive business practices affecting international trade and continue to explore possible use of the Recommendation of 1973 concerning a consultation and conciliation procedure on restrictive business practices affecting international trade.

218. The OECD Committe of Experts on Restrictive Business Practices will keep under review antitrust and competition policy problems identified in this report and try, as part of its future programme of work, to study these problems in greater depth in order to develop more adequate measures to remedy them. The Committee will in particular keep in touch with all endeavours at the international level to deal with antitrust and competition policy problems connected with multinational enterprises.

ANNEX 5: RECOMMENDATION OF THE COUNCIL CONCERNING ACTION
AGAINST RESTRICTIVE BUSINESS PRACTICES AFFECTING INTERNATIONAL
TRADE INCLUDING THOSE INVOLVING MULTINATIONAL ENTERPRISES
(Adopted by the Council at its 469th Meeting on 20th July, 1978)
[The Representative for Turkey abstained]

The Council,

Having regard to Article 5(b) of the Convention on the Organisation for
Economic Co-Operation and Development of 14th December, 1960;

Having regard to the Declaration on International Investment and Multinational Enterprises adopted by the Governments of OECD Member countries on 21st June, 1976;

Having regard to the Report of the Committee of Experts on Restrictive
Business Practices of 10th February, 1977 on the restrictive business practices of multinational enterprises [RBP(77)1-MNE];

Considering that restrictive business practices may have harmful effects
on international trade whether they emanate from purely national or from
multinational enterprises;

Considering that the restrictive business practices of multinational enterprises do not differ in form from those operated by purely national enterprises but that they may have a more significant impact on trade and competition due to the fact that multinational enterprises generally tend to wield
greater market power, that they play a relatively greater role in the process of
national and international concentration and that the restrictive business
practices they engage in have more often an international character;

Recognising that, in the present state of international law and of the laws
on restrictive business practices of Member countries, control of practices
affecting international trade, including those involving multinational enterprises, raises many difficulties, especially in assembling necessary information
held outside the jurisdiction of the country applying its law, in serving process
and in enforcing decisions in relation to enterprises located abroad;

Recognising that the solution to these difficulties cannot at present be
found in an international convention establishing control of restrictive business practices affecting international trade owing mainly to the still differing
attitudes adopted by countries toward restrictive business practices and in
particular to their varying national legislations in this field.

Considering, however, that the difficulties in controlling restrictive business practices affecting international trade, including those involving multinational enterprises, may be allevitaed by simultaneous efforts in the fields of
national legislation on restrictive business practices and of international co-
operation particularly within the OECD framework, it being understood that
such co-operation should not in any way be construed to affect the legal
positions of Member countries, in particular with regard to such questions of
sovereignty and extraterritorial application of laws concerning restrictive
business practices as may arise;

I. RECOMMENDS the Governments of Member countries to consider the following action:

(1) to adopt new or supplement existing measures on restrictive business practices so as to prohibit or control effectively such practices, particularly:

    (a) actions adversely affecting competition in the relevant market by abusing a dominant position of market power by means of, for example, anti-competitive acquisitions; predatory behaviour toward competitors; unreasonable refusal to deal; anti-competitive abuse of industrial property rights; discriminatory (i.e. unreasonably differentiated) pricing and using such pricing transactions between affiliated enterprises as a means of affecting adversely competition outside these enterprises;

    (b) cartels or other restrictive agreements which without justification adversely affect or eliminate competition;

(2) to develop, consistent with established rules of international law and taking international comity into account appropriate national rules to facilitate investigation and discovery by their respective competition authorities of relevant information within the control of an enterprise under investigation, where such information is located outside their respective national territories and when its provision is not contrary to the law or established policies of the country where the information is located;

(3) to allow, subject to appropriate safeguards, including those relating to confidentiality, the disclosure of information to the competent authorities of Member countries by the other parties concerned, whether accomplished unilaterally or in the context of bilateral or multilateral understandings, unless such co-operation or disclosure would be contrary to significant national interests;

(4) to facilitate, through conclusion of or adherence to bilateral or multilateral agreements or understandings, mutual administrative or judicial aid in the field of restrictive business practices;

(5) whilst vigorously enforcing their legislation on restrictive business practices, to make use as far as possible of the OECD procedures on co-operation between Member countries in the field of restrictive business practices affecting international trade so as to facilitate consultation and resolution of problems.

II. INSTRUCTS the Committee of Experts on Restrictive Business Practices to keep under review this Recommendation and to report to the Council when appropriate.

ANNEX 6: RECOMMENDATION OF THE COUNCIL CONCERNING
CO-OPERATION BETWEEN MEMBER COUNTRIES ON RESTRICTIVE
BUSINESS PRACTICES AFFECTING INTERNATIONAL TRADE
(Adopted by the Council at its 501st Meeting on 25th September, 1979)

The Council,

Having regard to Article 5(b) of the Convention on the Organisation for Economic Co-operation and Development of 14th December, 1960;

Having regard to the Recommendation of the Council of 5th October, 1967, concerning Co-operation between Member Countries on Restrictive Business Practices Affecting International Trade [C(67)53(Final)];

Having regard to the Recommendation of the Council of 3rd July, 1973, concerning a Consultation and Conciliation Procedure on Restrictive Business Practices Affecting International Trade [C(73)99(Final)];

Having regard to the Note by the Committee of Experts on Restrictive Business Practices on Co-operation between Member Countries on Restrictive Business Practices Affecting International Trade [C(79)154];

Recognising that restrictive business practices may constitute an obstacle to the achievement of economic growth, trade expansion and other economic goals of Member countries such as the control of inflation;

Recognising that the unilateral application of national legislation, in cases where business operations in other countries are involved, raises questions as to the respective spheres of sovereignty of the countries concerned;

Recognising that restrictive business practices investigations and proceedings by one Member country may, in certain cases, affect important interests of other Member countries;

Considering therefore that Member countries should co-operate in the implementation of their respective national legislation in order to combat the harmful effects of restrictive business practices;

Considering also that closer co-operation between Member countries is needed to deal effectively with restrictive business practices operated by enterprises situated in Member countries when they affect the interests of one or more other Member countries and have a harmful effect on international trade;

Considering moreover that closer co-operation between Member countries in the form of notification, exchange of information, co-ordination of action, consultation and conciliation, on a fully voluntary basis should be encouraged, it being understood that such co-operation should not, in any way, be construed to affect the legal positions of Member countries with regard to questions of sovereignty, and in particular, the extra-territorial application of laws concerning restrictive business practices, as may arise;

I. RECOMMENDS to the Governments of Member countries that insofar as their laws permit:

A. Notification, Exchange of Information and Co-ordination of Action

1.(a) when a Member country undertakes under its restrictive business practices laws an investigation or proceeding involving important interests of another Member country or countries, it should notify such Member country or countries in a manner and at a time deemed appropriate, if possible in advance and in any event at a time that would facilitate comments or consultations; such advance notification would enable the proceeding Member country, while retaining full freedom of ultimate decision, to take account of such views as the other Member country may wish to express and of such remedial action as the other Member country may find it feasible to take under its own laws to deal with the restrictive business practices;

(b) where two or more Member countries proceed against a restrictive business practice in international trade, they should endeavour to co-ordinate their action insofar as appropriate and practicable;

2. through consultations or otherwise, the Member countries should co-operate in developing or appying mutually satisfactory and beneficial measures for dealing with restrictive business practices in international trade. In this connection, they should supply each other with such relevant information on restrictive business practices as their legitimate interests permit them to disclose; and should allow, subject to appropriate safeguards, including those relating to confidentiality, the disclosure of information to the competent authorities of Member countries by the other parties concerned, whether accomplished unilaterally or in the context of bilateral or multilateral understandings, unless such co-operation or disclosure would be contrary to significant national interests.

B. CONSULTATION AND CONCILIATION

3.(a) a Member country that considers a restrictive business practice investigation or proceeding being conducted by another Member country to affect its important interests should transmit its views on the matter to or request consultation with the other Member country;

(b) without prejudice to the continuation of its action under its restrictive business practices law and to its full freedom of ultimate decision, the Member country so addressed should give full and sympathetic consideration to the views expressed by the requesting country, and in particular to any suggestions as to alternative means of fulfilling the needs or objectives of the restrictive business practice investigation or proceedings;

4.(a) a Member country that considers that one or more enterprises situated in one or more other Member countries are or have been engaged in restrictive business practices of whatever origin that are substantially and adversely affecting its interests may request consultation with such other Member country or countries, recognising that the entering into such consultations is without prejudice to any action under its restrictive business practices law and to the full freedom of ultimate decision of the Member countries concerned;

(b) any Member country so addressed should give full and sympathetic consideration to such views and factual materials as may be provided by the requesting country and, in particular, to the nature of the restrictive business practices in question, the enterprises involved and the alleged harmful effects on the interests of the requesting country;

(c) the Member country addressed which agrees that enterprises situated in its territory are engaged in restrictive business practices harmful to the interests of the requesting country should attempt to ensure that these enterprises take remedial action, or should itself take whatever remedial action it considers appropriate, including actions under its legislation on restrictive business practices or administrative measures, on a voluntary basis and considering its legitimate interests;

5. without prejudice to any of their rights, the Member countries involved in consultations under paragraphs 3. or 4. above should endeavour to find a mutually acceptable solution in the light of the respective interests involved;

6. in the event of a satisfactory settlement of the consultations under paragraphs 3. or 4. above, the requesting country, in agreement with, and in the form accepted by, the Member country or countries addressed, should inform the Committee of Experts on Restrictive Business Practices of the nature of the restrictive business practices in question and of the settlement reached;

7. in the event that no satisfactory solution can be found, the Member countries concerned, if they so agree, should submit the case to the Committee of Experts on Restrictive Business Practices with a view to conciliation. If the Member countries concerned agree to the use of another means of settlement and do not therefore submit the case to the Committee they should, if they consider it appropriate, inform the Committee of such features of the settlement as they feel they can disclose.

II. INSTRUCTS the Committee of Experts on Restrictive Business Practices:

1. to examine periodically the progress made in the implementation of the provisions set out in paragraphs 1 and 2 of Section I above;

2. to consider the reports submitted by Member countries in accordance with paragraph 6 of Section I above;

3. to consider the requests for conciliation submitted by Member countries in accordance with paragraph 7 of Section I above and to assist, by offering advice or by any other means, in the settlement of the case between the Member countries concerned;

4. to report to the Council as appropriate on the application of the present Recommendation.

III. DECIDES that this Recommendation repeals and supersedes the Recommendations of the Council of 5th October, 1967 and of 3rd July, 1973 referred to above.

Supranational Regulation of Transnational Corporations: The UNCTAD and CTC Efforts

JAMES D. KUREK

The focus of this article is the current United Nations' efforts designed to influence the activities of transnational corporations (TNCs) and other participants in the foreign investment arena, with special attention being given to those provisions which deal with concentration. The efforts to be discussed are primarily centered in the U. N. Conference on Trade and Development (UNCTAD) and the U. N. Economic and Social Council's Commission on Transnational Corporations (CTC). Since the approach and methods employed by these two bodies differ in several significant respects, each will be considered separately. The concluding discussion examines a variety of views on the international control of TNCs generally, and the UNCTAD and CTC efforts in particular.

In recent years the activities of TNCs have been subjected to the ever increasing scrutiny of a wide variety of national governments. Concern over the activities of TNCs has arisen from the fact that a growing number are acquiring, literally, worldwide operations that command tremendous economic resources. One problem created by worldwide operations is that the management of these enterprises necessarily must take a global perspective in making corporate decisions; consequently, such a perspective might require corporate actions within a particular nation which are contrary to that nation's governmentally defined developmental, social, and economic objectives. A further problem created by the vast resources of TNCs is that such enterprises may gain a dominant position in a particular market or even an entire sector of a nation's economy, bringing concomitant problems of anti-competitive concentration.

From the TNC perspective, the economies of developing nations often offer an attractive environment for TNC direct investment. From the developing nation perspective, TNCs can provide the type and amount of capital investments that host governments desire to stimulate domestic growth. In fact, these nations tend to rely to a great extent on TNCs as the major sources of foreign investment capital, technical expertise, and technology transfers.[1] Therefore, it is understandable that many developing nations be-

James D. Kurek is a member of the class of 1981, University of Michigan Law School.

lieve they are particularly susceptible to undesirable TNC activities, viewing the sheer magnitude of TNC investments as a conduit by which TNCs develop the ability to control the national economy and direct social development. Such a surrender of sovereign power is considered by some developing nations to be as reprehensible as the colonial domination with which they previously had to contend.[2]

Although one apparent solution to these concerns would be the implementation of national laws designed to curb potential TNC abuses, it is at this point that the real dilemma facing national governments surfaces. Authorities are generally agreed that the high degree of geographic diversification and vast global resources possessed by TNCs render most attempts to control TNC activities through national laws largely ineffective, since the TNC has the capability to shift its resources and operations beyond any particular nation's jurisdictional reach, thereby creating at least the theoretical possibility that the TNC will circumvent national controls.[3] A potential answer to this dilemma would be a broader system of control implemented at the regional or international level, thereby lessening the TNC's ability to circumvent the law by shifting resources. However, certain problems inherent in this proposal make the effective implementation of such a system very difficult.

The major obstacle to an agreement among governments on a supranational legal framework capable of controlling TNC activities is the governments themselves. Inevitably, all national governments have their own unique developmental objectives in mind when they approach the problem of establishing any type of international regulatory framework. Since social and economic conditions vary greatly between individual nations, their objectives also vary, and thus it is difficult to reach a consensus on the appropriate framework designed to control TNCs. One solution might be for nations with similar developmental objectives to form a group to deal with this problem on a collective basis—for example, the OECD.[4] But, if several distinct groups should develop, this would still allow TNCs to choose, albeit in a more restricted manner, the law under which they would operate. Moreover, there would still exist a problem of coordination. If some countries sought to attract TNC investment at "any cost" (in terms of potential harm to developmental objectives) their actions could greatly impede even effective regional regulatory efforts. Therefore, the most appealing objective seems to be the development of some sort of supranational system for regulating TNCs that would be acceptable to virtually all nations of the world.

In light of these considerations, the most obvious forum for the development of a supranational framework to control TNC activities is the United Nations, since its membership includes most of the nations recognized in the world today. However, this forum highlights the problem of divergent national objectives, which is a key factor hindering a consensus solution to international problems, including the one discussed herein. Although a number of homogeneous groups exist within the U. N. structure, three major groups tend to be the focus of attention in the area of TNC regulation: (1) the highly industrialized developed countries (Group B), which control much of the world's economic power, (2) the developing countries (Group of 77), which by sheer numbers control the voting power in the U. N., and (3) the Communist bloc countries (Group D), whose nonmarket economics control substantial resources. Reference in the following discussion will be made to these groups as though their membership acts in a unified manner, although it must be remembered that great diversity may in fact exist within each group.

UNCTAD

Within UNCTAD two separate efforts have been undertaken that bear on TNC activities; the effort in the Committee on Transfer of Technology to develop an International Code of Conduct on Transfer of Technology, and the work in the Committee on Manufactures to develop a set of multilaterally acceptable equitable principles and rules related to restrictive business practices. Athough the latter effort is more relevant to the problem of corporate concentration, both endeavors may affect TNC activities.

The efforts to develop a code of conduct on transfer of technology began in 1974 when an UNCTAD working group proposed a code designed to aid developing countries in their efforts to control the international transfer of technology.[5] In particular, this proposal articulated some of the restrictive and abusive practices which can accompany the transfer of technology.[6] The working group called for initiatives to establish an international code,[7] and the UNCTAD secretary general appointed a Group of Experts for that purpose.[8] Although a draft code could not be agreed upon, the Group of 77 and the Group B nations offered separate drafts, reflecting their differing views on these issues.[9] The Committee on Transfer of Technology has since performed detailed studies of the effects of technology transfer on particular nations; although a code in this area has not yet been completed, a U. N. Conference on an International Code of Conduct on the Transfer of Technology is scheduled to hold its third session during the first six months of 1980 to work on the code.[10] Therefore, although this code does not directly address the specific issue of concentration, the regulation of technology transfer will necessarily affect the behavior and structure of TNCs.[11]

UNCTAD efforts in the area of restrictive business practices (RBPs) began in 1972 with the establishment of an Ad Hoc Group of Experts on RBPs to study the possible adverse impact of RBPs on developing country economies in their quest for development of trade and economic growth.[12] The experts submitted a report on RBPs and their relation to developing countries,[13] but this report was never used because these experts were not official representatives of their respective countries.[14] As a result, the Committee on Manufactures convened a Second Ad Hoc Group of Experts on RBPs, this time comprised of official representatives.[15] This Second Group was directed, *inter alia*, to identify those RBPs which adversely affect developing countries and to consider the formulation of a model antitrust law for developing countries.[16] Although the Second Group made some significant advances, reaching an agreement on some general principles and a model law, its efforts represented only the first steps toward a final agreement in this area.[17] It was resolved that the work of the Second Group should be expanded with a view toward developing a model law (or laws) to assist developing countries in formulating appropriate RBP policy and legislation.[18] To this end the UNCTAD secretary general appointed a Third Ad Hoc Group of Experts on RBPs.[19]

In the development of a set of multilaterally accepted equitable principles and rules on RBPs, the approach of the Third Group has been to accept various proposed texts and attempt to negotiate an "agreed text."[20] Close scrutiny of the most recent texts of these principles will provide some understanding of their potential affect on TNC activities, their concern with corporate concentration and their current stage of development.[21] The agreed set of objectives toward which the principles and rules should be framed contains the following statement concerning concentration:

> To attain greater efficiency in international trade and development,
> particularly that of developing countries in accordance with national
> aims of economic and social development and existing economic struc-
> tures, such as through:
> (a) The creation, encouragement and protection of competition;
> (b) Control of the concentration of capital and/or economic power . . . [22]

Further, the agreed objectives recognize the need "[t]o eliminate the disadvantages to trade and development which may result from the restrictive business practices of transnational corporations or other enterprises,"[23] and the need to adopt these principles and rules at the international level in order "to facilitate the adoption and strengthening of laws and policies in this area at the national and regional levels."[24] This language demonstrates that the UNCTAD intends to address TNC activities generally and TNC concentration specifically. In fact, a proposed Group D objective is to ensure that restrictive practices of TNCs do not impede national developmental objectives.[25] The Group of Experts' desire to control concentration is again shown in the agreed definitions and scope of application section. RBPs are generally defined as:

> . . . acts or behaviour of enterprises which, through an abuse *or acquisi-*
> *tion* and abuse of a dominant position of market power, limit access to
> markets or otherwise unduly restrain competition, having or being likely
> to to [sic] have adverse effects on international trade, particularly that of
> developing countries, and on the economic development of these coun-
> tries, or which through formal, informal, written or unwritten agreements
> or arrangements among enterprises have the same effects.[26]

Additionally, *dominant position of market power* is defined as "a situation where an enterprise, either by itself or together with a few other enterprises, is in a position to control the relevant market for a particular product or service or groups of products or services."[27] Although these definitions are vague and somewhat ambiguous in their specific terms, they indicate the Group's concern with corporate concentration. Again, the Group D proposal more specifically addresses TNC practices which might be used to gain a dominant market position.[28] In addition to the previously cited language, specific reference to TNCs and concentration can also be found in other sections of the principles.[29]

Although several sections to be included in the proposed code have been agreed upon, some key elements of the principles have yet to be finalized. The unresolved elements include the issue of whether the developing countries should be able to exempt certain domestic actions from these principles,[30] and whether the developing countries should be accorded preferential or differential treatment for their national enterprises.[31] If these exceptions are accepted the result might be a set of principles which would bind only the developed countries. Therefore, the developed countries have not been amenable to these proposals by the Group of 77.[32] Due to the requirement of unanimity in the negotiating conference and the practical necessity that the Group B nations must accept the principles if they are to be effective, a negotiated solution to these and other differences will undoubtedly be attempted at future UNCTAD meetings.[33]

To aid developing countries in formulating their own RBP legislation, the UNCTAD Secretariat has submitted a draft model law for regulating RBPs to the Third Ad Hoc Group of Experts.[34] However, any affirmative action in this area is likely to be deferred until the general principles on RBPs have been agreed upon.

CTC

The U. N. Commission on Transnational Corporations, operating under the auspices of the Economic and Social Council, has taken a different approach to the problem of TNC activities than that of the UNCTAD. The CTC has its beginnings in a 1972 ECOSOC resolution that called for the appointment of a Group of Eminent Persons to study the effect of TNCs on world development.[35] The Eminent Persons, with the aid of a report issued by the ECOSOC Secretariat,[36] produced a report,[37] which together with other reports issued by the ECOSOC Secretariat[38] provided the impetus for the establishment of the CTC and the Centre on Transnational Corporations.[39]

One purpose of the CTC was to evolve "a set of recommendations which, taken together, would represent the basis for a code of conduct dealing with transnational corporations."[40] The Centre was mandated to function under the guidance of the CTC.[41] In performing its function of developing a code of conduct for TNCs, a function assigned the highest priority,[42] the CTC has sought the opinions and advice of a wide variety of governmental and non-governmental experts.[43] The CTC's method in formulating the code has been to use an Intergovernmental Working Group, made up of official representatives of various nations, to consider proposals made by various nations and information gathered by the Centre.[44] The ultimate objective of the Working Group is to negotiate a single proposed code text prepared from the common elements of the various proposals which, once in final form, will be presented to the entire CTC.[45]

The CTC effort differs from the UNCTAD endeavors in two very significant respects. First, the code of conduct being developed by the CTC is designed to address a much broader range of TNC activities.[46] Predictably, its comprehensive nature makes it more controversial yet potentially more effective than the UNCTAD codes. Second, the negotiations within the Working Group have been on a single text developed from prior discussions in lieu of alternate text proposals by the Group of 77 or Group B nations. It is hoped that this approach will reduce the opportunity for the various groups to become too firmly entrenched in their own stated positions, and thus contribute to freer and more effective negotiations.[47]

Currently, although some tentative formulations of the code have been published,[48] a final draft has yet to be submitted to the CTC. It is worth noting that although the tentative draft contains a section on competition and RBPs, all work on this section has been postponed until relevant work in the UNCTAD is complete.[49] Therefore, the Working Group will only address the issue of TNC concentration after the UNCTAD code efforts are finished. In spite of this delay, negotiations continue on some of the unresolved provisions in the code.[50]

Concluding Observations on Efforts to Date

While the current international efforts to countrol TNC activities have not yet attained final form, the mere existence and potential of these endeavors has sparked considerable academic and other discussion on international attempts to control TNC activities and concentration. In this final section some of the competing views on the key unresolved issues involved will be presented.

One issue of heated debate is whether the current efforts, if and when they become final, would be binding on the various countries involved. Although it is recognized that a country's consent to a negotiated effort will entail some sort of moral obligation to conform national regulations to the standards developed, what is important is whether the standards will be *legally* binding on the particular countries accepting them. One commentator, in discussing the legally binding nature of the UNCTAD codes, notes that the "common understanding at the inception of UNCTAD was that its actions could not be binding."[51] Thus he concludes that the codes will not become binding international law unless they are universally accepted and thereby become customary international law.[52] Regarding the CTC code, the issue of implementation is currently under discussion, although it is generally conceded that a strictly binding code is not likely to result.[53] Therefore, it is likely that a particular country will be bound to these codes only if it so chooses.

Another unresolved issue is whether these codes should accord preferential treatment to the developing countries at the possible expense of the developed countries. As previously noted, this is a topic of current disagreement within UNCTAD.[54] On this issue one authority in particular advocates differential treatment as a compromise.[55] Specifically, he believes that according preferential treatment to the developing countries could be a means of achieving equal economic opportunity among the nations of the world, based upon the premise that unequal status can best be remedied by allowing unequal treatment which favors those who have been previously disfavored.[56] He also suggests that TNCs should be treated differently from domestic enterprises with no foreign operations, thus limiting the code's provisions to TNCs and allowing national governments to develop their own (perhaps discriminatory) regulations for domestic industries not involved in foreign investment.[57] Whether in fact the developed nations are ready to accept this sort of one-sided agreement is highly debatable.

The final, and perhaps broadest, issue concerns the ultimate efficacy of these efforts. Although ultimate resolution of the more specific issues will invariably determine the effectiveness of the codes, several commentators have nonetheless made some general observations in this regard. One authority believes that the conclusion of the present endeavors will serve as an intermediate step to future negotiations on a more general and effective regulatory agreement for TNC activities.[58] Others believe that these efforts will, at the very least, set a minimum standard for TNC behavior that both national governments and TNCs will embrace.[59] The TNCs may be likely to embrace these standards due to the fear that rejection of them could serve as the stimulus for future, even less desirable, regulations at both the national and international levels. Still others believe the standards enunciated in these codes could eventually be incorporated into national laws, particularly in those countries that presently lack any RBP legislation.[60] With respect to the specific development of an effective international antitrust law, some writers suggest that a drastic reconciliation of the various national values and objectives is necessary before an effective result in this area can be obtained.[61]

The entire issue of effectiveness may be ultimately resolved only when "the legal form, language and machinery for enforcement are agreed upon."[62] Although it is likely that the current negotiations and draft codes will have some impact on TNC behavior and national and international regulation of TNCs (in general and regarding concentration specifically), the extent of this impact cannot be measured with certainty until these efforts are finalized in a negotiated consensus to be reached by the various participating nations. Until then it is only possible to discuss the methods which might effect certain results, and ponder the eventual fate of these very ambitious endeavors.

NOTES

1. *See, e.g.,* Soloman, *Multinational Corporations and the Emerging World Order,* 8 Case W. Res. J. Int'l L. 329 (1976).

2. *Id.* at 332–35.

3. *See, e.g.,* Coonrod, *The United Nations Code of Conduct for Transnational Corporations,* 18 Harv. Int'l L.J. 273, 275 (1977); Barnet & Müller, Global Reach (1974). It should be noted that although the TNCs possess this capability it does not necessarily mean that they will in fact be willing to take such actions, due to the adverse reactions they might receive from the international community as a whole. Also, if a majority of the developing nations were to develop laws designed to control TNC activities, it is unlikely that the TNCs would be willing to forego the economic benefits which could nonetheless be gained in these markets.

4. The OECD has actually developed "guidelines for multinational enterprises" promulgated in June 1976, in OECD, Annex to the *Declaration of 21st June, 1976 by Government of OECD Member Countries on International Investment and Multinational Enterprises, reprinted in* 15 Int'l Legal Mats. 967 (1976). *See* Stockmann, *Reflections on Recent OECD Activities: Regulation of Multinational Corporate Conduct and Structure, supra.* But, these guidelines are not acceptable to the developing countries due to their voluntary nature, Coonrod, *supra* note 3, at 289; Schwartz, *Are the OECD and UNCTAD Codes Legally Binding?,* 11 Int'l Law. 529, 530 (1977), and because the OECD is an organization which represents the interests of most of the developed countries of the world, Coonrod, *supra* note 3, at

286 n.65. For a more general discussion of the OECD guidelines, *see* Chance, *Codes of Conduct for Multinational Corporations,* 33 Bus. Law. 1799, 1808 (1978); Hawk, *The OECD Guidelines for Multinational Enterprises: Competition,* 46 Fordham L. Rev. 241 (1977).

5. *See* UNCTAD, The Possibility and Feasibility of an International Code of Conduct on Transfer of Technology, U. N. Doc. TD/B/AC.11/22; GE.74–46032 (1974).

6. *Id.* at ¶¶ 24–29.

7. *Id.* at ¶¶ 141–50. This call also was made by the Intergovernmental Group on Transfer of Technology at its third session held at the Palais des Nations, Geneva from 15 to 26 July 1974, UNCTAD, Report of the Intergovernmental Group on Transfer of Technology on its Third Session ¶¶ 95–127, U. N. Doc. TD/B/520 (1974).

8. UNCTAD, An International Code of Conduct on Transfer of Technology ¶¶ 3, 5, U. N. Doc. TD/B/C.6/AC.1/2/Supp.1/Rev.1 (1975).

9. *See* UNCTAD, Report of the Intergovernmental Group of Experts on a Code of Conduct on Transfer of Technology, Annex I–III, U. N. Doc. TD/B/C.6/1 (1975). For a discussion of the content of these proposed drafts, *see* Joelson, *The Proposed International Codes of Conduct as Related to Restrictive Business Practices,* 8 Law & Pol'y Int'l Bus. 837, 860–61 (1976).

10. *See* UNCTAD Monthly Bull. No. 157 (1979).

11. For a more detailed discussion of this code, *see* Jeffries, *Regulation of Transfer of Technology: An Evaluation of the UNCTAD Code of Conduct,* 18 Harv. Int'l L.J. 309 (1977).

12. *See* UNCTAD Secretariat, Res. 73(III), U.N. UNCTAD, Report and

Annexes (Agenda Item 5) 82, U.N. Doc. TD/180(1972).

13. UNCTAD, Report of the *Ad Hoc* Group of Experts on Restrictive Business Practices in Relation to the Trade and Development of Developing Countries, U.N. Doc. TD/B/C.2/119/Rev.1 (1974). The Group listed some specific types of RBPs which are likely to have significantly adverse effects whether in developed or developing countries. It also found that TNC activities have a significant effect on the economic, social and political character of developing countries and that TNC behavior is not always in line with the particular nation's government policies; specific RBPs engaged in by TNCs were also mentioned. The Group concluded by calling for action in this area at both the national and international levels.

14. Joelson, *supra* note 9, at 858.

15. UNCTAD, Report of the Second *Ad Hoc* Group of Experts on Restrictive Business Practices ¶ 1, U.N. Doc. TD/B/600, TD/B/C.2/166, TD/B/C.2/AC.5/6 (1976).

16. *Id.* at ¶ 3.

17. *See Id.*; Joelson, *supra* note 9, at 858–59; Davidow, *Extraterritorial Application of U. S. Antitrust Law in a Changing World,* 8 LAW & POL'Y INT'L BUS. 895 (1976).

18. *See* UNCTAD Res. 96(IV), sec. III, ¶ 3, U.N. Doc. TD/217 (1976).

19. *See* UNCTAD, Interim Report of the Third *Ad Hoc* Group of Experts on Restrictive Business Practices to the Committee on Manufactures at its Eighth Session ¶ 3, U.N. Doc. TD/B/C.2/181, TD/B/C.2/AC.6/7 (1977).

20. In its first interim report, the Group evidenced its multiple-text approach by providing for Group of 77 proposals, Group B proposals, and an agreed text, *Id.*, Annex I. This approach has been followed in subsequent reports,

see, e.g., UNCTAD, Report of the Third *Ad Hoc* Group of Experts on Restrictive Business Practices on its First Session, Annex I & II, U.N. Doc. TD/B/C.2/AC.6/4 (1976); UNCTAD, Report of the Third *Ad Hoc* Group of Experts on Restrictive Business Practices on its Third Session, Annex I, U.N. Doc. TD/B/C.2/AC.6/10 (1977); UNCTAD, Report of the Third *Ad Hoc* Group of Experts on Restrictive Business Practices on its Fourth Session, Annex I, U.N. Doc. TD/B/C.2/AC.6/13 (1978). It should be noted that beginning with the Group's fifth session, UNCTAD, Report of the Third *Ad Hoc* Group of Experts on Restrictive Business Practices on its Fifth Session, U.N. Doc. TD/B/C.2/AC.6/18 (1978), and carrying through to its most recent session, UNCTAD, Report of the Third *Ad Hoc* Group of Experts on Restrictive Business Practices on its Sixth Session, U.N. Doc. TD/B/C.2/AC.6/20 (1979), the proposed text categories have included proposals by the Group D nations.

21. The most current text of the proposed and agreed principles appears in UNCTAD, Report of the Third *Ad Hoc* Group of Experts on Restrictive Business Practices on its Sixth Session, *supra* note 20, at ¶ 10, and is entitled "A Set of Multilaterally Agreed Equitable Principles and Rules for the Control of Restrictive Business Practices having Adverse Effects on International Trade, Particularly that of Developing Countries, and on the Economic Development of these Countries." The agreed principles are the result of unanimous acceptance at the negotiating conference, but they are subject to being reopened in subsequent negotiations.

22. *Id.* Agreed text, § A, 2.

23. *Id.* Agreed text, § A, 4.

24. *Id.* Agreed text, § A, 5.

25. *Id.* Proposals by Group D, § A, 6.

26. *Id.* Agreed text § B, Definitions, 1. [Emphasis added.]

27. *Id.* Agreed text, § B, Definitions, 2.

28. *Id.* Proposals of Group D, § B, Definitions, (v). This proposal, coupled with other Group D proposals (*e.g.*, *supra* note 25), reflects their rather ambivalent position, since they want to control the western TNCs while keeping their own highly concentrated state-owned industries beyond the reach of these controls.

29. *See, e.g., Id.* Agreed text, § B, Scope of application, 1, "[t]he principles and rules apply to restrictive business practices, including those of transnational corporations . . ."; *Id.*, Agreed text, § C, 1, "action should be taken in a mutually reinforcing manner at national, regional and international levels to eliminate, or effectively deal with, restrictive business practices, including those of transnational corporations . . ."; *Id.*, Agreed text, § D, 4, where the rules for enterprises include refraining from acquisitions through "mergers, takeovers, joint ventures or other acquisitions of control, whether of a horizontal, vertical or a conglomerate nature" where such acquisitions can lead to an abuse of dominant market power.

30. *Id.*, Proposals by Group of 77, § B, Scope of application, (v).

31. *Id.*, Proposals by Group of 77, § C, (v).

32. *See Id.*, Proposals by Group B, § B, Scope of application, (v); *Id.*, Proposals by Group B, § C, (v).

33. The work of the Third Ad Hoc Group of Experts underwent further negotiation and change at a recent U.N. Conference on RBPs held in Geneva from November 19 to December 7, 1979. UNCTAD MONTHLY BULL. NO. 156 (1979). Although the Conference did not adopt the principles and rules developed by the experts, some previously disputed issues were resolved; in particular, the conferees agreed that the code would be voluntary. Issues which remain unresolved include dispute settlement and the consideration of parent-subsidiary arrangements as RBPs. See ANTITRUST & TRADE REG. REP. (BNA) (Dec. 13, 1979) A–15. The Conference also resulted in some changes in the tentative code text, which are shown in excerpts from working papers at the Conference. ANTITRUST & TRADE REG. REP. (BNA) (Dec. 20, 1979) G–1—G–5. Although some disagreement exists concerning the characterization of the antitrust principles contained in this current draft, *Id.*, at A–12, the positive implications of this most recent effort are undisputed.

34. *See* UNCTAD Secretariat, First Draft of a Model Law or Laws on Restrictive Business Practices to Assist Developing Countries in Devising Appropriate Legislation, U.N. Doc. TD/B/C.2/AC.6/16 (1978).

35. *See* E.S.C. Res. 1721 (LIII), OFFICIAL RECORDS—53d Sess.—1972—Resolutions, U.N. Doc. E/5209 (1972).

36. E.S.C. Secretariat, Multinational Corporations in World Development, U.N. Doc. ST/ECA/190 (1973).

37. E.S.C., Report of the Group of Eminent Persons to Study the Role of Multinational Corporations on Development and on International Relations, U.N. Doc. E/5500/Add.l (pts. I and II) (1974).

38. E.S.C. Secretariat, The Impact of Multinational Corporations on the Development Process and on International Relations, U.N. Doc. E/5500 (1974); E.S.C Secretariat, The Impact of Transnational Corporations on the Development Process and on International Relations: Views of States on the Report of the Group of Eminent Persons, U.N. Doc. E/5595 and Add.l–6 (1974).

39. E.S.C. Res. 1908(LVII), U.N. E.S.C.—Official Records—57th Sess.—Resolutions, U.N. Doc. E/5570 (1974), at ¶ 6, established the Centre on Transnational Corporations (Centre) to function in an administrative capacity and to gather information on the various effects of TNCs, to aid the CTC in its work. *See infra* note 40. E.S.C. Res. 1913(LVII), U.N. E.S.C.—Official Records—57th Sess.—Resolutions, U.N. Doc. E/5570/Add.l (1974), at ¶ 1, established the CTC.

40. E.S.C. Res. 1913(LVII), *supra* note 39, at ¶ 3 (e).

41. *Id.* at ¶ 4.

42. *See* CTC, Report on the Second Session ¶ 9, U.N. Doc. E/5782 (1976).

43. The CTC was advised to seek such advice by E.S.C. Res. 1913(LVII), *supra* note 39, at ¶ 1 (d), while the Centre was instructed to gather and compile information on TNCs from an equally wide range of experts, CTC, Report on the Second Session, *supra* note 42, at ¶ 16.

44. *See* CTC, Report on the Second Session, *supra* note 42, at ¶ 11.

45. *Id.* at ¶ 13.

46. The most current tentative code text is entitled *Transnational Corporations: Code of Conduct; Formulations of the Chairman*, U.N. Doc. E/C.10/AC.2/8 (1978), *reprinted in* 1 CTC Rep. No. 6 (1979), at 5.

47. Statements of Mr. S. Mousouris, Secretary of the Working Group, at a symposium on TNC Concentration held at the University of Michigan Law School, November 9 & 10, 1979 (unpublished).

48. *See* 1 CTC Rep. No. 6, *supra* note 46. This draft includes provisions dealing with respect of national sovereignty, adherence to economic and developmental objectives, ownership and control, transfer pricing, disclosure of information, treatment of TNCs by the countries in which they operate, and intergovernmental cooperation.

49. *Id.* at 6.

50. Some of the unresolved issues include nationalization of TNCs and implementation of the code, *see* Statements of Mousouris, *supra* note 47. For a discussion of the current areas of concern within the CTC and future plans for this effort, *see* 1 CTC Rep. No. 6, *supra* note 46, at 3; 1 CTC Rep. No. 7 (1979), at 5. For a general discussion of the problem and issues involved in the development of this comprehensive code of conduct for TNCs, *see* Note, *Transnational Corporations—The United Nations Code of Conduct*, 5 Brooklyn J. Int'l L. 129 (1979); Coonrod, *supra* note 3.

51. Schwartz, *supra* note 4, at 531.

52. *Id.* at 536. There has in fact been recent agreement within UNCTAD that the RBP code will be voluntary. *See* Antitrust & Trade Reg. Rep. (BNA) (Dec. 13, 1979), *supra* note 33.

53. *See, e.g.,* 1 CTC Rep. No. 6, *supra* note 46, at 3, 11; CTC Secretariat, Transnational Corporations: Certain Modalities for Implementation of a Code of Conduct in Relation to its Possible Legal Nature, U.N. Doc. E/C.10/AC.2/9 (1978).

54. *See* text accompanying notes 30–32 *supra.*

55. Wex, *A Code of Conduct on Restrictive Business Practices: A Third Option,* 1977 Can. Y.B. Int'l L. 198 (1977).

56. *Id.* at 231.

57. *Id.* at 232.

58. *See* Wang, *The Design of an International Code of Conduct for Transnational Corporations,* 10 J. Int'l L. & Econ. 319 (1975).

59. *See, e.g.,* Chance, *supra* note 4, at 1820; Coonrod, *supra* note 3, at 306; Rubin, *Harmonization of*

Rules: A Perspective on the U.N. Commission on Transnational Corporations, 8 L. & POL'Y INT'L BUS. 875, 889 (1976).

60. Joelson & Griffin, *International Regulation of Restrictive Business Practices Engaged in by Transna-tional Enterprises: A Prognosis,* 11 INT'L LAW. 5, 20 (1977).

61. Kintner, Joelson & Vaghi, *Groping for a Truly International Antitrust Law,* 14 VA. J. INT'L L. 75, 97 (1973).

62. Note, 5 BROOKLYN J. INT'L L. 129, *supra* note 50, at 152.

Appendixes

Appendix 1:

Foreign Monopoly and Merger Law

This Appendix consists of brief descriptions of the monopoly and merger laws of several nations. These descriptions are not intended to provide a complete statement of any one nation's antitrust statutes and case law. Rather, they are included in this volume to permit the reader to observe the widely divergent approaches to the regulation of economic concentration.

These summaries may not contain the latest case law developments or statutory amendments. It is hoped, however, that they provide a sound starting point for investigation of the regulatory regimes of the nations included in this collection.

AUSTRALIA

LAW

Trade Practices Act, No. 51 of 1974 as amended by Acts Nos. 56 and 63, 1975; Nos. 88 and 157, 1976; Nos. 81, 111, and 151, 1977; Nos. 206 and 207, 1978.

Synopsis
The Trade Practices Act (the Act) of 1974 inaugurated an era of aggressive antitrust policy in Australia. Modeled on the Sherman and Clayton Acts, Part IV of the Act makes a wide variety of anticompetitive practices illegal. Although the Australian economy is composed largely of small- and medium-sized firms, Sections 46 and 50 of the Act demonstrate the Australian government's desire to control economic concentration. The former forbids monopolistic behavior; the latter forbids anticompetitive mergers.

The Act does not make acquisition of market control illegal. Once a corporation gains power to determine prices or control production or distribution of "a substantial part of the goods or services in a market" however, it is subject to the per se prohibitions set forth in Section 46. Specifically, a monopolist cannot:

1. eliminate or substantially damage a competitor in any market;
2. prevent the entry of a person into any market;
3. deter or prevent a person from competing in any market.

Certain conduct is exempted from the monopolization prohibition, including practices relating exclusively to the export of goods or supply of services outside of Australia.

Section 50 seeks to prevent anticompetitive mergers. Patterned after Section 7 of the Clayton Act, 15 U.S.C. § 18 (1976), this section provides that:

> A corporation shall not acquire, directly, or indirectly, any shares in the capital, or any assets of a body corporate if—
> (a) as a result of the acquistion, the corporation would be, or be likely to be, in a position to control or dominate a market for goods or services; or
> (b) in a case where the corporation is in a position to control or domi- nate a market for goods or services—
>
> > (ii) the acquisition would, or would be likely to, substantially strengthen the power of the corporation to control or dominate [any market in which the corporation is a competitor].

For purposes of Section 50 only, a *market* is defined as a substantial market for goods or services in Australia or in a state.

Under Part VII of the Act, a corporation can petition the Trade Practices Commission (Commission) for authorization of a proposed merger. If authorization is obtained, the applicant is protected against subsequent actions alleging that the authorized merger violates the Act.

The Commission is a five-member panel charged with administration of the Act. In addition to granting authorization for proposed mergers and other potentially anticompetitive agreements, the Commission can investigate alleged violations of the Act and bring charges against alleged violators in the Australian Industrial Court. The Commission does not have power to enforce its own orders.

The Trade Practices Tribunal (Tribunal) is a quasi-judicial body that reviews Commission decisions regarding authorization applications. The Tribunal applies the same tests as the Commission in its review of authorization applications. If necessary, the Tribunal may modify or set aside the Commission's decisions. As with the Commission, the members of the Tribunal are appointed by the governor general and enjoy substantial independence from the legislative and executive branches of government.

Exclusive jurisdiction for violations of the Act lies with the Industrial Court. If a violation is established, the offender is subject to an injunction, a fine of up to $50,000 in the case of a person and $250,000 in the case of corporations, and liability for damages resulting from violation of the Act. If a merger is found to be illegal, the acquiring firm can also be ordered to divest itself of the acquired assets or shares.

In actions brought by the Commission or the minister of business and commerce, any of these remedies can be requested. In actions filed by private parties, the plaintiff can request either injunctive relief (except in the case of allegedly anticompetitive mergers) or compensation for damages directly resulting from the defendant's anticompetitive acts.

The Act does not make any restrictive trade practice a crime. However, because the civil fines imposed by the Act are similar to criminal penalities, the Australian Federal Court has required that parties alleging violations of the Act bear a standard of proof greater than the preponderance of evidence standard normally required in civil litigation.

CASES

Top Performance Motors Pty. Ltd. v. Ira Berk (Queensland) Pty. Ltd., (1975) 5 Argus L.R. 465.
Trade Practices Commission v. Vaponordic (Australia) Pty. Ltd., (1975) 6 Argus L.R. 248.
Trade Practices Commission v. Sharp Corporation of Australia Pty. Ltd., (1975) 8 Argus L.R. 255.
Quadramain Pty. Ltd. v. Sevastapol Investments Pty. Ltd., (1976) 8 Argus L.R. 555.
Re Queensland Co-operative Milling Association Ltd., (1976) 25 F.L.R. 169.
Trade Practices Commission v. Guest's Garage Pty., [1976] A.T.P.R. ¶ 40–016.
Re Howard Smith Industries Pty. Ltd., (1977) 15 Argus L.R. 645.
Phelps v. Western Mining Corporation Ltd., [1978] A.T.P.R. ¶ 40–077.
Re Tooth & Co. Ltd., [1978] A.T.P.R. ¶ 40–084.
Trade Practices Commission v. Ansett Transport Industries (Operations) Pty. Ltd., [1978] A.T.P.R. ¶ 40–071.
Western Australia Football League, Inc. and the West Perth Football Club, Inc., [1979] A.T.P.R. ¶ 18–017.

SECONDARY SOURCES

Breyer, *Five Questions about Australian Anti-Trust Law* , 51 AUSTL. L. REV. 28 (1977).
D'Aloisio, *Trade Practices Act 1977: Restrictive Trade Practices and Mergers*, 52 L. INST. J. 380 (1978).
Giles, *The Role of the Trade Practices Commission when Appearing before the Trade Practices Tribunal in Support of its Determinations*, 51 AUSTL. L.J. 199 (1977).
Gummow, *Abuse of Monopoly: Industrial Property and Trade Practices Control*, 7 SYDNEY L. REV. 339 (1976).
Harrison, *Joint Ventures and the Trade Practices Act 1974: The American Approach and its Applicability to Australia*, 3 AUSTL. B. L. REV. 117 (1975).

Lucas, *Monopolization and the Shopping Centre Developer*, L. & Soc'y J. 209 (1977).

Pengilley, *Section 45 of the Trade Practices Act—the Law and Administration to Date*, 8 FED. L. REV. 15 (1976–77).

Pierce, *Effect on Competition of Corporate Acquisitions as a Factor in Authorisation Applications to the Trade Practices Commission*, 9 FED. L. REV. 71 (1978).

Santow, *Mergers and the Commonwealth Trade Practices Act 1974*, 49 AUSTL. L.J. 52 (1975).

Santow & Gonski, *Mergers After the Trade Practices Act 1974–77*, 52 AUSTL. L.J. 132 (1978).

Wallace, *The Constitutional Reach of the Trade Practices Act and the Liability of Corporate Officers*, 52 AUSTL. L.J. 682 (1977).

Wallace, *Public Benefit and Authorisation Determinations under the Trade Practices Act 1974*, 4 AUSTL. B. L. REV. 175 (1976).

G. WIDMER, RESTRICTIVE TRADE PRACTICES AND MERGERS (1977).

Williamson, *Trade Practices Law—Its Implications for Mining and Petroleum Joint Ventures*, 1 AUSTL. MINING & PETROLEUM J. 59 (1977).

BELGIUM

LAW

Belgian Act of 27 May 1960 on Protection Against the Abuse of Economic Power ("Moniteur Belge" of 22 June 1960); Article 36 of the Law of 30 December 1970, as amended by Law of 17 August 1973 on Notification of Mergers and Acquisitions (B.S.G. of 8 September 1973).

Synopsis

Article 1 of the Belgian Act of 27 May 1960 on Protection Against the Abuse of Economic Power (the Act) defines *economic power* as the power of individuals or corporations, acting alone or in concert, to exert a "dominating influence" over merchandise supplies or prices, capital markets, or service prices. However, under Article 2, an "abuse of economic power" exists only when persons holding economic power "prejudice the public interest" by engaging in practices which distort or restrict competition, economic freedom, or the development of production or trade. No well-defined categories of abuse are enumerated in the Act, and the mere holding of a dominant market position is not considered a per se violation. Rather, a dominant position must be used to the detriment of "the public interest" as determined by the competent authorities.

A very detailed multilevel investigative procedure is established for determining whether an abuse of economic power exists. The reporting commissioner conducts the initial investigation; the Council for Economic Disputes (the Council) serves as the administrative tribunal with the authority to decide not to proceed; and the minister of economic affairs can institute proceedings, aid in the investigation, and participate in a final decision for the Council. If this procedure results in an affirmative finding of abuse of economic power, then the minister suggests proposals for conciliation, makes recommendations in the event of noncompliance with the proposals, issues a cease and desist order if the recommendations are not followed, and institutes, at his discretion, civil or criminal proceedings should any of the above methods fail to achieve the desired result. Actual enforcement of the Act has had limited success, since most actions brought thus far have involved limited private interests rather than at the general public interest, and thus have not been covered by the Act.

The 1970 notification statute requires that the minister of economic affairs, the minister of finance, and the secretary of state for regional economy be notified of any transfer to non-Belgians of a one-third capital interest in a Belgian enterprise having funds of at least B.Frs.100 million. Additionally, the minister of finance must authorize any public offer for purchase or exchange of Belgian securities made by Belgian individuals living abroad or by Belgian companies under foreign control. Failure to obtain proper authorization can lead to a public notice by the minister which prohibits anyone from aiding the transaction. These notification requirements are limited to mergers and acquisitions by foreign participants, thus giving the government a means of controlling foreign direct investment.

SECONDARY SOURCES

COMPETITION LAW IN WESTERN EUROPE AND THE USA, (Gijlstra & Murphy, eds., 1976) (with looseleaf supplements).
OECD—GUIDE TO LEGISLATION ON RESTRICTIVE BUSINESS PRACTICES, Vol. I (1964).
[1974] COMM. MKT. REP. (CCH) ¶ 21,521 *et seq.*

BRAZIL

LAW

Antitrust Law No. 4134 (1962); Regulations to the Antitrust Law, Decree 52–025 (1964).

Synopsis
Brazilian Antitrust Law No. 4134 (the Act) seeks to "eliminate abuses of economic power referred to in Article 148 of the Federal Constitution." Article 2 of the Act prohibits the following conduct:

1. Manipulation of markets or elimination of competition, by means of agreements, accumulation of companies or shares, mergers or other

associations, concentration of capital, accumulation of managerial
control, cessation of business activity, or obstruction of the formation
or operation of other companies;

2. Arbitrary increases in profits of natural or actual monopolies by raising prices without need for expansion or other just cause;

3. Creation of monopolistic conditions [defined below] or excessive
speculation for the purpose of promoting a temporary increase in
prices by cutting back on productive capacity, any form of attempted
monopolization, withholding goods from a market with a view toward creating a shortage, or use of artificial means to cause price
fluctuations;

4. Formation of economic groupings of companies which restrict free
actions of buyers and sellers by discriminating as to prices or services to the purchase of a product or service;

5. Unfair competitive practices, such as demanding exclusive promotional advertising or making prior agreements as to prices or other
benefits when dealing with government officials.

Monopolistic conditions is defined as those conditions "in which a company
or group of companies so controls the production, distribution, and sale of a
product or service that it exercise a preponderant influence on prices."

The statute requires registration of corporate agreements. Article 72 requires that documents referring to the establishment, transformation, merger,
or association of companies, or changes in the articles of incorporation, cannot
be registered without broad disclosure of relevant information regarding the
share ownership, operation, purpose, and location of the corporate enterprise.
Disclosure of financial information concerning the partners and directors of
the enterprise is also required.

Article 74 prohibits certain types of contracts entered into without prior
government scrutiny and approval:

Unless approved and registered with CADE [described below], any contracts, agreements, or conventions of any kind . . . shall be void if made
for any one of the following purposes:

(a) to put production on par with consumption;
(b) to control a market;
(c) to standardize production;
(d) to stabilize prices;
(e) to divide markets between companies, whether of production or
distribution;
(f) to restrict distribution in such a way as to harm equivalent or substitute goods.

Chapter II of the statute establishes a federal government agency—the
Administrative Council for Economic Defense (CADE)—that is charged

with enforcement of Brazilian antitrust laws. CADE is given extensive investigatory powers. A general counsel is established to assist CADE with legal advice and to insure that CADE's regulations and pronouncements are enforced.

CADE is divided into five sections. The Economic Group performs economic, statistical, and general quantitative analysis. The Control Group supervises nationalized enterprises. The Auditing Group supervises the accounting of all Brazilian firms. The Administrative Group provides basic administrative and support services for CADE. The Regional Inspectorates are charged "with the task of representing and assisting CADE in the performance of the attributes conferred upon them by law and these regulations."

CADE has sole responsibility for investigations into, and prosecutions of, "abuses of economic power." State and local authorities are not permitted to conduct their own investigations; rather they must submit their allegations to CADE for enforcement. Individuals can also bring possible violations of the antitrust laws to the attention of CADE. However, the statute vests exclusive authority to prosecute and enforce the law in CADE. Thus, Brazilian antitrust laws do not recognize a private right of action for antitrust violations.

The remedies available to CADE in enforcing the law are quite substantial. Fines can range from five to ten thousand times the highest minimum wage in the country on the date of CADE's decision. The fine is assessed even if the defendant agrees to terminate the illegal activity. In addition to the fine, CADE can require that the company correct its practices and come into compliance with the law within a certain period of time. If the defendant does not comply within this time period, or if after being corrected the defendant again engages in the illegal activity, CADE can impose another fine—double the previous fine. Moreover, if a defendant's pledge to refrain from illegal conduct is broken, the statute provides for a mandatory expropriation of corporate assets.

Enforcement of fines requires judicial process. In lieu of collecting a fine, CADE can petition the Federal District Court of the state where the defendant company is located for imposition of government control over the company. The government-appointed administrator is obligated to take steps necessary to eliminate the abuses that required government intervention. Once the abuses are eliminated, the government administrator may be removed and the corporation returned to private administration.

Government directorship does not affect the normal operation of the defendant firm; the only change in operation is the placement of a government official at the pinnacle of power. However, should the majority of those responsible for the administration of the company refuse to cooperate with the government administrator, a judge can order the government administrator to assume full responsibility for the company. Further, a judge can dismiss any company official who attempts to prevent the government administrator from carrying out his or her duties.

CANADA

LAW

Combines Investigation Act, R.S.C. 1970; as amended S.C. 1974–75–76 c. 76, 1977 c. 28; Foreign Investment Review Act, S.C. 1973, c. 46, as amended; Bill C–13, an act to amend the Combines Investigation Act (introduced into Parliament on November 18, 1977; the Bill would have to be reintroduced to be considered again).

Synopsis
The Combines Investigation Act (the Act) defines a merger as any acquisition by one or more persons, whether by purchase or lease of shares or assets, or any control over or interest in the business of an competitior, supplier, customer, or any other person whereby competition is or is likely to be lessened contrary to the interest of consumers, producers, or the general public. A monopoly exists when one or more persons substantially control the business in which they are engaged, and have operated, or are likely to operate, such business against the public interest.

Sections 5 to 14 describe the functions of the director of investigation and research. Private citizens can apply for an inquiry by the director if they believe that someone has or will commit a merger. The Director will commence an inquiry when he receives such an application, has reason to believe such an inquiry should be instituted, or has been directed by the minister to make such an inquiry. The director can require production of a business' tax returns. The director also has broad powers to search properties and to seize evidence relevant to his inquiry. This evidence is admissible in any hearing.

Sections 16 through 22 establish the Restrictive Trade Practices Commission (RTPC), provide for submission of evidence by the director, authorize publication of RTPC reports, and establish the right of an investigated party to be represented by counsel. The RTPC hears evidence of the director and the defenses of the parties involved. The RTPC then makes a report to the minister containing a review of the evidence, a conclusion as to the effect on the public interest of the arrangements, and a recommendation as to remedies. The RTPC has substantial investigatory powers.

The director can make a general inquiry into monopolistic conditions on his own initiative or when authorized by the minister.

Section 33 provides that every person who is a party or privy to or knowingly assists in a merger or monopoly is guilty of an indictable offense and is liable to imprisonment for up to two years or to a fine not exceeding $5,000 or both. Section 20 grants judges the power to prohibit or to dissolve a merger or monopoly.

Under Bill C–13 the Competition Board is substituted for the Restrictive Trade Practices Commission. The Board has as its objective the examination of trade practices referred to it. The Board can examine mergers and monopolies as well as other trade practices. Violation of the merger provisions of the Act is no longer considered a criminal offense under Bill C–13.

Bill C–13 also replaces the previous director of investigation with the competition policy advocate. The Canadian Cabinet appoints the advocate and deputy competition policy advocates. The advocate's functions are essentially the same as the director's, but his quasi-judicial responsibilities include a greater number that are reviewable by the Competition Board. The advocate also has a more active role in presenting the government's position before administrative bodies.

In lieu of proof "beyond a reasonable doubt" of detriment to the public, the bill substitutes a "preponderance of the evidence" standard. The Board, if the advocate meets this standard, can prohibit or dissolve any merger that substantially lessens competition.

A merger is defined broadly as any acquisition or establishment by a person of any control over or interest in the whole or any part of the business of another, whether in a trade, industry, or profession. A joint venture is included within the definition of a merger if it includes the creation of a new corporation.

The provisions of the proposed law are applicable to both conglomerate and vertical mergers. Only horizontal mergers whose effect is to place more than 20 percent of the market in the hands of the acquirer are subject to review by the Board.

The participating companies to a proposed merger can defend the propriety of their merger on grounds that it will increase the efficiency of the Canadian economy. If the Board is satisfied that a merger has brought about or will probably bring about a substantial increase in efficiency, it cannot issue a remedial order. However, even if the merger increases efficiency, the Board must rule against the merger if it would create monopoly in the relevant market. Bill C–13 also addresses the coordination of merger review under the Act with merger review under the Foreign Investment Review Act.

The purpose of the Foreign Investment Review Act (FIRA) is to allow foreign direct investment or takeover of Canadian businesses only if such action significantly benefits the Canadian economy. The Review Act lists several factors to consider in deciding whether to approve a foreign acquisition. These factors are directed toward determining whether foreign control will promote efficiency or competition in the Canadian economy.

The FIRA applies to acquisition of control of any Canadian enterprise except Crown corporations, certain tax-exempt enterprises, associated business enterprises, and small business enterprises. The FIRA also applies to establishment of all new businesses.

All companies seeking foreign acquisitions or direct investments covered by the FIRA must give notice to the Foreign Investment Review Agency (the Agency). The minister, a member of the Queen's Privy Council appointed by the governor to administer the FIRA, can also demand such notice if he believes such foreign proposals or actual investments have occurred. After the Agency is notified, the minister will assess whether the foreign investment is or will likely be of significant benefit to Canada. If the minister finds the investment is of significant benefit, then he will make a recommendation to approve the investment to the governor in council. Involved parties have the right to represent themselves before the governor. If the governor decides the investment is of significant benefit, he shall allow the investment. But if he does not make such a finding, the governor in council must deny the proposed investment. Section 13 provides that investments are allowed if the governor in council issues no order within sixty days after he is notified by the agency of the proposed or actual investment.

Sections 15 through 18 provide for investigations. These sections grant the minister broad powers with respect to searches, seizures, and obtaining relevant evidence.

Sections 19 to 23 concern remedies available to the minister to obtain compliance with his orders. The minister can obtain an injunction against a company violating his order. The minister can also seek an order by a superior court to render an investment nugatory or an order to comply with the undertaking. Anyone who does not comply with a superior court order is subject to a contempt citation.

Sections 24 to 27 establish penalties for offenses under the FIRA. Failure to give notice of a proposed investment is an offense punishable by a fine of no more than Canadian $5,000. Any obstruction of an investigation under the FIRA is an offense punishable by a fine of no more than Canadian $5,000 or imprisonment of not more than six months or both.

REGULATIONS

Foreign Investment Review Regulations—under the Foreign Investment Review Act: SOR/77–226, P.C. 1077–606, *gazetted* March 23, 1977 *as amended by* SOR/78–589, P.C. 1978–2309 *gazetted* August 9, 1978.

Sections 3 through 5 give interpretations of *noneligible person, gross assets and gross revenue,* and *notices.* The regulations also describe the information the applicant must provide to the Agency. The regulations require the applicant to summarize its proposal, give detailed information on the financial status of the acquiring and acquired businesses, and provide details of the applicant's plans for the Canadian business enterprise. The information sought is designed to facilitate a determination of whether a foreign investment significantly benefits Canada.

CASES

R. v. K. C. Irving Ltd. and three other Corporations, 72 D.L.R.2d 12 N.B. 488 (S.C.C. 1977). A corporation can defend a charge of merger or monopoly under the Combines Investigation Act by arguing its anti-competitive acts are not detrimental because of economic gains from a merger or monopoly unrelated to the merger's effects on competition. A court in a merger or monopoly case must weigh the detriment of lost competition against the value of economic gains from the merger or monopoly to determine whether such merger or monopoly is detrimental to the public.

R. v. F. W. Woolworth Co. Ltd., 46 D.L.R.2d 345, 18 C.C.C.2d 23, 3 Ont. R. 2d 630 (C.A.) (1974), *rev'g.* 11 C.C.C.2d 562, 11 C.P.R.2d 229, 21 C.R.N. 8. 371 (Ont. H.C.T.)—Prohibition order under Combines Investigation Act must relate to the offense for which conviction was obtained. Such an order should be made only if the evidence shows a deliberate and flagrant disobedience and the likelihood of continuation in the absence of prohibition.

R. v. Canada Safeway Ltd., 41 D.L.R.2d 264, 14 C.C.C.2d 14, 12 C.P.R.2d 3 (1973), 1 W.W.R. 210 (Alta. S.C.T.P.) (1974)—Court can prohibit acts directed toward commission of an offense under the Combines Act.

R. v. Allied Chemical Canada Ltd., et al., 69 D.L.R.3d 506, 29 C.C.C.2d 460, 24 C.P.R.2d 22, 6 W.W.R. 481 (B.C.S.C.) (1975)—Discusses the difference between conspiracy charges and the offense of formation of a monopoly.

R. v. Canadian General Electric Co. Ltd., et al., 75 D.L.R.2d 664, 34 C.C.C.2d 489, 15 Ont.R.2d 360, 29 C.P.R.2d 1 (H.C.J.) (1976)—Detriment to the public, a necessary element of a monopoly violation, must be shown to flow from the operation of the shared monopoly and not from collateral acts which may be the subject of another charge.

ADMINISTRATIVE PROCEEDINGS

Reports by Restrictive Practices Commission
Prior to the 1970s, none of the reports relating to mergers of the Restrictive Trade Practices Commission resulted in convictions of corporations. On January 14, 1971, the RTPC issued a report that found that the substantial control of the large lamps business in Canada by Canadian General Electric Company Limited, Canadian Westinghouse Company Limited, and Sylvania Electric (Canada) Ltd. resulted in a monopoly situation; therefore, such business operated to the detriment of the public. The report recommended periodic review of the customs duties on electric lamps to ensure that the tariff was not used to insulate Canadian manufactures from competition by outside suppliers to the disadvantage of users in Canada. On September 2, 1976, the accused were convicted of two counts of monopoly. On April 13, 1977, fines totaling $550,000 were imposed for monopoly and other offenses as follows: Canadian General Electric Co. Ltd. $300,000; Westinghouse Canada Ltd. $150,000; G.T.E. Sylvania Ltd. $100,000.

In other proceedings referred directly to the Attorney General of Canada, four charges of merger and monopoly were brought against K. C. Irving Ltd., a newspaper chain. On January 24, 1974, the accused was convicted and fines totaling $150,000 were imposed on April 2, 1974. An order of divestiture was issued on July 10, 1974. The accused successfully appealed the convictions, sentences & order. The Crown lost its appeal to the Supreme Court of Canada on November 16, 1976.

REPORTS UNDER THE FOREIGN INVESTMENT REVIEW ACT

Since the institution of FIRA, most foreign takeovers have been approved. If the Cabinet finds some combination of the following factors, the proposed merger will usually be approved:

1. the merger increases employment;
2. the merger constitutes a new investment;
3. the merger will increase resource processing or use of Canadian parts and services;
4. the merger will increase exports;
5. the merging corporation is owned partially by Canadian interests;
6. the merger will improve productivity and efficiency;
7. the merger will enhance technological development;
8. the merger will improve product variety and innovation;
9. the merger will have beneficial impacts on competition; or
10. the proposed merger is compatible with industrial and economic policies.

Thus, as the FIRA has been enforced so far, only extremely unattractive foreign mergers have been disallowed.

List of Disallowed Cases
Fiscal 1975/76. During this period, 22 out of 132 foreign takeovers were disallowed. The following lists the applicants who were disallowed and the nature of their business:

1. Ambassador Bridge Inc./Canada Transit Co., which operates the Canadian side of the Ambassador Bridge.
2. Avco Financial Services Canada Ltd./certain assets of La Corporation de Finance Bonaccord Ltée, a finance company.
3. Canadian Canners Ltd./Robert G. Tamblyn Paper Box Ltd., a producer of folding paper boxes.
4. Ciba-Geigy Canada Ltd./Stewart Seeds Ltd., a producer of cereal and corn seed.
5. Corbetts Ltd./Maurice Rousseau & Cie. Ltée, a distributor of automotive replacement parts, accessories, and supplies.

6. De Lavel Turbine Inc./Williams Machines, Ltd., True Forge Ltd., and certain assets of material Processing Division of Havlik Enterprises Ltd., engaged in custom machine work.
7. Kibun Co. Ltd./North Sea Products Ltd., a processor of fish.
8. Lacroix, L., Fils S.A./Dominion Cigarette Tube Co. Ltd., a manufacturer of cigarette tubes and related manufacturing machinery.
9. Larochelle et Frères Ltée/La Boulangerie Racine Ltée, a bakery firm.
10. Meyer Laboratories Inc./Neo Drug Co., which packages and distributes ethical drugs.
11. Micco Equipment Co./Ferguson Supply Ltd., and Arctic Terex Ltd., distributors of off-highway machinery and equipment.
12. Perolin-Bird Archer Ltd./British-American Chemical Co. Ltd., a manufacturer of industrial chemicals.
13. Quebec Ready Mix Inc./Carriere Hebert Inc., an operator of a quarry.
14. Quebec Ready Mix Inc./Sables Laves Inc., an operator of a quarry.
15. Sonotone Corp. (Canada) Ltd./Burgess Battery Division of Gould Manufacturing of Canada Ltd., which manufactures dry cell batteries, flashlights, lanterns, and rolled zinc.
16. Syntex Ltd./Mowatt & Moore Ltd., a manufacturer of pharmaceutical products.
17. Turbex Ltd./certain assets of George Laird & Son Ltd., which sells fuel oil and home comfort equipment.
18. UPS Ltd./Delivero (Canada) Ltd., which delivers small parcels.
19. UPS Ltd./Grenoble Distribution Ltd., which delivers small parcels.
20. Lacroix, L., Fils S.A./Central Tobacco Manufacturing Co. Ltd., a manufacturer of cigarette tubes and related manufacturing machinery.
21. WCI Canada Ltd.,/the appliance business of Westinghouse Canada Ltd., a manufacturer and distributor of major household appliances and electrical industrial equipment.
22. WCI Canada Ltd./the appliance division of Westinghouse Canada (second submission), a manufacturer of major household appliances and electrical industrial equipment.

Fiscal 1976/77. During this period, 19 out of 172 foreign takeovers were disallowed.

1. Blackwood Hodge (Canada) Ltd./Tobin Tractor (1957) Ltd., which sells, services, and rents construction and industrial equipment.
2. Brady Industries Ltd./Bray-Dor Industries Ltd., which fabricates, installs, and repairs industrial doors.
3. Brewster Transport Co. Ltd./Jasper Sky Tram Ltd., which operates an aerial tramway.
4. C & J Clark Canada Ltd./Calderone Shoe Co. Ltd., which retails footwear.
5. Carisbrook Industries Inc./the Crawford-Collingwood Ontario Division of Indian Head Inc., a manufacturer of pillows and cushions.

6. Dow Jones & Co. Inc./Irwin-Dorsey Ltd., a textbook publisher and distributor.
7. Dresser Industries Canada Ltd./General Abrasive (Canada) Ltd., which manufactures aluminum oxide, silicone, carbide, and aluminum zirconia.
8. Dresser Industries, Inc./Jarco Services, Ltd., which leases hydraulic bumper jars to the petroleum industry.
9. E.G. & G., Inc./Radionics Ltd., which distributes and services electronic testing and research equipment.
10. Fuji Photo Film Co. Ltd./R & H Products Ltd., a distributor of photographic equipment and supplies.
11. General Mills Canada, Ltd./Regal Toy, Ltd., a manufacturer of toys.
12. Gulf Oil Canada Ltd./Mosbacher Oil & Gas Ltd., engaged in exploration for, and the development of, petroleum and natural gas fields.
13. Hayes-Dana Ltd./Western Wheel & Parts Ltd., which sells and services heavy-duty truck components.
14. Lafarge Concrete Ltd.-Lafarge Beton Ltée/Argus Agregates Ltd., which crushes and processes aggregates.
15. N.V. Indivers/Canadian Vac-Hyd Processing Ltd., which sells and services computer peripheral equipment.
17. Simon & Schuster Inc./Simon & Schuster Canada Ltd., a paperbook publisher and distributor.
18. State Electric Co. Ltd./D. Thompson Ltd., and D. Thompson (Western) Ltd., which are electrical contractors.
19. Welltech Inc./Gamache Well Servicing Ltd., Prairie Gold Servicing Co., Well Servicing Holdings Inc. and Dow Well Servicing Ltd., which engage in oil and gas well completion, servicing, and workover.

Fiscal 1978/79. During this period, 25 out of 323 proposed foreign mergers were disallowed.

1. Baker Material Hanling Corp./Otis Elevator Co. Ltd.'s facilities to distribute imported forklift trucks.
2. Bank Building and Equipment Corp./Cooper Appraisals Ltd., which is engaged in general property appraisal.
3. Bulk Transport Service Inc./Soulanges Cartage & Equipment Co. Ltd., which hauls bulk cement and construction materials.
4. CFMG Inc./which will acquire the fuel, heating, and home comfort equipment business of S. Anglin Co. Ltd.
5. Colorcraft Corporation/Triple Print Film Labs Ltd., which is engaged in mail-order photo-finishing.
6. Comshare Inc./Comshare Ltd., which operates a computer service bureau.
7. Creusot-Loire Steel Corp./Brace-Meuller-Huntley (Canada) Ltd., which warehouses machine and tool steels and aluminum bars.
8. Dow Jones & Co. Inc./Irwin-Dorsey Ltd., which distributes textbooks.

9. Editions Etudes Vivantes Ltée/Les Edition Julienne Inc., which publishes French language textbooks.

10. Ex-Cell-O Corp./Davidson Rubber Co. Ltd. and Associates, which manufacture automotive instrument panel crash pads and armrests.

11. Gelco Corp./B.D.C. Ltd., which provides a courier service.

12. Hillbrand Industries Ltd./Terra-Flex Ltd., which designs and manufactures trackmounted off-highway vehicles.

13. Hongkong and Shanghai Banking Corp., The/Marmid Financial Services Ltd. and M.M. Builders Funds Ltd., 1. which is a holding company and 2. which is engaged in construction financing.

14. Kaiser Engineers Inc./Henry J. Kaiser Company (Canada) Ltd./La Compagnie Henry J. Kaiser (Canada) Ltée, which is a consulting engineering business.

15. Louisiana-Pacific Canada Ltd./Salmo Forest Products Ltd., which operates a sawmill.

16. Meadows, Thomas, & Co. Canada Ltd./Allan & Johnston Ltd., which is a customs broker.

17. National Distillers and Chemical Corp./Emery Industries Ltd., which sells specialty chemicals.

18. Norton Simon Inc./Avis Transport of Canada Ltd., which rents and leases cars and trucks.

19. Parker-Hannifin Corp./Joly Engineering Ltd., which manufactures precision mechanical components.

20. Pentos Ltd./certain assets of The Master's Collection, namely facilities to publish religious recorded music and to distribute religious musical records, tapes, and sheet music.

21. Produits Petroliers Champlain Ltée/retail business of Petrole Moderne Ltee, which wholesales and/or retails gasoline and fuels.

22. Robin Hood Multifoods Ltd./Fred Martin Agencies Ltd., which imports sporting goods, supplies, and equipment.

23. Seismograph Service Corporation/Central Development Exploration Ltd., which collects seismic data.

24. Unilever United States, Inc./1. Nacan Products Ltd. 2. Lepage's Ltd. 3. Foodpro National Inc., 1. which produces adhesives, resins, and speciality starch products; 2. which produces and sells adhesives and allied home care products and decoration aids; 3. which produces additives and imports and sells stabilizers, emulsifiers, natural smoke extracts, and soya proteins.

25. United Technologies Corp./Otis Elevator Co. Ltd., which manufactures elevators.

SECONDARY SOURCES

Canada Parliament Senate, *Proceedings of the Standing Senate Committee on Banking, Trade and Commerce*, 2, 8, 23 February; 1, 8, 15 March; 5 April 1978 (1978).

Comment, *The Canadian Foreign Investment Review Act: Red, White and Gray*, 5 L. & Pol'y Int'l Bus. 1 (1973)

Donaldson & Jackson, *The Foreign Investment Review Act*, 53 Can. B. Rev. 171 (1975).

C. Flavell, Canadian Competition Law: A Business Guide (1979).

C. Goff & C. Reasons, Corporate Crime in Canada: A Critical Analysis of Anti-Combines Legislation (1978).

G. Hughes, A Commentary on the Foreign Investment Review Act, (1975).

J. Langford, Canadian Foreign Investment Controls (1975).

Merger Policy, 22 Antitrust Bull. 673 (Fall 1975).

Note, *Competition Policy in Canada: A Comment on Bill C–13*, 43 Sask. L. Rev. 137 (1978–79).

J. Rowley & W. Stanbury (eds.), Competition Policy in Canada: Stage II, Bill C–13 (1978).

Spence, *The Foreign Investment Review Act of Canada*, 4 Syr. J. Int'l L. & Comm. 303 (1976–77).

W. Stanbury (ed.), Papers on Bill C–13: The Proposed Competition Act (1977).

W. Stanbury & Cook, Competition Policy: The Retreat Begins, Canadian Consumer 36 (February 1978).

H. Strikeman, The Foreign Investment Review Act (1974).

Symposium, *Canadian Antitrust Laws and Their Impact Upon U.S. Firms*, 44 A.B.A. Antitrust L.J. 463 (1975).

EUROPEAN ECONOMIC COMMUNITY

LAW

Articles 85 and 86, Treaty Establishing the European Economic Community, 298 U.N.T.S. 4300 (1958).

Synopsis

Multinational enterprises operating in the European Economic Community come under the ambit of the general competition laws: Articles 85 and 86 of the Treaty of Rome and subsequent regulations and directives. Article 85 prohibits agreements between undertakings and concerted practices that may affect trade between member states, and which are designed to prevent or distort competition in the Common Market. Article 86 prohibits abuse of a firm's dominant position in a substantial part of the Common Market. Both articles list examples of the behavior they prohibit.

The Commission of the European Communities (Commission) has proposed a regulation concerning prior notification of mergers of corporations with turnovers in excess of 1.25 billion units of account. This regulation was expected to help deal with the competitive threat of multinational corporations. The Council of the European Communities (Council) has declined to adopt the regulation.

The Commission has been working with the OECD to develop guidelines for multinational corporations, specifically in the area of service of documents, enforcement of decisions, and competitive behavior. It has also formulated a regulation that would allow the creation of a European Company—a community-wide corporation formed under standards promulgated by the Commission. This regulation has not been adopted by the Council.

The Court of Justice and the Commission have used Articles 85 and 86 of the Treaty of Rome against foreign corporations if these corporations' acts threaten competition in the Community. Though the Commission has espoused the "effects doctrine" as a means of obtaining jurisdiction over foreign corporations, the Court of Justice has only allowed jurisdiction over these firms in two types of circumstances: first, if the foreign corporation acts directly within the Community to restrain competition; or second, if the corporation's subsidiary commits an act in restraint of competition within the Community, and the subsidiary is not wholly independent of the parent.

Article 86, dealing with abuse of dominant position, has been applied to mergers with at least one firm in the Community where the merger will distort competition in the Community. This use of Article 86 greatly affects foreign corporations, since they often engage in such mergers.

The procedure and remedies for competition cases are found in several Commission regulations. Two regulations are most important. Regulation 17/62 gives the Commission the necessary powers to investigate threats to competition and to fine those corporations that violate the competition laws. It also confirms the Court of Justice's jurisdiction under Article 173 to review Commission decisions in this area.

Article 3 of Regulation 17/62 grants the Commission power to issue cease and desist orders. Whether this power encompasses divestiture orders has not been decided by the court of Justice. In *Europemballage & Continental Can Co. v. E.C. Commission,* [1973] E.C.R. 215, the court ordered Continental Can Co. to divest itself of an acquired company because the merger violated Article 86. However, the court reversed the Commission on the merits, never reaching the issue of divestiture. The regulation allows both member states and individuals to bring alleged violations of the competition laws to the attention of the Commission. Regulation 67/67 grants block exemptions from competition laws in certain circumstances.

In *Multinational Undertakings and the Community,* BULLETIN OF THE EUROPEAN ECONOMIC COMMUNITIES, No. 15 (Supp. 1973) the Commission explained its policies toward multinational corporations. It has tried to fit foreign corporations into the framework of the general competition laws, according them extra surveillance due to their propensity to harm competition more than smaller national firms. Although the Commission desires to work from a free enterprise theory of competition, it realizes that the size of multinational corporations mandates a considerable degree of control over them. The Commission also desires that European firms grow in order to meet the competitive threat from foreign corporations. The Commission, however, does not discriminate on the basis of nationality in the application of competition laws to multinational corporations. The Court of Justice, although allowing the Commission leeway to formulate policy in the area, insists that standards must be promulgated to protect the rights guaranteed under the Treaty of Rome.

CASES

Beguelin Import Co. v. G.L. Import-Export S.A., [1971] E.C.R. 949. Belgian parent company cannot grant the exclusive right of sale of a Japanese product to its French subsidiary if this harms competition in the Community.

Imperial Chemical Industries v. E.C. Commission, [1972] E.C.R. 619. Non-Community firm engaged in price-fixing with various Community firms claimed the concerted action was carried out by its subsidiary in the Community. The court ruled it had jurisdiction over the non-Community parent firm because its subsidiary was not autonomous from the parent.

Europemballage Corporation and Continental Can Co. v. E.C. Commission, [1973] E.C.R. 215. Continental Can Co., already controlling a substantial share of the Community can market, acquired its leading Dutch competitor. The court ruled that Article 86, dealing with abuse of dominant position, can prevent the merger from taking place if it threatens the product's supply structure.

Commercial Solvents Corp. v. E.C. Commission, [1974] E.C.R. 223. This case, involving jurisdiction over a U.S. parent firm because of the acts of its Italian subsidiary, solidifies the court's use of the "economic unity" theory of jurisdiction.

United Brands Co. v. E.C. Commission, [1978] E.C.R. 207. In this case, involving certain pricing and distribution practices of the multinational corporation United Brands concerning the sale of bananas in the Community, the court held that a corporation cannot seek to eliminate a competitor if such elimination would have effects on the pattern of competition in the Common Market.

SECONDARY SOURCES

European Commission, *Multinational Undertakings and the Community,* BULL. OF THE EUROPEAN COMMUNITIES (Supplement 15/73 November 8, 1973).

Hawk, *Antitrust in the EEC—The First Decade,* 41 FORDHAM L. REV. 229–92 (1971).

B. Hawk, United States, Common Market and International Anti-
    trust: a Comparative Guide (1979).
Note, *European Economic Community Antitrust Law: The Continental Can
    Decision—Forerunner of a New European Anti-Merger Policy?* 47
    Tulane L. Rev. 829 (1973).
Temple Lang, *Regulating Multinational Corporate Concentration—the Eu-
    ropean Economic Community,* 2 Mich. Y.B. Int'l Leg. Stud. 144
    (1981).
Wolfe & Montauk, *Antitrust in the European Economic Community: An
    Analysis of Recent Developments in the Court of Justice,* 18 Santa
    Clara L. Rev. 349 (1978).

FEDERAL REPUBLIC OF GERMANY

LAW

Act Against Restraints of Competition (ARC), Third Chapter: Market-
Dominating Enterprises, §§ 22–24b.

Synopsis
Prior to the passage of the ARC in 1957, the German legal tradition's theory
of freedom of contract legitimized private restrictive agreements. The first
legislation to address restrictive business practices, the Cartel Ordinance of
1923, granted a generally unexercised power to act against coercive practices. The period of National Socialism highlighted the Cartel Ordinance's
ineffectiveness as cartels became the compulsory means for obtaining the
government's planned economy objectives.

During the postwar allied occupation, the United States, Britain, and
France each instituted laws against restrictive business practices in accordance with the Potsdam Agreement's mandate to eliminate "excessive concentration of German economic power." These laws were replaced in 1957 by
the ARC.

In 1966 the first amendment to the ARC strengthened its enforcement
provisions, especially with respect to vertical agreements and market-
dominating enterprises. In 1973 the second amendment to the ARC instituted stricter abuse control over market-dominating enterprises and certain
mergers. In 1976 the third amendment to the ARC extended merger control
to newspaper enterprises of only local or regional significance.

Currently the legislature is considering a fourth amendment to the ARC
to render more effective the provisions covering merger control, abusive practices of market-dominating firms, the ban on discrimination, nonbinding
price recommendations, export cartels, and the exempted areas of banking,
insurance, and public utilities.

The ARC applies to all restraints on competition, including mergers,
having an effect on German territory. There are statutory exceptions, such as

public transportation enterprises, to the application of the statute. However, the ARC applies to other partly or wholly owned state enterprises unless there are express provisions to the contrary.

The general provisions of the ARC concerning market-dominating enterprises apply to monopolies. Market domination exists if an enterprise is not exposed to significant competition, or if it occupies a superior market position as defined by general criteria including the financial resources of the enterprise. The Federal Cartel Office (FCO) is authorized to prohibit abusive market-dominating conduct; it employs the "comparative market" concept as a test for abusive conduct. Abusive behavior exists if the market-dominating enterprise acts in a manner that would be impossible if it was exposed to substantial competition. Demands of specified prices or terms and conditions of sale are such abusive practices. In addition to prohibiting abusive practices, the cartel authority may declare the related contracts void. The FCO can prevent market-dominating enterprises from charging prices exceeding a specified limit. The FCO, however, cannot itself establish prices, terms, and conditions in place of the enterprises.

Mergers do not per se restrain competition. ARC Section 24 authorizes the FCO to prohibit mergers between or among enterprises if the merger is expected to result in or strengthen a position of market domination. However, if the participating enterprises prove that the merger's detrimental effect on competition is outweighed by its overall economic advantages, or is justified by an overriding public interest, the federal minister of economics may grant permission for the merger, subject to possible restrictions and requirements.

The ARC establishes regulatory jurisdiction over mergers through the "effects" test or theory. Mergers occurring abroad are considered to have domestic effects if foreign participants have subsidiaries in Germany or if at least one German enterprise participates in a merger that influences the structural conditions for domestic competition.

ARC Sections 23 and 24(a) require reporting of most consummated mergers, as well as certain proposed mergers. These notification requirements operate independently from the FCO's prohibitory power; that is, notification can be required although no remedial action will be taken. The FCO can thus observe concentration activity regardless of the possibility of market domination. Merged enterprises must notify the FCO if: (1) a domestic market share of 20 percent is obtained or increased by the merger, or if one of the enterprises possesses a 20 percent market share in another market, or (2) the enterprises during the business year prior to the merger had at least 10,000 combined employees or a combined turnover of at least 500 million DM.

The FCO may prohibit completed mergers only within one year after notification. A completed merger that the FCO has prohibited is dissolved unless the federal minister of economics otherwise permits.

Enterprises proposing to merge must notify the FCO if at least two of the participating enterprises each had sales of 1 billion DM or more during the preceding fiscal year. Notification of mergers in the newspaper business is required if two of the participating enterprises each have sales of 50 million DM. Mergers not subject to control involve comparatively small enterprises and markets, or restraints of competition which do not produce an effect in a substantial part of the Federal Republic of Germany.

An independent Monopoly Commission reviews the information supplied by merging enterprises, and evaluates the development of enterprise concentration in the Federal Republic of Germany. The Commission issues a report every two years.

ARC Section 38 specifies that an offense is committed by any person who willfully or negligently disregards an order of the FCO, violates a prohibition, or fradulently furnishes or uses incorrect information to influence a prohibition proceeding of the FCO. The offender may be fined up to 10,000 DM plus three times the additional revenues realized as a result of the violation.

The ARC's provisions are designed primarily to protect the public interest. Claims by private parties for damages resulting from a violation of the ARC are allowed under the ARC; however, these claims can only be lodged against market-dominating enterprises and only if an order issued pursuant to ARC Section 22 (abusive conduct) is deemed to be directly protective of individual interests. A damage claim requires a showing that the defendant acted willfully or negligently in violating the protective order. Injunctive relief is also available, and it does not require a showing of willful or negligent conduct. These private actions are subject to a three-year statute of limitations. There is no provision for private actions with regard to mergers.

CASES

WuW/E BGH 1299—"Strombezugspreis." ARC Sections 22–24a do not protect the individual interests absent an expressly protective order.

WuW/E BGH 1377—"Zementmahlanlage." Established point at which the acquisition of assets is sufficiently significant to constitute a merger subject to the reporting requirements.

WuW/E OLG 1467—"BP." Concerns proof of an absence of significant competition between or among oligopolists.

WuW/E BKA 1482; KVR 4/75—"Vitamin B–12." Federal Supreme Court confirmed the FCO's authority to order lower prices in response to an abusive market-dominating practice although the specific order here was overruled.

WuW/E BKA 1517—"Bituman Verkaufsgesellschaft." Merger improved competition by the entrance of a strong competitor which weakened an existing oligopoly.

WuW/E BKA 1526; WuW/E BGH 1445; WuW/E OLG 1645; KVR 2/76—"Valium-Librium." FCO order to lower prices overruled.

WuW/E BKA 1571—"Kaiser-VAW." Merger improved competition by resulting in an increased number of strong competitors.

WuW/E OLG 1599; WuW/E BGH 1435—"Vitamin B–12." Federal Supreme Court recognized the "comparative market" concept for determining abusive pricing by comparing alleged abusive behavior with behavior of enterprises exposed to substantial competition.

WuW/E BKA 1625; WuW/E OLG 1745—"Sachs." Strengthening of market-dominating position occurs if a dominant enterprise would become part of a concern which has significant financial resources.

WuW/E OLG 1637—"Weichschaum." Enterprise's assurances can avert pro-hibition order or partial dissolution.

KartV 34/67 of 18 February 1969. Sale conditioned on exclusive five-year buying agreement, *i.e.,* tying arrangement, is an abuse of a market-dominating position.

BGHST 24 of 12 July 1973—"Olfeldrohre." Federal Supreme Court held that the existence or absence of "effects" for application of the ARC must be judged in connection with the rule of substantive law invoked in the specific case.

KVR 2/78 of 29 May 1979. Federal Supreme Court held that an acquisition completed abroad is subject to notification requirements according to the effects theory and the independent notification procedure of ARC Section 23.

SECONDARY SOURCES

Barnikel, *Abuse of Power by Dominant Firms: Application of the German Law,* 14 Antitrust Bull. 221 (1969).

German Federal Cartel Office Decision in the Metro Case, 13 Antitrust Bull. 1017 (1968).

Gunther, *Ten Years of the German Federal Cartel Office: Review of Past and Future Trends,* 13 Antitrust Bull. 1435 (1968).

Heil and Vorbrugg, *Antitrust Law in West Germany: Recent Developments in German and Common Market Regulation,* 8 Int'l Law. 349 (1974).

Hollman, *Antitrust Law and Protection of Freedom of the Press in the Federal Republic of Germany,* 24 Antitrust Bull. 149 (1979).

Markert, *The Application of German Antitrust Law to International Restraints of Trade,* 7 Va. J. Int'l L. 47 (1967).

———, *The Control of Abuses by Market-Dominating Enterprises Under German Antitrust Law,* 11 Cornell Int'l L.J. 275 (1978).

———, *The New German Antitrust Reform Law,* 19 Antitrust Bull. 135 (1974).

Muller, *The Impact of Mergers on Concentration: A Study of Eleven West German Industries,* 25 J. Industrial Econ. 113 (1976).

Niehus, *The New German Merger Law,* 48 Taxes 372 (1970).

OECD, Committee of Experts on Restrictive Business Practices. Annual Reports on Competition Policy in OECD Member Countries (since 1973).

———. Comparative Summary of Legislations on Restrictive Business Practices (1978).

Risenkampff, Law Against Restraints of Competition (1977).

———, *Recent Developments in German Antitrust Law*, 30 Bus. Law. 1273 (1975).

Risenkampff and Gerber, *German Merger Controls: The Role of Company Assurances*, 22 Antitrust Bull. 889 (1977).

Stockmann and Strauch, *Germany*, in World Law of Competition (von Kalinowski ed. 1979).

FRANCE

LAW

Price Ordinance No. 45–1483 of 30 June 1945 as amended, Articles 50–59; Ordinance No. 45–1484 of 30 June 1945; Penal Code, Article 419; Act No. 77–806 of 19 July 1977.

Synopsis
French economic policy underlies competition policy. The dominant theme of that policy since World War II has been price control. The Price Ordinance of 1945 was used primarily to fight price increases; it was only partially considered to be the legal basis for a general policy of maintaining competition and facilitating the development of free enterprise in a market economy.

Article 50 of the Price Ordinance No. 45–1483 prohibits activities of dominant enterprises which may have the effect of interfering with the normal operation of the market. The minister of the economy may require enterprises that have abused a dominant position to amend or annul the acts and transactions from which the abuse arises. The minister may also require such enterprises to take necessary steps to reestablish either the *status quo ante* or adequate competition. If injunctions issued by the minister are violated, fines may be assessed against the enterprises. Exemption provisions are extensively utilized where there has been legislative approval or where the activities further economic progress as proven by the parties to an agreement. In practice, the law has not been rigorously applied.

There is no system for the notification or registration of restrictive agreements in France. However, restrictive agreements can be investigated at the administrative level if inquiries are made to the appropriate ministry. The minister of the economy may refer the matter to the Commission on Competition (Commission). The Commission may bypass this referral process and examine the case on its own initiative at the behest of other interested parties. The Commission may issue an opinion as to the lawfulness of the practices and make remedial proposals to the minister. The minister of the economy then decides what measures are to be taken, *i.e.*, closing the case, fining the violators, or remitting the case to the Public Prosecutor's Office for criminal proceedings against the parties.

The French Government encouraged mergers through the 1960s and into the 1970s as a simple answer to problems created by the small size of the average French firm in contrast with the large size and innovative practices of U.S. competitors. European "merger fever" during the 1960s ran highest in France.

Recently, however, the French government articulated its concern for the effects of mergers on inflation in the Act No. 77–806 of 19 July 1977. This Act purports to serve the government's inflation control objectives by authorizing action against unlawful cartels and abuse of dominant positions and by introducing some form of control over concentrated operations. The government's adoption of a policy that gradually frees prices is also significant because it changes the direction of competition policy away from price control, toward the regulation of the structural causes of inflation. The 1977 Act establishes control of mergers above a certain size for the first time in France. This Act also provides for selective control of concentrated industries which impede competition without adequately contributing to economic and social progress. The Act applies to the activities of concentrated enterprises if such enterprises impede competition and their annual sales exceed 40 percent of domestic consumption on a national market in the case of similar or substitute goods, products or services, or 25 percent of domestic consumption if such goods are of a different nature and not substitute goods. Mergers or other agreements between firms that exceed these thresholds may be prohibited or modified. The Act No. 77–806 established punitive measures to be taken against unlawful cartels and abuse of dominant positions. With respect to cartels and market-dominating enterprises, the Act establishes a system of administrative fines, a procedure for injunctions, and arrangements to encourage interested parties to inform the Commission on Competition of allegedly illegal arrangements.

Article 53 sets forth sanctions for unlawful cartels and abuse of dominant positions. An enterprise may incur a maximum fine of 5 percent of turnover for an Article 50 offense or Frs. 5 million in the case of associations, trade organizations, or commercial interest groups. The minister of the economy imposes the fine pursuant to the Commission on Competition's opinion. In cases where settlements are reached, the minister and the parties may agree to a system of lighter penalties which have a maximum fine of Frs. 100,000.

The minister may enjoin an enterprise engaged in practices in restraint of trade. The enterprise may also be ordered to restore competition. For abuse of dominant position, the minister may order the enterprise to amend or cancel agreements or to take measure to reestablish adequate competition. If the enterprise does not comply with the injunction, the minister may impose a fine. The Commission on Competition may also propose that an Article 50 case be remitted to the Public Prosecutor's Office. If the minister does so it enables both a public prosecution and a civil action for damages resulting from the offense.

To date the government has not aggressively enforced these new concentration provisions. However, following enactment of the 1977 Act, the government published four texts to clarify and bring its provisions into operation. These texts demonstrate the government's new determination to develop and enforce competition policy.

The Act establishes an optional notification system regarding activities of concentrated industries. Enterprises can voluntarily notify the minister of the economy who may either make no objection to the proposed action or who may refer the matter to the Commission on Competition for further scrutiny. The Commission may issue an Opinion within the limits of which the appropriate minister may require that the enterprises involved take necessary measures to insure or reestablish adequate competition. Such a decision must be made within eight months of notification.

Absent voluntary notification, the minister of the economy or the chairman of the Commission may order an inquiry to determine whether enterprises have concluded any illegal acts or agreements. There is no time limit for decisions initiated by the government's own inquiry into the nature of a business concentration.

An appeal lies for abuse of powers from all decisions taken by the government under this Act.

ADMINISTRATIVE PROCEEDINGS

Opinions delivered by the Technical Commission on Combines and Dominant Positions and by the Competition Commission.

Position Regarding Competition in the Carbon Dioxide Industry and on the Market for that Product, Official Bulletin No. 15 of the Price Services, 23 August 1969. The Commission found the existence of a dominant position but no evidence of anticompetitive practices. It recommended continued careful review of the industry with a conclusion in two years as to the existence of a cartel or any discriminatory practices.

Boycotting of the Limouzy Haulage Company by the GLAM, Opinion of 18 December 1970, Official Bulletin No. 6 of the Price Services, 17 March 1971. The Commission found the boycott to eliminate Limouzy from the sheephide processing market had the characteristics of a restraint of competition. Since no economic benefits resulted from the boycott and because of mitigating circumstances (Limouzy's objective was to acquire a quasi-monopoly), the Commission did not subject GLAM to criminal proceedings.

Practices Restricting Competition among Plastic Bottle Crate Manufacturers, Opinion of 17 March 1971, Official Bulletin No. 19 of the Price Services, 30 October 1971. The Commission recommended that the case be referred to the public prosecutor for violating Article 59 *bis* of the Price Ordinance concerning the abuse of a dominant position through restrictive contracts.

Exclusive Dealing Agreements Involving Exclusive Territorial Rights and Geographical Allocation of Markets; Concerted Action in Connection with Public Tenders, Opinion of 8 November 1974, Official Bulletin No. 5 of the Price Services, 1 February 1975. The Commission considered the submission of uniform bids upon invitation to tender as enabling the enterprises grouped within an economic cooperation group to compete with larger enterprises in regard to national contracts. Thus, the effect was not to restrict or distort competition but to strengthen it, and the agreements were permitted.

Situation with Regard to Competition in the Distribution of Spectacle Frames, Opinion of 4 June 1975, Official Bulletin No. 9 of the Price Services, 13 March 1976. The Commission found the generalized use by all opticians of a trade price scale, without reference to their true costs, to be an abusive cartel situation. However, the Commission recommended that, if a competitive situation did not emerge after direct retail price control, an information campaign would be launched to draw consumer's attention to the absence of binding price scales and the unlawfulness of such price scales. This marks a new direction for the Commission in allying consumers by keeping them informed of anticompetitive practices.

Competitive Situation in the Production and Distribution of Sound Recordings, Opinion of 17 May 1977, Official Bulletin No. 5 of the Price Services, 10 February 1978. Uniform price system violated Art. 59 but was not a restriction on competition because of the industry's need to expand.

Practices in Restraint of Competition in the Marketing of Non-Refillable Lighters, Opinion of 11 May 1978, Official Bulletin No. 13 of the Price Services, 1 June 1978. The Commission imposed heavy fines on three companies responsible for nearly 80 percent of the distribution of lighters to tobacconists. The companies had placed restrictions on freedom to purchase a small firm's disposable lighter and provisions restricting freedom of marketing. In addition to the fines, the Commission ordered the companies to cease these practices and revoke all measures restricting free competition in the trade.

Practices in Restraint of Competition Found to Exist in the Sector of Non-Skid Tire Studs for Motor Vehicles, Opinion of 8 June 1978, Ministerial decision of 26 July 1978. Practices in restraint of competition were found to exist in the sector of nonskid tire studs for motor vehicles. The Commission held that agreements or practices designed to harmonize prices violated the prohibition on cartels, and that the companies in question should renounce all agreements in restraint of competition, including the exclusive supply provisions. Although the minister did not refer the case to the public prosecutor, he did require a follow-up report on the restoration of competition.

SECONDARY SOURCES

Clement, *An Appraisal of French Antitrust Policy*, 19 ANTITRUST BULL. 587 (1974).
Dubois, *French Economic Interest Groups and the Rules of Competition*, 14 ANTITRUST BULL. 667 (1969).
French Technical Commission on Agreements and Dominating Positions, 13 ANTITRUST BULL. 1035 (1968).
Kobak, *Three Approaches to the Bureaucratic Dilemma: The Administration and Enforcement of the Antitrust Laws of the United States, France and the Common Market*, 23 ALA. L. REV. 43 (1970).
OECD, ANNUAL REPORTS ON COMPETITION POLICY IN OECD MEMBER COUNTRIES.
OECD, COMPARATIVE SUMMARY OF LEGISLATIONS ON RESTRICTIVE BUSINESS PRACTICES (1978).
OECD, GUIDE TO LEGISLATION ON RESTRICTIVE BUSINESS PRACTICES (1968).
Plaisant, *French Legislation Against Restrictive Trade Practices*, 10 TEX. INT'L L.J. 26 (1975).
Plaisant, *France* in WORLD LAW OF COMPETITION (Von Kalinowski ed. 1979).
VENTURINI, MONOPOLIES AND RESTRICTIVE TRADE PRACTICES IN FRANCE (1971).

GREAT BRITAIN

LAW

Fair Trading Act, 1973, c. 41, §§ 1–11, 44–56, 63–76.

Synopsis
The Fair Trading Act of 1973 is the major law governing mergers and the exercise of monopoly power in Great Britain. It defines monopoly as an enterprise that occupies 25 percent of the market. The Act also created an Office of Fair Trading that is headed by an independent director general responsible only to Parliament. The director general is empowered to make monopoly and oligopoly references to the newly named Monopolies and Mergers Commission (Commission), though only the Board of Trade can refer mergers to the Commission. The Act also implemented provisions concerning consumer protection, restrictive labor practices, and pyramid selling. Further, it extended the registration requirements of the 1956 and 1968 Restrictive Practices Acts to services; thus, all restrictive agreements and information agreements affecting the product and service markets come under the scrutiny of the Monopolies Commission. The secretary of state and the director general of fair trading each have power to refer scale and complex monopoly situations to the Commission for investigation and report. A scale monopoly may exist when one person, company, or group of interconnected companies sup-

plies or acquires at least one-quarter of the market share in a particular market for goods or services. A complex monopoly may exist when at least one-quarter of the market share in a particular market for goods or services are supplied by or sold to two or more persons, unconnected companies or group of companies who prevent or restrict competition in the supply of goods or services.

If the director general determines that a monopoly situation exists, or may exist, he can refer it to the Commission for investigation. Any such reference must relate to the supply of all goods or services of a particular description; it cannot relate to the activities of a named person, company, or companies. The Commission cannot investigate a monopoly situation unless the matter has been formally referred to it.

A monopoly reference requires the Commission to consider whether, in fact, a monopoly situation exists. If the Commission determines one does exist, it must decide, first, who is favored by the situation; second, whether the favored persons are taking steps to exploit or maintain the situation; and third, whether any of the favored persons' acts or omissions are attributable to the existence of the monopoly situation. Also, the Commission examines whether the monopoly situation operates against the public interest and how that aspect can be remedied.

When the Commission reports that a monopoly situation exists and operates against the public interest, the minister of the appropriate state and industry may, by order, give effect to the report. In so doing, the minister takes into account any recommendations of the Commission and the advice of the director general. Noncompliance with an order is not a criminal offense. Individuals or the Crown may enforce orders by bringing a civil action "for an injunction or interdict or for any other appropriate relief." The director general is responsible for monitoring merger activities in order to identify situations that qualify for investigation. Mergers qualify for investigation if, first, two or more enterprises merge and cease to be distinct; second, at least one of the enterprises does business in the United Kingdom or is under the control of a corporation incorporated in the United Kingdom; third, the merger has occurred within six months; and fourth, the enterprises are both engaged in supply of goods or services of the same description, and either have between them at least one-quarter of the market for those goods or services, or the gross value of the assets taken over exceeds £5 million.

A merger may only be referred to the Commission by the secretary of state on the advice of the director general. The Commission is directed to consider any relevant matter, but the following matters are mentioned in the legislation for guidance: competition, the interests of the consumer, costs and innovation, a balanced distribution of industry and employment in the United Kingdom, and the export market. All merger reports must be published and presented to Parliament. If a report is made with adverse findings, the secretary of state may ask the director general to negotiate assurances from the parties as to their future conduct. Also, the secretary may prohibit a proposed merger or dissolve an existing merger.

The new U.K. Competition Bill (now in the committee stage in the House of Commons) contemplates selective investigation and control of practices which have, or are intended or likely to have "the effect of restricting, distorting or preventing competition in connection with the production, supply or acquisition of goods in the United Kingdom or any part of it or the supply or securing of services in the United Kingdom or any part of it."

It empowers the director general to carry out preliminary investigations of conduct that may have this effect. Following an investigation, the director general will publish his findings. If he identifies an anticompetitive practice, he may request the Commission to investigate further and report whether the practice is against the public interest; as an alternative, the director general may accept a voluntary remedy (undertaking) from the enterprise relating to the practice. Following adverse findings by the Commission, the secretary of state may ask the director general to seek an undertaking from the enterprise or he may make an order prohibiting the particular practice or remedying its adverse effects.

The Competition Bill also provides, in part, for a new investigative method of scrutinizing activities of nationalized industries and certain other bodies. Additionally, it enables the secretary of state to require the director general to investigate prices or charges of major public concern.

The Competition Bill is expected to be out of the committee stage by March, 1980.

ADMINISTRATIVE PROCEEDINGS: MONOPOLIES

Supply of Chlordiazepoxide and Diazepam (Librium and Valium); 899 H.C. DEB. (1975–76) 12 November 1975, col. 1543–47. In 1973, Parliament ordered a 40 percent decrease in the price of Librium and a 25 percent decrease in the price of Valium. In settlement negotiations, Roche agreed to pay the government approximately £3¾ million in excess profits from 1970–73, to participate in a voluntary price regulation scheme, and to reduce the price of Valium and Librium to one-half their 1970 level.

Supply of Building Bricks; 913 H.C. DEB. (1975–76) 17 June 1976, col. 221–23. One manufacturer supplying more than one-third of the building market, was found not to operate against the public interest.

Barrister's Services—the supply by her Majesty's Counsel alone of their services, and Advocate's services—the supply by Senior Counsel alone of their services; 914 H.C. DEB. (1975–76) 7 July 1976, col. 543–45. Restrictions requiring senior and junior counsel for certain actions were deemed to create a monopoly operating against the public interest.

Restrictions of Advertising by Solicitors, Advocates and Barristers; 916 H.C. DEB. (1975–76) 29 July 1976, col. 320–24. Advertising prohibitions for solicitors created a monopoly situation operating against the public interest. The prohibitions restricted entry to the field and decreased competition and efficiency. The minister asked the director general to discuss with the relevant professional bodies the implementation of new rules.

Restrictions on Advertising by Veterinary Surgeons, Stockbrokers and Accountants; 916 H.C. DEB. (1975–76) 6 Aug. 1976, col. 1209–15. Restrictions on advertising created a monopoly situation that operated against the public interest. The minister asked the director general to consult with the appropriate professional bodies to implement the Commission's recommended rules and safeguards.

Revised Undertakings Given by Oil Companies Regarding Retail Supply of Petrol; 916 H.C. DEB. (1975–76) 3 August 1976. Pursuant to the minister's request, the director general obtained comprehensive agreements from the oil companies regulating supply agreements for various petrol products and leases and licenses of company filling stations.

Supply of Diazonium Sensitized Copying Materials; 927 H.C. DEB. (1976–77) 2 March 1977, col. 191–93. One company supplied over 50 percent of the U.K. market but the Commission determined the monopoly was not operating against the public interest. However, the Commission discovered twenty-two industry-wide restrictive agreements that had not been registered and were subsequently terminated.

Supply of Cat and Dog Foods; 935 H.C. DEB. (1976–77) 20 July 1977, col. 543–44. Two companies each controlled more than 25 percent of the market, but their profits, prices, and efficiency indicated the monopolies did not operate against the public interest.

Supply of Frozen Foodstuffs for Human Consumption; 919 H.C. DEB. (1975–76) 10 November 1976, col. 165–66. One company supplied over one-quarter of frozen foodstuffs in the U.K. The Commission found the company was efficient and its prices were not excessive. However, it recommended discontinuance of the company's practice of giving discounts to retailers for reserving space in freezers.

Supply of Indirect Electrostatic Reprographic Equipment; 922 H.C. DEB. (1976–77) 16 December 1976, col. 744–78. Rank Xerox Ltd. supplied at least one-third of the market. Though the Commission found the company generally not be operating against the public interest, it criticized certain of Xerox's practices, including group discounts. Xerox remedied some of the criticized practices, and the minister asked the director general to consult with Xerox to end the others.

Supply of Wheat Flour and Bread Made from Wheat Flour; 935 H.C. DEB. (1976–77) 14 July 1977, col. 261–62. Three companies required their flour-using subsidiaries to buy flour from the group's own mills. This foreclosed 51 percent of the market and the Commission determined it was done to restrict competition. However, the Commission concluded that effective competition existed to the extent allowed by the substantial statutory control of the industry and that the situation did not operate against the public interest. The Commission discovered twenty-two restrictive trade agreements that had not been registered and these were subsequently abandoned.

Wholesaling of Newspapers and Periodicals; Press Notice, Department of Press and Consumer Protection, June 1, 1978. Wholesale suppliers of national newspapers and periodicals refused to supply certain retailers. Though this constituted a complex monopoly situation, the Commission determined it was cost-efficient for wholesalers to limit the number of retailers they supplied and to select them on the basis of location and service standards.

Supply and Export of Ceramic Sanitaryware; Press Notice, Department of Prices and Consumer Protection, August 31, 1978. One company and its wholly owned subsidiary controlled over 25 percent of the domestic market. However, its profits were not excessive and price similarity in the industry reflected effective competition. Thus, the Commission determined the monopoly did not operate against the public interest. Control of 31 percent of the export market was found not to operate against the public interest because of competition from the international market.

MERGERS

Amalgamated Industrials Limited; 912 H.C. DEB. (1975–76) 26 May 1976, col. 274–75. The Commission found a consummated merger to be contrary to the public interest. It restricted the acquired company's progress, lessened the company's contribution to the balance of payments, and caused serious labor problems. The minister asked the director general to consult with the acquiring company to limit its holdings to no more than 10 percent of the stock of the acquired company.

Pilkington Brothers Ltd./U.K. Optical and Industrial Holdings Ltd.; 928 H.C. DEB. (1976–77) 24 March 1977, col. 590. The Commission expected the merger to operate against the public interest because of decreased incentive to meet the needs of the domestic market for glass and plastic lenses, and decreased ability to compete on the international market. The secretary of state asked the director general to obtain an undertaking from Pilkington Brothers to refrain from any merger activity with U.K. Optical.

Babcox & Wilcox Ltd./Herbert Morris Ltd., 926 H.C. DEB. (1976–77) 23 February 1977, col. 571–73. Three members of the Commission determined the acquisition would be against the public interest, and recommended limiting Babcox's holdings in Herbert Morris to 10 percent. However, the secretary of state took no action on the report.

The British Petroleum Company Ltd./Century Oil Group Ltd.; Press Notice, Department of Prices and Consumer Protection, May 31, 1977. The

Commission determined the merger would be against the public interest because it might restrict development of Century's refining activity,
tend to decrease price competition and customer-oriented research,
and end the largest independent producer of lubricants in the U.K.
The director general received an undertaking from British Petroleum
to refrain from any merger activity with Century Oils.

*Rockware Group Ltd./Redfern National Glass Ltd.; United Glass
Ltd./Redfern National Glass Ltd.; Annual Report of the Director General of Fair Trading,* 1978, at 93–94. The Commission expected both
mergers to operate against the public interest by diminishing competition and domestic supply and increasing imports. The director general
was asked to seek, and did receive, undertakings from the companies
to forego the proposed mergers.

SECONDARY SOURCES

Annual Report of the Director General of Fair Trading, 1974 et seq.

Cawthra, *Learning to Live with EEC Rules of Competition,* 126 New L.J.
493–94, 593–94, 691–92 (1976).

Dixon, *Economic Effect of Exclusive Dealing and Ownership Control: The
U.K. Petrol Cases Revisited,* 18 Antitrust Bull. 375–90 (1973).

Department of Prices & Consumer Protection, A Review of Monopolies and Mergers Policy (Green Paper, Cmnd. No. 7198, 1978).

Department of Prices & Consumer Protection, A Review of Restrictive Trade Practices Policy (Green Paper, Cmnd. No. 7512, 1978).

Gribbin, *Recent Antitrust Developments in the United Kingdom,* 20
Antitrust Bull. 377–410 (1975).

Gribbin, *The United Kingdom 1977 Price Commission Act and Competition
Policy,* 23 Antitrust Bull. 405–39 (1978).

Harding, *Injury Occasioned By Infringements of the EEC Rules of Competition: Remedies in English Law,* 7 Anglo-Am. L. Rev. 290–306 (1978).

Johnson and Apps, *Interlocking Directorates Among the U.K.'s Largest Companies,* 24 Antitrust Bull. 357–69 (1979).

Kintner, Joelson, and Griffin, *Recent Developments in United Kingdom Antitrust Law,* 19 Antitrust Bull. 217–55 (1974).

Maloney, *Hoffmann-LaRoche—Aggregated Rebates,* 127 New L.J. 41–42
and 141–42 (1977).

Monopolies Commission Reports

OECD. Guide to Legislation on Restrictive Business Practices, Vol.
II.

Pass and Hawkins, *Exclusive Dealing, Supplier Ownership of Outlets and the
Public Interest: The Petrol Case,* 18 Antitrust Bull. 567–95 (1972).

Rhinelander, *Roche Case: One Giant Step for British Antitrust,* 15 Va. J.
Int'l L. 1–38 (1974).

Wyatt, *Company Merger and Competition in the United Kingdom and the EEC,* 124 New L.J. 31–3, 149–50 (1974).

IRELAND

LAW

Restrictive Trade Practices Act (No. 11 of 1972), Acts of the Oireachtas, 553.

Synopsis
The Restrictive Practices Act of 1972, and the orders promulgated pursuant to it, provide a comprehensive system of investigation and control of market-dominating enterprises and monopolies. Section 4 of the Act empowers the Restrictive Practices Commission to establish rules to insure the fair supply and distribution of goods. These rules are not enforceable, and depend on voluntary compliance. However, § 8 of the Act empowers the minister of industry and commerce (minister) to issue fair trade orders that are legally enforceable. Section 19 provides courts jurisdiction to enforce orders. Section 20 declares that anyone who contravenes an order is guilty of an offense. Offenses are defined in § 23; they range from fines of £100 to £5000 and imprisonment for up to six months.

The third schedule to the Act sets forth categories of individual or group practices that violate the Act, including: unjust elimination of competitors, restrictions of the supply of goods, creation of barriers to entry, territorial division of markets, private monopolization, and all other acts or agreements that "operate against the common good or are not in accordance with the principles of social justice."

Sections 13 through 16 of the Act establish and define the functions of the Examiner of Restrictive Practices. The examiner is appointed by the minister. The examiner investigates any aspect of: (a) the supply and distribution of goods or the provision of a service, (b) the operation of an order under the Act; or (c) the operation of Fair Practice Rules. Where a potential trade abuse is found it must be submitted in a report to the Restrictive Practices Commission or the minister.

Section 5 empowers the Restrictive Practices Commission to conduct inquiries into unfair trade practices at the request of the minister or examiner. It may also conduct an inquiry on application by a private party who lodged a prior request with the examiner that was denied. In conducting an inquiry, the Commission may summon witnesses and order discovery. Section 8 requires the Commission to report its findings and recommendations to the minister. To remedy an abuse, the Commission may establish fair practice rules, or the minister may declare legally enforceable restrictive practice orders.

Comprehensive Orders governing supply and distribution in eleven industries were issued through 1976.

CASES

Report of the Board of Examiner: Motor Spirit, 1971; Restrictive Practices (Motor Spirit) Order, No. 18 of 1972, No. 15 of 1975. In April 1970, the Commission, at the request of the minister, announced an inquiry into retail outlets for motor spirits. The Commission learned that company stations accounted for 31 percent of total motor spirit sales, and that three major companies accounted for a high proportion of sales through company outlets. The Commission recommended, in part, that there should be a halt to the growth of new company outlets for three years to permit freer entry into the market. The minister issued an order that incorporated the recommendation, and the order was renewed, with slight modification, in 1975.

Report of Examiner: Iron and Steel Scrap, 1972. A government-owned steel company held a monopoly position for certain types of steel. It used a graduated rate scale that resulted in its supplies being channeled through a single supplier. This forces all scrap dealers to deal through only that supplier. The Commission concluded that "it is impossible to justify, in a protected market for scrap, the range and composition of the graduated price scale" adopted by the steel company for its purchases. This procedure created "a formidable and unnecessary barrier to entry into trade in scrap with the company, foster[ed] a monopoly in merchant scrap sales to the company," and served to create a situation in the trade which "seriously impedes free and fair competition." The Commission recommended revision in the purchase scale for scrap, and removal of the sole supplier of scrap from the steel company's board. The minister accepted these recommendations. Enforcement by order was not necessary because the government controlled the steel company.

SECONDARY SOURCES

OECD, COMPARATIVE SUMMARY LEGISLATION ON RESTRICTIVE BUSINESS PRACTICES, Tables IX, X (1978).

OECD, GUIDE TO LEGISLATION ON RESTRICTIVE BUSINESS PRACTICES, Vol. II (1970, looseleaf update).

Walsh, *Restrictive Business Practices in Ireland: Legislation and Administration,* 19 ANTITRUST BULL. 803, 850 (1974).

ISRAEL

LAW

Restrictive Trade Practices Law 5719–1929; as amended in 1973.

Synopsis

The Israeli antitrust statute prohibits anticompetitive agreements between enterprises and provides for control of concentrated industries through ministerial discretion.

Arrangements that restrict competition, whether undertaken by a formal cartel or pursuant to an implicit agreement within an industry, are illegal unless exempted by statute or sanctioned by the Restrictive Trade Practices Board. Violations are criminal offenses and parties to the agreement are subject to private tort liability. Tacit consent to an agreement, combined with an interest in its operation, is sufficient to establish an individual as a party.

Agreements negotiated by trade unions, by agricultural marketing organizations, by conglomerates with their subsidiaries, as well as those involving intellectual property, international air, or sea carriage (where the minister of transport has been consulted), or exclusive dealing between suppliers and resellers are afforded statutory exemption. Parties involved in other agreements must register as cartels with the Board and determine their effect on the public interest. While the statute provides that the Board should refer to considerations set forth in the British Restrictive Practices Act of 1956 as indicative, nonexhaustive, criteria for this determination, applicants bear the burden of demonstrating that the benefits of cartelization to the public as a whole outweigh any damage that will result to identifiable sections of the society. An autonomous government official, the controller of restricted trade practices, is charged with representing the public interest before the Board. Cartels may be granted provisional, temporary, conditional, or partial authorization. All dispositions may be modified or cancelled by subsequent decisions of the Board and are subject to review by the Supreme Court.

The minister of commerce has discretionary power to declare that a particular industry has reached a level of concentration sufficient to justify government control of the entire industry. The level of concentration is not defined with reference to control of the relevant market by several firms. Rather, it is defined with reference to the size of the largest "commercial unit" in that market. *Commercial unit* is defined as "a single corporation; a corporation and its subsidiaries; the several subsidiaries of a single corporation; several corporations with predominantly interlocking directorates; a corporation and its controlling interests; or several corporations controlled by a single interest."

Once the minister of commerce and industry determines an industry's concentration level is monopolistic, that industry becomes subject to ministerial control with regard to the price, quality, and amount or method of production. Such control is imposed in response to proposals by the controller of restrictive trade practices, based upon findings that the existence of monopoly has led to unsatisfactory economic results.

Dispositions by the Restrictive Trade Practices Control Board create no *stare decisis* effect upon subsequent applications. However, some fairly consistent principles of decision are discernible.

The attainment of lower prices is considered to be inherently in the public interest so long as agreements which facilitate this do not interfere with other policy goals. Price stabilization, however, is not a public interest goal in itself. Furthermore, provision for public supervision of price increases is insufficient justification for agreements which tend to eliminate competition. Assertions that a cartel will improve efficiency, quality, or service must be supported by substantial evidence, including a showing of the degree of cartelization necessary to attain the projected benefits. That a cartel agreement would insure the continued existence of an advantageous branch of the Israeli economy will not justify registration where the agreement could do so only by protecting firms that are inefficient or that are threatened with the technological obsolescence of their capital plants, even where there exists a government policy encouraging investment in the affected industry. Government initiated or approved export cartel plans through which industry members levy charges upon domestic sales to fund export subsidies have been approved. Other assertions of export benefit, however, may be dismissed as *de minimis* or as requiring the imposition of disproportionate cost upon consumers.

CASES

Dagan Flour Mills, Ltd. v. Minister of Commerce and Industry 26 P.D. 292 (1972–I).
Shimoni v. Ulamei Lehayim, Ltd. 25 P.D. 824 (1971–I).

ADMINISTRATIVE DECISIONS

Association of Liquor Manufacturers Res. Prac. File No. 3 (1961).
Chemochlor, Ltd. v. Controller of Restrictive Trade Practices Res. Prac. File No. 39 (1961).
In re Tifereth Hasharon Registered Partnership Res. Prac. File No. 138 (1962).
Bicycle Tyres-Gamid, Ltd. v. Controller of Restrictive Trade Practices Res. Prac. File No. 2 (1961).
Hadar-B, Shaplin, Ltd. v. Controller of Restrictive Trade Practices Res. Prac. File No. 31 (1961).
United Zincographers, Ltd. v. Controller of Restrictive Trade Practices Res. Prac. File No. 13 (1961).
Luxor Lighting, Ltd. Res. Prac. File No. 15 (1962).
In Re PACA, Ltd. Res. Prac. File Nos. 7, 24 (1962).
Osem Food Manufacturing, Ltd. v. Controller of Restrictive Trade Practices Res. Prac. File No. 60 (1961).
Yitzher Israel Oil Manufacturing, Ltd. v. Controller of Restrictive Trade Practices Res. Prac. File No. 174 (1964) and Res. Prac. File No. 261 (1970).
Israel Plywood, Ltd. v. Controller of Restrictive Trade Practices Res. Prac. File No. 202 (1965).
Aderet Co. v. Controller of Restrictive Trade Practices Res. Prac. File No. 248 (1968).
Cargel, Ltd. v. Controller of Restrictive Trade Practices Res. Prac. File No. 265 (1969).

SECONDARY SOURCES

Jaffe, *Cartel Control in Israel,* 12 ANTITRUST BULL. 931 (1967).

Kaplan, *Israeli Antitrust Policy—A Different Approach Towards Antitrust by an Emerging Nation,* 26 RECORD OF ASSOCIATION OF THE BAR OF THE CITY OF NEW YORK 389 (1971).

Kestenbaum, *Israel's Restrictive Trade Practices Law: Antitrust Misadventures in a Small Developing Country,* 8 ISRAEL L. REV. 411 (1973).

Shefer, *A Critique of the Implementation of the Trade Restraints Law in Israel,* 16 ANTITRUST BULL. 415 (1971).

Shefer, *Guidelines for Legislation on Monopolies and Restrictive Practices in Small Economies,* 15 ANTITRUST BULL. 781 (1970).

JAPAN

LAW

Law concerning the Prohibition of Private Monopolization and the Preservation of Fair Trade (Antimonopoly Act), Law No. 54 of 1947, as amended by Acts Nos. 214 of 1949, 259 of 1953, and 63 of 1977.

Synopsis

Japan's Antimonopoly Act of 1947 is modeled after U.S. antitrust legislation. Enacted under the auspices of the Occupation Forces, the Antimonopoly Act was designed to be the basic law governing industry, and, as such, to provide the legal foundation for a strong free enterprise system. The Antimonopoly Act controls private monopolization, unreasonable restraints of trade, stockholding, interlocking directorates, mergers which may substantially restrain competition, and unfair business practices. However, the numerous exemptions subsequently enacted restrict the application of the statute in several industries. The Antimonopoly Act is administered by the Fair Trade Commission (FTC) which exercises its powers independently, although it is administratively attached to the prime minister's office.

The Act's history demonstrates that its enforcement in Japan has differed markedly from antitrust enforcement in the United States. For example, private antitrust actions for money damages have as yet played little role in the Act's enforcement. Furthermore, there have been only four criminal actions since 1947 against violators under Section 73, which permits the FTC to file an accusation with the public prosecutor when it determines the Act has been violated.

The Antimonopoly Act proscribes ". . . private monopolization, unreasonable restraint of trade and unfair business practices, by preventing the excessive concentration of economic power and by eliminating unreasonable restraint of production, sale, price, [and] technology, . . . through combinations, [and] agreements, ..." Section 3 prohibits an entrepreneur from effecting a private monopoly or engaging in unreasonable restraints of trade, although private monopolization is not a per se violation of the Act. Section 6 extends the statutory provisions to international trade; Section 8 lists activities which trade associations may not undertake; and Section 13 places restriction on interlocking directorates. Up to 1977, the FTC took action in six cases of private monopolization.

Section 2(5) defines a *prohibited private monopolization* as "business activities by which any entrepreneur, either individually, or in combination with, or in conspiracy with other entrepreneurs or in any other manner, excludes or controls the business activities of other entrepreneurs thereby causing a substantial restraint of trade contrary to the public interest." The Tokyo High Court has stated that any substantial restraint of trade is inherently contrary to the public interest.

Sections 10 (restriction on acquisition of stock), 15 (restriction on mergers or consolidations), and 16 (restriction on acquisition of assets) prohibit mergers or acquisitions of businesses where the effect may be substantially to restrain competition in any field of trade or where unfair business practices have been employed. Proposed mergers or acquisitions must be reported to the FTC thirty days in advance of the transaction. The FTC must act within the thirty-day period if it determines that the proposed transaction violates the above prohibition and should be enjoined. These sections, unlike the provisions concerning private monopolization under Section 2(5), require only the probability of a substantial restraint of trade to prohibit a merger or acquisition. However, the FTC has not been particularly active in the merger area. In the few cases that have arisen, none of the proposed mergers have been prohibited.

The *Yawata-Fuji Merger Case* in 1968 has been the most controversial merger case to date. The Yawata Steel Company and the Fuji Steel Company, which had constituted the Japan Steel Company prior to World War II, sought to reconstitute the Japan Steel Company and restore the prewar status quo. The FTC initiated proceedings to block the merger alleging substantial restraints of competition in four product areas. The two companies proposed a compromise whereby they would make a partial transfer of their facilities to their competitors and give technical assistance to their competitors. A consent decision was accepted by the FTC permitting the merger on that basis.

The Antimonopoly Act has been amended on three occasions, the most recent in May 1977, when, for the first time in the history of Japanese competition policy, the Diet passed an amendment which strengthened the Antimonopoly Act. Included in the 1977 amendments are new provisions relating to surcharges on profits by illegal cartels; structural controls providing for regulation of industries where an enterprise holds a 50 percent market share or two enterprises hold a 75 percent market share, and where the economic performance of the industry has been unsatisfactory; establishment of a reporting system for enterprises participating in parallel price increases; FTC hearing procedures; reinstitution of restrictions on stockholding by large corporations or financial companies; and an increase in maximum criminal fines for a violation of the Act.

The Antimonopoly Act empowers the FTC, a quasi-judicial agency modeled after the U.S. Federal Trade Commission, to enforce the Act's provisions. There are three ways in which a violation may be brought to the attention of the FTC. First, any person having knowledge of a violation may request the FTC to take appropriate measures to remedy the illegality. However, the FTC retains discretion as to whether it should commence proceedings on the basis of such a report. Second, the public prosecutor may file a report with the FTC when a violation is discovered, although this procedure is seldom used in practice. Third, the FTC can commence an *ex officio* investigation.

If it becomes clear from an FTC investigation that a violation exists, the FTC may either recommend that the violator refrain from its illegal conduct or it may institute formal proceedings against the violator. If the concerned party accepts the FTC recommendation, a decision is issued on that basis without formal trial. If the FTC initiates formal proceedings, a trial takes place in which FTC investigators bring their findings before administrative law judges. During the trial the defendant may accept both the investigators' facts and the application of law to those facts as presented in the FTC's complaint, but contest the FTC's proposed remedies. If the Commission agrees to modify its proposed abatement measures, the trial is terminated and a consent decision is issued. If neither a recommendation nor a consent decision is issued, a decision is rendered upon completion of a formal trial. Therefore, three types of decisions may result from an FTC investigation: recommendation decisions, consent decisions, and formal decisions. All three types of decisions are legally binding, and violation of a decision is an offense punishable by imprisonment or fine.

A defendant whose conduct has been found to be illegal may appeal the FTC decision to the Tokyo High Court, which has exclusive jurisdiction over FTC decisions. The FTC's findings of fact are binding on the Tokyo High Court and the introduction of new evidence is generally not allowed. An FTC decision is subject to reversal if it is not based on substantial evidence or if it is found to be unconstitutional, in which case, the Court may remand the case to the FTC for further proceedings. Through 1977, thirty-one cases had been appealed to the court and in fifteen cases, the FTC's decision was affirmed.

Violations of the Antimonopoly Act are subject not only to the various orders rendered by the FTC including, for example, orders under a 1977 provision for disgorgement of profits gained by cartel participants through illegal activities, but also to criminal penalties. Private monopolization and unreasonable restraint of trade are the violations for which the heaviest penalty is imposed—imprisonment for not more than three years or a fine of not more than 5 million yen. However, criminal proceedings are initiated only upon accusation by the FTC so that alleged violations can be judged by FTC personnel having special economic and expert knowledge.

Section 25 of the Act also provides money damages for private actions. Any person who has been injured because of a violation of the Act is entitled to indemnification for actual damages. The claim for damages under the Act can only be made after a final decision, in which case the FTC's decision is conclusive evidence of the illegality of the defendant's conduct. To date, only three private actions have been concluded. If no FTC decision has been issued with regard to the particular conduct, an injured party may still bring an action under § 709 of the Civil Code, which authorizes general tort claims.

Chapter 6 of the Antimonopoly Act sets forth exceptions to the Act for certain acts of public utility enterprises, rights exercised under the patent, copyright, and tradmark acts, and acts of various cooperatives. In addition, land transportation, insurance, and certain other activities are exempted from the Antimonopoly Act by virtue of the "Act concerning Exemption from the Application of the Act concerning Prohibition of Private Monopoly and Maintenance of Fair Trade." Shipping cartels also are exempted from the Antimonopoly Act by virtue of the Marine Transportation Act of 1949.

The 1953 amendments to the Antimonopoly Act exempted certain depression cartels and rationalization cartels. Separate exemption laws also were enacted about this time. These exemption laws include the "Export Trading Act of 1952" (now the "Export and Import Trading Act") and the "Temporary Measures Act of 1952 concerning the Stabilization of Specific Small and Medium-Sized Enterprises" (replaced by the "Small and Medium-Sized Enterprises Organization Act of 1957"). Today, in such industries as coal, machinery, and textiles, other statutes permit specific rationalization cartels to be formed in conjunction with particular promotional programs of government agencies. But, the number of exemption cartels has been decreasing yearly, from 1,040 in 1965, to 788 in 1978, and 492 in 1979.

CASES

Toho Co. Ltd. v. Fair Trade Commission, Tokyo High Court Decision of September 19, 1951. Contract for the lease of cinemas.

Toho Co. Ltd. and Another v. Fair Trade Commission, Tokyo High Court Decision of December 7, 1953. Exclusive dealing agreement between two companies for distribution of motion pictures.

Noda Shoyu Co. v. Fair Trade Commission, Tokyo High Court Decision of December 25, 1957. Private monopolization.

Miyagewa v. Gifu Shoko Shinyokumiai, Supreme Court Decision of June 20, 1977. Abuse of predominant position.

Ohkawa et al. v. Matsushita Electric Co., Tokyo High Court Decision of September 19, 1977. Private action requesting money damages for resale price maintenance.

Case of Idemitsu Kosan and 26 others, Tokyo High Court, formal proceedings initiated May 28, 1974. Criminal action for price fixing.

ADMINISTRATIVE PROCEEDINGS

Leading decisions of the Fair Trade Commission.
Case of the Yuasa Timber Co. Ltd. and 64 Others, Decision of August 30, 1949. Horizontal price fixing of plywood.
Case of the Noda Shoyu Co. Ltd. and 4 Others, Decision of April 4, 1952. Horizontal price fixing of soy sauce.
Case of the Snow Brand Dairy Co. Ltd. and 3 Others, Decision of July 28, 1956. Private monopolization concerning fresh milk.
Case of the Nippon Gakki Co. Ltd., Recommendation Decision of January 30, 1957. Illegal acquisition of stock by a musical instrument manufacturing company.
Case of the Mitsubishi Bank Ltd., Recommendation Decision of June 3, 1957. Abuse of dominant bargaining position by a financial institution.
Case of the Yawata/Fuji Merger, Consent Decision of October 30, 1969. Restraints of competition in a particular field of trade by merger.
Case of Toyo Seikan Kaisha Co. Ltd., Recommendation Decision of September 18, 1972. Private monopolization by shareholding.
Case of Hiroshima Railway Co. Ltd. and 4 Others, Consent Decision of July 17, 1973. Stockholding and interlocking directorates.
Case of Idemitsu Kosan Co. Ltd. and 11 Others, Recommendation Decision of February 22, 1974. Horizontal price fixing, quantitative restriction on petroleum sales.
Case of the Petroleum Association, Recommendation Decision of February 22, 1974. Quantitative restrictions on petroleum sales.
Case of the Chubu Yomiuri Newspaper Co. Ltd., Consent Decision of November 24, 1977. Sales at unreasonably low prices.
Case of the Gunma Asano Concrete Co. Ltd. and 5 Others, Recommendation Decision of June 5, 1978. First surcharge case; price fixing.
Case of Mitsukoshi, Formal proceedings were initiated on May 14, 1979. Abuse of dominant position.
Case of Komatsu Co. Ltd., Bucyrus-Erie Co., Formal proceedings initiated on October 12, 1979. First extraterritorial antitrust case; abuse of dominant position.

SECONDARY SOURCES

Ariga, *International Trade of Japan and the Antimonopoly Act,* 9 J. INT'L L. & ECON. 185–201 (1973).
Ariga and Reke, *The Antimonopoly Law of Japan and Its Enforcement,* 39 WASH. L. REV. 437 (1964).
E. HADLEY, ANTITRUST IN JAPAN (1970).

J.H. IYORI, ANTIMONOPOLY LEGISLATION IN JAPAN (1969).

K. KYOKAI (FAIR TRADE INSTITUTE), ANTIMONOPOLY LEGISLATION OF JAPAN (1977).

Matsushita, *The Antimonopoly Law of Japan* in FEDERAL BAR ASSOCIATION, MATERIALS FOR REGISTRANTS: US-JAPAN TRADE LAW CONFERENCE, June 6–7, 1979 (1979).

OECD, COMPARATIVE SUMMARY OF LEGISLATION ON RESTRICTIVE BUSINESS PRACTICES (1978).

OECD, GUIDE TO LEGISLATION ON RESTRICTIVE TRADE PRACTICES (1968).

Sawada and Brown, *American Japanese Antitrust Law,* 2 INT'L L. BULL. 13 (1963).

TRADE BULLETIN CORPORATION, JAPAN INDUSTRY SERIES: JAPAN'S ANTIMONOPOLY POLICY IN LEGISLATIVE AND PRACTICAL PERSPECTIVE, Vol. XX (1968).

Yamamura, *The Development of Antimonopoly Policy in Japan: The Erosion of Japanese Antimonopoly Policy,* 1947–64, 2 STUDIES IN L. & ECON. DEV. 1 (1967).

MEXICO

LAW

Constitution Article 28 (Mex.); Organic Law Associated with Article 28, 85 D.O. 1161 (August 31, 1934); Regulations to the Organic Law, 88 D.O. 112 (February 1, 1936); Codigo Penal Article 253 (Mex.); Codigo Civil Article 1910 (Mex.).

Synopsis
Article 28 of the Constitution of 1917 states:

> The law shall punish severely and the authorities shall effectively prosecute every concentration or association in one or a few hands of goods of primary necessity for the purpose of obtaining a rise in prices; every act or proceeding which prevents or tends to prevent free competition . . . every agreement or combination, in whatever manner it may be made, to prevent competition . . . and to compel consumers to pay exaggerated prices; and in general, whatever constitutes an exclusive and undue advantage in favor of one or more specified persons and to the prejudice of the public in general or of any social class.

Constitutionally-established exceptions include labor union activity, authorized associations of producers selling directly in foreign markets, and specified state-created monopolies (telegraph, postal service, federal banks, etc.). The 1934 Organic Law adopted pursuant to Article 28 of the Constitution forbids the existence of monopolies, defined in Article 3 of the Organic Law as any situation deliberately created which allows one or more persons to fix prices or set quotas on services with resulting injury to the general public or a specified social class. Under Article 4 a rubuttable presumption of the existence of monopoly is raised by any concentration of goods of necessary consumption, any price-fixing agreement or combination made without authorization or regulation from the government, or any commercial or industrial situation willfully created to fix prices on goods or set quotas on services. The 1936 regulations to the Organic Law provide that government authorization will generally be granted to price-fixing agreements or combinations if the organization seeking authorization can demonstrate that the proposed agreement will result in any of the following: integration of an industry line permitting price reductions, suppression of intermediaries to obtain less costly distribution, elimination of one or more goods from product lines without unjustly raising prices, creation of a competitor, reduction of commercial activities because they have ceased to be economically useful to the public, adoption of quality control rules or ethical standards, exportation of goods without prejudice to national consumption, adoption of cost-minimizing production and distribution techniques, or any other activities which by their nature demonstrate it is not their aim to impose prices that harm the public.

The Organic Law defines other conditions that raise a presumption concerning activity which "tends" to be a monopoly. Since these conditions show only a tendency toward monopolization, the penalty is one-half that of an Article 4 violation. Under Article 5 these conditions include the importation of goods which may result in unfair competition, unauthorized voluntary destruction of goods to raise prices by lowering supply, unregulated benefits to consumers such as rebates, and sales of goods below cost. However, sales of goods below cost is allowed if the goods are new on the market, the market price is below cost, or the goods are sold at an auction or bankruptcy proceeding.

The Organic Law excepts from the definition of a monopoly any authorized industrial or public services operating under official price schedules and any industries in which the government participates as shareholder or partner.

The Organic Law establishes a fine of 100 to 10,000 pesos for persons who violate Article 1. In the case of continued unlawful conduct a new sanction will be imposed every day. In addition to this penalty, the federal executive, together with the National Council on Economics, is empowered to take steps to restore competitive market conditions by fixing maximum prices on goods, forcing the sale of goods held off the market, forcing the furnishing of withheld services, and promoting competition by granting subsidies or franchises.

The federal executive is also empowered to take action pursuant to the decreed Powers of the Federal Executive in Economic Matters, Feb. 1 D.O.

1936, which grants regulatory authority to the federal executive without specific reference to antitrust. This law applies to business activity related to certain types of merchandise such as goods of necessary consumption, raw materials, and products of fundamental industries. Luxury item industries are specifically excluded from the scope of this law. The decree empowers the federal executive to impose maximum prices on goods, force the sale of goods held from the market, regulate the distribution of goods to avoid unnecessary intermediary steps, regulate imports and exports, force raw material producers to satisfy domestic demand before exporting, and impose rationing and priority systems when a product's demand exceeds its supply. Persons who violate this law face fines of 100 to 20,000 pesos or confinement for ninety days.

Alternatively, a plaintiff may seek remedies through provisions in the Penal Code. Article 253 of the Penal Code of the Federal District of Mexico punishes the following acts with up to nine years imprisonment and a fine of up to 150,000 pesos: monopolizing goods of primary necessity with the intent to obtain price increases by restricting the flow of goods; impairing competition by creating barriers to entry; restricting output of goods with intent to obtain higher prices; exporting goods without authorization; selling goods of primary necessity for excessive profits or any other acts which violate the provisions of Article 28 of the Constitution. In addition, a court may order suspension of operation for one year or the dissolution of the enterprise. Under Article 30 of the Penal Code, a plaintiff can seek restitution and indemnification for any damage caused to him.

Either individuals or the National Council on Economics, representing the government, can initiate an antitrust action. The National Council on Economics, a federal agency, is in charge of regulating national economic matters including trade and more specifically any illegal monopoly activity. The provisions of the Civil and Penal Codes and the Organic Law of Article 28 of the Constitution do not preempt but supplement each other. Therefore all three statutory provisions are channels available to the plaintiff.

CASES

Amparo Administrativo en Revision Promovide por Estevez Adelfonso, 43 Seminario 781, 786 (1935).

Amparo Civil Directo promovide por miguel Kuri Awad, 108 Seminario 1655 (1951).

Amparo Administrativo in Revision promovido por Mexican Petroleum Company, 57 Seminario 818 (1938).

SECONDARY SOURCES

Browning, *A Comparative Glance at the Anti-Monopoly Laws of the United States and Mexico,* 42 TEXAS L. REV. 577 (1964).

THE NETHERLANDS

LAW

Economic Competition Act of 28 June 1956, as amended by the Act of 16 July 1958.

Synopsis

The Economic Competition Act (Act) deals with two subjects: *regulation of competition* which is defined as "any agreement or decision governed by civil law, regulating economic competition between owners of enterprises"; and *dominant position* which is defined as "a factual or legal relationship in trade or industry involving a predominant influence by one or more owners of enterprises on a market for goods or servies in the Netherlands." Actions are brought by the government only when such actions are deemed to be in the public interest. Any private action by interested third parties is limited to filing complaints with the government.

Section 2 of the Act requires notification to the minister of economic affairs of any "regulation of competition" within one month after such regulation comes into being. However, the minister may grant exemptions to the notification requirement, and have in fact done so for certain types of agreements (for example, joint purchase or sale agreements, agreements regarding exclusive selling or purchasing rights, and others).

The minister can make a competition regulation binding on an entire branch or sector of a trade or industry for a period not to exceed three years, where such an action is deemed to be within the public interest. However, the minister may invoke an Order in Council which declares that specific elements of regulations of competition are not valid for a period of five years, again only where the public interest requires such an action.

This authority has been invoked regarding, respectively, collective resale price maintenance and individual resale price maintenance for certain durable consumer products, and agreements restricting competition which require binding arbitration of disputes. This prohibition may be and in fact has been extended in these areas by periodic statutory enactments. Before the minister can take any of these actions, however, the matter is referred to the Economic Competition Commission, which is a Crown-appointed panel of independent experts who act in an advisory capacity, giving consideration to both the competition regulations and claims of dominant position. The Commission publishes a notice of public hearings, and all interested parties may present their positions at that time. Also, the Commission has the power to make otherwise secret information public for the purpose of informed public involvement in the hearing process.

Ministerial decrees under the Act must be complied with by all enterprises operating in the Netherlands (whether foreign or domestic), but the Act does not have extraterritorial effect. Noncompliance with a ministerial decree can give rise to criminal sanctions, although in practice damage remedies are more common. The government has instituted relatively few investigations under the Act, due mainly to the high burden of proof required to establish a violation contrary to the public interest. Draft legislation has been submitted to the Parliament to amend the statute's approach to control of horizontal and vertical price arrangements, making such arrangements prima facie contrary to the public interest, with the enterprise bearing the burden of showing that its actions fall within one of the specific exceptions allowed; this legislation is likely to be adopted in the near future. Recommendations have also been made for the development of premerger controls; action in this area, however, is unlikely in the near future.

SECONDARY SOURCES

Boot & de Jong, *Chapter 20, Economic Law,* in INTRODUCTION TO DUTCH LAW FOR FOREIGN LAWYERS (Fokkema, Chorus, Hondius & Lisser eds. 1978).
OECD, GUIDE TO LEGISLATION ON RESTRICTIVE BUSINESS PRACTICES, VOL. V (1964).
[1972] COMM. MKT. REP. (CCH) ¶ 27,005 *et seq.*

REPUBLIC OF SOUTH AFRICA

LAW

Regulation of Monopolistic Conditions Act, No. 24 of 1955, as amended by the Regulation of Monopolistic Conditions Amendments Acts, Nos. 14 of 1958, 48 of 1975, 23 of 1976, and 75 of 1978.

Synopsis
The Regulation of Monopolistic Conditions Act of 1955, as amended (Act) empowers the minister of economic affairs to control, prevent, or eliminate monopolistic practices "detrimental to the public interest." The Act also empowers the Board of Trade and Industries to conduct investigations into alleged monopolistic conditions and to make recommendations to the minister of economic affairs.
The Act applies to:

(a) Every agreement, arrangement, or understanding, whether legally enforceable or not, between two or more companies;
(b) Every business practice or method of trading, including any method of fixing prices;
(c) Every act or omission on the part of any person, whether acting independently or in concert with any other person;
(d) Every situation arising out of the activities of any person or class or group of persons;

which by directly or indirectly restricting competition, has or is calculated to have, the effect of—

(i) restricting the output or disposal of any commodity;
(ii) limiting the facilities available for the production or distribution of any commodity;
(iii) enhancing or maintaining prices;
(iv) preventing the production or distribution of any commodity by the most efficient or economic means;
(v) preventing or retarding the development or introduction of technical improvements or the expansion of existing markets or the opening up of new markets;
(vi) preventing or retarding the entry of new products or distribution into any branch of trade or industry; or
(vii) preventing or retarding the adjustment of any branch of trade or industry to changing circumstances.

Specific types of monopolistic practices may be prohibited by the Board of Trade and Industries, or a cease and desist order may be issued to a particular party within a specific trade. However, takeover bids are actually aided by a provision of the South African Companies Act which stipulates that when a bidding company acquires 90 percent of another company's outstanding shares, the remaining 10 percent must be relinquished to the bidding company.

South African law does not specifically prohibit monopolies or require prior government approval for mergers. It more closely resembles the British system than the U.S., in that mergers and voluntary agreements are permissible if deemed to be in the public interest. Since the Act provides no definition of *public interest,* the Board of Trade and Industries has to weigh the advantages and disadvantages of the monopolistic condition and conclude on the preponderance of the evidence, and in light of its own assessment of the facts, whether the monopolistic condition in question is justified. A merger that creates "monopolistic conditions" may be dissolved.

In the period 1955 to 1976 the minister of economic affairs ordered the Board of Trade and Industries to conduct eighteen investigations into suspected monopolistic conditions of which fifteen had been completed through 1979. Only four prosecutions resulted in convictions through 1976. Furthermore, the minister has only irregularly issued directives to undertake an investigation. During two five-year-periods, no directives were given to the Board of Trade and Industries. Investigations that were undertaken were quite lengthy—more than two years on the average—and even in those investigations for which the minister of economic affairs issued an order, very little was done to enforce such orders prior to 1974.

Nonetheless, Section 18 of the Act provides for fines or imprisonment or both for specified violations. Section 8(1) provides that any person who fails to comply with an order issued by the minister of economic affairs, and based upon the Board of Trade and Industries' investigation into suspected monopolistic conditions is guilty of an offense and liable for a fine not exceeding R 20,000 (ten thousand pounds) or imprisonment not exceeding five years, or both. Any person who fails to comply with the Board of Trade and Industries' investigation by submitting requested information or who knowingly furnishes false information is likewise guilty of an offense and liable to a fine not exceeding five thousand pounds or imprisonment not exceeding two-and-one-half years, or both.

Merger and acquisitions policy will be substantially changed by the report of the Mouton Commission (Commission) (published in 1977), if the government accepts the Commission's recommendations. Although a draft bill embodying some of the recommendations of the Commission was published for general information in February 1978, it appears, as a result of criticism, that the draft is being reconsidered by the Department of Commerce. The Mouton Commission contends the Act's main weakness lies in its inability to deal effectively with the merger problem. While the Act may be used to dissolve harmful concentrations that result from horizontal and vertical mergers, conglomerates may fall outside the Act. The Commission also questions the wisdom and efficacy of compulsory dissolution of consummated vertical and horizonal mergers. The Commission concluded that the decision to entrust enforcement of the Act to the Board of Trade and Industries rather than an autonomous body has interfered with proper implementation of the legislation. The Commission considered it unrealistic to expect the Board of Trade and Industries to be an impartial judge and effective policeman of those firms with which the Board had been closely linked and whose growth and well-being had been its primary task for years.

The Commission's proposals concerning mergers are:

(a) Since the Commission is not in favor of the per se prohibition of economic concentration, or of behavior which causes such concentration, the proposal concerns the need to provide in the legislation for the investigation of mergers, takeovers and other methods of acquiring control on an individual basis in accordance with the requirements of the public interest;

(b) the Commission is not in favor of an elaborate system for the scrutiny of mergers, takeovers and other forms of acquiring control involving provision for pre-notification and criteria, such as total assets or market shares for the screening of amalgamations. Apart from the demands on time and manpower which such a system would involve and which the country can ill afford it would not cover "creeping" takeovers, *i.e.*, the purchase of shares over a period until control of another company is obtained;

(c) there should be established a quasi-judicial body which may be called the Merger Tribunal presided over by a judge or by some other independent person together with at least two further members experienced in, or with the knowledge of, the problems in this field;

(d) the Tribunal would have the power not only to forbid a takeover to proceed but also to break it up once it had been completed and to break up the results of a "creeping" takeover or indeed any form of conglomerate if it considers it in the public interest to do so;

(e) the Tribunal should complete its investigation and report its decision to the Minister within three months after the date of reference, and the Mnister must convey his decision to the relevant parties within two weeks after receipt of the Tribunal's decision; and

(f) the Commission considers that the existing maximum fine of twenty thousand Rand can no longer be considered adequate and favors an increase in the maximum fine.

SECONDARY SOURCES

MacGregor, Mergers, Acquisitions, and Shareholders (1979).

VENEZUELA

LAW

Decision 24 of the Commission of the Cartagena Agreement, Common Regime of Treatment of Foreign Capital, Patents, Licenses and Royalties, reprinted in 16 Int'l Legal Mat. 138 (1977), commonly known as the Andean Foreign Investment Code (AFIC) and incorporated into Venezuelan law by Decree 2,031, Feb. 8, 1977, reprinted in 16 Int'l Legal Mat. 1531 (1977) and in *Gac. Of.* 31,171 (Feb. 9, 1977) (Ven.) and Decree 2,442, Nov. 8, 1977, *Gac. Of.* 2,100 Ex. (Nov. 15, 1977) (Ven.).

Synopsis
In order to encourage domestic financial and technological development, Venezuela has enacted legislation that regulates foreign investment and multinational corporate activity in Venezuela. The AFIC and Decree 2442 require that all new and existing foreign investments be registered with and approved by the government. Loans from foreign sources to Venezuelan enterprises must receive prior government approval; all contracts to import technology, or license patents or trademarks must also be approved and registered. Failure to comply with these registration requirements will result in the loss of the right to remit earnings or capital, to make payments on principal or interest, and to transfer royalties abroad.

The Foreign Investment Agency (SIEX), responsible to the Venezuelan Ministry of Finance, is a government agency charged with supervising all foreign investments. If a direct foreign investment is to be approved, such approval must come from SIEX within 180 days after a completed application is filed. Aggrieved enterprises can appeal an adverse decision of SIEX.

All foreign enterprises investing in Venezuela after December 31, 1974 must agree to transform themselves into "mixed" or "national" companies within fifteen years. For the purpose of this provision the expansion of an existing investment is treated as a new investment. In a mixed enterprise foreign investors hold less than 50 percent of the stock; an enterprise is considered national when foreigners own less than 20 percent of its shares. When computing percentages, citizens of other Andean Common Market countries can be treated as Venezuelan nationals.

Certain sectors of the Venezuelan economy are reserved for national companies. One such sector is public services, which includes telecommunications, mail, drinking water, electricity, sanitation, and security. The following industries are also limited to national companies: domestic transportation services, advertising, television, Spanish language newspapers and magazines, and retail firms. Certain companies are exempt from national and mixed company requirements: companies selling goods made in Venezuela, companies providing services, such as computer software or rental cars, and firms importing capital equipment.

In the area of technology transfer, domestic development is the principal goal. Royalty payments between a majority foreign-owned subsidiary and its parent or affiliates are prohibited, and such payments may not be deducted from taxable income. Foreign enterprises that have agreed to convert into national or mixed enterprises are exempt from this proscription, however. If a foreign company transfers technology to a Venezuelan subsidiary, it is obligated to train Venezuelan personnel in the use of the transferred technology.

Recently there has been an effort to regulate the commercially restrictive practices of Venezuela's domestic enterprises. The Venezuelan legislature is presently considering a bill that would prohibit most acts and agreements that create or threaten to create a monopoly situation. Under the proposed legislation certain types of cartel arrangements are permissible, including those for supply, payment, and quantity discount standards, standardization of goods, uniform trade practices, promotion of export sales, and production of agricultural goods. However, with all such exceptions the enterprise must notify the government of the agreement; government approval will be granted only if the parties prove that the same result cannot be reached by other means and establish that the agreement will not prejudice the means of production or supply.

The proposed law also prohibits price-fixing agreements, although it permits resale price maintenance arrangements. The statute does not automatically prohibit agreements that limit the use of goods or services acquired by price-fixing agreements, nor does it bar tying arrangements. Instead the government reserves the right to examine these arrangements and, if necessary, void them. The bill also prohibits agreements concerning licenses, patents, designs, or industrial secrets that impose substantial limitations on the acquiring party, except when the limitation or improvements relate to a price agreement between the parties, or to sales in a foreign market.

The bill also authorizes the prohibition of all economic abuses by market-dominating enterprises. To this end it will control merger, acquisitions, and transfer of assets. It will accomplish this by requiring the parties involved to notify the government of such agreements when it is probable that an enterprise will acquire 20 percent of an industry market or that an enterprise already possessing such market power shall increase it. The proposal in general terms limits abusive pricing, purchase and sales restrictions, and price discrimination. The penalties for violations of the proposed statute are fines, calculated as a percentage of paid income tax, and prison terms.

SECONDARY SOURCES

Brewer-Corias, *Regimen de competencia entre empresas publicas y empresas privados en la sistima venezolana,* [1978] PONENCIAS VENEZOLANAS 261–300.

Carl & Johnson, *Venezuela and the Andean Common Market,* 7 DEN. J. of INT'L L. 151–196 (1978).

White, *La legislacion antimonopoica y el control del poder economico en America Latina: recien tendencias,* 28–29 DERECHO DE LA INTEGRACION 35–59 (1978).

Appendix 2: Recent United States Legislative Antitrust Proposals

PETROLEUM INDUSTRY COMPETITION ACT, S. 82.

Introduced on January 18, 1979, by Senator Bayh.
Referred to the Judiciary Committe.
Facilitates the creation and maintenance of competition in the petroleum industry, and requires divestment of certain assets of vertically-integrated oil companies.

Within five years of its enactment, makes it unlawful for any major producer, transporter, refiner, marketer, or other person owning refining, production, or marketing assets to control any interest in refinery, transport, or marketing assets.

Anyone covered by these provisions must submit to the Federal Trade Commission within eighteen months of enactment a plan for divestment of the prohibited assets. The required divestment must occur within five years.

Violations of the Petroleum Industry Competition Act incur civil penalties of up to $100,000 for individuals and up to $1 million for corporations.

Creates Temporary Petroleum Industry Divestiture Court having exclusive jurisdiction of matters arising under this Act.

ANTITRUST ENFORCEMENT ACT, S. 300.

Introduced on January 31, 1979, by Senator Kennedy.
Referred to the Judiciary Committee; Hearing March 9, 1979.
Reported as amended S. REPT. No. 96–239, July 10, 1979.
Amends Clayton Act Section 4 to allow those injured by antitrust violations to recover damages whether or not they have dealt directly with the defendant.

Allows as partial or complete defense that plaintiff has passed on to others who are entitled to recover under Clayton Act some measure of what would otherwise constitute plaintiff's damages.

Limits recovery of foreign governments to actual damages, and permits such suits in U.S. courts only if the foreign state's laws forbid the same conduct which is the subject of suit under the Clayton Act.

Amends Multidistrict Litigation Act to permit the Judicial Panel on Multidistrict Litigation to consolidate related civil antitrust actions.

Authorizes court to award attorney fees to prevailing defendants upon showing of plaintiff's bad faith in bringing suit.

SMALL AND INDEPENDENT BUSINESS PROTECTION ACT, S. 600.

Introduced on March 8, 1979, by Senator Kennedy.
Referred to the Judiciary Committee; Hearing March 8, 1979.
Prohibits mergers which would result in control of a majority of assets if each party has sales exceeding a certain amount.

Establishes affirmative defense that the transaction will enhance competition, result in substantial efficiencies, or within one year before consummation, the parties have divested one or more viable business units, the assets and revenues of which are equal to or greater than those of the smaller party to the transaction.

Endows attorney general and Federal Trade Commission with enforcement authority. Grants injunctive relief to private parties under same terms as Section 16 of the Clayton Act.

PETROLEUM MARKETING MORATORIUM ACT, S. 723.

Introduced on March 21, 1979, by Senator Durkin.
Referred to the Judiciary Committee.
Prohibits any major market shareholder directly or indirectly engaged in production, refinery, or transportation of petroleum products from acquiring, operating, or controlling any retail outlet for marketing petroleum products not already acquired, operated, or controlled by it by enactment date.

Establishes a fine of $100,000 and/or imprisonment up to ten years for violations, and adds a further civil penalty up to $10,000 a day during continuation of violation.

Provides that anyone injured as a result of the above provisions may bring an action to enforce compliance, enjoin, or for damages.

UNFAIR COMPETITION ACT, S. 938.

Introduced on April 10, 1979, by Senator Mathias.
Referred to the Judiciary Committee; Senate Hearing December 6, 1979.
Amends Clayton Act Section 4 to include Section 801 of Revenue Act of 1916. Section 801 prohibits importation of foreign goods to be sold in United States at prices less than market value if act done with intent of destroying or injuring U.S. industry, preventing establishment of an industry in the United States or restraining or monopolizing any part of trade and commerce in such

goods in this country. The proposed Unfair Competition Act would amend Section 801 by adding that injury or restraint or monopoly must result from such conduct to be illegal. It would also add provisions authorizing the court to cause any other parties it deems necessary to resolution of the dispute to appear. If defendant fails to comply with any discovery order or other order of the court, the amendment provides, the court has authority to enjoin further importation into the United States or distribution in interstate commerce of same articles alleged in the proceeding to have been sold illegally.

Amends penalty provisions of Section 801 to increase the fine from $5,000 to $50,000.

ANTITRUST CONSENT DECREE ENFORCEMENT ACT, S. 958.

Introduced on April 10, 1979, by Senator Kennedy.
Referred to the Judiciary Committee.
Amends Clayton Act Section 5 to provide remedies for enforcement of antitrust judgments. Any individual damaged by violation of antitrust judgment may notify the attorney general that the judgment is not being complied with. Prevailing private parties may recover costs of action and reasonable attorney's fees.

Provides penalty for violation of judgment up to $10,000. Each day a violation continues may be considered a separate violation.

THE ANTITRUST RECIPROCITY ACT, S. 317.

Introduced on February 1, 1979, by Senator DeConcini.
Referred to the Judiciary Committee.
Limits the standing of foreign sovereigns to sue under antitrust laws.

Amends Clayton Act Section 4 by limiting the damages foreign sovereigns may recover to actual damages, and by providing that no foreign state may maintain an action in the United States unless the attorney general, within 120 days after commencement of an action, has certified to the relevant court that the United States is entitled to sue in that foreign state's courts and that the foreign sovereign has laws prohibiting restrictive business practices which are enforced against those within its territory.

INTERNATIONAL TRADE AND INVESTMENT REORGANIZATION ACT, S. 377.

Introduced on February 2, 1979, by Senator Roth.
Referred to the Governmental Affairs Committee; Hearing July 23, 1979.

Establishes a Department of International Trade and Investment as an executive department. This Department would assume many of the functions and duties of other bodies, *i.e.* Special Representative for Trade Negotiations, secretary of state, and Department of State, that relate to commercial activities.

COMPETITION IMPROVEMENTS ACT, S. 382.

Introduced on February 7, 1979, by Senator Kennedy.
Referred to the Judiciary Committee; Hearing March 6, 1979.
Prohibits federal agencies from taking any action that has the effect of lessening competition. Requires each independent regulatory agency to establish procedures within one hundred and twenty days after enactment which provide for notification of the attorney general of important pending agency actions.

EXPORT TRADE ASSOCIATION ACT, S. 864.

Introduced on April 4, 1979, by Senator Danforth.
Referred to the Banking, Housing & Urban Affairs Committee.
Encourages U.S. exports by establishing office within Department of Commerce to promote formation of export trade associations through the Webb-Pomerene Act. Makes provisions of Webb-Pomerene Act applicable to exportation of services and transfers responsibility for administering Act from the Chairman of the Federal Trade Commission to the secretary of commerce.

Amends Section 2 of the Webb-Pomerene Act to exempt export trade associations from the antitrust laws in certain circumstances.

Only federal agencies have standing to sue the export association. Individuals may file a petition requesting the appropriate enforcement action.

(No Title) S. 980.

Introduced on April 23, 1979, by Senator Mathias.
Referred to the Judiciary Committee.
Amends Clayton Act by providing that no foreign sovereign may maintain an action under Section 4 unless its laws would have forbidden the same conduct upon which its action is based. The foreign state's laws must authorize the government and U.S. citizens to recover damages in its courts. Limits foreign sovereign potential recovery to actual damages.

(No Title) S. 1010.

Introduced on April 10, 1979, by Senator Mathias.
Referred to the Governmental Affairs Committee; Senate Hearing October 31, 1979.
Establishes Commission on the International Application of Antitrust Laws. Commission shall make comprehensive recommendations regarding international aspects of U.S. antitrust law, and make periodic reports to president and Congress. Commission has power to hold hearings and subpoena witnesses.

OIL WINDFALL ACQUISITION ACT, S. 1246.

Introduced on May 24, 1979, by Senator Kennedy.
Referred to the Judiciary Committee; Hearing June 19, 1979.
Reported as amended, S. REP. No. 9–444, December 4, 1979.
Amends Clayton Act by adding limitation on acquisitions and mergers where the acquiree has assets in excess of $100 million in the energy business, or assets of $50 million and not in the energy business, and the major producer would control a majority of those assets.

The bill does not prohibit acquisitions which enhance competition in United States domestic or foreign commerce, or materially increase energy exploration, extraction, production, or conversion; the bill does not apply to joint ventures.

The bill presumes that assets acquired in the energy business within three years are the subject of a single acquisition.

(No Title) S. 1413.

Introduced on June 26, 1979, by Senator Jackson.
Referred to the Energy & Natural Resources and Judiciary Committees; Senate Hearing October 3, 1979.
Extends the antitrust exemption for oil companies that participate in the Agreement on an International Energy Program. Section 252(j) of Energy Policy & Conservation Act of 1975 is amended by striking out "June 30, 1979" and inserting "January 19, 1986."

EXPORT TRADE ACTIVITIES ACT, S. 1499.

Introduced on July 12, 1979, by Senator Roth.
Referred to the Banking and Housing & Urban Affairs Committees; Hearing September 17, 1979.

Encourages the formation and utilization of export trade associations. Gives the Federal Trade Commission exclusive jurisdiction to certify and supervise such associations, which are exempt from the antitrust laws as long as they refrain from certain conduct.

Individuals have standing to bring actions against an association only if the Federal Trade Commission determines its activities constitute certain prohibited conduct.

Repeals Webb-Pomerene Act as of the ninetieth day of Export Trade Activities Act's enactment.

(No Title) S. 1744.

Introduced on September 13, 1979, by Senator Inouye.
Referred to the Banking and Housing and Urban Affairs Committees; Senate Hearing September 17, 1979.
Amends Export Trade Act to encourage increased utilization of the Act, to expand exemptions provided under the Act, to clarify U.S. government policy with respect to administration of the Act, and to assist U.S. exporters in international trade competition.

(No Title) S. 1871.

Introduced on October 10, 1979, by Senators Metzenbaum, Thurmond, and Jackson.
Referred to the Energy & Natural Resources Committee.
Reported, amended, without written Senate report October 16, 1979; passed Senate as reported (Voice) October 17, 1979; amended to contain text of H. 4445 as passed (Voice) October 22, 1979; passed House as amended (Voice) October 22, 1979; Senate agreed to unanimous consent agreement regarding consideration (Voice) October 29, 1979; House amendments agreed to by Senate with amendments (Roll-call) October 30, 1979; Pursuant to HOUSE RES. 478, bill returned to Senate November 8, 1979; amended on Senate floor (Voice) November 16, 1979; Conferees appointed by House November 26, 1979; Conferees appointed by Senate November 27, 1979; agreed to by Senate (Voice) November 28, 1979; Conferees Report filed, H. REP. No. 96–669 November 28, 1979; agreed to by House (Voice) November 29, 1979; to president November 29, 1979; approved (P.L. 96–133) November 30, 1979.

Extends existing antitrust exemption for oil companies that participate in Agreement on International Energy Program, by Amending Section 252(j) of the Energy Policy & Consideration Act of 1975 by striking out "June 30, 1979" and inserting "June 30, 1980."

ANTITRUST ENFORCEMENT IMPROVEMENTS ACT, S. 1980.

Introduced on November 6, 1979, by Senators Hatch, Thurmond, Cochran, Helms, Laxalt.
Referred to the Judiciary Committee.
Provides for more efficient and equitable enforcement of the antitrust laws by eliminating adjudicative function of the Federal Trade Commission. Vests that function in federal district courts and retains in the Federal Trade Commission its authority to investigate alleged violations of antitrust provisions. Confers authority on the Federal Trade Commission to bring civil actions in federal district courts.

Amends Clayton Act by investing federal district courts with jurisdiction to prevent violations of Clayton Act. Requires U.S. attorneys under direction of the attorney general to institute proceedings in equity.

FOREIGN INVESTMENT DISCLOSURE ACT, H. R. 158.

Introduced on January 15, 1979, by Representative Brodhead.
Referred to Interstate and Foreign Commerce Committee.
Amends Securities Exchange Act of 1934 to require disclosure by foreign investors acquiring more than 5 percent of equity securities in U.S. corporations having assets greater than $1 million. The president may prohibit such acquisitions to protect national security and the domestic economy or to further foreign policy. The president shall prohibit such acquisitions if he determines the foreign investor has caused, attempted, or conspired to cause any person to discriminate against a U.S. company, because that company has been dealing with a country with which the United States has diplomatic relations.

ENERGY COMPETITION ACT, H. R. 508.

Introduced on January 15, 1979, by Representative Kastenmeier.
Referred to the Judiciary Committee.
Makes it unlawful for any person involved in production of petroleum or petroleum products to acquire any coal, uranium, or geothermal power asset; to buy, own, or control any of the above energy sources after three years from enactment date; or to have any management personnel holding a controlling interest in any energy company in the United States.

Attorney general requires those covered to submit within one year of the date of this bill's enactment a plan for divestment of prohibited assets within three years.

For knowing violations there is a penalty of up to $500,000 for individuals, or imprisonment, or both. For corporations, the penalty is $5 million and up to a ten-year suspension of the right to do business.

COMPETITIVE ENERGY DEVELOPMENT ACT, H. R. 2345.

Introduced on February 22, 1979, by Representative McKinney.
Referred to the Interstate and Foreign Commerce Committee.
Requires the Federal Trade Commission (Commission) to monitor energy-related industries under criteria established in consultation with the Department of Energy to measure the level of competition in alternative energy source markets. If the Commission determines such criteria have been violated, it may issue an order to show cause at a hearing. The person must come forward with reasons why he should not be held responsible for non-competitive or anticompetitive situations.

The Commission may make recommendations to any governmental entity to take action which that entity has authority to carry out.

SMALL AND INDEPENDENT BUSINESS PROTECTION ACT, H. R. 3169.

Introduced on March 21, 1979, by Representative Seiberling.
Referred to the Judiciary Committee.
Prohibits mergers between two or more parties, one having assets greater than $2 billion and the other having assets of $350 million; or if one party has assets exceeding $350 million and the other has 20 percent or more of the sales in a significant market.

Establishes affirmative defense that transaction will substantially enhance competition, efficiencies, or that within one year the parties will divest one or more business units whose assets and revenues are equal to or greater than those of the smallest party.

Attorney general and the Federal Trade Commission have the authority to enforce compliance. Injunctive relief for private parties is available under same terms as Section 16 of the Clayton Act.

FOREIGN INVESTORS LIMITATION ACT, H. R. 3182.

Introduced on March 22, 1979, by Representative Gaydos.
Referred to the Interstate & Foreign Trade Committee.
Amends Securities Exchange Act of 1934 to restrict non-U.S. citizens from acquiring more than 35 percent of nonvoting securities or more than 5 percent of voting securities of any issuer registered under the Act.

PETROLEUM INDUSTRY COMPETITION ACT, H. R. 3346.

Introduced on March 29, 1979, by Representative Mottl.
Referred to the Judiciary Committee.
Requires divestment of vertically-integrated petroleum companies. Makes it unlawful for any major petroleum producer, refiner, transporter, or marketer to own or control any interest in stages of production it is not presently involved in.

The Federal Trade Commission shall require each person covered by Section 4 to submit plans for divestment within three years.

Penalties for willful violation are $500,000 for an individual and/or imprisonment not more than ten years; for corporations, the same amount and/or suspension of the right to do business in interstate commerce for up to ten years.

ENERGY ANTIMONOPOLY ACT, H. R. 4295.

Introduced on June 4, 1979, by Representative Luken.
Referred to the Judiciary Committee.
Amends Clayton Act by prohibiting major oil producers, or subsidiaries thereof, from merging or consolidating with any person engaged in commerce. Prohibits acquisition of an amount of stock or other share of capital of any person engaged in commerce so as to enable such producer to control such other person or acquire a majority of his assets, if he has assets over $100,000,000.

CARTEL RESTRICTION ACT, H. R. 4661.

Introduced on June 28, 1979, by Representatives Gore and Scheuer.
Referred to the Interstate & Foreign Commerce and Judiciary Committees.
Amends Federal Trade Commission Act to require persons subject to the Act to submit reports regarding certain business activities conducted by them in foreign states to enable the Federal Trade Commission to determine whether such activities involve anticompetitive practices.

In actions brought to enforce this Act or the antitrust laws the court may not decline to exercise jurisdiction solely because it would require an examination of official action of a foreign state, except where the foreign state acted in its sovereign capacity.

COMPETITION IN GASOLINE MARKETING ACT, H. R. 4682.

Introduced on June 28, 1979, by Representative Kostmayer.
Referred to the Judiciary Committee.

To restore and provide competition in marketing of motor fuel by prohibiting the control, operation, or acquisition of marketing outlets by petroleum refiners, producers, distributors. Such interests must be disposed of within two years after enactment.

A knowing violation invokes a penalty of up to $100,000 and/or imprisonment up to ten years. A violation by a corporation shall be deemed to be a violation by the individual directors, officers, receivers, trustees, or agents. It is the duty of the attorney general to commence a civil action for appropriate relief upon violation.

If a producer, refiner, or distributor fails to comply with Act's requirements, any retailer may maintain a civil action against it.

PETROLEUM COMPANY HOLDINGS ACT, H. R. 4733.

Introduced on July 10, 1979, by Representative Mottl.
Referred to the Interstate and Foreign Commerce & Judiciary Committees.
Prohibits major petroleum producers, refiners, and marketers from acquiring, owning, or controlling any business (or interest therein) outside of the petroleum industry, effective beginning three years after this bill's enactment.

The Federal Trade Commission shall require those subject to this Act to submit within one year a plan for divestment of the interests prohibited by the Act. The plan must accomplish the divestment within three years of the date of enactment.

The Commission shall institute suits in federal district courts requesting the issuance of such appropriate relief to assure compliance.

A knowing or willful violation of this Act carries a penalty of $500,000 and/or imprisonment. A corporation may stand to lose the right to engage in commerce for up to ten years and/or the above fine. Provides for civil penalty up to $100,000 for violation of lawful Commission orders.

SPECIAL ENERGY PROSECUTION ACT, H. R. 5776.

Introduced on November 1, 1979, by Representative Glickman.
Referred to the Interstate & Foreign Commerce and Judiciary Committees.
Creates special prosecutor for audit, review, investigation, and prosecution of violations by major oil companies of the Federal Trade Commission Act, the Sherman and Clayton Acts, and other antitrust laws.

(No Title) H. R. 6292.

Introduced on January 24, 1980, by Representative Long.
Referred to the Judiciary Committee.
Restores and promotes competition in the marketing of gasoline by prohibit-

ing the control, operation, or acquisition of marketing outlets by petroleum refiners, producers, and distributors.

(No Title) H. Res. 125.

Introduced on February 15, 1979, by Representative St. Germain.
Referred to the Rules Committee.
Creates a select committee to investigate nationalization of the oil industry.

Annotated Bibliography

Corporate concentration of both a national and transnational character is one of the more oblique topics in antitrust literature. Books and articles in the area tend to focus on narrow aspects of this issue, or on the regulatory efforts of particular countries and international organizations. The annotations which follow highlight some of the leading writings on industrial concentration.

COMPENDIA OF ANTITRUST LEGISLATION

OECD. Guide to Legislation on Restrictive Business Practices. Paris: OECD. Texts, explanatory notes, decisions, bibliography in four volumes updated periodically cover OECD member countries, the European Coal and Steel Community, and the European Community legislation on restrictive business practices.

OECD Committee of Experts on Restrictive Business Practices. Annual Reports on Competition Policy in OECD Member Countries. Paris: OECD. Annual reports issued since 1973, covering developments in government regulation of restrictive business practices in individual countries.

————. Comparative Summary of Legislation on Restrictive Business Practices. OECD, 1978. Tabular summaries of legal attitudes adopted by OECD member countries, the European Communities, and the European Free Trade Association toward twenty-two elements of the control of restrictive business practices. This information is supplemented with references to laws, regulations, comments, and decisions contained in the OECD Guide to Legislation on Restrictive Business Practices.

von Kalinowski, Julian O. World Law of Competition. New York: Matthew Bender, 1979. Multivolume series compiling detailed explanations and translations of U.S., European, and EEC competition law written by experts in the field.

EVIDENTIARY AND PROCEDURAL ISSUES

Amram, Phillip W. *Explanatory Report on the Convention on the Taking of Evidence Abroad in Civil or Commercial Matters.* 12 Int'l Leg. Mat.

327, 343 (1973). The author was the rapporteur to the Hague Conference on Private International Law Commission that produced the Hague Evidence Convention. His report explains each article of that convention.

Hollman, Hermann H. *Problems of Obtaining Evidence in Antitrust Litigation: Comparative Approaches to the Multinational Corporation.* 22 TEX. INT'L L.J. 461, 483 (1976). Surveys legal provisions for extraterritorial discovery as well as problems encountered by antitrust authorities in Belgium, the Netherlands, Germany, and the European Communities Commission.

Jones, David Lloyd. *Letters Rogatory—Privilege Against Self-Incrimination: Infringement of United Kingdom Sovereignty.* 37 CAMB. L.J. 244–49 (1978). Concise discussion of the legal issues in *Rio Tinto Zinc Corporation and Others v. Westinghouse Electric Corporation* [1977] 3 W.L.R. 430, 492 (C.A.); [1978] 2 W.L.R. 81 (H.L.).

Katz, Brian E. *Ordering the Production of Documents Abroad—The Tenth Circuit's Approach: In Re Westinghouse Electric Corp. Uranium Contracts Litigation.* 1978 UTAH L. REV. 361–74. Reviews the case background and the "balancing of interests" approach adopted by the Tenth Circuit in *Westinghouse.* Katz discusses the factors the court weighed in holding that a Canadian corporation need not produce discovery that would require it to violate a Canadian criminal law. He concludes by suggesting that the balancing test is proper and proposes a framework for properly weighing competing interests.

Maher, Laurence W. *Time Uranium and the Legislative Process.* 9 FED. L. REV. 399–426 (1978). This article reviews the passage of the Australian legislation responsible for blocking documentary production to Westinghouse. The author severely criticizes the Australian Parliament for its haste in passing the legislation and the alarming vagueness and breadth of the Act.

Note. *Discovery in Great Britain: The Evidence (Proceedings in Other Jurisdictions) Act.* 22 CORNELL INT'L L.J. 323–42 (1978). Examines the Evidence Act in the context of antitrust actions. It focuses on the kinds of discovery available in the United Kingdom to American litigants, the pitfalls that can defeat discovery, and how these pitfalls can be avoided or exploited.

Note. *Discovery of Documents Located Abroad in U.S. Antitrust Litigation: Recent Developments in the Law Concerning the Foreign Illegality Excuse for Non-Production.* 14 VA. J. INT'L L.J. 747–74 (1974). Analyzes the conflict between domestic discovery orders and foreign nondisclosure laws in case law. Suggests that international law norms and empirical observations of international agreement for cooperation at the diplomatic level would be a partial solution.

Note. *Foreign Nondisclosure Laws and Domestic Discovery Orders in Antitrust Litigation.* 88 YALE L.J. 613–28 (1979). Argues that the principles of *lex fori* (a domestic forum controls its own procedure) and international comity are irreconcilable in determining whether U.S. courts should order discovery that would conflict with foreign nondisclosure laws. The author surveys approaches to the problem and advocates a flexible four-step approach at the discovery stage.

Note. *Taking Evidence Outside of the United States.* 55 B.U.L. REV. 368–86 (1975). Practical guide for taking evidence abroad under the Federal Rules of Civil Procedure and the Hague Evidence Convention.

Reports on the Work of the Special Commission on the Operation of the Hague Evidence Convention on the Taking of Evidence Abroad in Civil or Commercial Matters. 17 INT'L LEG. MAT. 1417–41 (1978). Reports discussions on problems that have arisen under the Convention. Specifically, the reports consider whether the Convention's application to "civil or commercial" matters includes American administrative tribunals, and the proper definitions of *evidence* and *pre-trial discovery*, as those terms are used in the Convention.

Shenefield, John. *Extraterritorial Impact of U.S. Antitrust Laws.* [1978] 5 TRADE REG. REP. (CCH) ¶ 50,386 (remarks delivered Aug. 9, 1978). The Assistant Attorney General, Antitrust Division, contends that U.S. "objective territorial" jurisdiction in antitrust cases is reasonable, reviews foreign discovery and antitrust policy in this regard, and discusses the implications of the *Timberlane* decision. Regarding foreign nondisclosure laws, he states that: "the Antitrust Division may be left with no choice but to press the courts, as a practical matter, to ignore this particular type of foreign legislation."

Sklaver, Harvey. *Obtaining Evidence in International Litigation.* 7 CUM. L. REV. 233–54 (1976). Sklaver, a practicing attorney, discusses extraterritorial discovery pursuant to 18 U.S.C. §§ 1781–84 (1970), which governs the issuance of letters rogatory and the Hague Convention on the Taking of Evidence Abroad in Civil or Commercial Matters.

SMIT, HANS. INTERNATIONAL COOPERATION IN LITIGATION: EUROPE. Columbia University School of Law Project on International Procedure, 1965. Dated but complete survey of cooperation in discovery that is granted and sought by sixteen Western European nations.

Sutherland. *Rio Tinto-Zinc Corporation v. Westinghouse Electric Corporation: Extraterritorial Jurisdiction in Antitrust Matters.* 5 MONASH U.L. REV. 76–85 (1978). An Australian law professor reviews the House of Lords' *Westinghouse* opinion, and urges the need for an international antitrust convention to maintain harmony between Western trading partners.

Obtaining Foreign Discovery and Evidence for Use in Litigation in the United States. 13 INT'L LAW. 3–42 (1979). Three articles by practicing attorneys are included: Canter, *Existing Rules and Procedures,* at 3, which discusses foreign attitudes toward American discovery and evidence abroad; Collins, *Opportunities for and Obstacles to Obtain-*

ing Evidence in England for Use in Litigation in the United States, at 27, which gives practical advice from a British solicitor; and Bond and Boyd, *Opportunities for and Obstacles to Obtaining Evidence in France for Use in Litigation in the United States*, at 35, which gives practical advice from a French *avocat a la cour* and an American practitioner. Also, the Richmond District Court Judge who presided over the *Westinghouse* discovery requests describes his fifth amendment and immunity rulings in the case. Mehrige, *The Westinghouse Uranium Case: Problems Encountered in Seeking Foreign Discovery and Evidence*, at 19.

Wood, Jeffrey L., and Cannener, Victor M. *The International Uranium Cartel Litigation and Legal Implications.* 14 Tex. Int'l L.J. 59–114 (1979). Thoroughly discusses the nuclear industry, the Westinghouse uranium litigation, and its discovery proceedings.

ACT OF STATE AND SOVEREIGN COMPULSION

Graziano, Anthony W., Jr. *Foreign Governmental Compulsion as a Defense in United States Antitrust Law.* 7 Va. J. Int'l L. 100–45 (1967). Good background on extraterritorial enforcement of U.S. antitrust laws. Analyzes the extent to which foreign law, foreign sovereignty, and foreign governmental compulsion affect the application of U.S. antitrust laws to business activity abroad.

Note. *Development of the Defense of Sovereign Compulsion.* 69 Mich. L. Rev. 888–913 (1971). Explores the doctrinal basis and practical difficulties of the sovereign compulsion doctrine promulgated in *Interamerican Refining.* Suggests an alternative balancing approach to the inflexible *Interamerican* rule whereby a court weighs such factors as impact of compelled activity on American foreign and economic policy, scope of foreign government's directive, degree of actual compulsion, impact upon competition and commerce, nationality of defendant and defendant's prior knowledge of the restraint.

Note. *State Action Exemption from the Antitrust Laws.* 50 B.U.L. Rev. 393–416 (1970). Considers the *Parker v. Brown* "state action" exemption and the difficult distinction between "state action" (which confers antitrust immunity on private actions) and state involvement insufficient to generate immunity. The Note concludes that "state action" should not be found on the basis of state presence or state approval alone. Rather, courts should apply the doctrine only if the state exerts independent influence in approving any scheme and ultimately approves all proposals.

Note. *The State Action Exemption in Antitrust: From Parker v. Brown to Cantor v. Detroit Edison Co.* 77 Duke L.J. 871–908 (1977). Analyzes the impact of *Cantor* on the *Parker* state action exemption emphasizing the further complications of the state action inquiry resulting from the decision.

Pansius, David K. *The Pitfalls of Act of State Analysis in the Antitrust Context: A Critique of Hunt v. Mobil Oil.* 6 DENVER J. INT'L L. & PL. 749–75 (1977). Analyzes *Hunt's* holding that the Act of State Doctrine bars inquiries into the motivation of sovereign acts. Pansius suggests *Hunt* errs by equating inquiry into motivation of an act with inquiry into the validity of that Act. The article proposes a two-part test plaintiffs must meet to recover for alleged antitrust violations: (1) the sovereign act which results in injury must be significantly attributable to independent efforts of the private defendant, and (2) these efforts must involve the abuse of the state's legitimate policy-making processes.

Symposium. *American Antitrust Law and Foreign Governments.* 13 J. INT'L L. & ECON. 137–63 (1978). Compilation of articles discussing the application of U.S. antitrust laws to the alleged international uranium cartel, impingement of antitrust laws on procurement of documents located abroad, and State Department perspectives on antitrust enforcement abroad.

ECONOMIC IMPACT OF MERGER CONTROL

Aaronovitch, Sam, and Sawyer, Malcom C. *Mergers, Growth and Concentration.* 27 OXFORD ECON. PAPERS 136–55 (1975). Isolates the effect of mergers on concentration by developing a set of alternate assumptions regarding the growth of acquired firms had mergers not occurred. The separate effect of each of four factors causing concentration to change is measured. These factors include the relative growth of surviving firms and disappearance through acquisition.

Bain, JOE S. INTERNATIONAL DIFFERENCES IN INDUSTRIAL STRUCTURE. New Haven: Yale University Press, 1966. Seminal work in the field, although the methodology may be a bit dated. Studies of India, France, the United States, Great Britain, Italy, Canada, and Sweden. Bain concludes by finding allocative inefficiencies caused by too small-scale production in plants accounting for over one-half the work force in countries outside the United States and the United Kingdom. Legal toleration of cartelization is put forward as a tentative explanation for these inefficiencies.

Gort, Michael, and Hogarty, Thomas F. *New Evidence on Mergers.* 13 J. L. & ECON. 167–84 (1970). Changes in the concentration of aggregate assets among the two hundred largest manufacturing firms for the period of 1948–67 are compared with the ratio of acquired assets to total assets of these firms to estimate the relative contribution of mergers to changes in concentration of aggregate assets.

Laiken, S.N. *Financial Performance of Merging Firms in a Virtually Uncon-strained Legal Environment*. 18 ANTITRUST BULL. 827–51 (1973). Analyzes merging firms during a period and in a country—Canada—where mergers encountered no substantial legal obstacles. Performance measures include profitability, stability of income stream, and size distribution.

McGowan, John J. *Effect of Alternate Antimerger Policies on the Size Distri-bution of Firms*. YALE ECON. ESSAYS (1965). Studies the effect of legal policies regarding mergers on the size distribution of firms. Utilizes a Markov chain model to estimate the effect of mergers on size distribu-tion and then tests various hypothetical policies.

———. *International Comparisons of Merger Activity*. 14 J. LAW and ECON. 233–50 (1971). Comparative study of the characteristics of merger behavior during the 1950s and early 1960s in the United States, Great Britain, France, and Australia. McGowan shows that some intercountry differences in characteristics of merger activity, such as size distribu-tion, may be explained by differing competitive environments, which in turn may be caused by varying institutional and legal arrangements regarding mergers and competition.

Müller, Jürgen. *The Impact of Mergers on Concentration: A Study of Eleven West German Industries*. 25 J. INDUS. ECON. 113–32 (1976). Covers the periods 1958–65 and 1965–71. The change in concentration is broken down into four components: internal growth, displacement, mergers, and the effect of entry and exit. The study found mergers and internal growth to be the dominant factors, and to be of roughly equal importance. It also found that the level of concentration did not decrease in a rapidly growing market.

Peltzman, Sam. *The Gains and Losses from Industrial Concentration*. 20 J. L. & ECON. 229–63 (1977). Theoretical exposition of the notion that the persistence of above-average rates of return in highly concentrated industries is the product of market disequilibrium. Peltzman found that cost-shift induced disequilibrium benefitting large firms dispro-portionately accounted for such high rates of return, and concluded that attacking concentration would do economic harm by preventing the realization of such cost-reducing efficiencies.

Pfunder, Plaine, and Whittemore. *Compliance with Divestiture Orders under Section 7 of the Clayton Act: An Analysis of the Relief Obtained*. 17 ANTITRUST BULL. 19–180 (1972). Makes analysis based on 114 dives-titure cases, and studies those elements of the divestiture process that are likely to have an anticompetitive impact. The authors pinpoint two fundamental misperceptions pervading the compliance mechanism: (1) that a remedy causing injury or inconvenience to a defendant is a penalty and inappropriate as civil relief, and (2) that defendant's ownership of the assets to be divested entitles him to direct the course of compliance. Where traditional structural relief would be effective, authors argue for stricter enforcement of time limits, required establishment of newly independent entities in most cases, and appointment of a trustee to direct all defendant's activities concerning compliance. In highly concentrated, oligopolistic industries, authors argue that divestiture inadequate. Suggest that Section 1 Sherman Act can be used to invalidate pre-1950 asset acquisitions which Section 7 Clayton Act doesn't reach. Also suggest that dividing oligopolistic industries into smaller parts is legally feasible and such restructure will not harm owners of oligopolistic corporations if the component parts of the company are able to obtain their own economies of scale.

Utton, M.A. *On Measuring the Effects of Industrial Mergers.* 21 Scottish J. Pol. Econ. 13–28 (1974). Criticizes previous attempts to measure the effect of mergers on efficiency and profitability as ignoring the dynamic nature of the merger process. Utton then examines British data on mergers and concludes that merged firms' profitability tends to be lower than that of internal growth firms.

White, Lawrence J. *Industrial Organization and International Trade: Some Theoretical Considerations.* 64 Am. Econ. Rev. 1013–20 (1974). Compares monopoly and competition, and demonstrates that under conditions of uncertain world demand, monopoly results in more imports than does competition. A theoretical result of empirical interest in light of the policy argument that increased concentration by monopoly may enhance the ability to compete on world markets.

CANADA

Borgsdorf, Charles W. *Virtually Unconstrained Environment for Mergers in Canada.* 18 Antitrust Bull. 809 (1973). Short history of the case law concerning mergers in Canada. Borgsdorf demonstrates that merger policy up to 1973 promoted business acquisitions by weak statutes and probusiness interpretations by the courts of legislative language. However, the author may have underestimated the importance of the merger reform movement beginning in 1971.

Brewster, Kingman, Jr. Law and United States Business in Canada. National Planning Association and Private Planning Association of Canada, 1960. Analyzes the application of Canadian law to United States corporate subsidiaries and the extraterritorial extensions of United States law to American companies in Canada. Brewster's analysis, while somewhat dated, provides support for the conclusion that Canadian economic activity is limited by the provisions of U.S. law.

Canada's Merger Muddle. 270 Economist 80–81 (1979). Argues that both foreign and domestic mergers in Canada have increased dramatically during the 1970s and that the number of conglomerate mergers has risen. The article notes the weakness of the national government's merger policies compared with those of Quebec and British Columbia.

GLOBERMAN, STEVEN. MERGERS AND ACQUISITIONS IN CANADA. Mississauga: Minister of Supply and Services Canada, 1977. Uses statistical analysis to support the thesis that pre-1970 merger policy in Canada was ineffective. However, Globerman concludes that the Foreign Investment Review Act should reverse trends in merger activity. In addition, Globerman also demonstrates through regression analysis that Canadian merger activity has paralleled that of the United States.

GOFF, COLIN H., and REASONS, CHARLES E. CORPORATE CRIME IN CANADA: A CRITICAL ANALYSIS OF ANTI-COMBINES LEGISLATION. Scarborough: Prentice-Hall of Canada, 1978. Summarizes the political history of Canadian merger and monopoly policies. Goff and Reasons provide a strong case for the proposition that enforcement of Canadian merger laws has been a disaster, although they are perhaps too pessimistic about future developments in reform of the merger laws.

KINTNER, EARL W., and JOELSON, MARK R. AN INTERNATIONAL ANTITRUST PRIMER. New York: Macmillan Co., 1974. Background material on the Combines Investigation Act and its administration by the Canadian government. Kintner and Joelson provide insight into the 1971 proposed amendments to the Act. The authors also describe merger policies of other countries.

LEVITT, KARI. SILENT SURRENDER: THE AMERICAN ECONOMIC EMPIRE IN CANADA. New York: Liveright, 1970. Although slanted against U.S. corporate activity in Canada, it would be unfair to characterize Levitt as totally biased. Levitt provides statistics to support his thesis that American corporate control of Canadian industries has been destructive. The author shows that merger policy has helped promote American control of Canada.

McFetridge, D.G. *The Emergence of a Canadian Merger Policy: The ERCO Case.* 11 ANTITRUST BULL. 1–11 (1974). Explaining the emergence of a Canadian merger policy, McFetridge emphasizes that, prior to *ERCO*, Canada had no operative merger policy. McFetridge also specifies that economic factors in Canada require the existence of highly concentrated industries. After tracing the history of *ERCO*, McFetridge concludes that it represents a new approach to mergers which emphasizes prohibitory orders to restrain the market power of the acquiring firm.

ROSENBLUTH, GIDEON, and THORBUN, HUGH G. CANADIAN ANTI-COMBINES ADMINISTRATION 1952–1960. Holland: University of Toronto Press, 1963. Analyzes legislative and administrative developments in merger policy before 1970. Although the authors use numerous statistics and tables to characterize anticombines policy in Canada, their study suffers from a lack of critical analysis.

ROWLEY, JOHN W., and STANBURY, WILLIAM THOMAS. COMPETITION POLICY IN CANADA: STAGE II. BILL C–13. Quebec: Institute for Research on

Public Policy, 1978. A thorough exposition of the legislative proposals for reform of Canada's merger laws. Rowley and Stanbury explain the details of recent legislative proposals and provide insight into the political forces preventing passage of major reforms.

EEC

European Commission. *Multinational Undertakings and the Community.* BULL. OF THE EUROPEAN COMMUNITIES. Supplement 15/73 Nov. 8, 1973. Commission report on its efforts to develop a program of dealing with multinational corporations. An important insight into the Commission's views on the inability of European firms to compete with multinational corporations, and the draft regulation concerning the threat to competition posed by multinational corporations.

Guyenot, Jean. *The Continental Can Case: A European View.* 8 J. OF WORLD TRADE L. 107–12 (1974). Posits that the court in *Continental Can* disliked the Commission's expansion of article 86 to control MNC mergers. Consequently, the Commission may be derailed from setting itself up as the sole agency in control of the European economy.

Hawk, Barry. *Antitrust in the EEC—The First Decade.* 41 FORDHAM L. REV. 229–92 (1971). Analyzes the Commission's functional view of antitrust, stressing its free enterprise approach to competition policy. Hawk could have made a better analysis of the Court of Justice's role in developing the Community's antitrust policy.

Howell, Joel. *Extraterritorial Application of Antitrust Legislation in the Common Market: The Dyestuffs Case.* 12 COLUM. J. OF TRANSNAT'L L. 169–81 (1973). Analyzes the Court of Justice's and Commission's handling of the effects doctrine in light of the "Dyestuffs Cases."

Note. *European Economic Community Antitrust Law: The Continental Can Decision—Forerunner of a New European Anti-merger Policy?* 47 TULANE L. REV. 829–51 (1973). Explains *Continental Can* as the beginning of a Commission policy of discouraging American multinational corporations from engaging in mergers with European firms that could lead to monopolistic control of a market. This is a break with the prior policy of ignoring takeovers by American firms.

Note. *The Common Market Responds to the American Challenge: The Proposal for a European Company.* 45 S. CAL. L. REV. 1168–1183 (1972). Representative of several articles describing the Commission's formulation of a draft regulation establishing a European Company. Such a company would help European firms meet competition from American multinational corporations. This note tries to reconcile the European Company with the Commission's overall approach to competition.

Swacker, Frank. *Foreign Business Operations under U.S. and Common Market Antitrust Laws.* 19 BUS. LAW. 493–509 (1964). An analysis early in EEC organs in antitrust policy. Demonstrates that the roles of the various organs solidified very early in EEC history.

von der Groeben, M. *Competition Policy as Part of Economic Policy in the Common Market.* 10 ANTITRUST BULL. 911–31 (1965). Relates the Commission's conception of antitrust to its economic plan for Europe. Von der Groeben, a Commission member, encourages "rational" mergers in the EEC, but warns against giant foreign firms dominating markets in Europe.

Wolfe, Jonathan, and Montauk, Richard. *Antitrust in the European Economic Community: An Analysis of Recent Developments in the Court of Justice.* 18 SANTA CLARA L. REV. 349–425 (1978). Explains the court's ability to make antitrust law due to the fluidity of the law and the novel fact situations. Wolfe and Montauk provide a sound analysis of *Commercial Solvents.*

FEDERAL REPUBLIC OF GERMANY

Barnikel, Dr. Hans-Heinrich. *Abuse of Power by Dominant Firms: Application of the German Law.* 14 ANTITRUST BULL. 221–47 (1969). Examines cases arising under statutory provisions regarding abuse of market domination, prohibition of discrimination, and termination of resale price maintenance. Barnikel concludes that the Federal Cartel Office was initially influenced by theoretical arguments about competition concepts but became more pragmatic in order to apply effective abuse control.

German Federal Cartel Office Decision in the Metro Case. 13 ANTITRUST BULL. 1017–33 (1968). Analyzes German Federal Cartel Office's decision involving an interesting test of abuse of market power. The office found the functional interchangeability of goods, in the sense of usefulness to the consumer, to be the decisive criterion for defining the relevant market; the market conduct is abusive when it impedes competition.

Gunther, Eberhard. *Ten Years of the German Federal Cartel Office: Review of Past and Future Trends.* 13 ANTITRUST BULL. 1435–72 (1968). Reviews the FCO's enforcement of the Act Against Restraints of Competition. Analyzes the application of ARC to contractual restraints of competition and criticizes the lack of concentration control (prior to the 1973 merger control law) and far-reaching exemptions of individual sectors. Concludes that FCO enforcement insufficiently addressed the purpose of ARC to maintain and foster competition throughout the economy. Compares and contrasts different systems of antitrust law attempts to promote competition.

Heil, Paul W., and Vorbrugg, Georg. *Antitrust Law in West Germany: Recent Developments in German and Common Market Regulation.* 8

INT'L LAW. 349–86 (1974). Describes the 1973 Act amending the Act Against Restraints of Competition and developments in EEC antitrust law affecting American enterprises doing business in Germany. Heil and Vorbrugg discuss the *Europemballage Case* wherein the European Court of Justice accepted the doctrine of abuse-aimed mergers.

Hollman, Hermann H. *Antitrust Law and Protection of Freedom of the Press in the Federal Republic of Germany.* 24 ANTITRUST BULL. 149–68 (1979). Examines the Third Amendment to the Act Against Restraints of Competition relating to questions of economic concentration and freedom of expression in Germany's print media. The amendment lowers the tolerance criteria for controlling mergers of companies engaged in the press market. Hollman concludes that this attempt to control newspaper mergers comes too late to apply to the most important cases, *i.e.*, economic concentration in the newspaper market is a current reality. He also describes a proposed statute drafted by the Federal Ministry of the Interior as potential instrument for addressing press concentration by providing for a policy of general journalistic orientation of a newspaper, for journalistic codetermination.

Markert, Kurt E. *The Application of German Antitrust Law to International Restraints of Trade.* 7 VA. J. INT'L L. 47–67 (1967). Compares the application of German antitrust law to international restraints of trade with U.S. antitrust enforcement. In theory, ARC § 98(2) permits even more extensive application of German law than U.S. law, but in practice, German law is applied far less extraterritorially than U.S. law. In general, the ARC was not rigorously enforced during its first ten years, and, in particular, practical difficulties in securing evidence have made formal action against foreign enterprises undesirable. However, the cautious policy of the Federal Cartel Office was expected to change as international antitrust coordination and cooperation remove some of the obstacles to international enforcement.

——. *The Control of Abuses by Market-Dominating Enterprises Under German Antitrust Law.* 11 CORNELL INT'L L.J. 275–301 (1978). Analyzes German Competition law's conduct-oriented approach to regulating market-dominating enterprises and the comparative relevance of this approach to American antitrust experience. Concludes that while German conduct control of monopolistic practices as compared with the American dissolution control has practical limitations, American antitrust enforcement practice can benefit from analysis of German attempts to define market domination.

——. *The New German Antitrust Reform Law.* 19 ANTITRUST BULL. 135–56 (1974). Reviews merger and abuse of market-dominating position contra provisions of the 1973 Second Amendment to the Act Against Restraints of Competition. Markert concludes that the new law closes two serious gaps in the coverage of antitrust law by including mergers and restrictive concerted actions. The improvements outweigh the exemptions provided in §§ 5(b), 28 and 38(2). Foresees that a separate system of national controls might be unnecessary should the European Community adopt a satisfactory merger control system.

Niehus, Rudolf J. *The New German Merger Law.* 48 TAXES 372–81 (1970). Discusses the tax-free merger law enacted in 1969 with illustrations of qualifying tax-free mergers.

Risenkampff, Alexander, and Gerber, David J. *German Merger Controls: The Role of Company Assurances.* 22 ANTITRUST BULL. 889–912 (1977). Discusses the German Federal Cartel Office's policy of considering assurances or promises of parties subject to merger control. Traces the legal and policy development of this practice since 1975; the negative response of the Monopoly Commission; the positive response of the legislature; the judicial requirement in the *Bayer-Metzeler* decision that such assurances must be taken into account by the Federal Cartel Office. Analyzes, evaluates, and compares the assurance practice with U.S. consent decree practice. Concludes that the assurance practice facilitates cooperative planning between the government and industry with regard to the structure of industrial competition. The practice yields a bargaining capacity to the Federal Cartel Office's decisions which is of practical value.

———. LAW AGAINST RESTRAINTS OF COMPETITION. Koln: Verlag Dr. Otto Schmidt KG, 1977. German and English translation with explanation of the Law Against Restraints of Competition (Gesetzgegen Wettbewerbsbeschränkungen-WEB).

———. *Recent Developments in German Antitrust Law.* 30 BUS. LAW. 1273–88 (1975). Reviews the merger control provisions and other competition control provisions of the 1973 amendment to the German Law Against Restraint of Competition. Riesenkampff concludes that the Federal Cartel Office's administrative practice became more stringent in the imposition of fines and interpretation of the law since the 1973 revisions.

FRANCE

Clement, B. *An Appraisal of French Antitrust Policy.* 19 ANTITRUST BULL. 587–603 (1974). Examines the requirements of a successful restrictive business practices action, and the scope, features, and impact of French legislation. Clement concludes that while the competitive environment has improved in France, the rate of industrial and trade concentration and the oligopolistic pattern of markets have altered the form and lessened the vigor of competition.

Dubois, Jean-Pierre. *French Economic Interest Groups and the Rules of Competition.* 14 ANTITRUST BULL. 667–703 (1969). Examines the economic importance of legally created economic interest groups (EIGs) with regard to cooperative undertakings among enterprises and rules of competition. Concludes that the present form of EIGs does not fulfill the aim of increased competition.

French Technical Commission on Agreements and Dominating Positions. 13 ANTITRUST BULL. 1035–62 (1968). Report for the years 1963–66 on the growing number of judgments regarding agreements and dominating positions. Includes excerpts from the September 1967 summary report of the operation of the provisions of French law about cartels and dominant firms published by the Technical Commission on Combines and Dominant Positions. Cases concern small metal fabrications, electric lamps, and waterproofing services.

Kobak, James B., Jr. *Three Approaches to the Bureaucratic Dilemma: The Administration and Enforcement of the Antitrust Laws of the United States, France, and The Common Market.* 23 ALA. L.R. 43–97 (1970). Analyzes French, U.S., and EEC antitrust law and procedure. Kobak concludes that the EEC, and, to a lesser extent, the United States, must deal with the problem of integrating central and regional authorities into the same enforcement scheme; such a problem hardly exists in France. In France the informal administrative stage is more important than the judicial stage of antitrust enforcement. In the EEC the administrative stage is more formal and more visible while in the U.S. the administrative stage is the most visible of all. This visibility encumbers the decision-making process with procedureal minutiae.

Plaisant, Rene. *French Legislation Against Restrictive Trade Practices.* 10 TEX. INT'L L.J. 26–45 (1975). Examines French antitrust legislation in light of the principle of freedom of commerce and industry, Article 419 of the Penal Code and the Ordinance of June 30, 1945, Article 59 *bis*. Concludes that French antitrust enforcement does not aim to disturb existing market structure, is flexible due to its administrative rather than judicial character, and with respect to agreement practices, is oriented toward the single criterion of pricing. The article relates to the antitrust situation in France before the Act of 19th July 1977.

GREAT BRITAIN

Cawthra, B.I. *Learning to Live with EEC Rules of Competition.* 126 NEW L.J. 493–94, 593–94, 691–92 (1976). Short survey focusing on notification of agreements to EEC and the conflict between national and Community laws in trademarks, patents, and merger control.

Dixon, Donald. *Economic Effect of Exclusive Dealing and Ownership Control: The U.K. Petrol Cases Revisited.* 18 ANTITRUST BULL. 375–90 (1973). Discusses supplier control of petrol distribution as it relates to distribution costs, market entry, and nonprice competition. Concludes with criticism of conventional competitive model as applied to situation by a previous article (Pass, *infra*).

DEPARTMENT OF PRICES AND CONSUMER Protection. A REVIEW OF MONOPOLIES AND MERGERS POLICY. Green Paper, Cmnd. No. 7198 (1978). Consultative Document prepared by the Secretary of State for Prices and Consumer Protection. Surveys economic effects of monopolies and mergers and the operation of competition law in the U.K., EEC, and other countries. Recommends, in part, changing from a favorable to a neutral presumption of mergers as being in the public interest.

————. A REVIEW OF RESTRICTIVE TRADE POLICY PRACTICES. Green Paper, Cmnd. No. 7512 (1978). Consultative Document prepared by the Secretary of State for Prices and Consumer Protection. Reviews restrictive trade practices policy in the U.K., EEC, and other countries. Recommends procedural changes to provide for more flexible and efficient regulation of restrictive agreements.

Gribbin, J.D. *Recent Antitrust Developments in the United Kingdom.* 20 ANTITRUST BULL. 377–410 (1975). Reviews history of U.K. antitrust policy through the Fair Trading Act of 1973. Discusses political and economic background of the trade acts and concludes with a survey of the first year of the 1973 Act's operation.

————. *The United Kingdom 1977 Price Commission Act and Competition Policy.* 23 ANTITRUST BULL. 405–39 (1978). Reviews the economic factors leading to the Act, the Act's philosophy and its provisions. Discusses first six months of the Act's operation and summarizes its investigation reports through end of February 1978. Focuses on the relations between the law and other U.K. competition laws.

Harding, C.S.P. *Injury Occasioned by Infringements of the E.E.C. Rules of Competition: Remedies in English Law,* 7 ANGLO-AM. L. REV. 290–306 (1978). Discusses the possible applications of English common law actions to infringements of Articles 85 and 86 of the Treaty of Rome.

Johnson, P.S., and Apps, R. *Interlocking Directorates Among the U.K.'s Largest Companies.* 24 ANTITRUST BULL. 357–69 (1979). Discusses legal and economic consequences of interlocking directorates and provides preliminary evidence on the importance of the phenomenon among the U.K.'s largest companies. Focuses on the manufacturing sector and the insurance, banking, and finance sector.

Kintner, Earl; Joelson, Mark; and Griffin, Joseph. *Recent Developments in United Kingdom Antitrust Law,* 19 ANTITRUST BULL. 217–55 (1974). Practical guide to the U.K.'s antitrust laws. Analyzes and synthesizes the U.K.'s accession to the EEC and its enactment of the 1973 Fair Trading Act.

Maloney, M.T. *Hoffmann-LaRoche—Aggregated Rebates.* 127 NEW L.J. 41–42, 141–42. The author summarizes the Commission report that fined

Hoffmann-LaRoche for aggregated rebates and criticizes the report for its wide-ranging and ambiguous *obiter dicta*.

Monopolies Commission Reports. Reports on competitive situation in industries referred to the Monopolies Commission by the Director General or Board of Trade, and reports on whether referred mergers are against the public interest.

Pass, C.L., and Hawkins, H.K. *Exclusive Dealing, Supplier Ownership of Outlets and the Public Interest: The Petrol Case.* 18 ANTITRUST BULL. 567–95 (1972). Supports the Monopolies Commission Report on Petrol in the United Kingdom. Agrees, in principle, that supplier control of petrol distribution need not operate against the public interest, but suggests an ownership control limitation for dominant suppliers.

Rhinelander, L.H. *Roche Case: One Giant Step for British Antitrust.* 15 VA. J. INT'L L. 1–38 (1974). Comprehensive summary of the issues and legal procedures involved in trying to force Roche to lower its prices for valium and librium. Concludes by assessing possible effects of the case on European and American antitrust law.

Wyalt, D.A. *Company Merger and Competition in the United Kingdom and the E.E.C.* 124 NEW L.J. 31–33, 149–50 (1974). Surveys background, workings, and philosophy of U.K. and EEC merger laws.

STATE-CONTROLLED ECONOMIES

Baker, Donald. *Antitrust Remedies Against Government-Inspired Boycotts, Shortages, and Squeezes: Wanderings on the Road to Mecca.* 61 CORNELL L. REV. 911–49 (1976). Concluding there are no antitrust remedies against government cartels such as OPEC. Baker focuses instead on remedies against corporations involved in foreign governmental schemes to restrain trade. His discussion is useful for its inventory of possible foreign governmental-created antitrust problems, but somewhat dated, in view of developments since the enactment of the Foreign Sovereign Immunities Act.

Connor, John, Jr., ed. LEGAL ASPECTS OF DOING BUSINESS WITH THE U.S.S.R. AND EASTERN EUROPE. New York: Practicing Law Institute, 1977. Essays on the business and trade problems that Western businesses encounter when trading with the state monopolies of Eastern Europe and the Soviet Union. Connor ties characteristics of state trading to actual consequences in a business setting in discussions of contract terms and conditions, compensation and license agreements, license restrictions, and buying and selling cooperation among Western firms dealing with state traders.

Joelson, Mark, and Griffin, J.P. *The Legal Status of Nation-State Cartels Under United States Antitrust and Public International Law.* 9 INT'L LAW. 617–45 (1975). Explores sovereign immunity issues, the act of state doctrine, and enforcement jurisdiction in connection with antitrust laws and government cartels. While the Foreign Sovereign Immunities Act seems to have stripped foreign governments of some of the immunity assumed by Joelson and Griffin, they identify intractable problems of politics and the limits of judicial action that the Act has not changed.

Note. *American Antitrust Liability of Foreign State Instrumentalities: A New Application of the Parker Doctrine.* 11 CORNELL INT'L L.J. 305–22 (1978). Several types of foreign government instrumentalities are defined and matched with what the author proposes are appropriate tests for deciding issues of sovereign immunity and foreign sovereign compulsion under the *Parker* doctrine. A thorough treatment of recent case law and an imaginative forecast of problems that could arise as more foreign state enterprises transact business with and in the United States.

INTERNATIONAL CODES OF CONDUCT

Chance, Steven K. *Codes of Conduct for Multinational Corporations.* 33 BUS. LAW. 1799–1820 (1978). Discusses international efforts to develop a code of conduct relating to the activities of multinational corporations and the potential place of such a code in national legal systems.

Davidow, Joel, and Chiles, Lisa. *The United States and the Issue of the Binding or Voluntary Nature of International Codes of Conduct Regarding Restrictive Business Practices.* 72 AM. J. INT'L L. 247–71 (1978). Overviews the varying attitudes concerning the implementation of transnational restrictive business practices regulations. The authors consider the position of the United States in light of recent administrative statements expressing an interest in developing country concerns, and they discuss the potential for effectuating this policy in a code of conduct regarding restrictive business practices.

Griffin, Joseph P., and Joelson, Mark R. *International Regulation of Restrictive Business Practices Engaged in by Transnational Enterprises: A Prognosis.* 11 INT'L LAW. 5–28 (1977). Discusses the different positions taken by the developing and the developed countries regarding transnational enterprises resulting from divergent economic objectives and the impact of this conflict on efforts to develop international standards for restrictive business practices.

Hawk, Barry E. *The OECD Guidelines for Multinational Enterprises: Competition.* 46 FORDHAM L. REV. 241–76 (1977). Discusses recent international efforts to deal with multinational enterprises emphasizing the "Guidelines for Multinational Enterprises" established by the OECD in 1976. Hawk analyzes the specific language of each provision of the competition guidelines.

Joelson, Mark R. *The Proposed International Codes of Conduct as Related To Restrictive Business Practices.* 8 L. & POL'Y INT'L BUS. 837–74 (1976). Discusses the adverse effects of restrictive business practices on national economies, with particular emphasis on the economies of developing countries. Joelson also summarizes previous international efforts to regulate these practices, including the OECD and UNCTAD efforts.

Kintner, Earl W.; Joelson, Mark R.; and Vaghi, Peter J. *Groping for a Truly International Antitrust Law.* 14 VA. J. INT'L L. 75–100 (1973). Discusses the need for international antitrust regulation due to the ineffectiveness of national laws in the transnational sphere. The authors set forth criteria to be considered in forming an international regulatory system.

Note. *The United Nations Code of Conduct for Transnational Corporations.* 18 HARV. INT'L L.J. 273–307 (1977). Discusses the perceived need for new international arrangements to deal with transnational corporations, and the variance in attitudes between home and host countries. The Note discusses United Nations efforts with special emphasis placed on the potential benefits of the code being developed by the United Nations Commission on Transnational Corporations.

Note. *Transnational Corporations—The United Nations Code of Conduct.* 5 BROOKLYN J. INT'L L. 129–53 (1979). Discusses the purposes and issues underlying the formation of the UNCTAD code of conduct for transnational corporations.

Raman, K. Venkata. *Transnational Corporations, International Law, and the New International Economic Order.* 6 SYRACUSE J. INT'L L. & COM. 17–76 (1978). Discusses the viewpoints of developing countries concerning various aspects of transnational corporate operations.

Rubin, Seymour J. *Harmonization of Rules: A Perspective on the U.N. Commission on Transnational Corporations,* 8 L. & POL'Y INT'L BUS. 875–93 (1976). Discusses the development and status of the Commission and its potential for success in developing internationally acceptable standards for transnational corporate activity.

The United Nations Conference on Trade and Development Secretariat. *Considerations for the Drafting of a Model Law or Laws on Restrictive Business Practices to Assist Developing Countries in Devising Appropriate Legislation.* 22 ANTITRUST BULL. 831–55 (1977). Deals with three issues: the reasons for restrictive business practices legislation, present restrictive business practices controls in twelve developing countries, considerations relevant to the drafting of a model law. The policy considerations expressed in the article reflect current attitudes within UNCTAD toward a restrictive business practices code.

Wex, Samuel. *A Code of Conduct on Restrictive Business Practices: A Third Option.* 1977 CAN. Y.B. INT'L L. 198–235 (1977). Outlines the competing interests that must be considered in developing a code of conduct on restrictive business practices, and presents concrete proposals for resolution of this conflict, including: the allowance of preferential treatment for developing countries and a system of differential treatment for restrictive business practices having purely national effects.

Index